The United States in Asia

The United States in Asia

Robert G. Sutter

ROWMAN & LITTLEFIELD PUBLISHERS, INC.
Lanham • Boulder • New York • Toronto • Plymouth, UK

ROWMAN & LITTLEFIELD PUBLISHERS, INC.

Published in the United States of America
by Rowman & Littlefield Publishers, Inc.
A wholly owned subsidiary of The Rowman & Littlefield Publishing Group, Inc.
4501 Forbes Boulevard, Suite 200, Lanham, Maryland 20706
www.rowmanlittlefield.com

Estover Road, Plymouth PL6 7PY, United Kingdom

British Library Cataloguing in Publication Information Available

Library of Congress Cataloging-in-Publication Data

Sutter, Robert G.
  The United States in Asia / Robert Sutter.
    p. cm.
  Includes bibliographical references.
  ISBN-13: 978-0-7425-5648-5 (cloth : alk. paper)
  ISBN-10: 0-7425-5648-4 (cloth : alk. paper)
  ISBN-13: 978-0-7425-5649-2 (pbk. : alk. paper)
  ISBN-10: 0-7425-5649-2 (pbk. : alk. paper)
  eISBN-13: 978-0-7425-5717-8
  eISBN-10: 0-7425-5717-0
  1. Asia—Foreign relations—United States. 2. United States—Foreign relations—
Asia. 3. United States—Foreign relations—1989– I. Title.
  DS33.4.U6S87 2009
  327.7305—dc22

                                                                  2008009777

Printed in the United States of America

♾ ™ The paper used in this publication meets the minimum requirements of
American National Standard for Information Sciences—Permanence of Paper
for Printed Library Materials, ANSI/NISO Z39.48-1992.

Contents

Please see this book's website for a chronology:
http://www.rowmanlittlefield.com/isbn/0742556492

Acknowledgments

I wish to express special thanks to the many individuals who have helped to make this book possible. As noted in chapter 9, 175 Asia-Pacific affairs experts in the governments of nine Asian Pacific states graciously made themselves available for confidential interviews and consultations during the author's four research trips to the region from 2004 to 2007. Susan McEachern, editorial director of history, international studies, and geography at Rowman & Littlefield Publishers, provided expert guidance and support. Keith Gerver read and commented on the entire draft manuscript, offering many valuable suggestions and additions. Mary O'Loughlin produced a detailed timeline that provided the basis for the book's chronology of U.S.-Asian interaction and key political events in Asia since 1789, which can be found at http://www.rowmanlittlefield.com/isbn/0742556492.

Introduction

Is the United States in Decline in the Asia-Pacific?

A deepening crisis in the U.S. government over what to do about the deteriorating security situation in Iraq headed the list of American foreign policy preoccupations during the second term of the George W. Bush administration. The Democratic-led 110th Congress in 2007 began to register strong opposition to the president's policies, and public opinion sided with the congressional critics of the president. The Bush administration's handling of the Global War on Terrorism, the war in Afghanistan, efforts to curb Iran's and North Korea's nuclear weapons development, and related security issues was widely criticized. Democratic leaders asserted that Bush administration actions had made the United States less rather than more secure after the September 11, 2001, terrorist attacks on America. The Bush administration's policies and practices regarding economic, trade, welfare, social, and other issues affecting U.S. jobs and domestic well-being also came under attack. The attacks intensified with the downturn in the U.S. economy in 2008. Unpopular and facing a hostile Congress led by his opponents at home, and widely criticized abroad, President Bush appeared to fit the image of a political "lame duck" as he finished the last years of his term in office.[1]

Behind the widespread criticism and unpopularity of the Bush administration and its controversial leader were many other problems seen to affect American leadership abroad. The capacity of the U.S. government was challenged by the need to curb large government spending deficits. The failure of U.S. decision making in the war in Iraq and various scandals associated with U.S. foreign policy and the pursuit of the War on

Terrorism raised serious questions about the effectiveness of U.S. government procedures in foreign affairs.[2]

The massive and seeming intractable problems of the Middle East meant that U.S. leaders in the present and future U.S. administrations would have less time and inclination to deal with issues in other areas, including the Asia-Pacific. Pressing domestic priorities involving energy costs and consumption, environmental issues and global warming, Social Security, Medicare, and health care reforms seemed likely to demand the attention of U.S. leaders for some time to come, reducing the priority they would devote to foreign affairs in general and to the Asia-Pacific in particular. Divided government with a president of one political party facing a Congress led by another exacerbated the difficulties in U.S. government decision making. The unpopular war in Iraq added to trouble the U.S. armed forces was having in recruiting volunteers to serve in the military. Ballooning U.S. trade deficits with Asian exporters of manufactured products meshed with the steady decline of good-paying manufacturing jobs in the United States. These developments strengthened political forces in the Congress and among presidential aspirants in 2008 to adopt protectionist trade measures against these foreign exporters, exacerbating U.S. differences with many Asia-Pacific countries.[3]

This backdrop reinforced an already strong line of argument seen in prominent expert publications, think tank reports, media commentaries, and public opinion surveys that the United States was in decline in the Asia-Pacific, with some assessing that the long-standing U.S. role as the region's leading power was ending. While there was considerable sympathy with and support for the United States in the region following the September 11 terrorist attacks, U.S. actions, especially the war in Iraq, greatly alienated popular and elite opinion in most Asia-Pacific countries. Perceived U.S. unilateralism and arrogance over such issues as missile defense, environmental issues, and the Palestinian-Israeli conflict added to antipathy toward the United States.[4]

Asia-Pacific government officials often shared these negative views of the U.S. government actions and policies. They and elite and popular opinion also saw U.S. decision makers as being preoccupied with issues that seemed to ignore the main concerns of the Asia-Pacific region or that meshed poorly with those concerns. For instance, Southeast Asian officials often saw U.S. policy as inattentive to their nation-building, development, and security concerns that involved rapidly growing Asian multilateral cooperation and interaction. The U.S. government did focus new attention to Southeast Asia after September 11, but the focus was seen as narrowly centered on the U.S. concern with Southeast Asia as a so-called second front in the Global War on Terrorism. This led to dissatisfaction by Southeast Asian leaders seeking U.S. cooperation in areas of importance to them involving economic development and multilateral cooperation.[5]

Meanwhile, antiterrorist efforts strengthened U.S. concerns about nuclear weapons proliferation and for several years reinforced a tough U.S. stance toward North Korea's nuclear weapons development. The U.S. hard line toward Pyongyang alienated the South Korean government, which continued to pursue a policy of asymmetrical engagement under the rubric of the "sunshine policy" designed to ease tensions and encourage gradual change in North Korean policies and actions. It added to deep fissures in the U.S.–South Korean alliance and to regional anxiety about possible unilateral or assertive U.S. actions against North Korea that would destabilize Northeast Asia. More recently, the Bush administration's change in policy and its decision to adopt a more accommodating approach to North Korea, including serious bilateral talks with Pyongyang, led to an agreement among the concerned powers in the Six-Party Talks on February 13, 2007. The agreement and the more flexible U.S. posture were generally welcomed, though there remained numerous hurdles to overcome in carrying out this ambitious accord.[6]

More broadly, the widely perceived decline in the image of the United States in the Asia-Pacific, along with widely reported U.S. preoccupations, inattention, and seeming weaknesses of the Bush administration at home and abroad, came as Asian regional cooperation grew markedly within a rapidly expanding regional trade and investment network, with rising China at the center. China's growing economy attracted the lion's share of the Asian and world investment going to Asian countries. China's trade levels grew at almost twice the pace of its rapid economic growth. China soon became the largest or second trading partner of most of its neighbors. Attentive and accommodating Chinese diplomacy saw a marked improvement in Chinese relations with most Asian states. Chinese leaders also became among the most active in pursuing initiatives in Asian multilateral groups. China was in the lead in fostering greater Chinese and other Asian cooperation with ASEAN; in the Shanghai Cooperation Organization, involving Russia and four Central Asian states; and in the Six-Party Talks dealing with North Korea's nuclear weapons program.[7]

By contrast, U.S. policies and actions were seen as inadequate and reactive. Many commentaries warned of the United States becoming increasingly marginalized in the region as China rose in prominence. While China was rapidly winning support and goodwill through adroit diplomacy and the growth of China-regional economic ties, U.S. policies and actions were seen to continue to alienate regional opinion and to be inadequate in meeting the concerns and priorities of regional governments.[8]

In books, media commentaries, and government reports, eminent U.S. diplomats, academic experts, journalists, and government analysts recounted long lists of U.S. failings and regional challenges to the United States as they depicted a steady decline in the position of the United States in the Asia-Pacific region. The situation reached a point where regional governments often were said to resist or ignore the United States, while seeking to deal with issues by working with rising Asian powers, notably China, and with one another in burgeoning regional multilateral organizations. As America became increasingly less attractive and the image of the United States declined, the economically dynamic and diplomatically attentive Asian powers, again led by China, were sought out by governments and other international actors for cooperation and closer relations. Rapidly expanding intra-Asian trade networks continued to grow, meaning that Asian countries were trading more with one another and less with the United States, further reducing U.S. importance in the region.[9]

Looking out, many commentaries and assessments were pessimistic that the U.S. government would be able to reverse the perceived slide in U.S. image and influence in the Asia-Pacific region.[10] As noted above, heading the list of problems were U.S. government spending deficits and massive U.S. trade deficits, which suggested that economic resources might not be available for significant U.S. government initiatives. The drain of the Iraq War and other commitments in the Global War on Terrorism seemed to forecast a decline in U.S. military spending and preparedness in dealing with the Asia-Pacific. The Democratic-led 110th Congress worked to change U.S. trade and economic policies in directions that appeared to restrict open access to the U.S. market on the part of China and the other export-oriented economies of Asia, further alienating Asian opinion from the United States.

CONTEXT AND BALANCE IN ASSESSING THE UNITED STATES AND ASIA-PACIFIC

This book assesses the background, status, and outlook of U.S. relations with the Asia-Pacific region. The Asia-Pacific region is defined as the Asian countries east of Afghanistan, including states of what is known as Northeast, Southeast, South, and Central Asia, as well as such Asia-Pacific states as Australia, New Zealand, and the Pacific Islands. The assessment reviews salient developments in the United States and in the Asia-Pacific region that affect U.S. relations with the Asia-Pacific countries. It shows that American relations with the region are heavily influenced by the policies and actions of government leaders on both sides of the Pacific. They also are influenced by a range of economic, political, military, technological, and other forces that affect international affairs throughout the world and have particular impacts on the governments of the Asia-Pacific and the United States. How well the U.S. government policies and behavior mesh with the priorities and actions of counterparts in the Asia-Pacific will go far toward determining whether the course of American relations with the region will be smooth or difficult.

The assessment provides an inventory of the major strengths and weaknesses of American relations with the Asia-Pacific region, along with the significant points of agreement and disagreement between the United States and the governments and peoples of the region, at the end of the George W. Bush administration. As noted above, there is considerable discussion among specialists, commentators, and other observers about the importance and effectiveness of recent U.S. policies and interactions with the Asia-Pacific. Although there are notable exceptions,[11] widely held views see the United States in decline, with the U.S. leadership role in regional affairs undermined by a range of political, economic, and security problems. This assessment carefully considers these views in the context of past U.S. difficulties in the region. It finds that recent U.S. difficulties have not fundamentally undermined the main foundations of the leadership, power, and influence that the United States has exerted in the region for many years. It suggests U.S. policy options that will help to remedy prevailing difficulties while sustaining U.S. interests related to America's leading role in Asian and Pacific affairs.

The structure of the book is as follows:

- Chapter 1 provides the historical context of the U.S. relationship with the contemporary Asia-Pacific, highlighting the lessons of the past relevant to the present.
- Chapters 2–4 assess in priority order U.S. issues and concerns, including those reflected in U.S. domestic discussion and debate, regarding American policy toward Asia-Pacific countries and Asia-Pacific affairs.
- Chapters 5–8 assess the main determinants of the policies of Asia-Pacific governments and other regional actors and evaluate the priorities and concerns of important Asia-Pacific governments and other actors, including the actions of regional governments and leaders in burgeoning Asian multilateral organizations.
- Chapter 9 builds on the foundation provided by chapters 5–8 to make an overall assessment of the prevailing trends in the Asia-Pacific that flow from the already discerned determinants and priorities. This chapter shows how those trends challenge and support U.S. policy. Against this background, it compares U.S. strengths and weaknesses with those of China, the rising power widely portrayed as advancing to Asian leadership as the United States declines. The

chapter provides a generally positive view of continued U.S. leadership in the Asia-Pacific.
- Chapter 10 forecasts a continued role for the United States as the leading power in the Asia-Pacific region and offers recommendations on how U.S. relations with the Asia-Pacific could be improved.
- A detailed chronology of U.S.-Asian interaction and key political events in Asia since 1789 can be found at http://www.rowmanlittlefield.com/isbn/0742556492.

NOTES

1. Sara Thannhauser, "A Dangerous Inheritance: Converging Challenges That Will Face the Next American President" (Washington, D.C.: America's Role in the World Working Group, Institute for the Study of Diplomacy, Georgetown University, 2007); available at http://isd.georgetown.edu/Inheritance_Feb_26_2007 .pdf; Thomas Pickering and Chester Crocker, *America's Role in the World: Foreign Policy Choices for the Next President* (Washington, D.C.: Institute for the Study of Diplomacy, Georgetown University, 2008).

2. Richard Armitage and Joseph Nye, *CSIS Commission on Smart Power: A Smarter More Secure America*, 61–68 (Washington, D.C.: Center for Strategic and International Studies, 2007).

3. Casimir Yost, "Choices for America in the World," Scope Paper No. 4 (Washington, D.C.: America's Role in the World Working Group, Institute for the Study of Diplomacy, Georgetown University, 2007); available at http://isd.georgetown .edu/Scope_Paper_4_June_4_2007.pdf.

4. Jason Shaplen and James Laney, "Washington's Eastern Sunset: The Decline of U.S. Power in Northeast Asia," *Foreign Affairs* (November/December 2007): 82–97; Joshua Kurlantzick, "Pax Asia-Pacifica? East Asian Integration and Its Implications for the United States," *Washington Quarterly* 30, no. 3 (Summer 2007): 67–77.

5. Stanley Foundation, *New Power Dynamics in Southeast Asia: Issues for U.S. Policy Makers* (Muscatine, Iowa: Stanley Foundation, 2007).

6. International Crisis Group, "After the North Korean Nuclear Breakthrough: Compliance or Confrontation?" Asia Briefing No. 62, April 30, 2007; available at http://www.crisisgroup.org/home/index.cfm?l=1&id=4795.

7. David Shambaugh, "China Engages Asia: Reshaping the Regional Order," *International Security* 29, no. 3 (Winter 2004/05): 64–99; Joshua Kurlantzick, *Charm Offensive: How China's Soft Power Is Transforming the World* (New Haven, Conn.: Yale University Press, 2007).

8. Hugo Restall, "China's Bid for Asian Hegemony," *Far Eastern Economic Review*, May 2007, 10–14; Michael Vatikiotis and Murray Hiebert, "How China Is Building an Empire," *Far Eastern Economic Review*, November 20, 2003, 30–33.

9. Morton Abramowitz and Stephen Bosworth, *Chasing the Sun: Rethinking East Asian Policy* (New York: Century Foundation, 2006); Bates Gill, *Rising Star: China's New Security Diplomacy* (Washington, D.C.: Brookings Institution Press, 2007);

Kurlantzick, *Charm Offensive*; Stanley Foundation, *New Power Dynamics*; Shaplen and Laney, "Washington's Eastern Sunset."

10. "Come in Number One, Your Time Is Up," *Economist*, April 12, 2007, 12, http://www.the-economist.com/research/backgrounders/displaystory.cfm?story_id=9005261; Armitage and Nye, *CSIS Commission*.

11. Michael Yahuda, *The International Politics of the Asia-Pacific* (New York: RoutledgeCurzon, 2005); G. John Ikenberry, "America in East Asia: Power, Markets, and Grand Strategy," in *Beyond Bilateralism: U.S.-Japan Relations in the New Asia-Pacific*, ed. Ellis Krauss and T. J. Pempel, 37–54 (Stanford, Calif.: Stanford University Press, 2004); Victor Cha, "Winning Asia: Washington's Untold Success Story," *Foreign Affairs* 86, no. 6 (November/December 2007): 98–113.

1

+

Historical Lessons and the Evolution of U.S. Relations with the Asia-Pacific

The United States has a long record of active interaction with Asia-Pacific countries. The purpose of this chapter is to identify and explain lessons from this record that are relevant for the objective of this book—discerning the weaknesses, strengths, and outlook of contemporary U.S. relations with the Asia-Pacific region. The lessons are identified and explained in summary form in the first section of this chapter. Following that is a chronological narrative of major developments of U.S. relations with the Asia-Pacific that explains those lessons in more detail and provides background information for readers unfamiliar with the context of contemporary U.S. relations with the Asia-Pacific.

LESSONS OF HISTORY

The record of U.S. relations with the Asia-Pacific region surveyed in this chapter reveals several findings of relevance to contemporary U.S. relations with the region.

U.S. Interests: Economic, Values, and Strategic, Focused on Northeast Asia

Historically, U.S. relations with Asia were grounded in advancing trade and economic interests and promoting religious and other American values. The U.S. Navy sometimes preceded U.S. diplomats in opening relations with Asian governments in the nineteenth century, but the Navy's

1

mission focused heavily on fostering and protecting American commercial, missionary, and related interests.

Northeast Asia, especially China and Japan, was the focus of U.S. interest and has remained the top priority of the United States in Asia. The acquisition of the Philippines in the late nineteenth century gave the United States a modest stake in Southeast Asia. The United States generally cooperated with British, French, and other European colonial powers in Southeast Asia and South Asia. Central Asia was the preserve of tsarist Russia and later the Soviet Union.[1]

U.S. Reluctance to Lead: Major Costs and Risks of Leadership

The United States came late to leadership in the Asia-Pacific. After World War I, despite its position as a major world power and one of two principal powers in East Asia (Japan was the other), the United States was reluctant to undertake the risks, costs, and obligations of leadership. The United States used inexpensive diplomatic efforts to curb Japanese expansion in East Asia following World War I, the collapse of Russia, and the weakening of Britain, France, and other European powers. These efforts failed by the early 1930s, but the United States remained very reluctant to confront Japanese expansion.[2]

The Japanese attack on Pearl Harbor put the United States in the leading role in the armed conflict to destroy Japan's war machine and create a new order in Asia and the Pacific. The scope of U.S. interests spread widely to include Northeast and Southeast Asia, Australia and New Zealand, and many Pacific Island countries. South Asia was still ruled by U.S. ally Great Britain and Joseph Stalin's Soviet Union controlled Central Asia.[3]

U.S. leaders had ambitions for a post–World War II order in the Asia-Pacific region that featured a strong and united China friendly to the United States and newly independent countries in Southeast and South Asia. The ambitions ran aground on realities of Chinese division and weakness, refusal of the European colonial powers to withdraw from Southeast Asia, and emerging Cold War competition with the Soviet Union and its allies and associates. Reflecting a reluctance to bear the continued cost of strategic leadership in the Asia-Pacific, the U.S. government rapidly demobilized its military forces in the Asia-Pacific after World War II, apart from its occupation forces in Japan.[4]

Repeated Challenges to U.S. Leadership in the Asia-Pacific

U.S. calculations of military withdrawal and continued peace in Asia, as well as other U.S. interests in Asia, were fundamentally challenged by the emerging Cold War. The Soviet Union and China backed the North Korean assault on South Korea in June 1950. This followed the failure of U.S. policy in China. A Chinese Communist administration hostile to the United States rose in 1949 and aligned with Stalin's Soviet Union in a pact directed against the United States in February 1950. This posed major problems for the United States. The war in Korea saw three years of U.S. hard combat against mainly Chinese forces in Korea that resulted in more than thirty thousand U.S. dead. The experience reinforced in blood U.S. determination over the next two decades to take the lead, pay the costs, and run the risks in building and maintaining strategic, economic, and political bulwarks to "contain" the spread of Chinese- and Soviet-backed Communist expansion in the Asia-Pacific.[5]

American leadership in Asia was repeatedly and seriously challenged. U.S.-backed French forces failed in Indochina in 1954 in the face of Chinese-backed Vietnamese Communists. The United States moved in to become more directly involved as the main backer of the noncommunist regime in South Vietnam, leading by the 1960s to the commitment of hundreds of thousands of U.S. troops to the war there against Vietnamese Communist forces that were supported by the Soviet Union and China. China militarily confronted Chiang Kai-shek and U.S. forces in the Taiwan Strait twice in the 1950s, developed a nuclear bomb by 1964, and widely promoted "wars of national liberation" against U.S.-supported governments in Southeast Asia and elsewhere.[6]

The nadir of U.S. influence in the Asia-Pacific region and the most serious challenge to U.S. leadership in Asia since Pearl Harbor came with the collapse of the U.S.-backed governments in Cambodia and South Vietnam in 1975. These major U.S. defeats—despite enormous U.S. costs including fifty thousand dead—came amid a major U.S. economic crisis, brought on by the oil shocks and energy crisis of this time, and weak and divided U.S. governments following the resignation of President Richard Nixon and his pardon by President Gerald Ford. Anxiety among U.S.-supported governments in Northeast and Southeast Asia saw them maneuver internationally and take measures at home to compensate for the obvious decline in U.S. power. The United States and China also cooperated together to deal with the rise of Soviet power in the Western Pacific, Southeast Asia, and South Asia; they anticipated continued decline in U.S. regional power and influence in the Asia-Pacific region as Soviet dominance grew.[7]

Faulty Forecasts of U.S. Decline in the Asia-Pacific

Forecasts of U.S. decline in the Asia-Pacific proved incorrect. U.S. economic and military power at home and abroad, including in the Asia-Pacific region, rose markedly during the early 1980s. American resolve, backed by strong allies in Europe and Japan, prompted a new Soviet leadership under Mikhail Gorbachev to seek to ease tensions and reduce military competition and confrontation.

Nonetheless, a new challenge to U.S. leadership emerged in this period. For more than ten years, a wide range of respected specialists and commentators argued that the United States could not keep pace with Asia's rapidly rising great power, Japan. Japan was seen as so competitive in Asian and world markets that it was widely asserted that Japan was emerging as Asia's dominant power and the United States was gradually falling to second place in Asia-Pacific affairs. Such predictions lasted well into the first years of the post–Cold War period. They did not cease until Japan experienced several years of economic stagnation and deflation and U.S. economic and military power rose to new prominence in the 1990s.[8]

Current Challenges in Light of the Past

The current challenges to U.S. leadership in Asia that are reviewed in the introduction and elsewhere in this book are serious. However, they have not reached the level of the challenges faced by the United States in the Asia-Pacific at the start of the Cold War, during the Vietnam War, after the U.S. defeat in Indochina in 1975, and in the face of Japan's rise in the late 1980s. Most notably, unlike in those past instances, the United States today exerts military predominance, and the continued growth of the massive and globally influential U.S. economy undergirds an ability to exert continued strong U.S. leadership in Asian and world affairs.

Past assumptions of U.S. decline in the face of rising powers and challenges tended to exaggerate the U.S. weaknesses without assessing U.S. strengths, and they tended to exaggerate the strengths of the rising powers and challenges to U.S. leadership without assessing their weaknesses and limitations. Credible assessments dealing with contemporary U.S. difficulties in the Asia-Pacific would appear to call for better balance in considering both contemporary U.S. weaknesses and strengths, as well as similar balance in assessing the power and influence of rising powers and other regional challenges to U.S. leadership in the Asia-Pacific, before offering projections and recommendations. That is the intention of this study.

EVOLUTION OF U.S. RELATIONS
WITH THE ASIA-PACIFIC REGION

Looked at broadly, current U.S. policy represents the culmination of a long-standing pursuit of three sets of policy objectives toward Asia and the Pacific. First, the United States remains concerned with maintaining a balance of power in Asia favorable to American interests and opposed to efforts at domination of the region by hostile powers.[9] Second, U.S. economic interests in the region grow through involvement in economic development and expanded U.S. trade and investment. Third, U.S. culture and values prompt efforts to foster democracy, human rights, and other culturally progressive trends in Asia, along with other parts of the world. The priority given to each of these goals has changed over time. U.S. leaders have varied in their ability to set priorities and organize U.S. objectives as part of a well-integrated national approach to the Asia-Pacific.[10]

Roots of American Foreign Policy in the Asia-Pacific

The background of American foreign policy in the Asia-Pacific extends to the formative experiences of the late eighteenth and nineteenth centuries. At that time, the United States endeavored to be seen as a nation interested in peaceful and friendly dealings with the world. U.S. relations focused primarily on commercial and cultural affairs. American interaction with the Asia-Pacific, like U.S. relations with other parts of the world, was characterized by informal activities such as trade, missionary endeavors, and tourism. Military and diplomatic considerations played only a minor role and were almost always subordinate to commerce and shipping. Economic activities, in turn, were often secondary to cultural relations. American trade with Asia never amounted to more than a few percent of total U.S. trade, whereas thousands of Americans went to Asia as missionaries and in other nongovernmental and noncommercial capacities to bring American civilization to Asia. U.S. missionary, educational, and related initiatives were timely in that Japan, China, and Korea were in the midst of modernization—a process that benefited from the presence of American missionaries, educators, scientists, engineers, and travelers, who offered Asian elites and others needed advice and information. Thus, in the first phase in their encounter, which ended with the nineteenth century, America and the Asia-Pacific met at three levels—strategic, economic, and cultural—but the cultural dimension was clearly the most significant.

U.S. relations with China were the most active and important of American relations with the Asia-Pacific during this period. Beginning in the late eighteenth century, America's new freedom from British rule brought Americans loss of access to their previous British-controlled trade partners. This prompted an American search for new trading opportunities in China. Though actual U.S. trade with China remained relatively small, the China market often loomed large in the American political and business imagination. Meanwhile, U.S. officials in the latter part of the nineteenth century and the early part of the twentieth century sometimes sought to channel U.S. investment in ways that would preserve American commercial opportunities in China in the face of foreign powers seeking exclusive privileges and spheres of influence.[11]

Americans also were in the vanguard of Protestant missionaries sent to China in the nineteenth century. U.S. missionaries came in groups and as individuals, set to work initially in China's so-called treaty ports, and eventually grew to many hundreds working throughout China to spread the gospel and to carry out relief, education, medical, and other works of benefit to Chinese people. Part of a well-organized network of church groups that reached deep into the United States for prayers and material support, American missionaries explained Chinese conditions to interested Americans, fostering a sense of special bond between the United States and China. They also served as advisers to U.S. officials dealing with China and sometimes became official U.S. representatives in China. The missionaries' core interest remained unobstructed access to Chinese people for purposes of evangelization and good works carried out by themselves and their foreign and Chinese colleagues.[12]

Though commercial and missionary interests remained at the center of U.S. concerns in China well into the twentieth century, a related strategic interest also had deep roots. In 1835, several years before the first U.S. treaty with China in 1844, the United States organized the Asiatic Squadron, later called the Asiatic Fleet. This U.S. Navy group in 1842 began to maintain a regular presence along the China coast. Initially two or three vessels, it grew to thirty-one craft by 1860, before forces were recalled on account of the American Civil War. The flotilla varied in size after the Civil War, but was sufficiently strong to easily destroy the Spanish forces in Manila's harbor during the Spanish-American War in 1898. It protected American lives and commerce in China and throughout maritime East and South Asia, and it reinforced American diplomacy in the region.[13]

Strong American interest in commercial and missionary access to China seemed to contrast with only episodic American diplomatic interest in China. The U.S. government occasionally gave high-level attention to the appointment of envoys or the reception of Chinese delegations. Caleb Cushing, Anson Burlingame, and some other nineteenth-century U.S. envoys to China were well connected politically. Some of them endeavored to use their actions in China to influence broader U.S. policy or to advance their own political or other ambitions. American envoys sometimes came from the missionary community in China. On the other hand, the post of U.S. minister in China often was vacant, with an interim official placed in charge in an acting capacity. Generally speaking, whenever nineteenth-century American diplomats pushed for more assertive policies that involved the chance of significant expenditure of U.S. resources or political risk, Washington decision makers reflected the realities of limited U.S. government interest in the situation in China and responded unenthusiastically. This broad pattern continued into the twentieth century, although American officials from time to time took the lead in low-risk political and diplomatic efforts in support of unimpeded U.S. commercial and other access to China.[14]

China's unexpected defeat by Japan in the Sino-Japanese War of 1894–1895 led European powers to join Japan in seeking exclusive spheres of influence and commercial and territorial rights in China. Alarmed that free commercial access to China for Americans would be jeopardized, U.S. officials formulated a response that led to the so-called Open Door Notes of 1899 and 1900.

The 1899 notes sought the powers' agreement that even if they established special spheres in China, they would not discriminate against foreign trade or interfere with customs collection. They underlined U.S. interests in preserving equal commercial access to China and the preservation of the integrity of the Chinese Customs Service, a crucial source of revenue for the struggling Chinese government. Though generally unenthusiastic about the U.S. initiative, most concerned powers offered evasive and qualified responses, but all in effect endorsed the principles in the Open Door Notes.

As the United States and other foreign powers dispatched troops to crush the Boxer uprising and lift the siege of foreign legations in Beijing, the United States in July 1900 sent a second round of Open Door Notes that expressed concern for preserving Chinese sovereignty. The foreign powers again went along with the notes.[15]

U.S. policy makers repeatedly referred to the U.S. Open Door Policy following the issuance of the Open Door Notes. The William H. Taft administration in 1910 interpreted the policy to extend beyond equal trade opportunity to include equal opportunity for investment in China. The Woodrow Wilson administration in 1915 reacted to the Japanese Twenty-One Demands against China by refusing to recognize such infringements on the Open Door Policy. The related principles concerning U.S. support for the territorial integrity of China were featured prominently in the Nine Power Treaty of the Washington Conference during the Warren Harding administration in 1922 and in the nonrecognition of Japanese aggression in Manchuria during the Herbert Hoover administration in 1932. The Harry Truman administration sought Soviet leader Joseph Stalin's promise that the Open Door Policy would be observed in the Soviet-influenced areas of Manchuria following the Soviet military defeat of Japanese forces there in 1945. In general, American political leaders dealing with China throughout the twentieth century tended to refer to the Open Door Policy in positive terms, as a U.S. attempt to prevent China from being carved up into commercially impenetrable foreign colonies. Chinese interpretations often emphasized that Americans were more concerned about maintaining their own commercial access and were prepared to do little in practice in support of Chinese sovereignty.

Not surprisingly, the Americans with an interest in China tended to emphasize the positive features of U.S. policy and behavior. Thus, the United States was seen to have behaved benignly toward China, especially when compared with the European powers and Japan that repeatedly coerced and attacked China militarily. The U.S. government repeatedly voiced support for China's territorial and national integrity. Through missionary and other activities, including education activities that eventually brought tens of thousands of Chinese students for higher education in the United States by the 1940s, Americans also showed strong sympathy and support for the broader welfare of the Chinese people.[16]

U.S. officials, opinion leaders, and commentators tended to ignore or soft-pedal the negative features of U.S. relations with China. Most notable was the so-called exclusion movement that grossly discriminated against and often violently persecuted Chinese immigrants to the United States. The movement took hold in U.S. politics beginning in the 1870s and lasted for almost a hundred years. At first centered in western states with some significant concentrations of Chinese workers, the exclusion movement reflected widespread American prejudice against and fear of Chinese workers amid sometimes difficult economic times in the United States. American elites and common people took legal and illegal actions, including riots and the murder of hundreds of Chinese in the United States, to stop Chinese immigration to America and drive away those Chinese already in the country. Various state governments and the federal government passed an array of laws and the U.S. courts made a variety of decisions that singled out Chinese immigrants for negative treatment and curbed the legal rights of Chinese residents and Chinese citizens of the United States. The movement eventually broadened to include all Asians. The National Origins Act of 1924 barred all new Asian immigration. U.S. mistreatment of Chinese people in the United States became a major issue for the Chinese government, which complained repeatedly against unjust U.S. actions, but with little effect. It was the target of a Chinese anti-American boycott in 1905.[17]

Growing Strategic Interests and Economic Power

U.S. strategic interests in Asia-Pacific changed markedly at the end of the nineteenth century. The United States fought a war in the Philippines, started a naval expansion program, and acquired Pacific island possessions. The United States developed as a major power in the Pacific and, by extension, in nearby Asia as well. Simultaneously, American trade and investment in Asia grew. The United States exported industrial products and invested capital in railways and mines in East Asia, as well as elsewhere in the world.

The period between the Spanish-American War and World War I was a time of transformation in U.S. policy. By 1914, the United States had one of the largest navies in the world and operated naval bases in the Caribbean and the Pacific. The Panama Canal had just been opened. As the world's leading industrial producer, the United States had become a major exporter of manufactured goods, especially to Asia and Latin America.

The American experience in Asia had become as much military and economic as cultural. Thousands of American soldiers and sailors experienced warfare in the Philippines. Thousands served during the Boxer Rebellion in China at the turn of the century. Hundreds of marines were stationed in China to safeguard Beijing's access to the sea. The American military began considering the possibility of war with Japan, which, too, was developing and expanding its military power in the Asia-Pacific region. The United States did not contemplate a war with Japan in the immediate future, but it became concerned with maintaining some sort of balance of power in the region, a task it could not leave to others powers alone.

Economically, furthermore, there was strong competition between American and Japanese cotton textiles imported into Manchuria. The United States affirmed its interest in an economic "open door" as official policy in part in order to prevent Japan from establishing dominance over the China market. At the same time, economic ties between the United States and Japan grew. Japan shipped 30 percent of its exports to America. It obtained hundreds of millions of dollars of U.S. loans as it fought a war against Russia in 1905 and managed its expanding empire on the Asian mainland.

The cultural dimension of U.S. policy and relations with the Asia-Pacific also remained strong. The Progressive movement reinforced the American sense of mission. The reformist impulse found an outlet in Asia, particularly China, which was trying to transform itself into a modern state. Many reformers in China were open to Progressive emphasis on education; they were coming to the view that educational reform must precede other changes. In their efforts to chart a new political order for China following the collapse of the Manchu dynasty in 1911, some Chinese reformers also eagerly turned to the U.S. Constitution as a model. Japanese reformers, for their part, drew inspiration from American capitalism, and Japanese radicals from American socialism. Thus, the sense of cultural connections grew. But missing was a sense of order among the various aspects of America's relations with the Asia-Pacific. Balance-of-power politics, trade, and reform movements continued without a clear sense of priority or interrelationships.

President Woodrow Wilson provided more coherence for U.S. foreign policy in the Asia-Pacific and elsewhere in the world. He set out
a comprehensive definition of international affairs in which military,
economic, and cultural aspects were integrated in order to establish a
more progressive world order. International peace would be maintained
by a system of collective security, economic interdependence, and cultural change that would promote democracy and human rights every-
where. To carry out such a foreign policy, the United States would play
a military role in cooperation with other nations. U.S. resources would
be available to open up markets of the world; to help other countries
through loans, investment, and technology transfer; and to collaborate
with other advanced nations in the development of dependent areas.
American universalistic values and reformist ideals would be used to
transform world conditions. Of course, Wilson's conception was not just
an agenda of selfless ideals; it meshed international and national affairs
in ways that promoted U.S. interests.

For Asia and the Pacific, Wilson's approach called for an end to the
naval race with Japan and to the latter's attempted domination of China,
and it sought a new security arrangement on the basis of cooperation
with Japan, Great Britain, and other powers. U.S. policy challenged
Japan's and other nations' monopolistic economic enclaves in China and
called for outside powers to attempt anew the doctrine of the open door.
America promoted democratization in Asia and elsewhere and supported
reformist movements in China and Japan.

For a time, the Wilsonian agenda put an end to the wartime antagonism
between the United States and Japan. There was "collective security" in
the Pacific on the basis of naval disarmament agreements and other accords, such as those negotiated at the Washington Conference of 1921–
1922. American goods, capital, and technology flowed into China and
Japan. Japan shifted its China policy away from military toward economic
interests. During the decade of the 1920s, the Americanization of Japan
was promoted through the spread of American movies, consumer goods,
and, even more important, political, economic, and social values.

In contrast, the 1930s was a time of the rise to power of Japanese
leaders who were oriented toward military strength. Military expenditures grew much faster than the economy. To justify and support such
increases, the military undertook aggressive acts in China and prepared
for war against the Soviet Union, the United States, and Great Britain.
In order to pay for such expenditures, Japan sought to establish control
over resources and markets of the Asian continent and the European
colonies in Southeast Asia.

Japan undertook these ultimately destructive policies as part of a
misguided effort to establish an autarkic region, an area of economic

self-sufficiency in Asia that would, it was thought, enrich the country as well as contribute to financing the military force. The Great Depression and world economic crisis added impetus to Japan's effort and helped to undermine the Wilsonian system of global interdependence. Rather than relying on close economic relations with the United States and an open door in China, the Japanese decided to reduce their dependency on the West and monopolize markets and resources in Asia. The Japanese never quite gave up their fascination with, and even dependence on, America's material and popular culture, but Japanese leaders during the 1930s were determined to reduce the influence of the ideals of democracy, individualism, and human rights. To counter these influences, Japanese leaders focused on the absence of racial equality seen in the practice of U.S. policy at home and abroad. Japanese military leaders in the 1930s repeatedly asserted that their determination to get Westerners out of their region was Asia's answer to American (and Western) racial injustice.

World War II, U.S. Leadership, and the Cold War

The Americans' initial isolationist reaction to Japanese militarism and Nazi Germany's expansionism gave way to a new vision authored by President Franklin D. Roosevelt. Over time, he formulated what some refer to as a new Wilsonianism to bring the world out of the turmoil and chaos of the 1930s. Roosevelt's vision shared with the original Wilsonianism a commitment to an integrated world order—militarily, economically, and culturally. The United States would be more willing to augment its armed forces and to be involved in different parts of the world in order to maintain a balance of power. It also would cooperate more closely with a few other powers to police the world order. This was still selective security with a few carefully chosen partners, but with a greater readiness to use force. The past stress on the open door and interdependence remained, but the government, not just the private sector, would be ready to help other countries undertake economic change. At the same time, worldwide bodies, such as the International Monetary Fund (IMF) and the World Bank, would be established to monitor and ensure a more open international economic system. Roosevelt's "four freedoms" speech in January 1941 contained principles that were Wilsonian—such as human rights and self-determination—but it also mentioned new values such as social justice and racial equality, values of particular importance to Asians.

Roosevelt's vision defined a new phase of American relations with the Asia-Pacific. After defeating Japan, the United States and its allies (including China and other Asian countries and groups resisting Japanese aggression) would reestablish regional order on the basis of this definition. As codified at the Cairo, Yalta, and Potsdam conferences, as well as through various other meetings, the new regional arrangement would be based on close cooperation among the victorious nations, particularly America, China, Great Britain, and the Soviet Union. Japan would be disarmed and democratized. Korea would be unified and eventually become independent, and the European colonies in Southeast Asia would be ultimately granted independence, but in the meantime placed in a trusteeship scheme under the aegis of the United Nations. Economic liaisons would be fostered throughout the Asia-Pacific region.

Plans were one thing and realities something else, however. The Japanese attack on Pearl Harbor had thrust the United States into a leadership position in China, the Asia-Pacific, and in global affairs generally. Heading the Allied coalition that would eventually defeat the Axis powers, U.S. leaders focused on fighting the massive worldwide conflict and dealing with issues that would determine the postwar international order. In this context, the complicated conditions in China, notably the bitter rivalry between Chiang Kai-shek's Nationalists and the Communist forces under the direction of Mao Zedong, received secondary attention. As a result, American officials tended to follow paths of least resistance as they reinforced existing proclivities to back the Nationalists, who enjoyed broad political support in the United States. They avoided the difficult U.S. policy reevaluation that would have been required for U.S. leaders to position the United States in a more balanced posture in order to deal constructively with the Chinese Communists as well as the Chinese Nationalists. The drift and bias in U.S. policy, strengthened by interventions of U.S. presidential envoy and ambassador to China Patrick Hurley, foreshadowed the U.S. failure in China once the Communists defeated the Nationalists on mainland China in 1949 and moved in early 1950 to align with the Soviet Union against the United States in the Cold War.

Neither the government of Mao Zedong nor the Truman administration sought or foresaw a U.S.-China war in early 1950. The Americans were therefore surprised when North Korean forces, with the support of Soviet and Chinese leaders, launched an all-out military attack against South Korea in June 1950. The Chinese Communist leaders and their Korean and Soviet allies apparently calculated that the better-armed North Koreans would attain victory quickly without provoking major or effective U.S. military response. Thus, it was their turn to be surprised when the United States quickly intervened militarily in the Korean War and also sent the U.S. Seventh Fleet to prevent the anticipated Chinese Communist attack on Taiwan. U.S. forces and their South Korean allies halted the North Korean advance and carried out an amphibious landing at Inchon in September 1950 that effectively cut off North Korean armies in the South, leading to their destruction.

The string of miscalculations continued. With UN sanction, the U.S. and South Korean armies proceeded into North Korea. The Chinese Communists warned that they were prepared to resist the advance, but U.S. leaders thought the warnings were a bluff. By November, hundreds of thousands of Chinese Communist troops were driving the U.S. and South Korean forces south in full retreat. Eventually, the Americans and their allies were able to sustain a line of combat roughly in the middle of the peninsula, as the two armies faced off for two more years of combat, casualties, and destruction.

The complications of the postwar situation in Asia and the start of the Cold War severely undermined Roosevelt's idealistic vision for the Asia-Pacific after World War II. Principles of economic interdependence, human rights, and democracy remained. But these were now subordinated to an overall strategic conception in which military confrontation between the United States and the Soviet Union became the overriding framework of American policy. Asia became part of a global anti-Soviet coalition. American troops and bases were maintained in Japan, Korea, the Philippines, and eventually Taiwan and elsewhere. Japan was encouraged to rearm; defense alliances were established with these countries, Australia, and New Zealand. The Communist People's Republic of China (PRC), the U.S. foe in the bloody Korean War and the main adversary in Asia, was ostracized, denied recognition and trade.

The military-strategic considerations of the Cold War provided the key to Asian international affairs and American relations with the Asia-Pacific for at least two decades, the 1950s and the 1960s. Accounting for more than half of the world's income and industrial production at the end of World War II, the United States put forth billions of dollars and tens of thousands of lives to uphold the "containment" arrangement in the Asia-Pacific. It fought two wars for the same purpose.

It seems clear that the origins and consequences of the Korean and the Vietnam wars were part of the same picture, reflecting the primacy of strategic considerations in America's approach to Asia. What is subject to more debate is the notion that, had the vision of Franklin Roosevelt retained a stronger influence in postwar American policy, there might have been a greater readiness to come to grips with the profound social and cultural changes taking place in China, Korea, Vietnam, and elsewhere and to deal with them in an integrated fashion, not simply in the framework of global balance of power.

But that was not to be. In the interests of Cold War competition and the doctrine of containment, the United States for a time reversed Roosevelt's vision and supported the Western European powers as they tried to sustain colonies in Southeast Asia. The United States followed through with its commitment to provide the Philippines with independence and to contribute to economic rehabilitation in the country. But U.S. opposition to the Communist-led Hukbalahap and American demands for U.S. military installations saw the U.S. government align with conservative political forces in the Philippines. These actions seemed to underscore that U.S. policy was less interested in free democracy and broad economic development than in sustaining stability and preventing the spread of communism.

One consequence of America's Cold War strategy in the Asia-Pacific was Japanese economic growth and its spread to nearby noncommunist Asian states. American officials thought an economically healthy Japan would be the best guarantee against its falling under Soviet or Chinese influence. Washington helped Japan's reentry into the international economic arena through membership in organizations such as the General Agreement on Tariffs and Trade (GATT), the predecessor to the World Trade Organization (WTO), and the IMF. The United States even tolerated significant trade between Japan and the PRC, which, though small in comparison with Japanese trade with the United States or Southeast Asia, steadily grew in importance for China because of the latter's increasing alienation from the Soviet Union. Viewed from the perspective of intense U.S.-Japanese economic rivalry in the 1980s, it was remarkable that America was supportive of Japanese economic interests, as Japan appeared to give little in return. In part, this was because the 1950s and 1960s were periods of high U.S. growth, and until at least the late 1960s, the United States seemed able to afford to engage in a costly war in Southeast Asia and to remain calm even as Japan and European nations expanded their trade and industrial production and came to challenge American economic supremacy.

Nixon's Opening to China and Strategic Shift in the Asia-Pacific

The U.S.-PRC rapprochement, the U.S.-Soviet détente in nuclear arms, and the oil shocks of the 1970s shook the foundations of the Cold War system in the Asia-Pacific. The United States incorporated mainland China into the Asia-Pacific security system and turned to Asian countries to contribute much more toward their own defense as the United States withdrew more than 600,000 military personnel from the region under the terms of the "Nixon Doctrine." U.S. leaders now expected Japan, as well as European countries, to do more to help stabilize international economic conditions. Given a period of negative growth and double-digit inflation, the United States was no longer seen as the dominant international economic leader. It was more concerned with safeguarding narrow national interests.

With Japan and other allies, significant gaps developed between the security and economic aspects of U.S. relations. Trade disputes grew, U.S. voices criticized Japan for taking advantage of American military protection, and U.S. officials asked whether Japan should contribute more to regional security. Japanese leaders remained unwilling to devote more than 1 percent of GNP to defense. Japan's 1976 "general guidelines for defense policy" reiterated the nation's commitment to a small-scale military force for purely defensive purposes. To some American officials, China began to seem a more promising ally.[18]

Following the collapse of U.S.-backed regimes in South Vietnam and Cambodia in 1975, U.S. policy in Asia was in considerable disarray. Indeed, authority was challenged from several quarters in the United States. The Watergate scandal and ensuing resignation of President Nixon in 1974, followed by the Vietnamese Communist takeover of South Vietnam the following year, left American credibility badly damaged and its policies (especially toward Asia) uncertain in the eyes of both friends and adversaries. There was particular concern in the U.S. government just after the fall of Saigon that North Korea might think the time was again opportune to strike militarily against South Korea.

Within the United States, there was rising concern over issues of morality regarding both the ends and the means of foreign policy. America had become involved in a policy of détente, but the idea that there were good as well as bad Communists confused many people. Higher standards were demanded and additional constraints imposed upon the presidency. The War Powers Resolution placed new restrictions on the president's freedom to use military force. Congress passed laws requiring countries that received U.S. economic and military assistance to meet certain minimum (if vague) human rights standards domestically, and later the administration was required to publish an annual report on human rights conditions in all countries. Congress enacted numerous "legislative vetoes," requiring the president to provide Congress with notice of proposed arms deliveries and allowing it to block such actions.

U.S. Policy during the Carter and Reagan Administrations

President Jimmy Carter came to office holding many of the beliefs of the critics of the Vietnam War and of the Nixon-Kissinger emphasis on realism and balance-of-power policies. Carter seemed determined to shift the emphasis of U.S. policy from power toward morality and to give less attention to seeking specific short-term advantages over the Soviet Union. He had several genuine accomplishments: the Panama Canal treaty, the Camp David Accords between Egypt and Israel, and the establishment of full diplomatic relations with China. Yet the Carter administration was ultimately overwhelmed by a combination of events over which it had little control, combined with its own divisions and vacillation. Among the key events were the Iranian revolution and ensuing hostage crisis, the second oil shock, and growing and internationally expanding Soviet strategic military power.[19]

The Soviet Union became more assertive in several parts of the world. Notably, Moscow intervened militarily in Afghanistan at the end of 1979 to shore up the Communist regime there, which had seized power in a coup in 1978 but was threatened by internal conflicts and the growing strength of anticommunist tribesmen. The different approaches of Secretary of State Cyrus Vance and National Security Adviser Zbigniew Brzezinski in dealing with the Soviets were never clearly resolved by Carter until Soviet aggressiveness and Vance's resignation in the wake of a failed hostage rescue attempt in 1980 made the issue moot. Carter's public vacillation on such issues as developing a neutron bomb and his startling statement that he had learned more about the USSR as a result of the invasion of Afghanistan than he had ever known previously convinced many Americans that he was naïve, inept, and indecisive. Despite his emphasis in the late 1970s on rebuilding U.S. military power, there was a widespread American and foreign view that the U.S. position vis-à-vis the Soviet Union was deteriorating.

In the Asia-Pacific, Carter initially benefited from the lack of serious challenges faced by the United States after the fall of South Vietnam. Nonetheless, his administration from the outset faced a problem in the Asia-Pacific because of Carter's 1975 public statement that the United States should withdraw its ground troops from South Korea over the next several years. Carter had been critical of the Republic of Korea (ROK) for its suppression of human rights, and the "Koreagate" scandal involving alleged South Korean gifts of money to U.S. members of Congress in an attempt to secure continued American support of South Korea's military security had generated widespread criticism of Seoul. While President Carter insisted that U.S. Air Force units would remain in Korea and the U.S.-ROK Security Treaty would still be valid, South Koreans of all political persuasions were fearful that withdrawing U.S. troops would remove a key factor deterring North Korea. The Japanese government, along with most other Asian nations friendly with the United States, also was worried about what was seen as further American retreat from Asia and as another example of American unilateralism on an issue of vital interest to many Asian countries. Even China, though publicly calling for the removal of U.S. troops from Korea, was widely reported to have told U.S. officials that it understood the need for the continued presence of American ground troops in South Korea.

Several factors led Carter to reverse his position and agree early in 1979 to keep U.S. ground troops in South Korea. For one thing, there was little domestic political pressure pushing him to follow through on his promise. Moreover, opponents of the move pressed for a major intelligence study of the North Korean military forces, which in 1978 concluded that North Korean forces were much larger, better equipped, and more offensively oriented than previously thought, providing the justification Carter needed to shift his positions.

President Carter also was unsuccessful in efforts to normalize relations with Vietnam. His efforts ran into strong opposition in the United States. Other obstacles included Vietnamese demands that were seen as excessive by Carter administration leaders and the U.S. government's competing interest in pursuing closer strategic ties with China against the expanding Soviet Union and its associates in Asian and world affairs. Notably, Vietnam in late 1978 was strongly backed by the Soviet Union as it toppled the Chinese-backed Khmer Rouge regime in neighboring Cambodia. This set the stage for China to confront and attack Vietnam along the Sino-Vietnamese border in early 1979. The convergence of these developments prompted Carter administration negotiators to halt the normalization talks with Hanoi.

The Carter administration devoted considerable effort to completing the formal structure of U.S.-China normalization, begun during the Nixon administration, by establishing full diplomatic relations with the PRC. In relations with China, President Carter and National Security Adviser Brzezinski followed the pattern of secret diplomacy used successfully by President Nixon and National Security Adviser Henry Kissinger in early interaction with China. Thus, there was very little consultation with Congress, key U.S. allies, or the government in Taiwan regarding the conditions and timing of the 1978 normalization agreement. In contrast to the general congressional, media, and popular support that greeted the surprise Nixon opening to China, Carter and his aides were notably less successful in winning U.S. domestic support for their initiatives. Many in Congress were satisfied with the stasis that developed in U.S.-PRC-Taiwan relations in the mid-1970s and unconvinced that the United States had a strategic or other need to pay the price of breaking a U.S. defense treaty and other official ties with a loyal government in Taiwan for the sake of formalizing already existing relations with the PRC. Bipartisan majorities in Congress resisted the president's initiatives and passed laws, notably the Taiwan Relations Act (TRA), that tied the hands of the administration on Taiwan and other issues.

The Taiwan Relations Act was passed by Congress in March 1979 and signed by President Carter on April 10, 1979. The initial draft of the legislation was proposed by the administration to govern U.S. relations with Taiwan once official U.S. ties were ended in 1979. Congress rewrote the legislation, notably adding or strengthening provisions on U.S. arms sales, opposition to threats and use of force, economic relations, human rights, and congressional oversight. Treating Taiwan as a separate entity that would continue to receive U.S. military and other support, the law appeared to contradict the U.S. stance in the U.S.-PRC communiqué of 1978 establishing official U.S.-PRC relations. Subsequently, Chinese officials and officials from Taiwan and their supporters in the United States competed to incline U.S. policy toward the commitments in the U.S.-PRC communiqué or those in the TRA. U.S. policy usually supported both, though it sometimes seemed more supportive of one set of commitments than the other.

President Carter's Asia policy played a significant role in the 1980 U.S. presidential campaign. Ronald Reagan attacked Carter's emphasis on human rights, which he argued was applied more strongly against U.S. allies than was appropriate. He castigated Carter's admission that the Soviet invasion of Afghanistan in late 1979 had taught him much about Soviet intentions and behavior as an indication of Carter's naïveté. Reagan also attacked Carter's policy toward Taiwan. Asserting for a time that he would restore official relations with Taipei, Reagan later backed away from this stance but still claimed he would base his policy on the Taiwan Relations Act.

After the 1980 election, continued rancor appeared likely between President Reagan, who took a hard-line foreign policy stance, and the Congress, which was divided between the Democratic-controlled House of Representatives and the Republican-controlled Senate. Over time, however, there emerged a growing spirit of bipartisanship in U.S. policy toward the Asia-Pacific region in the 1980s. In part this had to do with the fact that the administration's actions were seldom as strong as its rhetoric might have suggested. Democrats also came to see a need for the stronger U.S. defense and foreign policy that the Reagan administration advocated in the face of continued Soviet expansion. The administration and Democratic leaders also were willing to consult and compromise on key issues.

On sensitive issues regarding the authoritarian regime in South Korea, Reagan shortly after he took office invited South Korean president Chun Doo Hwan to the United States and gave him strong public backing. There apparently was at least an implicit agreement that President Chun would release prominent opposition leader and later democratically elected president of South Korea Kim Dae Jung and allow him to leave the country, which Chun did. President Reagan thus could point to an early success for quiet diplomacy, and Seoul felt that it had a firm friend in the White House.

The administration also formed policy and practices toward Japan in a calm and generally supportive manner. Instead of publicly criticizing Japan for not spending enough on defense, the focus was placed upon the appropriate roles and missions Japanese forces should undertake in conjunction with U.S. forces. Tokyo in 1981 accepted the primary responsibility for its own air defense and agreed to develop the capacity to help defend sea lanes a thousand miles to the east and south of Japan. Japan's steady though small increases in defense spending were regarded by the U.S. administration with satisfaction. Congressional criticism of Japan on such "burden-sharing" matters continued, but had no major effect on U.S. policy.

It took longer for the Reagan administration to come to a consensus on China policy. Reagan's pro-Taiwan rhetoric during the 1980 campaign and his initial period in office saw China respond strongly. The Chinese government put heavy pressure on the Reagan administration. It threatened a serious deterioration in relations due to various issues, especially continuing U.S. arms sales to Taiwan. Viewing close PRC-U.S. relations as a key element in U.S. strategy against the Soviet Union, Secretary of State Alexander Haig led those in the Reagan administration who favored maintaining close relations and opposed U.S. arms sales to Taiwan that might provoke China. For a year and a half, Haig and his supporters were successful in leading U.S. efforts to accommodate PRC concerns over Taiwan, especially arms sales, in the interest of fostering closer cooperation with China against the Soviet Union. The United States and China ultimately signed the August 17, 1982, communiqué in which the United States agreed gradually to diminish arms sales to Taiwan and China agreed it would seek peaceful reunification of Taiwan with the mainland. Subsequent developments showed that the vague agreement was subject to varying interpretations. President Reagan registered private reservations about this arrangement, and his administration also took steps to reassure Taiwan's leader of continued U.S. support.

Amid continued strong Chinese pressure tactics on a wide range of U.S.-China disputes, American policy shifted with Haig's resignation in 1982 and the appointment of George Shultz as secretary of state. Reagan administration officials who were at odds with Haig's emphasis on the need for a solicitous U.S. approach to China came to the fore. They were led by Paul Wolfowitz, who was chosen by Shultz as assistant secretary of state for East Asian affairs; Richard Armitage, the senior Defense Department officer managing relations with China and East Asia; and the senior National Security Council staff aide on Asian affairs and later assistant secretary of state for East Asian affairs, Gaston Sigur. While officers who had backed Haig's pro-China slant were transferred from authority over China policy, the new U.S. leadership contingent with responsibility for

Asian affairs shifted U.S. policy toward a less solicitous and accommodating stance with regard to China, while giving much higher priority to
U.S. relations with Japan. There was less emphasis on China's strategic
importance to the United States in American competition with the Soviet
Union, and there was less concern among U.S. policy makers about China
possibly downgrading relations over Taiwan and other disputes.

This position seemed more in line with the preferences of many in Congress, who had resisted efforts to cut back ties with Taiwan for the sake
of strengthening U.S. alignment with China against the Soviet Union. The
U.S. military buildup and the close U.S.-Japanese security relationship
seemed to reduce China's strategic importance to the United States. The
administration established a general consensus in the U.S. government
and with Congress for the first time since the controversy over the Carter
administration's secret move to normalize diplomatic relations with
China. By the mid-1980s, there was widespread agreement that the role
of the PRC in the U.S. policy calculus was less important than it had been
in the previous fifteen years. U.S. officials felt less compelled to make
additional sacrifices regarding Taiwan for the sake of ensuring close relations with the PRC.

The more moderate foreign policy of the Soviet Union in the Asia-
Pacific following the coming to power of Mikhail Gorbachev in 1985
reinforced stability in the balance of power in the region. At a minimum,
Moscow seemed interested by the latter 1980s in easing tensions around
its periphery, thereby gaining at least a temporary "breathing space" in
which to revive the ailing Soviet economy. At the same time, Gorbachev
highlighted political and economic initiatives designed to increase Soviet
influence abroad. Gorbachev had more difficulty expanding Soviet influence in Asia than in Europe, and he appeared to view an opening to China
as a key link in efforts to improve Soviet influence in the region. Soviet
leaders followed through on their repeated pledges to ease military tensions with China by addressing substantive Chinese security concerns.
Beijing summarized these concerns as the "three obstacles" to improved
Sino-Soviet relations: the Soviet military occupation of Afghanistan, Soviet military presence along China's northern border, and Soviet support
for Vietnam's military occupation of Cambodia.

U.S. Economic Weakness and the Rise of Japan

While the more stable security situation for U.S. interests in the Asia-
Pacific developed in the 1980s, a growing set of economic challenges
emerged. These challenges seemed fundamentally to undermine important U.S. interests and America's leading position in the region. Overall,
East Asian countries advanced rapidly in economic development in the

1980s. They doubled their percentage of world output—from 10 to 20 percent—in ten years. Their combined export trade expanded similarly, leading to huge surpluses with the United States ($27 billion in 1981, $105 billion in 1987). The decade saw American trade with East Asian countries surpass that with European countries. As the Asian economies grew, Asian investment began to enter the United States in order to finance part of its deficits. America and East Asia became economically more interdependent than ever.[20]

In retrospect, it appears ironic that just as resilient American power and obvious Soviet decline appeared to put to rest the widely perceived threat to American leadership posed by rising Soviet power, American strategists, specialists, and commentators began focusing on growing U.S. economic interdependence with Asia in the 1980s as marking a steady decline of U.S. influence and leadership in Asia. During the Cold War, America's ability to counter Soviet power and to promote economic growth and political stability abroad depended heavily on U.S. economic strength and willingness to make economic sacrifices in order to achieve military and political goals. Such U.S. costs included a large military budget, substantial foreign aid programs, and the free flow of exports of other countries to the U.S. market. By the 1980s, America's economic position was seen by many experts and pundits to be so seriously weakened that the nation's long-term ability to sustain its leading role in the world, and the Asia-Pacific in particular, was cast in doubt.

Among the salient reasons for the perceived U.S. economic decline was economic progress abroad, especially in East Asia. The Asian economies headed by Japan added competitive pressures on the U.S. economy not seen since before World War II, when foreign trade had a much smaller impact on the U.S. economy. At home, U.S. educational standards were widely reported to have declined, as had product quality, and businesses were seen to be giving increasing priority to short-term profits and financial mergers. Investment levels were inadequate for a more competitive international environment, as were low U.S. savings rates. The federal budget deficits rose, as did the U.S. dollar, and with it the U.S. trade deficit, greatly increasing pressures for protectionism.

The trend toward U.S. economic and trade protectionism grew for important reasons. The first was economic. In 1971, the United States had its first trade deficit since World War II. Trade deficits continued, increasing in size through most of the 1970s and the early 1980s, and averaged about $25 billion in 1979–1981. But a surplus in services meant that the United States had a current-account surplus and was earning and paying its way in the world, except briefly in 1977 and 1978.

From 1980, there was a dramatic rise in the trade account deficit, which in 1986 amounted to $153 billion. This was mainly due to a sharp rise in imports, from $245 billion in 1981 to $370 billion in 1986, while U.S. exports declined from $234 billion to $217 billion in the same period. The deficit in the trade balance with Asia, mainly East Asia, increased from $21.8 billion in 1981 to $95.7 billion in 1987. The total deficit for 1987 rose further to $159 billion, despite the fall in the value of the U.S. dollar that year. Exports rose to $253 billion, but imports continued to increase to $412 billion. These trade deficits made the United States a debtor nation for the first time since World War I. It soon became the world's largest debtor nation.[21]

The seeming economic weakness and decline of the United States came as Japan rose to great prominence in Asian and world affairs. The 1980s witnessed a sweeping change in the relative power of the United States and Japan. This change went well beyond the implications of the bilateral trade deficit, which remained around $50 billion annually even after the major drop in the value of the U.S. dollar in relation to the Japanese yen in the latter 1980s. As the persisting U.S. trade and budget deficits of the early 1980s led to a series of decisions in the mid-1980s that called for a major realignment of the value of the U.S. and Japanese currencies, the immediate result was to greatly strengthen Japan's ability to purchase U.S. goods and to invest in the United States. By the end of the decade, as the United States had reversed its previous position as the world's largest creditor and had become the world's largest debtor, Japan, with its stronger currency, became the largest international creditor.

Americans found it hard to compete with Japan in Asia and were seemingly unable to preserve market share even in the U.S. home market. Japan's growing investments in the United States led to complaints from some American constituencies. Moreover, Japanese industry seemed well positioned to use its economic power to invest in the range of high-technology products where U.S. manufacturers still had the lead. U.S. ability to compete under these circumstances was seen as being hampered by heavy personal, government, and business debt, a low savings rate, and other factors.

Based on its economic power and seemingly unstoppable competitiveness, Japan was able to steadily expand its role in the World Bank, the IMF, and such regional organizations as the Asian Development Bank. Investment and trade flows made Japan by far the dominant economic actor in Asia. U.S. leadership seemed to be in steady decline as Japan used its burgeoning investment and trade links to expand political influence in the Asia-Pacific region. While countries in Northeast and Southeast Asia were the main targets of Japanese economic networks of influence, countries in South Asia and the new republics in Central Asia, among others, actively sought Japanese aid and investment, while the United States seemed to have less to offer.

Post–Cold War Priorities

The collapse of communism in Eastern Europe and subsequently in the Soviet Union, the thaw in U.S.-Soviet relations, and the progress toward democracy and political reform in several former Soviet or Soviet-bloc states and other nations reinforced American interest in pursuing closer interaction with reforming Asian countries. These developments made cultural elements and values more important considerations in the making of American foreign policy. Those elements had remained strong in the Asia-Pacific even as overall U.S. influence in the region was seen to decline, notably in the face of economic problems and Japan's remarkable rise in influence.[22]

Democratization movements in China, South Korea, the Philippines, Taiwan, Burma, and elsewhere in the 1970s and 1980s were all inspired at least in some part by the American example. The 1989 student uprising in Beijing would not have been as massive or at least initially as successful without the knowledge that Americans were watching the event on television. The revolutionary innovations in information and communications technology, much of them products of American engineering, were weaving countries of the world closer together into a global network, and the sense of instantaneous communication was nowhere more pronounced than in the hitherto closed societies of Asia. Even in a more open society like Japan, there were forces tending to Americanize people's lifestyles further.

American society, too, was coming under increasing Asia-Pacific influences. The landmark immigration act of 1965 finally established color-blind U.S. immigration practices. When combined with various measures to resettle refugees, this development brought an influx of people from the Asia-Pacific region to the United States. Asians came to account for 2.4 percent of the U.S. population by the early 1990s. In the most populous U.S. state, California, the ratio was much higher, and there was an expectation that Asians might soon amount to one-third of the state's inhabitants. Immigrants from Vietnam, Korea, China, Taiwan, India, Thailand, Pakistan, Afghanistan, and other Asia-Pacific countries were much more visible in American society than they earlier had been. Americans became accustomed to varieties of Asian food, clothing, and religious practices. There also were hundreds of thousands of temporary visitors from Asia as tourists and students. In 1988, close to three million Japanese tourists came to America and more than 200,000 additional Japanese resided in the United States studying and working. The number of Korean and Chinese students in the United States seemed to have been even larger than the number of Japanese students.

The U.S. reaction to the Chinese government's crackdown on the Tiananmen Square demonstrations in June 1989 underscored the influence of culture and values in American foreign policy at that time. The Tiananmen massacre sharply changed American views about China. Instead of pursuing policies of political and economic reform, the leaders in Beijing were now widely seen as following policies antithetical to American values and therefore as unworthy of U.S. support. Rapidly changing U.S.-Soviet relations also meant that there was no longer a realpolitik or national security rationale of sufficient weight to offset the new revulsion with Beijing's leaders and their repressive policies.

Other parts of the world, meanwhile, saw political, economic, and security changes that attracted wide and generally positive attention from American people, media, interest groups, and legislators. Russia, some new republics of the former Soviet Union in Asia, and former Soviet bloc states like Mongolia were increasingly following policies of reform in their government structures and economies that seemed to be based on values of individual freedom, political democracy, and economic free enterprise that were well regarded in the United States. As a result, these American interest groups, media, and policy advocates tended at times to push U.S. government decision makers to be more forthcoming in negotiations and interaction with them involving arms control, trade, foreign assistance, and other matters.

The importance of this shift in domestic U.S. opinion regarding China and the former Soviet Union and Soviet bloc countries appeared to be of greater significance than it might have been in the past in determining the course of U.S. foreign policy. Since the start of the Cold War, the executive branch had been able to argue, on many occasions quite persuasively, that such domestic U.S. concerns with common values should not be permitted to override or seriously complicate realpolitik U.S. interests in the protracted struggle and rivalry with the USSR. Now that it was widely seen that the Cold War was ending and the threat from Moscow was ended or greatly reduced, the ability of the executive branch to control the course of U.S. foreign policy appeared somewhat weakened. The U.S. administration could no longer argue that the dangers of Cold War contention and confrontation required a tightly controlled foreign policy.

Indeed, following the end of the Cold War, Americans were deeply divided over foreign policy, and contending policy perspectives were not easily bridged to develop coherent policy toward the Asia-Pacific or other important areas. Because security issues and opposition to Soviet expansion no longer drove U.S. foreign policy, economic interests, democratization abroad, and human rights gained greater prominence. Various pressure groups and other institutions interested in these and other subjects also gained influence in policy making. Historically, such fluidity and competition among priorities were more often than not the norm. Woodrow Wilson and Franklin Roosevelt both set forth comprehensive concepts of a well-integrated U.S. foreign policy, but neither framework lasted long. The requirements of the Cold War were much more effective in establishing rigor and order in U.S. foreign policy priorities, but that era now was over.

In particular, the post–Cold War period saw substantial changes in the way foreign policy was made in the United States. There was a general shift away from the elitism of the past and toward much greater pluralism. This increased the opportunity for input by nongovernmental or lobby groups with interests in foreign policy.

The elitist model of foreign policy making included the following characteristics:

- Domination of the process by the executive branch, particularly by the White House, the State Department, and the Pentagon
- Presidential consultation with a bipartisan leadership in Congress and mobilization through them of broad congressional support for the administration's foreign policy
- Parallel consultations with a relatively small group of elites outside government, some of whom are specialists on the particular issue under consideration and others of whom have a more general interest in foreign policy as a whole
- Mobilization of public support through the major newspapers and television programs, other media outlets, and civic organizations

Gradually, however, this process was transformed in much more pluralistic directions to take on quite different characteristics:

- A much greater range of agencies within the executive branch involved in foreign policy, with the rise of the economic agencies (Commerce, Treasury, and the U.S. Trade Representative) of particular importance
- A seeming reallocation of power within government, away from the executive branch and toward Congress
- Much greater participation by nongovernmental organizations and lobbying groups that attempt to shape foreign policy to conform to their interests
- Much less consensus within Congress, and within the broader public, over foreign policy

In the 1990s, there was consensus that foreign policy should not be expensive. The fate of the international affairs budget in Congress after the Cold War indicated that Americans wanted foreign policy both to cost less and to give more benefit. Unfortunately, there was little agreement on how to accomplish this objective. Few Americans were aware that foreign policy spending accounted for less than 1 percent of the federal budget. There appeared to be different tendencies regarding post–Cold War foreign policy. These approaches seemed to divide into three schools of thought, though they were not necessarily exclusive. In particular, a U.S. leader demonstrated aspects of one tendency at some times and aspects of another tendency at other times. An understanding of what these schools stood for underscored how difficult it was to gauge the direction of U.S. policy toward the Asia-Pacific or other key areas of international concern.

One foreign policy school of thought was particularly prominent in the first half of the 1990s when troubled U.S. economic conditions and large government budget deficits added to a sense of relative decline of American power and its implications for U.S. ability to protect its interests. This approach called for the United States to work harder to preserve important interests while adjusting to limited resources and reduced influence. Advocates of this position expected continued international instability and a limited U.S. ability to respond. They observed that there was no international framework to shape policy; that U.S. policy must use a complex mix of international, regional, and bilateral efforts to achieve policy goals; and that security, economic, and cultural-political issues would compete for priority in policy making. They argued that in this uncertain environment, pressing domestic problems would take precedence over attention to international affairs and restrict financial resources available for foreign policy, defense, and international security. They also believed that policy making would remain difficult because the executive branch might remain under the control of one political party and Congress of the other party.

This school—reflected in the commentary of such leaders as former president George H. W. Bush, Henry Kissinger, and others—argued that these circumstances required the United States to work closely with traditional allies and associates. Regarding the Asia-Pacific, it contended that it was inconsistent with U.S. goals not to preserve long-standing good relations with Japan and other friends and allies in the Asia-Pacific whose security policies and political-cultural orientations complemented U.S. interests. It urged caution in policy toward other regional powers, namely, Russia, China, and India. All three countries were preoccupied with internal political-development issues and did not appear to want regional instability. All sought closer economic and political relations with the West and with other advancing economies. Washington would be well advised, proponents of this position said, to work closely with these governments wherever there were common interests. In considering U.S. assets available to influence regional trends, they called on the United States to go slow in reducing its regional military presence. The economic savings of cutbacks would be small, while the political costs could be high insofar as most countries in the Asia-Pacific encouraged the United States to remain active in the region to offset the growing power of Japan or China.

A second school was also particularly prominent during the troubled U.S. economic conditions of the early 1990s. It argued for major cutbacks in U.S. international activity, including military involvement, and a renewed focus on solving such domestic problems as crime, drug use, economic competitiveness, educational standards, homelessness, poverty, decaying cities, and transportation infrastructure. Variations of this view were seen in the writings of William Hyland, Patrick Buchanan, and other well-known commentators and in the political statements of Ross Perot and some segments of U.S. labor organizations. Often called an "America First" or "Neo-isolationist" school, it contended that the United States had become overextended in world affairs and was being taken advantage of in the current world security-economic system. It called for sweeping cuts in spending for international activities, favoring a U.S. pullback from foreign bases and major cuts in foreign assistance and foreign technical-information programs. It was skeptical of the utility of international financial institutions and the United Nations and of international efforts to promote free trade through the WTO. This school advocated termination of international economic talks that help to perpetuate a liberal world trading system, which it believed increased U.S. economic dependence and injured some American workers and industries. Some advocates favored trade measures that were seen as protectionist by U.S. trading partners.

A third position became much more prominent as U.S. economic conditions improved and government spending resumed increases amid record budget surpluses in the mid- and later 1990s. It argued that U.S. policy needed to promote U.S. interests in international political, military, and economic affairs more actively and to use U.S. influence to pressure countries that did not conform to the norms of an appropriate world order. Supporters of this position wanted the United States to maintain military forces with worldwide capabilities, to lead strongly in world affairs, and to minimize compromises and accommodations.

This school of thought had been present in American politics throughout the twentieth century. However, for several reasons, it was stronger in the middle and late 1990s than at any time since the 1960s. During the Reagan administration, after a prolonged period of introspection and doubt following the Vietnam War, oil shocks, and the Iran hostage crisis, the American public became much more optimistic about the future of the United States. This trend was reinforced by the end of the Cold War, a victory for the U.S.-backed system of collective security and for U.S. political and economic values. The outcome of the 1991 Persian Gulf War with Iraq further inspired confidence in U.S. military doctrine, equipment, and performance and in America's international leadership ability. The improved national and government economic conditions later in the 1990s reinforced this trend.

Those who supported this view acknowledged that America faced many serious international and domestic challenges, but they were optimistic that the United States could succeed in a competitive world economy. They also insisted that the United States was better positioned than any other country to exert leadership in the realm of ideas and values, political concepts, lifestyle, popular culture, and international organizations. They perceived a global power vacuum, caused notably by the collapse of the Soviet empire and the demise of communism, which allowed the United States to exert influence. Proponents of this view argued that Russia, China, and India would remain preoccupied with domestic problems. They acknowledged that Japan and Germany were economically powerful, but also saw them as uncertain regarding how to use their power; furthermore, they lacked American cultural attractiveness and influence.

In the mid- to late 1990s, advocates of this third tendency were most vocal in pressing for a strong policy in support of democracy and human rights. They argued for a more active foreign policy, which led some targeted countries to view U.S. policy as interference in other countries' internal affairs. The school's supporters opposed economic or trading policies of other countries that were seen as inequitable or predatory. They pressed for a strong policy against the proliferation of weapons of mass destruction. Members of this school also argued variously for sanctions against countries that practiced coercive birth control, seriously polluted the environment, harbored terrorists, or promoted the drug trade. They believed the United States should be more assertive in promoting humanitarian relief and in recognizing the legitimacy of people's right to self-determination. Republican leaders in Congress following the victory of the Republican Party in the 1994 congressional elections, including Speaker of the House Newt Gingrich, were seen to push this more assertive U.S. role in world affairs.

U.S. Asia-Pacific Policy in Flux: The Example of U.S. China Policy after the Cold War

A graphic example of the broad scope of contending interests and schools of thought in American policy toward the Asia-Pacific region in the post–Cold War period is the tortuous course of U.S. policy toward China.[23] Unexpected mass demonstrations centered in Beijing's Tiananmen Square and other Chinese cities in spring 1989 represented the most serious challenge to China's post-Mao leadership. Chinese leader Deng Xiaoping was decisive in resolving Chinese leadership differences in favor of hard-liners favoring a violent crackdown on the demonstrators and a broader suppression of political dissent that began with the bloody attack on Tiananmen Square on June 4, 1989. Reform-minded leaders were purged and punished.

Anticipating shock and disapproval to the Tiananmen crackdown from the United States and the West, Deng nonetheless argued that the negative reaction would have few prolonged negative consequences for China. The Chinese leader failed to anticipate the breadth and depth of U.S. disapproval that would profoundly influence U.S. policy into the twenty-first century. The condemnation was compounded by the unanticipated and dramatic collapse of Communist regimes in the Soviet bloc and other areas, leading to the demise of the Soviet Union by the early 1990s. These developments undermined the perceived necessity for the United States to cooperate pragmatically with China, despite its brutal dictatorship, on account of a U.S. strategic need for international support against the Soviet Union. Meanwhile, Taiwan's authoritarian government was moving steadily at this time to promote democratic policies and practices, marking a sharp contrast to the harsh political authoritarianism in mainland China and greatly enhancing Taiwan's popularity and support in the United States.

Taken together, these circumstances generally placed the clout in U.S.-China relations with U.S. leaders. Chinese leaders at first focused on maintaining internal stability as they maneuvered to sustain workable economic relations with the United States while rebuffing major U.S. initiatives that infringed on Chinese internal political control or territorial and sovereignty issues involving Taiwan and Tibet. As the Chinese government presided over strong economic growth beginning in 1993 and the U.S. and other international attention that came with it, Chinese leaders reflected more confidence as they dealt with U.S. pressure for change. However, they generally eschewed direct confrontation that would endanger the critically important economic relations with the United States unless China was provoked by U.S., Taiwanese, or other actions.

Effective U.S. policy toward China proved elusive amid contentious American domestic debate over China policy during the 1990s. That debate was not stilled until the September 11, 2001, terrorist attacks on America muffled for a time continued U.S. concerns over China amid an overwhelming American concern to deal with the immediate, serious, and broad consequences of the Global War on Terrorism.

After the Tiananmen massacre, President George H. W. Bush, with strong personal conviction about the importance of cooperative U.S. relations with China, strove to preserve mutual ties amid widespread American outrage and pressure for retribution and sanctions against the Chinese leaders. Bush was the U.S. chief executive most experienced in dealing with China, having served as the head of the U.S. Liaison Office in China in the mid-1970s. Accordingly, Bush took the lead in his own administration (1989–1993) in dealing with the severe problems in China-U.S. relations caused by the Tiananmen crackdown and the decline in U.S. strategic interest in China as a result of the collapse of the Soviet bloc. He resorted to secret diplomacy to maintain constructive communication with senior Chinese leaders, but the latter remained fairly rigid and were unable or unwilling to make many gestures to help Bush justify a continued moderate U.S. stance toward China amid wide-ranging U.S. skepticism and hostility in Congress, the media, and interest groups. While his administration officials said all high-level official contact with China would be cut off as a result of the Tiananmen crackdown, President Bush sent his national security adviser and the deputy secretary of state on secret missions to Beijing in July and December 1989. When the missions became known in December 1989, the congressional and media reaction was bitterly critical of the administration's perceived duplicity.

Bush eventually became frustrated with the Chinese leadership's intransigence and adopted a tough stance on trade and other issues, though he made special efforts to ensure that the United States continued most-favored-nation (MFN) tariff status for China despite opposition by a majority of the U.S. Congress and much of the American media. Reflecting more positive U.S. views of Taiwan, the Bush administration upgraded U.S. interchange with the Nationalist government by sending a cabinet level official to Taipei in 1992, the first such visit since official relations were ended in 1979. He also seemed to abandon the limits on U.S. arms sales set in accord with the August 1982 U.S. communiqué with China by agreeing in 1992 to a sale to Taiwan of 150 advanced F-16 jet fighters worth more than $5 billion.

Presidential candidate Bill Clinton used sharp attacks against Chinese government behavior, notably the Tiananmen crackdown, and President Bush's moderate approach to China to win support in the 1992 election. Clinton's attacks, though probably reflecting sincere anger and concern over Chinese behavior, also reflected a tendency in the United States, in the 1990s, to use China issues, particularly criticism of China and U.S. policy toward China, for partisan and other ulterior purposes. The president-elect, and U.S. politicians in following years, found that criticizing China and America's China policy provided a convenient means to pursue political and other ends. For candidate Clinton and his aides, using

China issues to discredit the record of Republican candidate Bush proved to be an effective way to take votes from the incumbent. Once he won the election and was in office, President Clinton showed little interest in China policy, leaving the responsibility to subordinates.

In particular, Assistant Secretary of State for East Asia Affairs Winston Lord in 1993 played the lead administration role in working with congressional leaders, notably Senate Majority Leader George Mitchell and a House of Representatives leader on China and human rights issues, Rep. Nancy Pelosi, and others to establish the human rights conditions the Clinton administration would require before renewing MFN status for China. The terms he worked out were widely welcomed in the United States at the time. However, the Chinese government leaders were determined not to give in on several of the U.S. demands, and they appeared to calculate that U.S. business interests in a burgeoning Chinese economy would be sufficient to prevent the United States from taking the drastic step of cutting MFN tariff treatment for China and risking the likely retaliation of the PRC against U.S. trade interests. Indeed, American business pressures pushed Clinton to intervene in May 1994 to reverse existing policy and allow for unimpeded U.S. renewal of MFN status for China.

Pro-Taiwan interests in the United States, backed by U.S. public relations firms in the pay of entities and organizations in Taiwan, took the opportunity of congressional elections in 1995 that gave control of the Congress to pro-Taiwan Republican leaders. They pushed for greater U.S. support for the island, notably seeking permission for a visit by Taiwanese president Lee Teng-hui to his alma mater Cornell University. Under heavy domestic political pressure, President Clinton intervened again and allowed Lee to visit the United States.

A resulting military confrontation with China in the Taiwan Strait involving two U.S. aircraft carrier battle groups saw the Clinton administration move to a much more coherent engagement policy toward China that received consistent and high-level attention from the president and his key aides and was marked by two U.S.-China summit meetings in 1997 and 1998. Progress included a U.S.-China agreement on China's entry into the World Trade Organization and U.S. agreement to provide permanent normal trade status for China. However, the new approach failed to still the vigorous American debate against forward movement in U.S. relations with China on a wide range of strategic, economic, political, and other issues.

As in the case of Clinton's attacks on George H. W. Bush, many of the criticisms of Clinton's engagement policy with China after 1996 were not so much focused on China and China issues for their own sake as they were on partisan or other concerns. Most notably, as congressional Republican leaders sought to impeach President Clinton and tarnish the reputation of his administration, they endeavored to dredge up a wide range of charges regarding illegal Chinese fund raising, Chinese espionage, and the PRC's wide deviations from international norms regarding human rights, nuclear weapons, ballistic missile proliferation, and other questions. They used these charges to discredit Clinton's moderate engagement policy toward China, and in so doing to cast serious doubt on the moral integrity and competence of the president and his aides.

The Clinton policy of engagement with China also came under attack from organized labor interests within the Democratic Party, some of which used the attacks on the administration's China policy as a means to get the administration to pay more attention to broader labor interests within the party. In a roughly similar fashion, social conservatives in the Republican Party used sharp attacks against continuation of U.S. most-favored-nation tariff status for China (a stance often supported by congressional Republican leaders) despite Chinese coercive birth control policies; they did this in part as a means to embarrass the Republican leaders and pressure them into paying more positive attention to the various agenda issues of the social conservatives.

During the 1990s, congressional disparagement of China and any moderation in U.S. policy toward China was easy to do and generally had benefits for those doing the criticism. The condemnation generated positive coverage from U.S. media, which were strongly critical of China. It generated positive support and perhaps some fundraising and electioneering support for the congressional critics from the many interest groups in the United States that focused censure on Chinese policies and practices at this time. The Chinese government, anxious to keep the economic relationship with the United States on an even keel, was disinclined to punish such congressional critics or take substantive action against them. More likely were Chinese invitations to the adversarial senators and representatives for all-expenses-paid trips to China in order to persuade them to change their views by seeing actual conditions in China. Furthermore, President Clinton, like President George H. W. Bush, often was not in a position to risk other legislative goals by punishing members critical of his China policy. In short, from a congressional perspective and a broader perspective in American politics, sharp criticism of China in the 1990s became, in political parlance, a "free ride," with many benefits for those doing the criticizing and few perceived drawbacks.

As Clinton and his White House staff took more control over China policy after the face-off with Chinese forces in the Taiwan Strait in 1996, they emphasized—like Bush before them—a moderate policy of engagement, seeking change in offensive Chinese government practices through a gradual process involving closer Chinese integration with the world economic and political order. The U.S.-China relationship improved, but also encountered significant setbacks and resistance. The president's more activist and positive policy of engagement with China saw such high points as the China-U.S. summits in 1997 and 1998, the Sino-U.S. agreement on China's entry into the WTO in 1999, and passage of U.S. legislation in 2000 granting China permanent normal trade relations status. Low points in the relationship during this time included strong congressional opposition to the president's stance against Taiwan independence in 1998; the May 1999 bombing of the Chinese Embassy in Belgrade and Chinese demonstrators trashing U.S. diplomatic properties in China; strident congressional criticism in the so-called Cox Committee report of May 1999 charging administration officials with gross malfeasance in guarding U.S. secrets and weaponry from Chinese spies; and partisan congressional investigations of Clinton administration political fund raising that highlighted some illegal contributions from sources connected to the Chinese regime and the alleged impact they had on the administration's more moderate approach to the PRC.

Lee Teng-hui added to Taiwan Strait tension that worried American policy makers when he asserted in July 1999 that Taiwan was a state separate from China and that China and Taiwan had "special state-to-state relations." Chinese leaders saw this as a step toward Taiwanese independence and reacted with strong rhetoric and some military actions and by cutting off cross-strait communication links.

George W. Bush became president in 2001 with a policy toward China that was tougher than that of his predecessor. Seeking to sustain economic relations with China, the new president was wary of China's strategic intentions and took steps to deter the PRC from using military force against Taiwan. Relations deteriorated when on April 1, 2001, a Chinese jet fighter collided with a U.S. reconnaissance plane, an EP-3, in international waters off the China coast. The jet was destroyed and the pilot killed. The EP-3 was seriously damaged but managed to make an emergency landing on China's Hainan Island. The American crew was held for eleven days and their plane much longer by Chinese authorities. Weeks of negotiations produced compromises that allowed the crew and plane to return to the United States, but neither side accepted responsibility for the incident.

Many specialists predicted continued deterioration of relations, but both governments worked to resolve issues and establish a businesslike relationship that emphasized positive aspects of the relationship and played down differences. The terrorist attack on America in September 2001 diverted U.S. attention away from China as a potential strategic threat. Preoccupied with leadership transition and other issues in China, Chinese leaders worked hard to moderate their previous harsh rhetoric and pressure tactics in order to consolidate relations with the United States.

Some specialists were encouraged by the surprising improvement in U.S.-China relations during the administration of George W. Bush. They tended to emphasize greater Chinese leadership confidence and maturity as the cause for the turnabout in relations, arguing that such self-assurance prompted the Chinese government to deal more moderately and with restraint regarding some of the seeming challenges posed by the new U.S. administration and its policies regarding Taiwan, weapons proliferation, ballistic missile defense, and the overall greater U.S. assertiveness and national security power in Asian and world affairs.[24]

Another group of specialists was less convinced that U.S.-China relations were destined to converge substantially over Asian and world affairs. These observers emphasized the importance of what they saw as the Bush administration moving fairly rapidly from an initial toughness toward China to a stance of accommodation and compromise. The shift toward a moderate U.S. stance prompted Chinese leaders to pursue greater moderation in turn in their overall approach to Asian and world affairs.[25]

A third view involved specialists who gave more weight to the Bush administration's firm and effective policies toward China, which were seen to have curbed assertive and potentially disruptive Chinese tendencies and served to make it in China's interests to avoid confrontation, seek better U.S. ties, and keep from challenging U.S. interests in Asian and world affairs. This view held that it was more China than the United States that took the lead in seeking better ties in 2001, and that greater U.S.-China cooperation in Asia-Pacific affairs depended not so much on Chinese confidence and maturity as on effective U.S. use of power and influence to keep assertive and disruptive Chinese tendencies in check and to prevail upon China to limit emphasis on its differences with the United States.[26]

In any event, the course of U.S.-China affairs was smoother than at any time since the normalization of bilateral relations. American preoccupation with the wars in Afghanistan and Iraq and the broader Global War on Terrorism meant that U.S. strategic attention to China as a threat remained a secondary consideration for American policy makers. Chinese leaders, for their part, continued to deal with an incomplete leadership transition and the broad problem of trying to sustain a one-party authoritarian political regime amid a vibrant economy and rapid social change. In this context, the two powers, despite a wide spectrum of continuing differences ranging from Taiwan and Tibet to trade issues and human rights, managed to see their interests best served by generally emphasizing the positive. In particular, they found new common ground in dealing with the crisis caused by North Korea's nuclear weapons program beginning in 2002, and the Chinese appreciated Bush's December 2003 warning to Taiwan's leader Chen Shui-bian to avoid steps toward independence for Taiwan that could lead to conflict in the Taiwan Strait.

Domestic criticism of U.S. policy toward China began to revive in 2005 as the war on terrorism wore on and the conflict in Iraq brought major setbacks for the Bush administration. Economic and trade issues dominated the China policy debate. The U.S. trade deficit with China that year amounted to more than $200 billion. By 2006, it was over $230 billion. China's current-account surpluses saw China collect more than $1 trillion in foreign exchange reserves and invest much of it in U.S. Treasury bills and other U.S. government investments. This interdependence was widely seen as a sign of U.S. weakness and reliance on a rising China, whose leadership was viewed with suspicion or wariness by many Americans. At the same time, congressional, media, and interest groups revived criticism of China on a variety of issues involving notably human rights and trade practices, international energy competition, and foreign relations with perceived rogue regimes. The Bush administration, some in Congress, and some U.S. interest groups endeavored to pursue constructive engagement and senior-level dialogues as means to encourage China to behave according to U.S.-accepted norms as a "responsible stakeholder" in the prevailing international order and thereby show that the positives in U.S.-China relations outweighed the negatives.[27]

NOTES

1. Akira Iriye, *Across the Pacific: An Inner History of American–East Asian Relations* (New York: Harcourt, Brace & World, 1967); Warren Cohen, ed., *Pacific Passage: The Study of American–East Asian Relations on the Eve of the 21st Century* (New York: Columbia University Press, 1996).

2. Akira Iriye, *After Imperialism: The Search for a New Order in the Far East, 1921–1931* (Cambridge, Mass.: Harvard University Press, 1965).

3. Ronald Spector, *Eagle against the Sun: The American War with Japan* (New York: Free Press, 1985).

4. John L. Gaddis, *The United States and the Origins of the Cold War, 1941–1947* (New York: Columbia University Press, 1972).

5. Robert M. Blum, *Drawing the Line: The Origins of the American Containment Policy in East Asia* (New York: W. W. Norton, 1982).

6. Akira Iriye, *The Cold War in Asia: A Historical Introduction* (Englewood Cliffs, N.J.: Prentice Hall, 1974).

7. Robert S. Ross, *Negotiating Cooperation: The United States and China, 1969–1989* (Stanford, Calif.: Stanford University Press, 1995).

8. James Fallows, "Containing Japan," *Atlantic Monthly* 263 (May 1989): 40–53; George R. Packard, "The Coming U.S.-Japan Crisis," *Foreign Affairs* 66 (Winter 1987/88): 348–67.

9. The U.S. Defense Department's Quadrennial Defense Review of 2006 said the United States "will also seek to ensure that no foreign power can dictate the terms of regional or global security. It will attempt to dissuade any military competitor from developing disruptive or other capabilities that could enable regional hegemony or hostile action against the United States or other friendly countries, and it will seek to deter aggression or coercion. Should deterrence fail, the United States would deny any hostile power its strategic and operational objectives." These stated objectives seem generally consistent with the United States seeking a favorable balance of power in the Asia-Pacific, though they also seem more assertive than past U.S. positions. U.S. Department of Defense, *Quadrennial Defense Review Report* (Washington, D.C.: Department of Defense, 2006), 30; available at http://www.defenselink.mil/pubs/pdfs/QDR20060203.pdf.

10. For sources in addition to those noted for the following historical assessment, see Robert Sutter, *East Asia and the Pacific: Challenges for U.S. Policy* (Boulder, Colo.: Westview Press, 1992), 15–27.

11. Warren I. Cohen, *America's Response to China: A History of Sino-American Relations* (New York: Columbia University Press, 2000).

12. John K. Fairbank and Suzanne W. Barnett, eds., *Christianity in China* (Cambridge, Mass.: Harvard University Press, 1985).

13. Michael Schaller, *The United States and China: Into the Twenty-First Century* (New York: Oxford University Press, 2002), 28.

14. Cohen, *America's Response to China.*

15. Michael H. Hunt, *The Making of a Special Relationship: The United States and China to 1914* (New York: Columbia University Press, 1983).

16. Cohen, *America's Response to China*; Schaller, *The United States and China.*

17. Schaller, *The United States and China*, 18–24.

18. Surveys for this period include Michael Yahuda, *The International Politics of the Asia-Pacific* (New York: RoutledgeCurzon, 2005), 72–94.

19. Surveys for this period include Robert Scalapino, Seizaburo Sato, Jusuf Wanandi, and Sung-Joo Han, eds., *Asia and the Major Powers: Domestic Politics and Foreign Policy* (Berkeley: University of California Press, 1988); see in particular William Barnds's chapter, "Trends in U.S. Politics and Their Implications for America's Asian Policy."

20. Surveys on these topics include Richard Cronin, *Japan, the United States, and Prospects for the Asia-Pacific Century* (Singapore: Institute for Southeast Asian Studies, 1992), and Takashi Inoguchi, *Japan's International Relations* (London: Pinter, 1991).

21. Sutter, *East Asia and the Pacific*, 25.

22. Sources for this section come from Robert Sutter, *U.S. Policy toward China: An Introduction to the Role of Interest Groups* (Lanham, Md.: Rowman & Littlefield, 1998), 10–17.

23. Surveys include David M. Lampton, *Same Bed, Different Dreams: Managing U.S.-China Relations, 1989–2000* (Berkeley: University of California Press, 2001); Jean Garrison, *Making China Policy: From Nixon to G. W. Bush* (Boulder, Colo.: Lynne Reinner, 2005); and Robert Suettinger, *Beyond Tiananmen: The Politics of U.S.-China Relations, 1989–2000* (Washington, D.C.: Brookings Institution Press,

2003). The account in this section is taken from Robert Sutter, *Historical Dictionary of United States–China Relations* (Lanham, Md.: Scarecrow Press, 2006), lxv–lxxv.

24. Kenneth Lieberthal, "Behind the Crawford Summit," Pacnet no. 44 (Honolulu: CSIS Pacific Forum, October 24, 2002).

25. Michael Swaine, "Reverse Course: The Fragile Turnabout in U.S.-China Relations," Policy Brief 22 (Washington, D.C.: Carnegie Endowment for International Peace, 2003).

26. Hugo Restall, "Tough Love for China," *Wall Street Journal*, October 21, 2002, A14.

27. Kerry Dumbaugh, *China-U.S. Relations: Current Issues and Implications for U.S. Policy*, CRS Report RL33877 (Washington, D.C.: Congressional Research Service, Library of Congress, 2007).

2

✛

U.S. Priorities and Concerns Regarding China and Korea

Greater fluidity and debate over U.S. foreign policy after the Cold War created a range of controversial issues in American policy toward the Asia-Pacific region. For much of the post–Cold War period, the policy debates in the United States often were not linked directly to significant changes in the behavior of Asia-Pacific governments or other international circumstances. Instead, they more frequently reflected the concerns of a variety of U.S. government and nongovernmental actors that were seeking changes in U.S. policy and developments in the Asia-Pacific for their own reasons. These concerns had their roots inside the United States, especially in revised perceptions of American interests in the Asia-Pacific in the post–Cold War environment. In general, such domestically driven initiatives tended to push harder than in the past to have a wider range of U.S. policies and practices in the region conform more closely to U.S.-supported political, economic, and security norms.[1]

These domestic U.S. actions and proposals had major impacts on U.S. policy toward China and North Korea during this period. They often supported a harder line in U.S. policy toward both countries. They had lesser but sometimes important influence in determining the priorities of U.S. policy toward other Asia-Pacific countries, as well.

Domestically driven American interests caused U.S. relations with People's Republic of China (PRC) to be preoccupied with a large number of issues of often intense policy debate. American policy toward North Korea also remained sensitive and frequently controversial within the United States, especially as North Korea's continued development of nuclear weapons rubbed against stronger U.S. concerns to curb nuclear weapons proliferation. In a related development, frictions also grew in U.S. alliance relations with South Korea, notably over what to do about North Korea.

Elsewhere in the region, U.S. relations with Burma, and occasionally also with Indonesia, Vietnam, and Cambodia, prompted sometimes-strident discussion and debate on some issues in the United States, mainly related to human rights and good governance. U.S. relations with Japan remained crucial to the American position in the region, and U.S. relations with India grew markedly in importance in recent years. Some economic, security, and political issues prompted significant U.S. concerns in both cases, though broad support for the close U.S. alliance relationship with Japan and the burgeoning U.S. strategic partnership with India did not seem to be in doubt.

U.S. relations with Russia ran hot and cold after the demise of the Soviet Union, but both Moscow and Washington most of the time saw their interests as best served by limiting confrontation and seeking common ground. Russian policy in Asia was not a major concern in U.S. foreign policy, though important U.S. interests were negatively affected by large-scale Russian arms sales to China and Russian support for efforts to limit and reduce the American presence in Central Asia.

This chapter describes and assesses U.S. priorities and issues of concern raised in the post–Cold War policy debates in the United States regarding China and Korea. Chapters 3 and 4 go on to describe and assess the situation vis-à-vis the generally less salient issues of concern raised in the post–Cold War policy debates in the United States regarding other countries and entities in the Asia-Pacific.

The terrorist attacks on America, the U.S.-led war against the Taliban regime in Afghanistan, and the U.S.-led assault against the Saddam Hussein regime in Iraq substantially changed American policies and priorities in the Asia-Pacific. The scope of U.S. military activities and presence spread to Central Asia, and the United States became for the first time the leading foreign power in South Asia. Increased U.S. interest in Southeast Asia focused on combating terrorist groups. The campaign against terrorism and the related conflicts in Afghanistan and Iraq preoccupied U.S. policy makers. They absorbed media attention that had been used in the recent past by congressional critics, U.S. interest groups, and other domestic entities interested in promoting particular initiatives in U.S. policy toward the Asia-Pacific. As a result, the salience of these domestically driven U.S. policy initiatives was reduced.

The upsurge in domestic pressure to have U.S. policies and practices in the Asia-Pacific conform more closely with U.S.-supported norms that emerged after the Cold War abated after the September 11, 2001, attacks on America, and they did not begin to revive until 2005. At that time, the failings of U.S. administration policies in Iraq headed the list of complaints from congressional, media, and other U.S. critics about Bush administration handling of foreign policy. The election of Democratic majorities in the House of Representatives and the Senate in 2006 prompted forecasts of major challenges to Bush administration policies regarding China, North Korea, and some other Asia-Pacific areas on the part of U.S. domestic critics determined to move U.S. policies and practices more in line with their concerns.[2]

Democratic Party candidates for the 2008 presidential election criticized Bush administration foreign and domestic policies, especially the war in Iraq. Republican candidates frequently avoided strong support for the unpopular president and his policies, though they tended to argue for continuation of existing policies favored by the Republican Party. Regarding issues involving U.S. relations with the Asia-Pacific region, Democratic candidates generally were critical of the Bush administration's free trade policies, which had seen the U.S. annual trade deficit with China approach $300 billion and coincided with the loss of good-paying manufacturing jobs in the United States. They also tended to take a tougher line than the White House on human rights, Tibet, and other issues in U.S.-China relations. Several of the Democratic candidates had been critical of the Bush administration's hard-line approach in negotiations over North Korea's nuclear weapons program. They appeared to welcome the administration's shift to a more forthcoming negotiating posture toward North Korea beginning in late 2006. Leading Democratic presidential candidates also opposed the U.S.–South Korea Free Trade Agreement that was signed in 2007.[3]

PRIORITIES AND ISSUES IN U.S. POLICY TOWARD CHINA

A close examination of the debates over issues in U.S.-China relations in the post–Cold War period generally appears to support the view that the U.S. debate over policy toward China at this time had more to do with developments in the United States, especially changed U.S. perceptions of Chinese government policies and behavior, than with changes in those Chinese policies and behavior. From one perspective, the Chinese authorities generally have been following broadly similar policies in the post–Mao Zedong (d. 1976) period designed to build national wealth and power, maintain territorial integrity and achieve unification with Taiwan, enhance the leadership of the authoritarian Communist Party, and improve the economic livelihood and social opportunities for the Chinese people. Their challenge to U.S.-supported norms regarding such subjects as human rights, weapons proliferation, environmental protection, the use of force to settle territorial disputes, and other sensitive issues have continued to wax and wane over the years. They often pose serious problems for the United States and U.S. interests (e.g., the U.S.-China differences over the recent Chinese military buildup in the Taiwan area), but on balance they probably are less serious today than they were in the Mao period or even during much of the rule of Deng Xiaoping.[4]

However, the shock of the 1989 Tiananmen Square incident and the end of the Cold War fundamentally changed the way the United States dealt with China. A prevailing pattern saw the U.S. administration generally continue to seek closer ties, including frequent high-level leadership meetings and various senior official dialogues, in order to develop areas of common ground while managing differences. The administration typically would highlight the many positive results from U.S.-China cooperation and dialogue. In recent years, these have included cooperation in facilitating mutually advantageous trade and investment relations and in managing such regional crises and threats as the Asian economic crisis of 1997–1998, the crises in 1994 and again beginning in 2002 over North Korea's nuclear weapons program, the 1998 crisis prompted by nuclear weapons tests by Pakistan and India, and the Global War on Terrorism beginning in 2001. Under the rubric of engagement or cooperation, U.S. government officials and their Chinese counterparts presided over an ever-increasing economic interdependence between the two countries, supplemented by growing cultural, political, and military contacts.

In contrast, a variety of U.S. groups were in the lead among American critics who applied pressure in Congress, through the media, and in other public discourse to encourage a firmer U.S. policy designed to press the Chinese government to align itself with U.S.-backed norms. Of course, each administration has had differences within its own ranks on how to deal with China, and the administrations have varied in their commitment to developing constructive ties and common ground with China. President Bill Clinton entered office with a strong inclination to take a harder line toward China, especially on human rights issues. However, his administration shifted course after a few years and strongly endorsed positive engagement with China.[5]

The George W. Bush administration initially emphasized the competitive as well as the cooperative aspects of U.S.-China relations. It gave more emphasis to U.S. relations with Japan and other regional allies than to relations with China as means for dealing with Asian affairs. It focused U.S. military planning on the implications of China's arms buildup, especially opposite Taiwan, and took strong positions on Taiwan, Tibet, human rights, and missile defense issues at odds with Chinese interests.

The EP-3 incident of April 1, 2001, saw China detain for eleven days the crew of a disabled U.S. reconnaissance aircraft that had collided with a

Chinese jet fighter over international waters near Hainan Island, killing the Chinese pilot and destroying the Chinese jet fighter. The impasse over the collision and detention, and the negotiations to return the plane, resulted in a halt in military and many other official contacts. The clouded relationship then began to improve; relations were on the upswing after the plane's return in July 2001 and high-level exchanges resumed, including a summit meeting in October 2001. The trend since that time has been toward closer cooperation between the U.S. and Chinese administrations.[6]

Many interest groups and individuals in the United States felt very strongly the need to change Chinese government behavior in their favored directions. They often opposed Chinese government practices on a wide range of human rights, security, economic, and other issues, seeing them as inherently wrong and against the interests of the United States. Some of these advocates had motives that related less to China and its government's behavior and more to partisan or other ulterior benefits they derived from taking a tough stand against Chinese practices. For example, issues in China policy were used in a partisan way between the Republican and Democratic parties, and even among contending groups within those parties. As noted in chapter 1, presidential candidate Clinton used China issues to discredit the leadership of his opponent, incumbent George H. W. Bush. Republican leaders in Congress then used China issues to discredit the leadership of President Clinton. Within the Democratic Party, some labor activists used China issues to press Clinton and the Democratic leadership to pay more attention to their policy agendas. Similarly, some social conservatives used China issues to press Republican leaders to pay more attention to their policy agendas.[7]

Reflecting a prevailing pattern in recent years, the U.S. executive branch generally continued to favor a policy of closer interaction and largely positive engagement with China. Administration officials appeared to judge that China believed good relations with the United States were important and that Chinese leaders made some shifts in their willingness to abide by international agreements, such as deciding to phase out China's nuclear cooperation with Iran, to join the World Trade Organization (WTO) or to assist the United States in the Six-Party Talks dealing with North Korea's nuclear weapons program. But this policy of closer interaction and positive engagement continued to generate opposition from many quarters, including from within the administration and notably from congressional and other critics who were pressuring the White House to take a tougher approach to China. For example, such pressure was evident in the wake of allegations in the late 1990s that China, in espionage activities at U.S. nuclear science labs, may have gained significant information helping it to develop better and more efficient nuclear weapons at a more accelerated timetable than could have been expected without such information.[8]

During the 1990s, congressional critics took advantage of the annual process of renewing China's most-favored-nation (MFN) status. The president was required to recommend renewal each year by June 3, and critics mustered their many arguments critical of China in the weeks before the recommendation. In a landmark vote with far-reaching consequences, the Congress in 2000 passed H.R. 4444, a bill that moved to eliminate this annual renewal process and give China what became known as Permanent Normal Trade Relations (PNTR).[9]

Backed by various groups opposed to Chinese government policies and practices, members of Congress who were critical of China's human rights and proliferation policies introduced measures that targeted sanctions against China more selectively. For example, the 105th Congress (1997–1999) considered a package of China-related measures, all critical of China, which touched on virtually every aspect of Sino-American concerns.[10] The 106th Congress (1999–2001) considered measures relating to enhancing Taiwan's security, improving U.S. knowledge on China's military affairs, and tightening safety precautions and restrictions on the U.S. transfer of technology to China.[11]

The 107th Congress (2001–2003) coincided with the start of the George W. Bush administration, which in its early months took several steps on Taiwan, Tibet, human rights, and other issues more strongly at odds with China than the previous U.S. administration. These actions were partly in response to pressure from congressional and other groups that advocated greater U.S. support for Taiwan and the Dalai Lama, and stronger criticism of China over human rights and other issues. Administration officials also emphasized the competitive as well as cooperative areas of U.S.-China relations and were less forthright in discussing U.S. determination to continue engagement with China. This more reserved approach shifted to greater cooperation following accommodating efforts by both administrations and the terrorist attack on America in 2001.[12]

Meanwhile, U.S. preoccupation with the war on terrorism, including the U.S.-led military attacks on Afghanistan and Iraq, made it more difficult for U.S. interest groups and other activists to gain the public and private attention they seemed to need in order to pressure for changes in U.S. policies toward China. Renewed U.S. domestic pressure regarding China-related issues did seem to reemerge beginning in 2005 when the burgeoning U.S. trade deficit with China headed the list of congressional concerns over the negative implications for the United States of the Bush administration's free trade policies toward China.

The election of the 110th Congress in November 2006 returned the Democrats to leadership positions in both houses of Congress. Forecasts regarding China focused on trade and economic issues, particularly on increasing congressional pressure to prompt the Chinese administration to revalue its currency upward in relation to the U.S. dollar and thereby end what was widely seen as an unfair Chinese advantage in U.S.-China trade relations.[13]

Congress and China Policy

To help to grasp the scope and depth of the recent U.S. domestic debate over China policy, it is instructive to review the issues that were raised in debates, notably in the U.S. Congress. Because of its receptivity to domestic political movements and constituent pressures, Congress has remained a focal point for those Americans and U.S. groups pressing for change in the country's policy toward China. The record of the post–Cold War debate in Congress over China policy is long and wide ranging. It deals with clusters of sensitive issues involving human rights and democratic political values, security issues, economic questions, and sovereignty issues, especially regarding Taiwan and Tibet. Highlights of the issues considered in congressional debate and actions noted below provide evidence of the broad range of American interests that were trying to influence policy toward China and the directions they wanted China policy to take. In general terms, the pattern shows that these groups often opposed improvements or other forward movement in U.S.-China relations until the Chinese government changed its policies and practices more in accord with U.S.-supported norms. The groups sometimes favored sanctions or other coercion to force the Chinese government to change, although U.S. business interests and others with a strong economic stake in China often were effective in sustaining constructive trade relations.

The overall impact of the interest groups and the actions of Congress served as a drag on forward movement in U.S.-China relations. There was little support for serious retrogression in key areas of U.S.-China relations or for a U.S. policy that would lead to military confrontation or strategic containment of China.[14] Meanwhile, beginning in 2001, U.S.-China relations experienced a few years of unusual stability, and Congress as a whole became less vocal and less active in proposing legislative moves regarding U.S.-China issues. The reasons for this did not appear related to any solution of the entrenched bilateral policy disputes such as those over human rights or Taiwan's status. These differences continued, and some reemerged with vigor with the revival of the congressional debates over China and some other U.S. issues in the Asia-Pacific beginning in 2005. Rather, other factors caused this interlude in congressional criticism of China, including:

- The incoming George W. Bush administration's initially tough stance toward China, deemphasis of U.S.-China engagement, and strong support for Taiwan were more in line with congressional views and the views of media and other critics than the policies of the outgoing Clinton administration had been.

- The Chinese administration, preoccupied with leadership transition and an array of difficulties at home, made repeated gestures to stabilize and improve U.S.-China relations.
- The war on terrorism and the conflicts in Afghanistan and Iraq filled the foreign policy agenda of the Congress, placing differences with China in a secondary category.[15]

A high point of revived congressional pressure on the administration's China policy came with the inauguration of the Democratic-controlled 110th Congress in 2007. While some forecast major challenges to existing U.S. China policy from domestic U.S. critics in the Congress and those working through the Congress, others saw a much more mixed outlook with pressures for a tougher U.S. China policy offset by important countervailing factors.[16]

Congress dealt with each of the issues noted below in a variety of ways, through press releases and statements reacting to U.S. media stories highlighting negative Chinese practices, legislation, hearings, so-called dear colleague letters, formal letters to the administration, speeches in and out of Congress, and other ways. The annual consideration of the president's decision to grant China normal trade relations (known earlier as MFN), now ended, provided a key focal point in the 1990s allowing most of these concerns to be aired fully in congressional deliberations and debate.[17]

Human Rights Issues

China's human rights abuses were among the most visible and constant points of contention in U.S.-China relations following the 1989 Tiananmen Square crackdown. China's human rights record since then has presented a mixed picture, with both setbacks and minor improvements providing plenty of ammunition for U.S. policy debate in the Congress and elsewhere. Among the more positive developments in China's human rights record, the Chinese government signed two key human rights agreements: the UN Covenant on Economic, Social, and Cultural Rights (October 27, 1997) and the International Covenant on Civil and Political Rights (March 12, 1998). The government also was allowing local, competitive elections in rural areas in China, and it implemented legislation to make political and judicial processes more transparent and to hold law enforcement officials more accountable for their actions.

Crackdowns against Dissidents and the Falungong Group

In 1999, American news accounts began to give wide coverage to reports that the Chinese government was arresting prominent activists and giving out harsh jail sentences for what most Americans considered to be routine and benign civil acts. On July 22, 1999, the government outlawed Falungong, a spiritual movement in China said to combine Buddhist and Taoist meditation practices with a series of exercises. The government arrested the movement's leaders, imposed harsh prison sentences, closed Falungong facilities, and confiscated Falungong literature. The Chinese government also cracked down on democracy activists trying to register a new independent political party, the Chinese Democracy Party. Promoters of the new party were convicted on subversion charges and given long prison sentences.[18]

At the same time, Chinese officials were harshly suppressing dissent among ethnic minorities, particularly in Tibet and in the Xinjiang-Uighur Autonomous Region in China's far west. In April 1999, Amnesty International issued a report accusing the Chinese government of gross violations of human rights in Xinjiang, including widespread use of torture to extract confessions, lengthy prison sentences, and numerous executions. Ruthless Chinese suppression continued as the Global War on Terrorism saw the Chinese administration brand dissidents in Xinjiang as terrorists, claiming some links to al-Qaeda and other international terrorist organizations. Although U.S. administration officials had warned after September 11, 2001, that the global antiterror campaign should not be used to persecute Uighurs or other minorities with political grievances against Beijing, some believe that the U.S. government made a concession to the PRC on August 26, 2002, when it announced that it was placing one small group, the East Turkestan Islamic Movement, on the U.S. list of terrorist groups.[19]

Chinese Prisons and Prison Labor

Prisons in China were widely criticized for their conditions, their treatment of prisoners, and their requirements that prisoners perform productive work. From the standpoint of U.S. policy, one issue was the extent to which products made by Chinese prisoners were exported to the American market, in violation of U.S. law. Because of concerns about prison labor exports, the United States and China had signed a memorandum of understanding (MOU) on the subject in 1992. In subsequent years, there were repeated allegations that China was failing to adhere to the agreement, and legislative initiatives pressured China to halt prison labor exports.

Meanwhile, periodic reports of Chinese security forces taking organs from executed prisoners and selling them on the black market prompted repeated congressional hearings, queries, and condemnations.[20]

Family Planning and Coercive Abortions

Bitter controversies in U.S. population planning assistance have arisen in recent years concerning China's population programs. Abortion, and the degree to which coercive abortions and sterilizations occur in China's family planning programs, was a prominent issue in these debates. Chinese officials routinely denied that coercion was an authorized part of national family planning programs, but they acknowledged that some provincial and local officials pursued coercive policies. Direct U.S. funding for coercive family planning practices was already prohibited under the provisions of several U.S. laws, as was indirect U.S. support for coercive family planning, specifically in China. In addition, legislation in recent years expanded these restrictions to include U.S. funding for international and multilateral family planning programs, such as the UN Population Fund (UNFPA), which had programs in China.[21]

Religious Freedom

Membership data on religious organizations in China suggest that the practice of religion continued to increase and the number of religious adherents continued to grow. Chinese officials decided in 1994 to tighten restrictions on religious practices, and one result was a marked increase in American criticism. Among other things, the restrictions prohibited evangelical activities and required all religious groups to register with the Religious Affairs Bureau (RAB). Registration required that religious groups reveal the names and addresses of members, their contacts in China and abroad, and details about leadership activities and finances. The RAB, charged with policing and regulating religious activities, was part of China's State Council and reported to the Communist Party's United Front Work Department. Its duties have been taken over by the State Administration for Religious Affairs in recent years.

U.S. government reports, including the Department of State's Annual Reports on International Religious Freedom and the report issued on May 1, 2000, by the U.S. Commission on International Religious Freedom, criticized Chinese government policies on religious practices and provided a focal point for congressional hearings and statements. Although some foreign commentators noted recent moderation and even encouragement by Chinese officials regarding freer religious practices, the strong U.S. criticism of China's record on religious freedom continued.[22]

Internet and Media Restrictions

The growth of the Internet, cell phone usage, and text messaging led to new Chinese regulations begun in 2005 that prompted some congressional hearings and other actions. A key issue was the extent to which U.S. Internet firms collaborated with Chinese authorities in helping the latter control Internet use in China.[23]

Issues in U.S.-China Security Relations

Once one of the stronger foundations of the relationship, U.S.-China security and military relations never fully recovered after they were suspended following the 1989 Tiananmen Square massacre. In October 1997, presidents Bill Clinton and Jiang Zemin announced they would improve military-to-military relations, including an increase in military contacts and agreement on a maritime safety accord meant to reduce the chance of accidents or misunderstandings at sea. The George W. Bush administration at first adopted a case-by-case approach in considering approval of military exchanges with China. The EP-3 incident resulted in a temporary halt to most military contacts. Some officials in the new U.S. administration, backed by observers in Congress, the media, and elsewhere, focused on China's military buildup regarding a Taiwan contingency involving U.S. military intervention and involvement. They pressed for stronger U.S. measures to deal with this situation, which in turn reinforced U.S.-China military competition and complicated bilateral military relations.[24]

The Bush administration, with support from many in Congress, took a tougher position against China's proliferation of weapons of mass destruction (WMD). In its first months, the administration sanctioned Chinese companies for WMD proliferation more times than the Clinton administration had in eight years. Legislation in the 109th Congress (2005–2007) called for a U.S. strategy to deal with China's rising military and related international power and prominence (P.L. 109-163), sanctions against foreign powers that transfer advanced weaponry to China (H.R. 2601), and the European Union to maintain its arms embargo against China (H.R. 57).[25]

One key security issue for the United States was China's track record of weapons sales, technology transfers, and nuclear energy assistance, particularly to Iran and Pakistan. Faced with U.S. pressure in recent years and for other reasons, China took a number of steps that suggested it was reassessing its weapons sales and assistance policies. Among other things, China in 1992 promised to abide by the Missile Technology Control Regime (MTCR) and acceded to the Nuclear Non-Proliferation Treaty (NPT). In 1993, China signed the Chemical Weapons Convention

(CWC); in 1996, it signed the Comprehensive Test Ban Treaty; and in 1997, it joined the Zangger Committee of NPT exporters. On January 12, 1998, President Clinton signed the required certifications to implement a nuclear cooperation agreement with China, citing clear assurances from China on nuclear nonproliferation issues. The actual U.S.-China Nuclear Cooperation agreement was signed in 1985. There appeared to be good prospects for U.S. nuclear reactor–related sales to China as a result of the visit of a senior U.S. official delegation to China in 2006.[26]

Congressional and other critics charged that confidence in China's nonproliferation policies was misplaced. They pointed out that for years reputable sources had reported that China was selling technology for WMD and ballistic missiles on the international market, primarily to Pakistan and the Middle East, notably Iran.[27]

Satellite Technology Transfer Allegations

Early in 1998, congressional attention also turned to U.S. satellite exports to China. According to the *New York Times* on April 13, 1998, a classified May 1997 report by the U.S. Department of Defense concluded that scientists from Hughes and Loral Space and Communications who were involved in studying the 1996 crash of a Chinese rocket launching a Loral satellite had turned over scientific expertise to China that significantly improved the reliability of China's missile launch abilities. The doomed Loral satellite had been granted an export license as a result of President Clinton's waiver of restrictions in Public Law (P.L.) 101-246 that related to satellite exports to China. After these allegations came to light, a special House select committee and a number of Senate committees investigated not only the administration's decision to grant the satellite export waiver but also the broader range of U.S. technology transfer policy with respect to China. Legislation in the 109th Congress to restrict transfers of U.S. satellites and satellite components to China included H.R. 5672.[28]

Allegations of Espionage

Beginning in the late 1990s, U.S. media sources reported about ongoing investigations of alleged Chinese espionage against the United States dating back to the 1980s. The most serious case involved China's alleged acquisition of significant information about the W88, an advanced miniaturized U.S. nuclear warhead, as a result of alleged security breaches at the Los Alamos nuclear science lab between 1984 and 1988. Another serious instance, first reported in late April 1999 by the *New York Times*, involved allegations that a Taiwan-born Chinese American scientist, Wen Ho Lee, had downloaded critical nuclear weapons codes, called legacy codes, from a classified computer system at Los Alamos to an unclassified computer system accessible by anyone with the proper password. Alleged Chinese espionage was featured prominently in the 1999 Cox Commission report. This congressional commission was sharply critical of the U.S. administration's counterespionage activities against China.[29]

Subsequently, the media focused attention on a complicated case involving an alleged Chinese double agent whose sexual relationship with senior FBI counterintelligence officers seemed to undermine the integrity of U.S. government efforts to curb Chinese espionage. Suspicions of Chinese spying were voiced in Congress when the State Department decided to purchase computers for use in classified communications from a Chinese company. The controversy caused the department to halt the purchase.[30]

Economic Issues

China was one of the world's fastest-growing economies, and trade analysts agreed that its potential as a market would increase significantly in the future. Issues involving trade with China factored heavily into U.S. policy debates. Between 1991 and 1996, U.S. exports to China increased by 90.5 percent, while imports from China surged by 171.4 percent. The U.S. trade deficit with China swelled accordingly, from a $17.8 billion deficit in 1989 to around $100 billion in 2000. It more than doubled in the five following years and was $232.5 billion in 2006.[31]

Economic issues were continuing sources of tension in U.S.-China relations. China's ineffectiveness in protecting U.S. intellectual property, its lack of transparent trade regulations, and its past high tariff rates all contributed to these debates. More recent issues related to the Chinese administration maintaining a low value for the Chinese currency relative to the U.S. dollar. At the October 1997 summit, Clinton and Jiang agreed to intensify talks on China's application to join the World Trade Organization. After often difficult negotiations, on November 6, 1999, U.S. and Chinese trade negotiators announced in Beijing that they had reached a WTO accord, which involved key Chinese concessions. China entered the WTO by the end of 2001. China's record of compliance with the many obligations it undertook in entering the WTO has been subject to mixed reviews in the Congress as well as by the George W. Bush administration and U.S. domestic groups.[32]

Most-Favored-Nation Status and Normal Trade Relations

The annual renewal of China's MFN status was a controversial irritant and a major focal point of debate in U.S.-China relations throughout the

1990s. Each year by June 3, the president recommended that Congress renew his authority to waive restrictions on China's MFN eligibility, thus effectively extending MFN status to China for another year. If recommended by the president, the renewal was automatic, and Congress need not act. The renewal could have been blocked, however, by enactment of a joint resolution of disapproval within a specified time frame. Indeed, joint resolutions of disapproval were introduced for China each year in the 1990s. Although none passed both houses, the House of Representatives voted on joint resolutions a total of eleven times (the Senate never had a recorded vote on a joint resolution of disapproval for China's trade status). In fact, most of the debate about China's MFN eligibility in the 1990s involved separate legislation that would have either placed new conditions on China's MFN eligibility or addressed a range of contentious issues other than MFN.[33]

In a move that ultimately eliminated the annual process for renewing China's trade status, the Congress in 2000 passed H.R. 4444, which granted China permanent normal trade relations. With this bill, China received the same trade status the United States accorded to all but a handful of other countries, without any annual review process or other restrictions applying. The grant was contingent on China joining the WTO, which happened in 2001.[34]

Intellectual Property Rights

China's lack of protection for intellectual property rights (IPR) was long an issue in U.S.-China relations and became more important in the 109th and 110th Congresses. According to calculations from U.S. industry sources in 2006, IPR piracy cost U.S. firms $2.5 billion in lost sales a year, and the IPR piracy rate in China for U.S. products remained estimated at 90 percent. Backed by Congress, U.S. administration officials repeatedly pressed Chinese officials to better implement IPR regulations.[35]

Currency Valuation

Until 2005, the PRC pegged its currency, the renminbi (RMB), to the U.S. dollar at a rate of about 8.3 RMB to the dollar—a valuation that many critics in Congress and elsewhere in the United States concluded kept the PRC's currency undervalued, making PRC exports artificially cheap and making it harder for American producers to compete. U.S. critics of the Chinese currency peg charged that the PRC unfairly manipulated its currency, and they urged Beijing either to raise the RMB's value or to make it freely convertible subject to market forces. On July 1, 2005, the PRC changed this valuation method, instead announcing it would peg the RMB to a basket of currencies. The resulting slow appreciation in the RMB from this action was not sufficient to assuage U.S. congressional concerns, however, and senators Charles Schumer and Lindsay Graham introduced legislation in the 109th Congress (S. 295) that would have raised U.S. tariffs on Chinese goods by 27.5 percent unless the PRC currency level appreciated. That legislation was not passed, but a series of bills on this subject were a focus of congressional attention on China in the 110th Congress.[36]

A related concern was Chinese purchases of U.S. Treasury bills and other U.S. government securities as a means of recycling China's massive trade surplus with the United States while maintaining a relatively low value of the Chinese currency relative to the dollar. The Chinese investments seemed very important to the stability of the U.S. economy. Some critics warned of U.S. overdependence on this type of investment by China.[37]

Bid for Unocal

The bid of a Chinese state-controlled oil company to acquire the American oil firm Unocal in 2005 set off an uproar in Congress and the media. The congressional debate over the alleged dangers of the transaction to U.S. energy security was so intense that the Chinese firm withdrew the bid after two months. Chinese investments in less sensitive areas of the U.S. economy were approved without serious challenge, though the proposed sale in 2007 of a computer security firm to a Chinese company linked to the PRC military raised concerns in Congress and the media.[38]

China's International Rise

A set of issues emerged in the 109th and 110th Congresses focused on the critical implications of China's economic growth and increasing international engagement and influence for U.S. economic, security, and political interests in various parts of the world. To feed its growing needs for resources, capital, and technology, Chinese officials, businesses, and others in 2005, 2006, and 2007 steadily and successfully sought trade agreements, oil and gas contracts, scientific and technological cooperation, and multilateral security, political, and economic arrangements with countries around its periphery and throughout the world. China's growing international economic engagement was backed by the country's growing military power and went hand in hand with expanding Chinese political influence. China notably used unconditional economic exchanges and assistance to woo governments and leaders seen as rogues or outliers by the United States and other developed countries. Chinese practices undercut Western pressure on these officials and governments. The PRC's increased influence extended to many key allies and associates of the United States and to regions such as Latin America where the United States exerted predominant influence.

Among the prominent signs of congressional concern over these trends, P.L. 109-163 urged the Bush administration to present to the Congress a comprehensive U.S. strategy to deal with China's economic, diplomatic, and military rise and included specific mention of what areas that strategy should address.[39]

Sovereignty Issues: Taiwan, Tibet, and Hong Kong

Taiwan

Taiwan remained the most sensitive and complex issue in U.S.-China relations. Beijing was engaged in a military buildup focused on a Taiwan contingency involving the United States. It refused to forswear the use of force should Taiwan declare independence from China, and Chinese officials repeatedly blocked Taiwan's efforts to gain greater international recognition. At the same time, officials in Taiwan were maneuvering for more international stature and for independent access to multilateral institutions.

Since 1978, when the United States had to break relations with Taiwan in order to normalize relations with Beijing, U.S. policy toward Taiwan had been shaped by U.S.-China communiqués and the Taiwan Relations Act (P.L. 96-8). Despite these pronouncements, in recent years, the Taiwan issue has posed delicate political problems for American policy makers. During his summit visit to China in June 1998, President Clinton made controversial statements about Taiwan that some interpreted as being a change in U.S. policy. According to a White House transcript of his remarks during a roundtable discussion in Shanghai on June 30, 1998, Clinton said in response to a question about Taiwan:

> I had a chance to reiterate our Taiwan policy, which is that we don't support independence for Taiwan, or two Chinas, or one Taiwan–one China. And we don't believe that Taiwan should be a member in any organization for which statehood is a requirement. So I think we have a consistent policy.

The president's statement was sharply criticized by many members of Congress and others who opposed what they viewed as a significant U.S. concession to Beijing at the expense of Taipei and U.S.-Taiwan relations.[40]

In 2001, the Bush administration provided the largest package of U.S. arms to Taiwan in ten years and allowed Taiwanese president Chen Shui-bian to tour more freely and to meet with congressional representatives during stopovers in the United States. President Bush publicly pledged to come to Taiwan's aid with U.S. military power if Taiwan were attacked by mainland China. These steps were welcomed in Congress, but they deepened Beijing's judgment that the United States would remain at odds with China over the Taiwan issue for the foreseeable future.[41]

As the Taiwan administration of President Chen beginning in 2003 advanced pro-independence proposals seen as destabilizing by the Bush administration, the U.S. president and his aides took steps to curb Taiwan's potentially dangerous actions. In general, these steps elicited only minor objections from the normally pro-Taiwan Congress. The 109th Congress did consider legislation that tried to strengthen U.S.-Taiwan military contacts, expressed strong opposition to an antisecession law directed at Taiwan that was passed by China in 2005, and supported a continuation of the European Union's embargo on arms transfers to China that, if lifted, might increase China's military strength against Taiwan.[42]

Tibet

In the late 1980s, Tibet became a recurring issue in U.S.-China relations. A number of factors contributed to the heightened interest, including the Dalai Lama's and the Tibetan community's ongoing international political activities, reports of human rights abuses and China's continuing repressive social and political controls in Tibet, and disputes among U.S. policy makers over the direction of American policy toward China. As a matter of policy, the U.S. government recognized Tibet as being part of China and affirmed that it had always done so, although some disputed the historical consistency of this position. Since normalization of relations with the PRC in 1979, Republican and Democratic administrations, favoring policies of engagement with China, sometimes sought to minimize areas of potential tension with Beijing where Chinese leaders took strong positions, such as on the question of Tibet's political status.[43]

The Dalai Lama had long had some strong supporters in the U.S. Congress and among other U.S. opinion leaders, and these continued to put pressure on the White House to protect Tibetan culture and accord Tibet greater status in U.S. law despite Beijing's strong objections. As a result of this public pressure, presidents George H. W. Bush and Bill Clinton each met with the Dalai Lama in the United States—meetings that were deliberately kept low-key and informal, but which nevertheless offended Chinese leaders. President George W. Bush went a bit further than his predecessors, meeting the Dalai Lama in the residence at the White House in May 2001.[44]

Congress in the 1990s attempted to insert language in Foreign Relations authorizations bills to create a special envoy for Tibet, with ambassadorial rank, to promote good relations between the Dalai Lama and Beijing and to handle negotiations with China on the Dalai Lama's behalf. Administration officials opposed the sovereignty implications of a special envoy provision, however, and a compromise of sorts was reached on October 31, 1997, when a State Department press statement reported that Secretary of State Madeleine Albright had designated Gregory B. Craig as a special coordinator for Tibetan issues within the State Department, adding to his ongoing role as director of policy planning. The special envoy provision was dropped from subsequent legislation. President George W. Bush appointed a more senior official, an undersecretary of state, as the State Department's special coordinator for Tibet.[45]

The Tibet issue flared again in U.S.-China relations in 2007 when Congress awarded the Congressional Gold Medal to the Dalai Lama in a public ceremony. President Bush met the Dalai Lama during his visit to Washington and took part in the congressional award ceremony. China protested strongly.[46]

Hong Kong

On July 1, 1997, Hong Kong reverted from British control back to Chinese sovereignty in a smooth transition. The former British colony became known as the Hong Kong Special Administrative Region (SAR) of the People's Republic of China. On the same day, Hong Kong officials inaugurated a new and controversial provisional legislature, a Beijing-appointed body that temporarily replaced Hong Kong's duly elected Legislative Council (LegCo). On May 24, 1998, elections for the first official LegCo of the SAR were held under agreements adopted on September 28, 1997, by the provisional legislature. Elections for the later LegCos followed.[47]

At the time they were put forward, the new election laws for the legislature and other bodies were criticized in the United States because they were seen as less democratic than those during the last years of British rule. Still, these election laws adhered to the major electoral requirements set in Sino-British agreements on Hong Kong.

U.S. policy toward Hong Kong was spelled out in the Hong Kong Policy Act (P.L. 102-383) enacted in 1992. Among other things, the Act declared Congress's support for the holding of free and fair elections for Hong Kong's legislature. In addition to requiring annual U.S. government reports on Hong Kong conditions through 2006 that were scrutinized by Congress, the Hong Kong Policy Act allowed the United States to treat Hong Kong more leniently than it did the PRC, on the condition that Hong Kong remained autonomous. Under the Act, the president had the power to halt existing agreements with Hong Kong or take other steps if he determined that Beijing was interfering unduly in Hong Kong's affairs.

China and the 110th Congress

The victory of the Democratic Party in the November 7, 2006, congressional elections underlined a broad desire of the American electorate for change in the policies and priorities of the Bush administration. In the House of Representatives, the Democratic Party moved from a deficit position of thirty seats against the Republican majority to an advantage of thirty seats, and in the Senate, it erased the Republicans' ten-seat advantage, gaining a one-seat majority.[48]

The implications of the Democratic victory seemed serious for U.S. policy in the Asia-Pacific and particularly for policy toward China, the focus of greatest controversy in the region. The Democratic majority of the 110th Congress, led by opinionated and often confrontational leaders Rep. Nancy Pelosi and Sen. Harry Reid, pressed for change in a partisan atmosphere charged by early preparations for the U.S. presidential election of 2008. The Democratic majority was forecast to pursue strong trade and economic measures that, if successful, would significantly disrupt U.S. economic relations with the region and the free trade emphasis of the Bush administration. Mainstream commentator Thomas Friedman predicted a civil war in American politics over the massive U.S. trade deficit and related economic issues with China. Democrats pushing more activist approaches regarding human rights and environmental initiatives added to the anticipated major complications in U.S. relations with China.[49]

In contrast with such dire warnings, however, factors of power, priorities, politics, and personalities diluted the push for substantive change in U.S. policy toward Asia in general and China in particular. Taking these factors into account resulted in a more balanced forecast of what the Democratic-led Congress could actually accomplish in changing U.S. policies and practices in the region. On the one hand, that forecast anticipated a wide range of congressional efforts and frequent episodes of congressional proposals, posturing, and maneuvers regarding U.S. policies and practices on China. On the other hand, it also showed that the impact of these congressional actions seemed unlikely to change the course of U.S. relations with China in major ways, at least during the term of the 110th Congress. The longer-term importance of these efforts and actions could prove to be more significant, though, if they assisted in electing a U.S. president and/or large congressional majorities in 2008 that would steer U.S. policy in directions favored by the current Democratic leadership of the House and the Senate.[50]

Power

The U.S. Constitution gave the executive the leading role in foreign affairs. In the face of a determined president like George W. Bush, the Democratic-led Congress appeared to have only a few levers to force change in areas that impact on U.S. relations with Asia and especially China. Congress played a direct role in any decision to extend the president's trade promotion authority, which allowed expedited congressional consideration of free trade agreements (FTAs), including one that was under negotiation with South Korea. The authority ended in mid-2007. Without it, congressional approval of this FTA and Bush administration consideration of additional FTAs in Asia or elsewhere were less likely. The relevance of this issue for China was indirect at best.

Congress also controls government spending—the "power of the purse." This can be used to block, redirect, or tailor administration requests for U.S. government spending and U.S. foreign assistance. But the relevance of this capability to China was low as well, especially since official U.S. aid was not allowed to go to China.

Congressional opposition can furthermore hold up and possibly halt administration personnel appointments or policy initiatives needing congressional approval. In its last years, though, the Bush administration did not appear to anticipate any major or controversial personnel changes in China nor any broader Asia policy initiatives requiring congressional action. Congressional oversight hearings, investigations, and reports promised to be much more numerous with the Democrats in control, but these usually lent only limited power to steer the course of U.S. policy.

Priorities

Democratic leaders in the House and Senate voiced varied priorities. They tended to focus initially on domestic issues such as raising the minimum wage, controlling government spending and deficits, strengthening job security for U.S. workers, preserving Social Security, and providing limited tax relief for middle-class taxpayers. Finding ways to change the adverse course of the U.S.-led war in Iraq dominated the foreign policy agenda.

Against this background, most issues affecting Asia received lower priority. Attention focused on finding ways to deal more effectively with the massive U.S. trade deficits and the perceived unfair trade and economic policies of countries in Asia, notably China. Some Democratic leaders and members favored a strong emphasis on human rights, labor conditions, and environmental concerns in fashioning U.S. policy toward China and other Asian countries, but others did not.

Politics

The bruising fight among House Democrats leading to the selection of Rep. Steny Hoyer as House majority leader against the wishes of Speaker-designate Pelosi was a reminder that the Democrats would not follow their leaders in lockstep as the Republicans had under Speaker Newt Gingrich following the Republican landslide victory of 1994. Even if Speaker Pelosi wanted to push House Democrats to follow her past leanings to be tough in relations with China and on other Asian issues regarding human rights and trade, the makeup of the Democratic caucus and likely committee leadership strongly suggested less-than-uniform support. The proportion of conservative Democratic members increased as a result of the 2006 election, and they were reluctant to press too hard on human rights, environmental, and other issues when important U.S. business and security interests were at stake. Many Democratic legislators supported free trade and resisted what they saw as protectionist measures against China, Japan, and other Asian trading partners proposed by their Democratic colleagues. They were backed by recent polling data of the Chicago Council on Global Affairs, which showed that Americans were fairly comfortable with the economic rise of China.

Personalities

Given the loose Democratic leadership control, individual members in key committee assignments mattered in the Democratic-led Congress and its approach to China issues. Because they differed among themselves on key issues, they were likely to have difficulty coming up with united positions in pressing for meaningful change in Bush administration policies regarding Asia, and China in particular.[51]

The public positions of House leader Pelosi and Senate leader Reid were tough on trade and related economic and human rights issues regarding China. Rep. Sander Levin and some other members of the House Ways and Means Committee and other economic policy committees also favored a tougher U.S. stance on trade issues, especially with China, and also with Japan on issues that affect key U.S. industries, notably autos. However, they were offset by committee moderates headed by the Ways and Means Committee's leading Democrat, Charles Rangel. In the Senate, the leading Democrat on the Finance Committee, Max Baucus, also held moderate views and was supported by others on the committee that eschewed protectionism.

Thomas Lantos, the Democratic chairman of the House Committee on International Relations, had a long record of vocal opposition to human rights violations, including those by China's authoritarian regime.

This meshed well with the views of Speaker Pelosi but was at odds with the large number of Democratic members who joined various working groups designed to foster pragmatic exchanges with, and more informed and effective U.S. policy toward, China. On balance, these groups moderated the congressional tendency to engage in "China bashing" seen during annual congressional debates in the 1990s on China's trading status with the United States.

In sum, prevailing circumstances seemed to argue for only modest change in U.S. policy toward China as a result of the Democratic victory in 2006. China's massive trade and foreign-exchange surpluses and perceived unfair currency and trading practices generated legislation and other actions to apply pressure on the Bush administration to toughen the U.S. approach to China, but they appeared to fall short of forcing significant protectionist measures against the PRC. Despite congressional pressure, the Bush administration's Treasury Department consistently refused to have China labeled a currency manipulator in its periodic reports to Congress. An increase in congressional rhetoric and posturing against Chinese human rights violations and other practices offending U.S. norms was balanced by growing congressional interest in working pragmatically with China in study groups and exchanges. Any congressional drive to press the Bush administration to increase support for Taiwan despite China's objections seemed offset by the turbulent political situation in Taiwan in the last years of the administration of President Chen Shui-bian and the fracturing of the Taiwan lobby in Washington as a result of partisan and divisive politics in Taiwan.

PRIORITIES AND ISSUES IN U.S. POLICY TOWARD KOREA

The United States has important interests on the Korean Peninsula involving security, economic, and political concerns.[52] The United States suffered more than 30,000 killed and 100,000 wounded in the Korean War (1950–1953). It agreed to defend South Korea from external aggression in the 1954 Mutual Defense Treaty, and U.S. leaders repeatedly affirmed that commitment in later years. In 2007, the United States maintained about 30,000 troops in South Korea to supplement the 650,000-strong South Korean armed forces. This force was intended to deter North Korea's numerically large (1.2 million troops) army. South Korea reciprocated American support, notably by supporting—with combat troops when required—U.S. military actions abroad. Tens of thousands of South Korean forces were an important part of U.S.-led efforts during the Vietnam War. In recent years, South Korea deployed more than 3,000 troops in support of the U.S.-led war in Iraq and also deployed some military forces to help the U.S.-led military effort in Afghanistan.

U.S. economic aid to South Korea between 1945 and 2002 totaled more than $6 billion, and U.S. military aid over the same period added more than $8.8 billion. Most economic aid ended in the mid-1970s as South Korea reached higher levels of economic development.

South Korea is a major economic partner of the United States. In 2005, two-way trade between the countries reached nearly $70 billion, making South Korea America's seventh largest trading partner. South Korea is far more dependent economically on the United States than the United States is on South Korea. In 2005, the United States was South Korea's third largest trading partner, second largest export market, third largest source of imports, and largest supplier of foreign direct investment (FDI). The United States used to be South Korea's largest trade partner, but that position went to China in 2003, and in 2005 the value of South Korean–Japanese trade also surpassed that of U.S.-South Korean trade, putting the United States in third place among South Korea's trading partners.[53]

Political, cultural, and personal ties between South Korea and the United States have deep roots and have remained strong. With the change of U.S. immigration policies and laws in the mid-1960s, large numbers of South Koreans settled permanently in the United States. Many became citizens and raised their children to be American citizens. Numbering about two million, Koreans are one of the larger groups in the ethnically pluralistic contemporary U.S. society. Religious, educational, and business ties also are deeply rooted, with many decades of constructive interaction.

Many important nongovernmental organizations were ahead of the U.S. government in encouraging and welcoming change in South Korea. They supported South Korea's economic growth in the 1970s and 1980s, and they were in the lead in backing South Korea's more turbulent transition from political authoritarianism to democracy in the late 1980s. The U.S. Catholic Conference of Bishops was among many American church groups that played an important role in support of South Korean activists and demonstrators seeking democratic reform in the face of sometimes harsh suppression by the authoritarian South Korean administration in the 1980s. During that difficult period of demonstrations and suppression in the South Korean capital, the Catholic cathedral in Seoul provided a sanctuary for the demonstrators, who were supported by Catholics, other Christians, and concerned American citizens.

U.S. issues and concerns on the Korean Peninsula in the post–Cold War period have focused on security issues. North Korea remains a serious threat, even after the demise of its previous backer, the Soviet Union, and moves by its remaining ally, China, to adjust support for North Korea in the interest of improving Chinese relations with South Korea and the United States. The United States has given top priority to dealing with North Korea's nuclear weapons program and development of ballistic missiles. U.S. approaches have swung widely from episodes of strong pressure backed by military force to periods of negotiations and even high-level engagement. Washington's policies and practices are driven by American debates on how best to deal with the North Korean threat amid sometimes radically changing maneuvers by the Pyongyang administration and the similarly volatile international reactions to those shifts.[54] The United States has had other strong differences with the brutally authoritarian North Korean regime, as well.

U.S. relations with South Korea deteriorated by the start of the twenty-first century, with various differences over dealing with North Korea, U.S. troop deployments in South Korea, defense burden-sharing questions, and trade issues. A prevailing pattern in the early twenty-first century saw U.S. relations with both North Korea and South Korea facing periodic crises that seemed difficult to resolve.[55]

Priorities and Issues in U.S. Policy toward North Korea

The pattern of U.S. policies and practices dealing with North Korea in the post–Cold War period has been erratic. Confrontation over North Korea's nuclear weapons program led to negotiations and the Agreed Framework accord of 1994. The Agreed Framework was controversial in the United States, though, and suspected North Korean cheating—along with North Korea's provocative ballistic missile testing—prompted renewed negotiations led by former U.S. defense secretary William Perry in 1999.

North Korea's abrupt shift toward reconciliation with South Korea, leading to a Pyongyang summit between North and South Korean leaders in 2000, had an important if temporary impact on the U.S. approach to the North Korean administration. For a time, senior leaders of the Clinton administration sought improved relations through widely publicized high-level dialogue.

The new U.S. administration of George W. Bush was divided and generally more wary than the previous U.S. government regarding the North Koreans. A harder U.S. line stalled progress in relations with North Korea. The situation sharply declined in late 2002 when North Korea responded harshly to U.S. accusations that it was secretly developing a highly enriched uranium nuclear weapons program and to the U.S. cutoff of oil to North Korea provided under terms of the Agreed Framework. North Korea broke its promises in the Agreed Framework, withdrew from the Nuclear Non-Proliferation Treaty, and proceeded with openly producing nuclear weapons.[56]

In a subsequent mix of U.S. pressure and negotiations that seemed to reflect continued strong differences within the Bush administration on how to deal with Pyongyang, American officials worked with China, and later with Japan, South Korea, and Russia, in multilateral discussions that came to be known as the Six-Party Talks, seeking to curb and end North Korea's nuclear weapons program. Those talks went through ups and downs, mainly in reaction to North Korean moves that in turn seemed to be in reaction to U.S. steps that sometimes stressed a hard line toward North Korea and sometimes a more flexible approach.

North Korea stayed away from the Six-Party Talks for much of 2004 and 2005. An agreement in principle governing a settlement of the North Korean nuclear issues was reached in the Six-Party Talks in Beijing in September 2005, but there was little progress after that. A major crisis emerged when North Korea conducted seven ballistic missile firings in July 2006 and on October 9, 2006, conducted a nuclear weapons test. This was followed by North Korea agreeing on November 1, 2006, to return to the Six-Party Talks and an agreement in those talks on February 13, 2007, that outlined steps to meet U.S. and North Korean concerns regarding the North Korean nuclear program and related issues.

The February 2007 agreement was widely seen as a first step in an uncertain process designed from the U.S. perspective to manage the consequences of—and over time to slow and ultimately end—North Korea's nuclear weapons development. North Korea, the United States, and the other participants in the Six-Party Talks followed through with actions in 2007 that saw the disabling of North Korea's overt nuclear installations and provision of aid to North Korea by the United States and other powers.[57]

The 1994 Agreed Framework

Concerned over reports in the late 1980s and early 1990s of North Korea's possible development of nuclear weapons, the George H. W. Bush administration took several actions aimed at securing from North Korea adherence to Pyongyang's obligations as a signatory of the Nuclear Non-Proliferation Treaty; North Korea had signed the NPT in 1985. Bush administration actions included the withdrawal of U.S. nuclear weapons from South Korea in late 1991. North Korea entered into two agreements, which specified nuclear obligations. In a denuclearization agreement signed in December 1991, North and South Korea pledged not to possess nuclear weapons, not to possess plutonium reprocessing or uranium enrichment facilities, and to negotiate a mutual nuclear inspection system. In January 1992, North Korea signed a safeguards agreement with the International Atomic Energy Agency (IAEA), providing for regular IAEA inspections of nuclear facilities. In 1992, North Korea rebuffed South Korea regarding implementation of the denuclearization agreement, but it did allow the IAEA to conduct six inspections between June 1992 and February 1993.[58]

In late 1992, the IAEA found evidence that North Korea had reprocessed more plutonium (potentially useful in producing a nuclear weapon) than the eighty grams it had disclosed to the agency. In February 1993, the IAEA invoked a provision in the safeguards agreement and called for a "special inspection" of two concealed but apparent nuclear waste sites at Yongbyon, North Korea. The IAEA believed that a special inspection would uncover information on the amount of plutonium that North Korea had produced since 1989. North Korea rejected the IAEA request and announced on March 12, 1993, its intention to withdraw from the NPT.[59]

The NPT withdrawal threat led to diplomatic talks between North Korea and the Clinton administration. Pyongyang "suspended" its withdrawal from the NPT when the Clinton administration agreed to a high-level meeting in June 1993. However, North Korea continued to refuse both special and regular IAEA inspections of facilities designated under the safeguards agreement. In May 1994, it also refused to allow the IAEA to inspect the eight thousand fuel rods it had removed from its five-megawatt reactor.

In June 1994, North Korean president Kim Il-sung reactivated a long-standing invitation to former U.S. president Jimmy Carter to visit Pyongyang. Kim offered Carter a freeze of North Korea's nuclear facilities and operations. Kim took this initiative after China reportedly informed him that it would not veto a first round of economic sanctions that the Clinton administration had proposed to members of the UN Security Council.

The Clinton administration reacted to Kim's offer by dropping its sanctions proposal and entering into a new round of high-level negotiations with North Korea. This negotiation led to the Agreed Framework of October 21, 1994. Two amending agreements were concluded in 1995: a U.S.–North Korean statement in Kuala Lumpur, Malaysia, in June, and a supply contract for the provision of nuclear reactors to North Korea, concluded in December.

The heart of the Agreed Framework and the amending accords was a deal under which the United States would provide North Korea with a package of nuclear, energy, economic, and diplomatic benefits; in return, North Korea would halt the operations and infrastructure development of its nuclear program.

U.S. officials emphasized that the key policy objective of the Clinton administration was to secure a freeze of North Korea's nuclear program in order to prevent North Korea from producing large quantities of weapons-grade plutonium through the operations of its planned 50- and

200-megawatt reactors and the existing plutonium reprocessing plant at Yongbyon. However, the Agreed Framework did not resolve the question of North Korea's existing achievements regarding the production and acquisition of plutonium and the production of nuclear weapons. The freeze did not prevent North Korea from producing a few nuclear weapons if, as U.S. and foreign intelligence reports estimated, North Korea had enough plutonium and sufficient technology to manufacture them. This shortcoming appeared to be a major weakness of the Agreed Framework, as was pointed out by U.S. and other critics. Critics also balked at the benefits provided to North Korea, including U.S.-supplied shipments of 500,000 metric tons of oil annually to North Korea and provision of two light-water nuclear reactors that were to be paid for mainly by South Korea and Japan. The accord also called for establishing full diplomatic relations and ending the U.S. economic embargo of North Korea, steps that critics in Congress and elsewhere were reluctant to take without major changes in North Korea's internationally aggressive and internally repressive policies and practices.

The Perry Initiative

In September 1998, North Korea launched a long-range ballistic missile over Japan, prompting great concern there. Concurrently there were disclosures of a possible hidden North Korean nuclear weapons site at Kumchangri, in North Korea. These developments prompted the Clinton administration to reassess its policy toward North Korea. The result was the Perry Initiative. Former secretary of defense William Perry, as special adviser to the president and secretary of state on North Korea, outlined a revised U.S. strategy in a report of October 1999. The Perry Report asserted that the Agreed Framework should continue in order to prevent North Korea from producing a "significant number of nuclear weapons." It recommended two sets of new U.S.–North Korea negotiations with the objectives of securing "verifiable assurances" that North Korea does not have a secret nuclear weapons program and "verifiable cessation" of North Korea's missile program. Perry recommended a step-by-step negotiating process. He proposed that, in return for commitments by North Korea on the nuclear and missile issues, the United States should normalize diplomatic relations with North Korea, relax economic sanctions against it, and "take other positive steps" to "provide opportunities" for the country. Perry added that such U.S. initiatives should be coordinated with similar actions by Japan and South Korea.[60]

The Clinton administration took an initial step in line with Perry's recommendations when it negotiated an agreement with North Korea in Berlin in September 1999 in which North Korea agreed to defer further missile launch tests in return for actions by the Clinton administration to lift major U.S. economic sanctions. The next planned step, a high-level North Korean visit to Washington, was stalemated over North Korea's demand of preconditions.

High-Level Dialogue, 2000

During 2000, the sudden thaw in North Korea's relations with South Korea, high-level meetings in U.S.–North Korean relations, and other indications of change in North Korea had an important effect on how U.S. and other observers viewed the situation and relevant issues on the Korean Peninsula. What had heretofore been widely considered as the most dangerous regional hot spot now became a focal point of speculation as to how far the thaw on the peninsula would go and what the implications would be for broader regional security concerns. Most notably, the changes in North-South Korean relations, highlighted during the summit meeting of the two top Korean leaders in Pyongyang on June 2000, led to a flurry of diplomatic activity as all major powers with concerns on the peninsula maneuvered for an advantageous position in the new, more fluid policy environment. The North-South changes also caused the United States and its allies in Seoul and Tokyo to consider whether and how the thaw on the peninsula would affect the size and scope of the U.S. military presence in South Korea and Japan that focused heavily on duties required in a possible Korean contingency.[61]

In June 2000, the Clinton administration officially announced the lifting of some economic sanctions against North Korea. North Korea responded by reaffirming its agreement to defer missile launch tests. Pyongyang sent a high-level official to Washington in October 2000, and this was followed by Secretary of State Madeleine Albright's visit to North Korea. These talks focused on the missile issue and particularly on a proposal made by North Korean leader Kim Jong-il to Russian president Vladimir Putin. According to Putin, Kim offered to make concessions on the missile issue (the scope of the proposed concessions was unclear) if the United States would organize a program to launch North Korean satellites into orbit.[62]

In ongoing bilateral talks, North Korea also was seeking its removal from the U.S. list of state sponsors of terrorism, which prevented U.S. backing of Pyongyang's membership in international aid organizations. For its part, the United States was pressing Pyongyang to make permanent its temporary moratorium on missile programs, to demonstrate a commitment to nonproliferation, and to provide evidence that it was no longer supporting terrorist groups.[63]

In the United States, there was considerable debate over the wisdom of the U.S. engagement of North Korea under terms of the 1994 Agreed

Framework, the so-called Perry process, and other diplomatic interaction and negotiations. Although Congress ultimately approved appropriations for assistance to North Korea that made it by far the largest recipient of U.S. aid in East Asia, this occurred amid considerable grumbling and controversy. Critics in Congress and elsewhere were quick to note that the North Korean military threat had not significantly changed, that Pyongyang continued to proliferate ballistic missiles and other WMDs to sensitive Third World countries and to develop its own missile and other WMD programs, and that North Korea's tight authoritarianism came at the expense of basic human rights, including the starvation of hundreds of thousands of its own citizens. The Clinton administration's consideration of a possible U.S. presidential trip following Secretary of State Albright's October 2000 visit to Pyongyang elicited an outpouring of criticism both within and outside of the U.S. government that the United States was going too far in "rewarding" North Korea with a high-level U.S. official visit while Pyongyang still threatened the South and its allies and oppressed its people.[64]

Issues during the George W. Bush Administration

The election of George W. Bush saw U.S.–North Korean policy undergo review. The Agreed Framework continued to be supported, and the United States continued support for South Korea's engagement with the North. However, U.S.–North Korean contacts were cut back, and negotiations on missile issues and other topics were held in abeyance. North Korea reacted with tough rhetoric and by stalling North-South relations, prompting some South Korean supporters of President Kim Dae Jung's engagement policy to press the United States to be more forthcoming toward North Korea.[65]

The result of the U.S. policy review, announced in June 2001, was a general approval for talks with North Korea, but with few hints of specific U.S. positions for those talks. North Korea avoided a formal response, while sharply attacking U.S. motives in official North Korean media. North Korea also refused forward movement in contacts with South Korea until the United States showed more flexibility. South Korean president Kim's engagement policy with North Korea stalled, and some in South Korea joined the North Korean media in blaming the Bush administration for the lack of progress. The U.S.-led war on terrorism begun in September 2001 soon diminished the attention U.S. policy makers paid to the Korean Peninsula, adding to a sense of drift in the U.S. government's policy toward North Korea.

The impasse broke badly for the United States with North Korea's decision in December 2002 to restart nuclear installations at Yongbyon that had been shut down under the U.S.–North Korean Agreed Framework of 1994 and its announced withdrawal from the Nuclear Non-Proliferation Treaty. North Korea's actions followed the reported disclosure in October 2002 that North Korea was operating a secret nuclear program based on uranium enrichment and the resulting decision of the Korean Energy Development Organization (KEDO) in November 2002 to suspend shipments of heavy oil to North Korea—a key U.S. obligation under the Agreed Framework. The developments threatened a North Korean "nuclear breakout," including open production of nuclear weapons.

The Bush administration agreed to participate in talks hosted by China that evolved into the so-called Six-Party Talks with the addition of South Korea, Japan, and Russia. The talks made little progress for over a year, however, amid U.S. demands that North Korea dismantle the nuclear program and efforts to contain and pressure the North through initiatives such as the Proliferation Security Initiative, an international effort supported by the United States to check the proliferation of WMDs to terrorists that was seen to be targeted in part against North Korea's proliferation behavior. North Korea remained truculent and claimed it had already built nuclear weapons and was preparing to build more.

An agreement on principles was reached in September 2005 in the Six-Party Talks that provided a framework for further talks and eased the crisis atmosphere. Greater U.S. flexibility in directly negotiating with North Korean delegates in the Six-Party Talks and in reaching the consensus agreement in September was welcomed by the other powers and more broadly in Asian and world affairs. The agreement came as a result of two sessions of protracted and difficult negotiations beginning in July, following a thirteen-month hiatus in the negotiations that saw repeated flare-ups of tensions, with North Korea refusing to rejoin the talks ostensibly on account of various critical U.S. statements and actions, and the United States showing signs of greater frustration, particularly as North Korea officially claimed it possessed nuclear weapons and took steps to build more.

By all accounts, the two rounds of Six-Party Talks in Beijing during July–August and September were difficult. The lead U.S. negotiator, Assistant Secretary of State for East Asian Affairs Christopher Hill, was allowed greater flexibility by the U.S. administration than his predecessor James Kelly in negotiating directly with North Korean delegates during the Six-Party Talks and in considering various approaches in reaching the U.S. goal of a verifiable dismantlement of North Korea's nuclear weapons program. Hill and other U.S. officials were modest in characterizing the significance of the September agreement on principles, asserting that it represented just the start of a process to which the United States was strongly committed.

The main issues needing to be dealt with included:

- *Scope of denuclearization.* The Bush administration insisted that North Korea's highly enriched uranium program be ended, along with other aspects of the North Korean nuclear weapons program. For its part, North Korea denied it had such a program and insisted on the right to build nuclear power reactors for peaceful uses. U.S. officials, led by President Bush, voiced strong opposition to this, though the United States went along with a provision in the September agreement accepting discussions on the issue at an appropriate time.
- *Sequencing of benefits and responsibilities.* While the Bush administration indicated a willingness to provide some benefits to North Korea if it took steps toward complete denuclearization, North Korea placed more emphasis on demands for U.S. security guarantees and U.S.-backed international assistance before moving forward substantially in meeting U.S. denuclearization goals.
- *Verification.* The United States sought a verification regime more intrusive than that set forth in the 1994 U.S.–North Korean Agreed Framework, while North Korea remained among the world's most secretive regimes, with a record of determination to hide sensitive military capabilities.

With the September 2005 agreement, the Six-Party Talks became more than ever the foundation for Bush administration efforts to manage the nuclear problem and broader issues with North Korea. Administration officials voiced determination to stick with the multilateral negotiations. They judged that North Korea would have great difficulty withdrawing from its commitments to denuclearize and "walking away" from China and its other negotiating partners.[66]

Nevertheless, over the next year North Korea appeared to thumb its nose at the United States, South Korea, China, and other participants in the Six-Party Talks as it carried out one provocation after another. Pyongyang carried out ballistic missile tests in July and made an official declaration in early October that it would be compelled by U.S. pressure to test a nuclear weapon. The provocations culminated in the North Korean nuclear weapon test on October 9, 2006. North Korea subsequently warned that it would test again or declare war in the face of U.S.-led sanctions, but it also agreed on November 1 to resume participation in the Six-Party Talks. The progress in North Korean–U.S. negotiations and the Six-Party Talks in late 2006 and 2007 prompted speculation but few hard facts on why North Korea seemed to sharply change course toward moderation following the crisis prompted by its October 2006 nuclear test.

The failure to halt North Korea's nuclear weapons program prompted recriminations but no immediate change in U.S. policy. On the one hand, the Bush administration reemphasized seeking a diplomatic solution through the Six-Party Talks dealing with the North Korean nuclear program and consulted closely with the other powers involved in those talks about seeking measures to press North Korea to resume the negotiations and reverse its nuclear program. Washington continued to refuse direct bilateral talks with Pyongyang, though it remained open to bilateral talks during sessions of the six-party negotiations.

On the other hand, the Bush administration sought a UN Security Council resolution and sanctions to punish North Korea and to curb North Korea's ability to develop and proliferate nuclear weapons and related weapons systems. It compromised with China and other concerned powers in reaching a broadly accepted Security Council resolution. It also reaffirmed U.S. determination to defend its interests and meet defense commitments to U.S. allies, notably South Korea and Japan. A prepared statement read by President Bush on October 9 seemed to underline conditions under which the United States would take military action against North Korea when it said, "The transfer of nuclear weapons or material by North Korea to states or non-state entities would be considered a grave threat to the United States and we would hold North Korea fully accountable of the consequence of such action." The mix of U.S. diplomacy and pressure prompted warnings from North Korea but few public objections from other powers.[67]

The United States and North Korea, along with China, worked over the next months and reached agreement to resume the Six-Party Talks in February 2007. At the talks, the parties discussed and reached an agreement on the actions to be taken in the "initial phase of the implementation" of the September 19, 2005, agreement. A concurrent dispute between the United States and North Korea that had resulted in the freezing of more than $20 million of North Korean assets in a Macao bank was gradually resolved with the United States accommodating North Korea's demands.

A series of parallel actions were announced on February 13, 2007: North Korea would take steps to shut down the Yongbyon facility, invite the return of IAEA personnel, and declare all of its nuclear programs. The United States agreed to start bilateral talks with North Korea on resolving bilateral issues, establishing full diplomatic relations, proceeding to remove North Korea from the U.S. restrictions imposed on state sponsors of terrorism, and removing the U.S. application of the Trading with the Enemy Act with regard to North Korea. Some of these steps would require actions by Congress, which remained wary of the North Korean regime even as progress was made toward reducing its nuclear weapons capability.[68] The United States and the other parties agreed to provide to North Korea an initial shipment of emergency energy assistance equivalent to 50,000 tons of heavy fuel oil. The six parties also agreed to establish working groups dealing with denuclearization of the Korean Peninsula, normalization of North Korea's relations with the United States and with Japan, economic and energy cooperation, and a Northeast Asia peace and security mechanism.

The reaction to the February 2007 agreement was mixed in the United States. Former George W. Bush administration officials that had pushed a hard line said it was a bad deal. Administration supporters said it signaled the beginning of complete denuclearization by North Korea. Democratic Speaker of the House Nancy Pelosi and other congressional critics who called for greater Bush administration flexibility in negotiating the accord welcomed the agreement. However, these critics also lamented that the accord in concrete terms seemed to represent little more than a return to the freeze and monitoring of the Yongbyon facilities that had existed under the Agreed Framework. From their view, Bush administration policy was now accepting a deal they already had in 2001, and the government efforts to press a harder line toward North Korea since then had led to the more negative situation of North Korea actually becoming a nuclear weapons state. They were uncertain that the vague wording of the February 2007 agreement and U.S. agreements with North Korea and other members of the Six-Party Talks would lead to an end of the North Korean nuclear weapons threat.

Progress seemed to be made as the year wore on, but the process was shrouded in secrecy. Adding to the mystery was a reported Israeli strike on an alleged Syrian nuclear installation that involved support from North Korea. What this episode meant for continued U.S. cooperation with North Korea remained unclear at the end of 2007.[69]

Other Issues

Ballistic Missile Testing and Proliferation. The United States remained concerned about North Korea's ballistic missile development and sales abroad. North Korea maintained a moratorium on flight testing of long-range missiles from September 1999 until July 2006. The 2006 test prompted efforts by the United States, Japan, and other concerned powers to bring the matter of North Korea's actions before the UN Security Council. The Security Council reached a compromise resolution on July 15, 2006, that denounced and demanded a halt to North Korea's ballistic missile activities, required international restrictions on transfers that could assist North Korea's missile programs, and urged North Korea to return to the Six-Party Talks. The North Korean actions reinforced ongoing U.S. and Japanese collaboration to establish ballistic missile defenses against the North Korean threat. The Clinton administration engaged in negotiations with North Korea over ballistic missile prolif- eration issues. The Bush administration subsequently condemned North Korea as a dangerous proliferator of missiles but offered no specific negotiating proposal on missiles.[70]

U.S. Terrorism List. North Korea sought removal from the U.S. list of state sponsors of terrorism. An important motive seemed to be to open the way for North Korea to receive financial aid from the World Bank and the International Monetary Fund (IMF). U.S. law required the United States to oppose such assistance to any country on the U.S. terrorism list. The South Korean government urged the United States to remove North Korea from the list, while Japan urged keeping North Korea on the ter- rorism list until it resolved Japan's concerns over North Korea's sanctu- ary for members of the terrorist Japanese Red Army organization and Japanese concerns over evidence that North Korea kidnapped and held Japanese citizens.[71]

Food Aid. In the face of reports of widespread famine and severe mal- nutrition in North Korea, the United States in the mid-1990s began sup- plying food aid to North Korea. By 2004, it had provided more than 1.9 million tons. The Bush administration then reduced food aid, citing North Korea's refusal to allow adequate access and monitoring of how the food was distributed and used. In 2007, the White House indicated that greater U.S. food aid would come in tandem with progress in implementing the February 2007 agreement at the Six-Party Talks on North Korea's nuclear weapons program.[72]

North Korean Refugees in China and Human Rights. The tens of thou- sands of North Koreans seeking refuge in China were an issue of some dispute between Congress and the Bush administration and a serious issue in U.S. relations with both China and South Korea. Beijing and Seoul chose to deal with the issue quietly, avoiding UN involvement and avoiding disrupting their respective relations with North Korea. The U.S. Congress was in the lead in pressing the Bush administration to take more forthright action in the United Nations and in relations with China and South Korea in order to safeguard these vulnerable migrants. Meanwhile, Congress also pressed the administration to take strong public measures to condemn the repressive North Korean regime and its gross violations of human rights. Its efforts saw the passage in 2004 of the North Korean Human Rights Act, which required numerous U.S. government actions and efforts to help safeguard human rights in North Korea. These steps were not welcomed by either China or South Korea, which continued to give higher priority to avoiding upset in their respective relations with North Korea.[73]

Priorities and Issues in U.S.–South Korean Relations

The United States has maintained a strong, multifaceted alliance relationship with South Korea that has for decades served vital interests of both sides. Beginning in the late 1990s, major changes in South Korean politics, public opinion, and elite viewpoints saw a major shift in South Korea's approach to North Korea and South Korea's attitude toward and interest in its alliance relationship with the United States. Under the George W. Bush administration, U.S. policy toward North Korea appeared to move in a direction opposite that of South Korea. South Korean–U.S. differences over policy toward the North, military alliance issues, trade policies, and other questions periodically reached crisis proportions. Leaders on both sides tended to see their interests best served by continuing the alliance, but persisting friction and disputes meant that the formerly close U.S.–South Korean alignment on Korean Peninsula issues and other international affairs was a thing of the past.[74]

Dealing with North Korea

Heading the list of issues in U.S.–South Korean relations was how to deal with North Korea. South Korean president Kim Dae Jung, inaugurated in February 1998, departed sharply from the more conservative South Korean policies of the past and adopted a more conciliatory approach to the North known as the "Sunshine Policy." Seoul pointedly disagreed with congressional and other U.S. critics of the Clinton administration's efforts at this time by negotiating with North Korea in pursuing and easing of tensions and understandings in accord with the Agreed Framework.[75]

In 2000, the dramatic summit meeting between North and South Korean leaders saw South Korea for a time take the lead from the United States in diplomacy with North Korea. A multifaceted North-South dialogue began on reuniting divided families, economic cooperation, and even military issues. Its progress was marred by stops and starts and by subsequent disclosures that the Pyongyang summit and resulting dialogue was prompted by large South Korean clandestine payments to North Korea.[76] Nevertheless, the South Korean government of Kim and his successor as president in 2003, Roh Moo Hyun, persisted with moderate policies toward North Korea. The policies were designed to ease tensions and bring gradual improvement in North-South relations by means of South Korean engagement efforts that called for asymmetrical South Korean concessions toward North Korea, despite the latter's often truculent and sometimes provocative behavior. More conservative South Korean politicians and public opinion disagreed with aspects of the Sunshine Policy, but the overall thrust of Seoul's asymmetrical engagement and normalization efforts with Pyongyang persisted without major controversy in South Korea.[77]

This broadly supported South Korean approach toward North Korea ran up against the Bush administration's harder line toward North Korea, resulting in repeated friction and open disputes. U.S. efforts to continue past practice and foster a united front with its allies Japan and South Korea in dealing with the North Korean threat foundered on strong differences between Washington and Tokyo, which favored a tougher approach, and Seoul, which favored moderation and flexibility. In the Six-Party Talks, South Korea's position was more in accord with China's and Russia's moderate stance toward North Korea than with the positions of the United States and Japan. Resentment festered in the South Korean government and among South Korean public opinion and opinion leaders over what was seen as misguided and arrogant hard-line U.S. policy positions toward North Korea.[78]

Military Issues and Alliance Relations

Since the late 1990s, government leaders and broad segments of opinion in South Korea have differed strongly with U.S. government leaders over the threat posed by North Korea. This exacerbated differences on how to deal with the North Korean nuclear weapons program in the Six-Party Talks and on whether to adopt a policy of engagement or containment in dealing with North Korea on other matters in international affairs and bilateral relations. In the past, there was close common understanding between U.S. and South Korean leaders on the prime mission of the U.S.–South Korean alliance: deterring the North Korean military threat. The George W. Bush administration strongly emphasized the threat posed by North Korea's nuclear weapons development, ballistic missile development and proliferation, and large conventional forces forward-deployed near the demilitarized zone (DMZ) separating North and South Korea. By contrast, South Korean leaders and public opinion tended to play down concern over the military threat from the North. The end of the Cold War and of support for North Korea by the Soviet Union, the marked decline in North Korea's economy, and progress in North-South relations headed the list of factors that prompted South Korean leaders and public opinion to adopt a more moderate attitude toward the North Korean threat than that of the U.S. government.

Declining South Korean fears of a North Korean invasion and threat, and progress in inter-Korean dialogue, added to debate in South Korea over the perceived negative implications for South Korea posed by the large U.S. military presence and other aspects of the alliance relationship. Long-standing opposition by some groups in South Korea to sensitive aspects of the U.S. military presence in South Korea and the U.S. alliance relations was reinforced by a younger generation of South Koreans who came of age under authoritarian South Korean regimes, which the young South Koreans tended to view unfavorably. These younger South Koreans came into positions of power in the administrations of Kim Dae Jung and Roh Moo Hyun, and they held negative views of U.S. government support for previous authoritarian South Korean governments.[79]

Changing South Korean government and public attitudes toward the alliance with the United States meant that incidents and issues resulted in strong South Korean public criticism. In the late 1990s, one issue was perceived U.S. resistance to Seoul's demands that the bilateral Status of Forces Agreement (SOFA) be amended to give South Korea greater jurisdiction over U.S. servicemen accused of crimes. The SOFA was ultimately amended to the at least temporary satisfaction of both governments in early 2001. Other contentious issues at that time were an errant U.S. bombing exercise that damaged a South Korean village and the disclosure that the U.S. Military Command had dumped dangerous chemicals in the Han River, which flows through Seoul. The United States and South Korea also engaged in tough negotiations over South Korea's desire to develop missiles with nearly double the range of the 180-kilometer limit established by a U.S.–South Korean agreement in 1979. The two governments, too, had to respond to reports that surfaced in 1999 claiming that, during the 1950–1953 Korean War, U.S. troops inflicted several atrocities on South Korean citizens or allowed South Korean troops under U.S. command to do so.[80]

In 2002, massive South Korean protests erupted when a U.S. military vehicle killed two South Korean schoolgirls and the U.S. military personnel driving the vehicle were acquitted in a U.S. court-martial. Presidential candidate Roh was elected in December 2002 after strongly criticizing the United States during his campaign. By 2004, polls found that more South Koreans viewed the United States as the biggest threat to South Korea rather than North Korea.[81]

Against the backdrop of these tensions in South Korean–U.S. alliance relations, the Bush administration in 2003 began a series of steps to alter the U.S. military presence in South Korea with an aim to bring deployments there more into line with U.S. plans in the Korean Peninsula and U.S. troop realignments in Asian and world affairs. The steps added to U.S.–South Korean friction and differences over their alliance relationship. The American actions called for the withdrawal of the U.S. Second Division, comprising about fifteen thousand troops, from a position just below the DMZ to bases about seventy-five miles south and the relocation of the U.S. base at Yongsan, housing some eight thousand U.S. military personnel in the center of Seoul, away from the city. (A 1991 agreement to relocate Yongsan never was implemented.) In mid-2004, the Pentagon disclosed a plan to withdraw 12,500 U.S. troops from South Korea by the end of 2005, and the United States rapidly withdrew one of two combat brigades of the Second Division to Iraq. Under South Korean pressure, the United States agreed to slow the withdrawal, but by 2008 U.S. forces in South Korea were to decline from 37,000 to 24,000. Proposed U.S. compensation efforts included upgrades worth $11 billion for U.S. forces in South Korea.[82]

The South Korean government voiced strong reservations over some of the U.S. decisions, although it eventually concluded agreements to facilitate the relocations and agreed in 2004 to assume the estimated $3–4 billion cost of relocating the Yongsan garrison. South Korea also continued some support for the cost of U.S. troops in South Korea. The cost in 2005 was about $3 billion annually, and South Korea's direct financial contribution for 2005 and 2006 was $681 million.

The changes in U.S. force deployments were accompanied by changes in the U.S. military command structure in Korea. During a summit meeting in September 2006, President Bush expressed support for President Roh's declared policy of regaining operational command from the United States over South Korea's armed forces during wartime. They agreed that the timing of the transfer should not become a political issue. This supported the South Korean president against domestic critics who feared a weakening of the U.S.–South Korean alliance. Bush affirmed that South Korea should not worry about U.S. support during an emergency. He declared, "My message to the Korean people is that the United States is committed to the security of the Korean peninsula."[83]

For South Korea, the transfer represented recognition of the country's independent defense capabilities and affirmed its equal role within the U.S.–South Korean alliance. Roh proposed a 2012 transfer date, and the U.S. military indicated in September 2006 that it was prepared to complete the transfer by 2009. The U.S. and South Korean defense ministers said following their meeting at the Pentagon in late September 2006 that the transfer would take place after October 15, 2009, but before March 15, 2012.

Political Issues

From one perspective, U.S. support for democratization in South Korea was a great success for U.S. policy. As South Korea moved from the authoritarian regimes of the past to more democratically based governments, U.S. officials were prominent in encouraging greater pluralism and democratic process. However, the process of democratization resulted in greater political instability and uncertainty in South Korea, exacerbating differences in the alliance relationship and raising questions for

U.S. policy makers about the South Korean government's ability to carry out burden sharing and economic reform programs sought by the United States. The Bush administration put priority on developing close relations with U.S. allies in East Asia and elsewhere, and relations with the South Korean leaders received careful attention. However, as noted above, major differences emerged on how to deal with North Korea and regarding sensitive issues in alliance relations, amid an upswing in negative public opinion polls in South Korea regarding the United States.[84]

Beginning in 2005, the United States was somewhat less in the negative spotlight of South Korean nationalistic public opinion as attention in South Korea focused on territorial and historical disputes with Japan. The rising South Korean infatuation with China also reached a plateau and appeared to take a dive when it became clearer that China disputed nationalistic Korean views on a historical kingdom ruling the peninsula and parts of what is now northeastern China. Meanwhile, Christopher Hill, the U.S. ambassador to Seoul whose brief record in U.S.–South Korean relations was the most positive in recent years, was appointed leading U.S. negotiator in the Six-Party Talks and concurrently assistant secretary of state for East Asian affairs. He and his South Korean counterparts endeavored to play down obvious differences between the two governments over policy toward North Korea in the interests of reaching agreements acceptable to all in the multilateral negotiations. Hill did not object to South Korea's intention in June 2005 to offer large-scale aid to North Korea if Pyongyang agreed to rejoin the six-party negotiations.

Hill was replaced as ambassador by the previous U.S. ambassador to Russia, a move that demonstrated the importance the U.S. government gave to this post and appealed to South Korean national pride. As noted above, U.S. and South Korean defense officials also made progress amid continuing differences on burden-sharing issues as the United States continued the realignment and streamlining of its forces on the peninsula. Meanwhile, President Bush generally emphasized the positive in his regularly scheduled meetings with his South Korean counterpart.[85]

Serious differences between the U.S. and South Korean governments over political issues, including foreign policy, also loomed large. President Roh had very low approval ratings and risked being considered a lame duck. He therefore sought and carried out successful meetings with U.S. leaders, including summit meetings with President Bush in June 2005 and in September 2006 that endeavored to paper over differences. At the same time, however, in other venues he emphasized views on how to deal with North Korea and international relations in Northeast Asia that were at odds with U.S. interests and traditional thinking on the U.S.–South Korean alliance relationship. He and his administration repeatedly played down North Korea as a security threat.

They emphasized Seoul's interest in playing a "balancer" role between the United States and Japan on the one hand and China on the other, thereby contrasting starkly with American views of the alliance as one of close U.S.–South Korean cooperation against the common enemy, North Korea. The South Korean president pressed the balancer idea presumably with an eye to safeguarding South Korea's growing trade and political ties with China by seeking to avoid having his country drawn into disputes between China and the United States and its ally Japan. Presumably on account of its difference with the U.S. policies toward North Korea and China, South Korea refused to join in U.S. ballistic missile defense efforts in Northeast Asia that were backed by Japan and also refused to join in the Proliferation Security Initiative.[86]

Economic Issues

The Asian economic crisis of 1997–1998 had a major effect on the South Korean economy. On November 21, 1997, Seoul sought assistance from the IMF. The bailout ballooned to $57 billion in December amid strenuous U.S. government and financial sector efforts to fend off a credit collapse in South Korea. By year's end, South Korea's currency had lost half its value relative to the U.S. dollar, the stock market was at its lowest point in ten years, eight of the top thirty Korean conglomerates had gone bankrupt or were seeking court protection from creditors, and international credit agencies were downgrading Korea's debt to near junk bond status.[87]

Economic conditions worsened in 1998 as the economy contracted by 6 percent. Strong recovery ensued in 1999, however, and the gross domestic product grew by more than 10 percent. Unemployment fell from 8.6 percent in February 1999 to 4.4 percent in November. Foreign exchange reserves, down to $4 billion in 1997, reached $73 billion at the end of 1999. U.S.–South Korean trade jumped from $40 billion in 1998 to $54 billion in 1999, according to the U.S. Department of Commerce. Imports from South Korea were $31 billion, while U.S. exports to South Korea stood at $23 billion.[88]

U.S. officials focused less on the overall trade deficit and more on South Korea's continued restrictions on market access for U.S. automobiles, pharmaceuticals, farm products, and other goods and services. Salient issues included U.S. concerns over steel imports from South Korea and over South Korean restrictions on U.S. beef exports to the country.[89] On the whole, the intensity of U.S.–South Korea trade disputes diminished from the late 1980s and early 1990s. As a result of reforms required under the IMF support package of 1997, South Korea opened to foreign investors, with the result that American companies and investors became significant shareholders in South Korean corporations, banks, and stock market shares. The U.S. trade imbalance with South Korea remained steady and relatively small, especially when compared with the large U.S. trade deficit with China. U.S. and South Korean officials also reportedly became more adept at managing trade disputes.[90]

Against this background, U.S. and South Korean officials announced in February 2006 their intention to negotiate a Korea-U.S. free trade agreement (KORUSFTA). The negotiations began later in the year and were completed in mid-2007. The accord still faced serious hurdles to implementation. Democrats in the U.S. Congress, including some presidential candidates, voiced opposition to the deal. The launching of the KORUSFTA was politically risky for both South Korea and the United States, as failure would almost certainly lead to serious recriminations. On the other hand, it was apparently deemed by both governments that a successful KORUSFTA would provide a significant boost to the U.S.–South Korean relations at a time of many difficulties, as noted above, and would produce important economic benefits for both countries. It would be the second largest FTA in which the United States is a participant and the largest for South Korea.[91]

NOTES

1. *East Asia and the Pacific: Issues at the End of the 105th Congress*, CRS Report 98-931F (Washington, D.C.: Congressional Research Service , Library of Congress, 1998).

2. Robert Sutter, "The Democratic-Led 110th Congress: Implications for Asia," *Asia Policy* 3 (January 2007): 125–50.

3. Council on Foreign Relations, *Campaign Blog: The Candidates and the World*, November 8, 2007, http://blogs.cfr.org/campaign2008/.

4. David M. Lampton, *Same Bed, Different Dreams: Managing U.S.-China Relations, 1989–2000* (Berkeley: University of California Press, 2001).

5. Ramon Myers, Michel Oksenberg, and David Shambaugh, eds., *Forging a Consensus: Making China Policy in the Bush and Clinton Administrations* (New York: Rowman & Littlefield, 2001).

6. Michael Swaine, *Reverse Course: The Fragile Turnabout in U.S.-China Relations*, Policy Brief no. 22 (Washington, D.C.: Carnegie Endowment for International Peace, 2003); Jean Garrison, *Making China Policy: From Nixon to G. W. Bush* (Boulder, Colo.: Lynne Reinner, 2005).

7. Robert Sutter, *U.S. Policy toward China: An Introduction to the Role of Interest Groups* (New York: Rowman & Littlefield, 1998), 35.

8. Shirley Kan, *China's Technology Acquisition: Cox Committee's Report—Findings, Issues and Recommendations*, CRS Report RL30220 (Washington, D.C.: Congressional Research Service, Library of Congress, 1999).

9. Wayne Morrison, *China-U.S. Trade Issues*, CRS Issue Brief IB91121 (Washington, D.C.: Congressional Research Service, Library of Congress, June 5, 2001).

10. Kerry Dumbaugh, *China and the 105th Congress: Policy Issues and Legislation, 1997–1998*, CRS Report RL30220 (Washington, D.C.: Congressional Research Service, Library of Congress, June 8, 1999).

11. Kerry Dumbaugh, *China-U.S. Relations*, CRS Issue Brief IB98018, updated November 17, 2000 (Washington, D.C.: Congressional Research Service, Library of Congress, 2000).

12. Kerry Dumbaugh, *China-U.S. Relations*, Issue Brief IB98018, updated July 17, 2001 (Washington, D.C.: Congressional Research Service, Library of Congress, 2001); Swaine, *Reverse Course.*

13. Kerry Dumbaugh, *China-U.S. Relations: Current Issues and Implications for U.S. Policy*, CRS Report RL33877 (Washington, D.C.: Congressional Research Service, Library of Congress, May 25, 2007).

14. Sutter, *U.S. Policy toward China*, 94.

15. Hugo Restall, "Tough Love for China," *Wall Street Journal*, October 21, 2002.

16. Bates Gill, *Meeting the Challenges and Opportunities of China's Rise* (Washington, D.C.: Center for Strategic and International Studies, 2006), 6–12.

17. As is clear in the notes below, the following discussion relies on reports on China-U.S. relations done by the Congressional Research Service of the Library of Congress. Other sources include *Congressional Quarterly Weekly Report* and *Congressional Quarterly Almanac.*

18. Tony Saich, *Governance and Politics of China* (New York: Palgrave, 2004), 83.

19. Dumbaugh, *China-U.S. Relations* (July 17, 2001), 5.

20. Dumbaugh, *China and the 105th Congress.*

21. Larry Q. Nowels, *U.S. International Population Assistance: Issues for Congress*, CRS Issue Brief IB96026 (Washington, D.C.: Congressional Research Service, Library of Congress, June 15, 2001).

22. "Religion in China: When Opium Can Be Benign," *Economist*, February 1, 2007, 25–28.

23. Erica Werner, "U.S. Lawmakers Criticize Yahoo Officials," *Washington Post*, November 6, 2007.

24. Testimony of CIA director George Tenet to the Senate Armed Services Committee, March 20, 2002, available at http://www.fas.org/irp/congress/2002_hr/031902tenet.html.

25. Kerry Dumbaugh, *China-U.S. Relations in the 109th Congress*, CRS Report RL32804 (Washington, D.C.: Congressional Research Service, Library of Congress, 2007), 20.

26. "Westinghouse Reactor Sale Reinforces U.S.-China Bilateral Collaborations," *WMD Insights* February 2007, http://www.wmdinsights.com/I12/I12_EA2_WestinghouseReactor.htm.

27. Shirley Kan, *Chinese Proliferation of Missiles and Weapons of Mass Destruction: Current Policy Issues*, CRS Issue Brief IB92056 (Washington, D.C.: Congressional Research Service, Library of Congress, October 30, 2001); Evan Medeiros, *Reluctant Restraint: The Evolution of China's Nonproliferation Policies and Practices, 1980–2004* (Stanford, Calif.: Stanford University Press, 2008).

28. Kan, *China's Technology Acquisition.*

29. Shirley Kan et al., *China: Suspected Acquisition of U.S. Nuclear Weapons Data*, CRS Report RL30143 (Washington, D.C.: Congressional Research Service, Library of Congress, 1999); Kan, *China's Technology Acquisition*.

30. Amy Argetsinger, "Spy Case Dismissed for Misconduct," *Washington Post*, January 7, 2005; Steve Lohr, "State Department Yields on PC's from China, *New York Times*, May 22, 2006.

31. Wayne Morrison, *China-U.S. Trade Issues*, CRS Report RL33536 (Washington, D.C.: Congressional Research Service, Library of Congress, April 23, 2007).

32. Wayne Morrison, *China and the World Trade Organization*, CRS Report RS20139 (Washington, D.C.: Congressional Research Service, Library of Congress, August 6, 2003).

33. *Foreign Affairs, Defense, and Trade Policy: Key Issues in the 107th Congress*, CRS Report RL30776 (Washington, D.C.: Congressional Research Service, Library of Congress, December 19, 2000), 22–23.

34. Morrison, *China and the World Trade Organization*.

35. Dumbaugh, *China-U.S. Relations in the 109th Congress*, 19.

36. Morrison, *China-U.S. Trade Issues*.

37. Ibid.

38. Dumbaugh, *China-U.S. Relations in the 109th Congress*, 4.

39. Ibid., 27.

40. Ibid., 9.

41. Bonnie Glaser, "Mid-Air Collision Cripples Sino-U.S. Relations," *Comparative Connections* 3, no. 2 (2nd Qtr 2001), 23–35, http://www.csis.org/media/csis/pubs/0102q.pdf.

42. Dumbaugh, *China-U.S. Relations in the 109th Congress*, 8.

43. Kerry Dumbaugh, *Tibet and China: Current Issues and Implications for U.S. Policy*, CRS Report RS20395 (Washington, D.C.: Congressional Research Service, Library of Congress, November 8, 1999).

44. Glaser, "Mid-Air Collision."

45. Steven Lee Myers, "The Jiang Visit: In Washington," *New York Times*, November 1, 1997.

46. Peter Grier, "Why Bush Risks China's Ire to Honor Dalai Lama," *Christian Science Monitor*, October 17, 2007.

47. Kerry Dumbaugh, *Hong Kong after the Return to China: Implications for U.S. Interests*, Issue Brief IB95119 (Washington, D.C.: Congressional Research Service, Library of Congress, June 10, 1998).

48. Robert Sutter, "The Democratic Victory in Congress: Implications for Asia," Brookings Northeast Asia Commentary, December 1, 2006, http://www.brookings.edu/opinions/2006/12northeastasia_sutter.aspx.

49. Thomas Friedman, "Will Congress View China as Scapegoat or Sputnik?" *New York Times*, November 10, 2006.

50. The analysis in and sources for this section are reviewed in Sutter, "Democratic-Led 110th Congress."

51. Robin Toner, "After Many Years, Now It's His Turn at the Helm," *New York Times*, January 8, 2007; Carl Hulse, "Leadership Tries to Restrain Fiefs in New Congress," *New York Times*, January 7, 2007.

52. Larry Niksch, *Korea: U.S.–South Korean Relations—Issues for Congress*, CRS Issue Brief IB98045 (Washington, D.C.: Congressional Research Service, Library of Congress, July 16, 2005), 1–2.

53. William Cooper and Mark Manyin, *The Proposed South Korea–U.S. Free Trade Agreement (KORUSFTA)*, CRS Report RL33435 (Washington, D.C.: Congressional Research Service, Library of Congress, May 24, 2006), 2–5.

54. Larry Niksch, *North Korea's Nuclear Weapons Program*, CRS Report RL33590 (Washington, D.C.: Congressional Research Service, Library of Congress, August 1, 2006).

55. Victor Cha, "Korea: A Peninsula in Crisis and Flux," in *Strategic Asia, 2004–2005: Confronting Terrorism in the Pursuit of Power*, ed. Ashley J. Tellis and Michael Wills, 139–62 (Seattle: National Bureau of Asian Research, 2004).

56. Charles L. Pritchard, *Failed Diplomacy: The Tragic Story of How North Korea Got the Bomb* (Washington, D.C.: Brookings Institution Press, 2007), 25–44.

57. Larry Niksch, *North Korea's Nuclear Weapons Developments and Diplomacy*, CRS Report RL33590 (Washington, D.C.: Congressional Research Service, Library of Congress, September 10, 2007).

58. Donald Oberdorfer, *The Two Koreas* (Reading, Mass.: Addison-Wesley, 1997); Nicholas Eberstadt, *The End of North Korea* (Washington, D.C.: AEI Press, 1999).

59. The account here is based on Niksch, *North Korea's Nuclear Weapons Program*. See also Joel S. Wit, Daniel B. Poneman, and Robert L. Gallucci, *Going Critical: The First North Korean Nuclear Crisis* (Washington, D.C.: Brookings Institution Press, 2004) and sources in Oberdorfer, *Two Koreas*.

60. William Perry, *Review of United States Policy toward North Korea: Findings and Recommendations* (Washington, D.C.: Department of State, Office of the North Korea Policy Coordinator, 1999).

61. *North Korea's Engagement: Perspectives, Outlook, and Implications*, Conference Report CR2001-01 (Washington, D.C.: U.S. National Intelligence Council, 2001).

62. Donald Gross, "Progress on All Fronts," *Comparative Connections* 2, no. 4 (4th Qtr 2000): 27–35, http://www.csis.org/media/csis/pubs/0004q.pdf.

63. Victor Cha, "Engaging North Korea Credibly," *Survival* 42, no. 2 (Summer 2000): 136–55.

64. Daniel Bob, *The 107th Congress: Asia Pacific Policy Outlook*, NBR Briefing no. 10 (Seattle: National Bureau of Asian Research, 2001), 8–9.

65. For the play-by-play on U.S. policy regarding Korea at this time, see Pritchard, *Failed Diplomacy*.

66. Robert Sutter, "The United States and Asia in 2005: Managing Troubles, Sustaining Leadership," *Asian Survey* 46, no. 1 (January/February 2006): 12–14.

67. Robert Sutter, "The United States and Asia in 2006: Crisis Management, Holding Patterns, and Secondary Initiatives," *Asian Survey* 47, no. 1 (January/February 2007): 12–14.

68. Susan Crabtree, "Bolton Lobbies on N.K. Deal," *The Hill*, October 23, 2007 http://thehill.com/leading-the-news/bolton-lobbies-on-n.k.-deal-2007-10-23.html.

69. Donald Gross, "Finally Progress on the Feb. 13 Joint Agreement," *Comparative Connections* 9, no. 2 (2nd Qtr 2007): 47–54, http://www.csis.org/media/csis/

pubs/0702q.pdf; Mark Mazzetti and William Broad, "The Right Confronts Rice over North Korea Policy," *New York Times*, October 25, 2007.

70. Ralph Cossa, *"Déjà Vu* All Over Again with North Korea," *Comparative Connections* 8, no. 3 (3rd Qtr 2006): 1–18, http://www.csis.org/media/csis/pubs/0603q.pdf.

71. Niksch, *Korea*, 8.

72. Mark Manyin, "U.S. Assistance to North Korea: Fact Sheet," CRS Report RS21834 (Washington, D.C.: Congressional Research Service, Library of Congress, January 3, 2007), 1.

73. Niksch, *Korea*, 9–10.

74. Victor Cha, "South Korea: Anchored or Adrift?" in *Strategic Asia, 2003–2004: Fragility and Crisis*, ed. Richard J. Ellings and Aaron L. Friedberg, 109–30 (Seattle: National Bureau of Asian Research, 2003).

75. Bob, *107th Congress*, 8–9.

76. Michael J. Green, "Three Scenarios for President Roh's Trip to Pyongyang: The Good, the Bad, and the Ugly," Pacnet no. 32 (Honolulu: CSIS Pacific Forum, August 13, 2007).

77. Choong Nam Kim, "The Roh Moo Hyun Government's Policy toward North Korea," *International Journal of Korean Studies* 9, no. 2 (Fall/Winter 2005): 1–34.

78. Pritchard, *Failed Diplomacy*, 101–45.

79. Niksch, *Korea*, 6.

80. Richard Baker and Charles Morrison, *Asia Pacific Security Outlook, 2000* (New York: Japan Center for International Exchange, 2000), 103–11.

81. Niksch, *Korea*, 12.

82. Ibid., 12–13.

83. Sutter, "United States and Asia in 2006," 17.

84. Cha, "South Korea: Anchored or Adrift?"

85. Author's observation of speech by U.S. ambassador Alexander Vershbow at the Council on U.S.-Korean Security Studies annual conference, Seoul, Korea, August 23, 2007.

86. Niksch, *Korea*, 15.

87. Tong Whan Park, "South Korea in 1998: Swallowing the Bitter Pills of Restructuring," *Asian Survey* 39, no. 1 (January/February 1999): 133–39.

88. Young-Kwan Yoon, "South Korea in 1999: Overcoming Cold War Legacies," *Asian Survey* 40, no. 1 (January/February 2000): 164–71.

89. Donald Gross, "Good Sense in Washington, a Big Question Mark in Pyongyang," *Comparative Connections* 3, no. 2 (2nd Qtr 2001): 36–45, http://www.csis.org/media/csis/pubs/0102q.pdf.

90. Cooper and Manyin, *Proposed South Korea–U.S. Free Trade Agreement*, 5.

91. Ibid., 25–27.

3

U.S. Priorities and Concerns
Regarding Japan, Southeast
Asia, and the Pacific

PRIORITIES AND ISSUES IN U.S. POLICY TOWARD JAPAN

U.S. relations with Japan were much less controversial than U.S. relations with China and Korea. They remained of central importance in American policy toward the region in the post–Cold War period. U.S.-Japan relations were often described by U.S. officials and specialists as the lynchpin of U.S. interaction with East Asia and the broader Asia-Pacific region.

Nevertheless, some debate continued among American policy makers, specialists, and opinion leaders regarding how much importance to devote to them. In broad terms, U.S. policy toward the Asia-Pacific since the 1960s saw President Richard Nixon and some later presidents give top priority to developing cooperative U.S. relations with China, and in the process neglecting or downgrading U.S. relations with Japan. In the post–Cold War period, as Japan was economically stagnating for a decade and its political leadership sometimes appeared weak, some in and out of government believed that the United States was better off seeking to enhance its interests and influence in the Asia-Pacific by working more closely with rising regional powers, notably China. Others strongly disagreed, however, and stressed that without Japan as an ally and without access to military bases in Japan, U.S. influence in the Asia-Pacific would be severely constrained. According to this view, despite China's rapid economic growth, it would take time for China to surpass the wealth of Japan. Moreover, common interests and values were said to bind the United States closely to Japan in an alliance relationship demonstrating mutual trust deemed essential in sustaining American security, economic, and political interests in the Asia-Pacific region.[1]

The George W. Bush administration in its early years clearly favored the latter view. Reflecting the judgments of a cohort of strongly pro-Japan leaders headed by Deputy Secretary of State Richard Armitage, the Bush administration's relations with Japan were given top priority in the Asia-Pacific and probably received more favorable U.S. administration attention than any other U.S. bilateral relationship during the early years of Bush's presidency. The improvement in U.S.-Japan relations was a notable bright spot in the administration's foreign policy record, which became mired in controversy and recriminations, particularly as a result of its decision to invade Iraq.[2]

In its later years, however, the Bush administration leaders came increasingly to rely on consultations and coordination with Chinese counterparts to manage salient Asia-Pacific hot spots, notably North Korea's nuclear weapons program and the Taiwan situation. On the one hand, U.S. leaders and Japanese leaders continued to reinforce political and economic cooperation and closer security ties, some of which served as a hedge against rising Chinese power and influence. On the other hand, American officials also came increasingly to rely on China to help to keep the North Korean and Taiwan situations stable as the Bush administration leaders focused on other issues, especially the deep crisis posed by the U.S.-led conflict in Iraq and related turmoil in the Middle East and Afghanistan.[3]

A range of issues and disagreements in U.S. relations with Japan in recent years is reviewed below. In general, they failed to change the overall positive direction and general convergence in the U.S.-Japan alliance relationship. The issues sometimes reflected U.S. domestic considerations influencing policy toward Japan. On balance, the review shows that U.S. policy toward Japan had few of the contentious issues that energized U.S. domestic constituencies and continued to complicate U.S. policy toward China and, to a lesser degree, Korea. Congress and concerned U.S. domestic advocates and interest groups did not place many serious obstacles before the Bush administration's efforts to upgrade the scope and depth of U.S.-Japan cooperation. Their overall concern about U.S.-Japan issues was moderate to low, especially when compared to the level of their concern regarding those with China and Korea.[4]

Overview: U.S.-Japan Cooperation and Interdependence

After the Cold War, the United States continued to work closely with Japan to build a strong, multifaceted relationship based on shared democratic values and mutual interest in Asian and global stability and development. The two governments followed through with agreements to adapt their security alliance to post–Cold War challenges, while they referred most trade disputes to the World Trade Organization (WTO). The United States and Japan long shared goals of mutual economic well-being and regional stability. In economic terms, the two countries became increasingly interdependent: the United States was Japan's most important foreign market, and Japan's market was the third most valuable single country for the United States, after Canada and Mexico. It was the fourth largest (after Canada, China, and Mexico) source of imports into the United States. The trade flow ran heavily in Japan's favor. At the end of 2000, the U.S. trade deficit with Japan stood at a record $81.3 billion, and it had increased to $88.4 billion in 2006. Japan was one of the largest sources of foreign investment in the United States (including portfolio, direct, and other investment).[5]

The U.S.-Japan alliance and the American nuclear umbrella gave Japan maneuvering room in dealing with its militarily powerful neighbors. It also supported an American strategic role in the Asia-Pacific. As the world's leading industrial democracies, the United States and Japan worked closely in dealing with international economic issues and other global and regional issues, ranging from nuclear nonproliferation to official responses to North Korea's nuclear program, peace efforts in Cambodia, and Chinese military assertiveness. Japan played an active role in support of the U.S.-led antiterrorism campaign begun after the terrorist attack on America in September 2001. Japan's use of military forces in support of the U.S.-led wars in Afghanistan and Iraq remained limited, however, reflecting controversy in Japanese politics and opposition by Japanese public opinion to using military forces abroad in this way. Prime Minister Junichiro Koizumi withdrew Japan's small contingent of military forces in Iraq after a few years, and Prime Minister Yasuo Fukuda was forced by political opposition to halt for a time Japan's use of military forces to refuel allied ships in the Indian Ocean involved in the war in Afghanistan.[6]

Periodic Strains in Relations

Relations periodically have been strained by differences over trade and economic issues and, less often, over divergent foreign policy stances. Strains arising from trade issues became intense in the 1980s but began to subside in the 1990s, as Japan's slow growth contrasted with the U.S. economy's steady expansion and rising international competitiveness, and, for a time, the widely watched U.S. trade deficit with Japan began to decline substantially.

The end of the Cold War and collapse of the Soviet Union called into question some of the strategic underpinnings of the alliance within both the American and Japanese governments and publics. After a period of strategic uncertainty in the two countries over how to respond to the post–Cold War situation in the Asia-Pacific, leaders on both sides saw their interests as best served by strengthening the U.S.-Japan alliance to support their respective strategic interests in the region.

Japan welcomed the U.S. Defense Department's Nye Initiative (named after Assistant Secretary of Defense Joseph Nye) in the mid-1990s, which was intended to reassure Japan and other regional states of the continued commitment of the United States to maintain its forward military deployment in Asia and the Western Pacific at about a hundred thousand troops. Japanese leaders, media, and opinion leaders also welcomed the so-called Nye-Armitage Report of 2000, a report of a nongovernment study group chaired by Joseph Nye and Richard Armitage that advocated closer U.S.-Japan security cooperation. A second Nye-Armitage report was issued in 2007.[7]

Tokyo watched with some unease the erratic course of U.S.-China relations and showed some disagreement with the Clinton administration's handling of North Korea. Japanese officials were uncomfortable with President Bill Clinton's June 1998 trip to China, which did not include a stop in Tokyo, and felt that in remarks in Shanghai he tilted too close to China's position on the China-Taiwan issue. Japan also was concerned, however, about deteriorating U.S.-China relations after the May 1999 bombing of the Chinese Embassy in Belgrade, revelations concerning Chinese espionage activities at U.S. weapons laboratories, and the failure of Clinton administration officials to reach an agreement on the terms for China's admission to the WTO during the April 1999 visit to the United States by Chinese premier Zhu Rongji.

Some in Japan worried that the George W. Bush administration's initially strong support for Taiwan and other measures might lead to regional instability contrary to Japanese interests. The Bush administration worked hard to develop close relations with Japan in dealing with the consequences of rising Chinese power and influence, though, and the Japanese government seemed reassured by this U.S. approach. There remained Japanese government concern that China's rise and importance to the United States in handling key issues like North Korea's nuclear weapons development might prompt the Bush government or a future U.S. administration to give higher priority to U.S. relations with China at the expense of those with Japan.[8]

Japan's own relations with China showed volatility and uncertainty. They received a setback during a November 1998 visit by Chinese president Jiang Zemin, who vocally and publicly criticized the Japanese government's refusal to include the word "apology" in part of the joint communiqué addressing Japan's past aggression in China. Prime Minister Keizo Obuchi's reciprocal visit to Beijing in early July 1999 was marked by the appearance of cordiality, as was Premier Zhu's visit to Japan in 2000, but analysts still saw deep differences in perspective.[9] Friction over historical and territorial issues and rivalry in Asian and world organizations became serious during the tenure of Prime Minister Koizumi (2001–2006). His insistence on annually visiting the controversial Yasukuni Shrine and war memorial exacerbated historical and nationalistic differences between the two countries, prompting Chinese leaders to refuse to meet with him. The public disputes subsided to some degree under his successors Shinzo Abe and Yasuo Fukuda, but few differences were resolved.[10]

The United States and Japan shared the same broad objectives regarding the unstable Korean Peninsula, but Japanese officials at times expressed a feeling of being left out of U.S. decision making or concern that the United States was following policies either too accommodating or too confrontational toward North Korea. Japan yielded reluctantly to pressure from the United States to pay about $1 billion toward the construction of two light-water nuclear power plants for North Korea under the October 1994 U.S.–North Korea Agreed Framework. The Japanese government maintained a firm position closest to that of the United States during the Six-Party Talks that began in 2003, and some Japanese officials were surprised by the shift toward greater flexibility and moderation in U.S. policy regarding North Korea seen in the agreement in those talks on February 13, 2007, that outlined steps to meet U.S. and North Korean concerns regarding the North Korean nuclear program and related issues. Japanese leaders repeatedly sought reassurance of U.S. support for Japan's interests in the negotiations with North Korea, in particular on the issue of Japanese citizens abducted by North Korean agents and taken to North Korea. Japan also for a time drew closer to the South Korean government headed by President Kim Dae Jung, including high-level military exchanges. Relations worsened under Prime Minister Koizumi, however, particularly as South Korea was as sensitive as China in reacting angrily to Koizumi's annual visits to the Yasukuni Shrine.[11]

Though he seriously alienated China and Korea, Koizumi worked closely with the Bush administration in fostering an important improvement in U.S.-Japan relations. His domestic reforms for the Japanese economy were warmly welcomed by the U.S. administration. Koizumi also adopted a more assertive Japanese foreign and national security policy that saw Japan stand together with the United States in offering strong political, economic, and military support for the Global War on Terrorism and the U.S.-led wars in Afghanistan and Iraq. Japan made its first-ever military deployments after World War II in noncombat support of the U.S. and allied forces in Afghanistan. In 2004, the Koizumi government also sent noncombat troops to Iraq, despite considerable domestic opposition. It cooperated closely with the Bush government in dealing with North Korea's nuclear program and with rising Chinese power and influence. Japan increased cooperation with the United States in bilateral missile defense research and development efforts. In 2005, the United States and Japan announced a sweeping agreement to strengthen military cooperation. The plan called for U.S. forces to be realigned and for Japan to take on a more active (albeit noncombat) role in maintaining regional and global security. The planned changes were intended to complement the broader U.S. Defense Department goal of deploying a more stream-lined and mobile force in the Asia-Pacific.[12]

The expanding Japanese military role exacerbated tensions in Japan's relations with China and South Korea, complicating U.S. policy and rela-tions with key allies Japan and South Korea and with Asia's ascendant power, China. Koizumi's assertive foreign policy stance was welcomed by the Bush government and met approval amid a rising sense in Japan of nationalism and vulnerability (to North Korea and China, in particu-lar). The Koizumi and subsequent Abe governments also stressed Japan's bid for a permanent seat in the UN Security Council and efforts to revise Japan's constitution to eliminate clauses prohibiting Japanese participa-tion in collective security arrangements. The Abe government also em-phasized closer alignment with the United States and other Asia-Pacific democracies, notably Australia and India. The Fukuda administration gave less emphasis to this initiative, which was controversial in China. The United States generally supported Japanese policies, though China and South Korea showed reservations and opposition.[13]

Global Issues in U.S.-Japan Diplomatic and Security Relations

The dominant theme in U.S.-Japan relations in recent years has been deepening alliance cooperation across a range of issues since the Septem-ber 11, 2001, terrorist attacks. Prior to traveling to Asia in November 2005, President Bush described Prime Minister Koizumi as "one of the best friends that I have in the international arena." During a summit between the two leaders in Kyoto in November 2005, Koizumi said that the closer U.S.-Japan relations are, the "easier for us [Japan] to behave and estab-lish better relations with China, with South Korea, and other nations in Asia."[14] Prime ministers Abe and Fukuda also endeavored to show close convergence with the United States and to build strong personal relation-ships with the U.S. president.[15]

Counterterrorism Cooperation

Following the terrorist attacks of September 11, 2001, the Koizumi gov-ernment initiated a series of unprecedented measures to protect American facilities in Japan and to provide nonlethal "rear-area" logistical support to U.S. military operations against al-Qaeda and the Taliban regime in Afghanistan. The latter mainly took the form of at-sea replenishment of fuel oil and water to U.S., British, French, and other allied warships operating in the Indian Ocean. The dispatch of Japan's Maritime Self-Defense Force (MSDF) was the first such deployment since World War II. Beginning in 2001, a small flotilla of Japanese transport ships, oilers, and destroyers provided about 30 percent of the fuel used by U.S. and allied warships, and Japan's Air Self-Defense Force (ASDF) conducted hundreds of airlift support missions for U.S. forces. On June 10, 2005, the Japanese government decided to extend its antiterrorism law for two years but to reduce its Indian Ocean deployment. The continued limited role of a Japanese naval ship providing refueling for allied ships in the Indian Ocean ended because of opposition in the Japanese Diet in late 2007. Prime Minister Fukuda pledged to try to resume the refueling operation. Meanwhile, Japan also became the second leading donor country (after the United States) for Afghanistan relief and reconstruction.[16]

Support for U.S. Policy toward Iraq

While strongly preferring a clear United Nations role in resolving the U.S.-British confrontation with Saddam Hussein's government in Iraq, Japan nonetheless gave almost unqualified support to the Bush administration's position. During an open debate in the UN Security Council, Japan was one of only two out of twenty-seven participating countries (the other being Australia) to support the U.S. contention that even if the UN inspections were strengthened and expanded, they were unlikely to lead to the elimination of Iraq's weapons of mass destruction. In 2003–2005, Japan provided $1.5 billion in grant assistance to Iraq, pledged to provide $3.5 billion in yen loans, and agreed to a phased cancellation of 80 percent of the approximately $7.5 billion in debt Iraq owed Japan. In addition, the Koizumi government deployed about six hundred military personnel—mainly ground troops—to carry out humanitarian aid and reconstruction activities in Iraq. The forces were withdrawn in 2006.[17]

United Nations Security Council Reform

In 2004, Japan accelerated its long-standing efforts to become a permanent member of the UN Security Council by forming a coalition with Germany, India, and Brazil (the so-called "G-4") to achieve nonveto membership for all countries. Though the Bush administration backed Japan's bid, it did not support the G-4 proposal and opposed taking a vote on expanding the Security Council until a "broader consensus" on reforming the entire organization was reached. After the G-4 bid failed in the run-up to the UN's Millennium Summit in September 2005, Koizumi reportedly indicated that in the future Japan would have to coordinate more closely with the United States in order to achieve its goal. Abe and Fukuda welcomed Bush administration pledges of support for Japan's seeking a permanent Security Council seat, though the immediate importance of the issue seemed to subside following the failure of the G-4 bid. Under UN rules, to become a new member of the Security Council, Japan would need to obtain support from two-thirds of all UN member countries.

At that time, Japan was the second largest contributor to the UN regular budget, paying more than 20 percent of the total, more than twice the percentage paid by the third largest contributor. After investigations revealed that mismanagement had allowed millions of dollars to be lost in the oil-for-food program for Iraq, Japan joined the United States and other donors in threatening to withhold part of its funding if drastic reforms were not adopted.[18]

Kyoto Protocol and Climate Change

Japan is the fourth leading producer of so-called greenhouse gases, after the United States, China, and Russia. Under the Kyoto Protocol, which Tokyo ratified in 2002, Japan was obligated to reduce its emissions to 6 percent below its 1990 levels by 2010. Japanese industry shared many of the concerns of U.S. industry about the cost and feasibility of achieving these reductions, but the Japanese government placed high value on its support of the accord. It expressed dismay over the Bush administration's decision to back away from the protocol.

In 2005, Japan joined with the United States, China, India, South Korea, and Australia in a new, nonbinding agreement. The Asia-Pacific Partnership on Clean Development and Climate called on the six nations to cooperate on the development and diffusion of technology to combat climate change, reduce pollution, and promote energy security. The group was designed to complement the Kyoto Protocol, but some environmentalists criticized the arrangement for its absence of requirements, particularly on greenhouse gas emissions, and for being a part of a suspected U.S. strategy to prevent the Kyoto Protocol from being renewed after it expires in 2012.[19]

Regional Issues in U.S.-Japan Diplomatic and Security Relations

Korean Peninsula

Japan's policy toward North Korea has hardened in recent years, drawing Japan closer to the tough position adopted in the Six-Party Talks until

2007 by the Bush administration. Japan insisted on North Korea abandoning its nuclear weapons and development programs. At times, Japan promised substantial aid in return. The Japanese government took steps to squeeze North Korea with restrictions on economic and trade relations with Japan. It also participated in the U.S.-led Proliferation Security Initiative (PSI), which guards against proliferation of weapons of mass destruction (WMD) from North Korea and other international proliferators. Japan took the lead in seeking UN measures against North Korean ballistic missile tests in July 2006 and nuclear weapons test in October 2006.

The issue of Japanese citizens kidnapped in the 1970s and 1980s by North Korean agents drove the governments of prime ministers Koizumi and Abe to a harder stance toward North Korea. The Bush administration and the U.S. Congress supported Japan's insistence on a full accounting of the fate of those abducted. The North Korea Human Rights Act (P.L. 108-333) passed the 108th Congress and was signed by President Bush in October 2004. It required that U.S. nonhumanitarian assistance to North Korea depend on "substantial progress" toward North Korea fully disclosing information on the abductees. Prime Minister Fukuda took power amid reports of rapid progress in U.S.–North Korean relations that might undercut Tokyo's hard line with Pyongyang over the Japanese abducted by North Korea, and he sought support from Bush on this issue.[20]

At times, Japan encouraged the United States to adopt a more flexible position in talks with North Korea. Outside the framework of U.S.-led Six-Party Talks, Koizumi pursued an independent channel of diplomacy with North Korea and held summits with North Korean leader Kim Jong-Il in September 2002 and May 2004. Koizumi and his successor Abe made normalization of Japan's relations with North Korea contingent on a settlement of the nuclear and abduction issues.

The Japanese government adjusted to the notably more flexible Bush administration stance in the Six-Party Talks exemplified by the February 13, 2007, agreement on procedures for the talks. Some Japanese officials expressed concern about the seemingly abrupt shift in U.S. policy and what this meant for Japan's continued firm posture toward North Korea. There was particular concern in Japan that the United States would seek to remove North Korea from the U.S. list of state sponsors of terrorism before North Korea had provided information on Japanese abductees satisfactory to Japan.[21]

Japan-China Rivalry

Despite extensive economic ties and growing interdependence, Japan-China differences over a wide range of nationalistic, political, historical, and defense issues grew in the early twenty-first century. These developments posed problems for the Bush administration, which was called upon repeatedly by Americans and Asians to take positions that were designed to ease these differences and reduce regional tensions. In general, the U.S. government adopted a low posture, trying to avoid taking sides while calling on the two countries to resolve differences through amicable discussions and negotiations.

In April 2005, large-scale anti-Japanese demonstrations broke out in at least nine Chinese cities, including a violent protest in Shanghai that damaged the Japanese consulate as well as shops that catered to the large Japanese expatriate community. The Chinese authorities at first were passive in allowing the protesters to organize and did not take strong measures to stop the violence until a few days had passed.

Beijing and Tokyo faced a series of disputes over territorial rights in the East China Sea, which is potentially rich in oil and gas reserves. Japan considers the area surrounding the Senkaku/Diaoyu islands to be part of its exclusive economic zone (EEZ). The Japanese Self-Defense Forces detected periodic Chinese military activities in the area, including a submarine incursion close to Okinawa and a fleet of warships near a disputed gas field.

Beijing, for its part, criticized the strengthening U.S.-Japan security relationship and Japan's increasingly public concern for Taiwan's security. In another indication of shifting relations, Japan cut its assistance to China in half from 2000 to 2005 and sought to phase out the program by the end of the decade.[22]

Prime ministers Abe and Fukuda avoided visits to the controversial Yasukuni Shrine that had strongly angered China during Prime Minister Koizumi's years in office. Koizumi visited the shrine repeatedly, despite Chinese objections. Fukuda endeavored to increase the thaw in Chinese-Japanese relations begun under Abe, but substantial differences remained between the two Asian powers.[23]

Historical Issues Dividing Asian Powers

Historical grievances, particularly those centered around Japan's behavior during and preceding World War II, continued to aggravate Japan's relations with its neighbors, notably China and South Korea. The most sensitive issue in recent years involved the visits of Japanese politicians to the Yasukuni Shrine, a Shinto shrine that honors Japanese soldiers who died in war. The millions enshrined include several Class A war criminals. Chinese leaders emphasized repeatedly that Prime Minister Koizumi's annual visits to the shrine constituted a major obstacle in Sino-Japanese relations. In a related vein, Japan came under fire regarding some of its history textbooks for schoolchildren. China and South Korea maintained that some texts misrepresent Japan's past by downplaying the atrocities committed by Japanese soldiers against civilian populations.

The disputes with Japan affected Chinese and South Korean views of the United States. Critics in China and South Korea attacked the Bush administration's reluctance to take sides in these historical disputes. The U.S. House of Representatives passed a resolution in 2005 (H.Con.Res. 191) that commemorated the sixtieth anniversary of the Pacific War and affirmed the judgments rendered by the international war crimes tribunal in Tokyo after World War II. In recent years, Congress proposed bills and amendments on behalf of surviving U.S. prisoners of war forced to work for Japanese companies who were seeking compensation for forced labor and torture. The 110th Congress also passed legislation in the House on the issue of Japan's treatment of the claims of "comfort women," who were widely seen to have been coerced to provide sexual services for Japanese troops during World War II.[24]

Military Issues

Deepening Cooperation

Japan and the United States are military allies under a security treaty concluded in 1951 and revised in 1960. Under the treaty, the United States pledges to assist Japan if it is attacked, and Japan grants the United States military base rights on its territory. The alliance was directed against the Soviet Union during the Cold War, but as the Cold War ended, a number of new issues emerged that gave the security relationship continued relevance.[25]

In October 2005, at a Security Consultative Committee meeting (SCC, also known as the 2+2 meeting) of the Japanese and U.S. foreign and defense ministers, the two sides released an interim report, *Transformation and Realignment for the Future*, announcing several significant steps that would expand the alliance beyond its existing framework. As U.S. personnel and facilities in Japan were realigned as part of a broader U.S. Defense Department strategy of deploying a more streamlined and mobile force, Japan was to take a more active role in contributing to global stability, primarily through increased coordination with the U.S. military. Features of the new arrangement included a reduction in the number of U.S. Marines in Japan, the relocation of a problematic air base in Okinawa, the deployment of an X-band radar system to Japan as part of a missile defense system, expanded bilateral cooperation in training and intelligence sharing, and Japan's acceptance of a U.S. nuclear-powered aircraft carrier based at the Yokosuka Naval Base.[26]

Proposed command structure changes coming from the October 2005 report and later decisions saw establishing an U.S. Army deployable headquarters at Camp Zama in Japan. Camp Zama would also be a base for a rapid response headquarters for the Japanese Ground Self-Defense Forces. A bilateral and joint operations center was planned at Yokota Air Base, near Tokyo, in order to enhance coordination between Japanese and U.S. air and missile defense commands. And the headquarters of the Third Marine Expeditionary Force, commanding 7,000–8,000 marines, was to move from Okinawa to Guam.

Many of the agreements' more controversial elements faced continued obstacles. Local Japanese politicians in areas identified to host new facilities and troops protested loudly. That all was not going smoothly in U.S.-Japan defense relations—reportedly over base realignment and the long-standing sensitive issues involving moving air bases in Okinawa—was evident in Defense Secretary Donald Rumsfeld's October 2005 visit to Asian capitals for defense-related consultations that bypassed Japan. The U.S. and Japanese security officials did reach agreements on these issues later that month, but a March 2006 deadline on base realignment passed without an expected agreement. In May 2006, the two sides concurred on a plan to restructure their military alliance. This notably involved extensive U.S. force redeployments (e.g., moving 8,000 U.S. Marines from Okinawa to Guam) and the costs of those redeployments (Japan would pay construction and other costs of facilities development, and the United States would pay operational costs arising from implementing the deal).[27]

The most recent alliance overhaul built upon 1997 revised defense cooperation guidelines that granted the U.S. military greater use of Japanese installations in times of crisis and referred to a possible limited Japanese military role in areas near Japan for minesweeping, search and rescue, and surveillance. The Clinton administration began discussions with Japan over an expanded role for Japan in supporting U.S. forces in any future East Asian crises. President Bill Clinton and Prime Minister Ryutaro Hashimoto issued a Joint U.S.-Japan Declaration on Security on April 17, 1996. The new defense cooperation guidelines were agreed to on September 24, 1997, replacing guidelines in force since 1978. The United States and Japan then had to negotiate implementing agreements. The Japanese Diet began passing implementing legislation in late 1998, amid considerable public controversy.[28]

The crises most often mentioned involved Korea and the Taiwan Strait. Japan traditionally barred its Self-Defense Forces (SDF) from operating outside Japanese territory, in accordance with Article 9 of the 1947 constitution, the so-called no war clause. Japanese public opinion strongly supported the limitations placed on the SDF. However, since 1991, Japan has allowed the SDF to participate in a number of United Nations peace-keeping missions.

American officials favored a more flexible interpretation of Article 9 that would permit the SDF to support U.S. forces directly in regional conflict contingencies. The Japanese government in the 1990s took the position that the Japanese military could counterattack a country that launched missiles at Japan, but a number of East Asian countries, including China, opposed even that enlargement of Japan's military role. China warned the United States and Japan not to expand defense cooperation in ways that would affect China's interests, including relations with Taiwan. In 2001, proposals that the Japanese SDF support U.S.-led military actions against Afghanistan and in Iraq were supported in Japan, while Chinese, Korean, and other reservations were downplayed.[29]

At the 2+2 meeting in February 2005, secretaries Condoleezza Rice and Rumsfeld, along with their Japanese counterparts, outlined a more global and integrated vision of the alliance, specifically mentioning issues related to the Korean Peninsula and the Taiwan Strait as "common strategic objectives" for "peaceful resolution." Defense officials continued to stress, however, that the Japanese military was not to be involved in combat missions but instead would be limited to contributions of logistical support.[30]

Defense technology sharing was an important security issue beginning in the late 1980s, starting with a troubled and controversial program to co-develop and jointly produce a new Japanese fighter aircraft, the FSX (now in the Japanese inventory as the F-2). The Clinton administration pressed Japan to develop jointly a theater missile defense (TMD) system for the defense of Japan against missile attacks, and Japan and the United States agreed in August 1999 to begin cooperative research and development over the next five to six years on a theater missile system. Proponents of TMD justified it on the basis of North Korea's missile program, but China's large and growing array of ballistic missiles also seemed to figure into Japanese calculations. China strongly opposed the program. Prime Minister Koizumi announced in December 2003 that Japan would acquire the ground-based U.S. Patriot Advanced Capability 3 (PAC-3) system and the ship-based U.S. Standard Missile 3 (SM-3) system. Japan reportedly planned to deploy missile defense systems around major Japanese cities in 2007. In 2005, it was announced that the missile defense efforts would cost more than $1 billion over nine years.[31]

Meanwhile, Japan sustained various independent defense programs and postures. Japan's National Defense Program Guidelines (NDPG) approved in December 2004 called on Japan to become more engaged militarily in the Indian Ocean region from the Middle East to Southeast

Asia, advocated military exports to the United States for development of joint missile defense, mentioned China as security problem (the first such mention in a five-year plan), and supported increasing the size of Japanese rapid reaction forces, whose main mission was to prevent infiltration from North Korea.[32]

Constitutional Restrictions: Article 9

In general, Japan's U.S.-drafted constitution remained an obstacle to closer U.S.-Japan defense cooperation. The prevailing interpretation of Article 9 in the constitution forbade engaging in "collective defense"— that is, combat cooperation with the United States against a third country. Article 9 outlaws war as a sovereign right of Japan and prohibits "the right of belligerency." It says that land, sea, and air forces, as well as other war potential will never be maintained. In the past, Japanese public opinion strongly supported the limitations placed on the SDF, but this opposition has softened in recent years. Since 1991, Japan has allowed the SDF to participate in noncombat roles in a number of UN peacekeeping missions and with the U.S.-led coalition dealing with Afghanistan and in Iraq. These moves often were accompanied by serious political debate in the Japanese Diet, in the media, and among the Japanese people.[33]

U.S. Bases and Burden Sharing

There are a large number of contentious issues in U.S. relations with Japan that involve U.S. forces stationed in Japan, particularly in Okinawa. For more than twenty years, the United States has pressed Japan to share the burden of the costs of American troops and bases. Under a host nation support agreement in force at the time, Japan in 2000 provided about $2.5 billion annually in direct financial support of U.S. forces in Japan, about 77 percent of the total estimated cost of stationing U.S. troops there.[34] According to a U.S. Defense Department report, Japan in 2004 provided $4.4 billion in direct and indirect host nation support, which was 75 percent of the total cost of maintaining troops in Japan. In January 2005, Japan agreed to provide $1.2 billion in direct support for U.S. forces in each of the next two years. Working out the cost of relocating eight thousand U.S. Marines from Okinawa to Guam proved difficult, but in 2006 Japan agreed to pay construction and facilities development costs related to the move.

U.S. forces on the island of Okinawa were at the center of large-scale protests in Okinawa in September 1995 following the abduction and rape of a Japanese schoolgirl by three U.S. servicemen. The U.S. and Japanese governments concluded an agreement worked out by the Special Action Committee on Okinawa (SACO) on December 2, 1996, under which the U.S. military would relinquish some bases and land on Okinawa (21 percent of the total bases' land) over seven years. Implementing this agreement was difficult.[35]

Economic Issues

Despite Japan's post–Cold War economic slump and recent slow recovery, U.S. trade and other economic ties with Japan remain highly important to U.S. national interests and are sometimes issues of controversy in the U.S. Congress. By the most conventional method of measurement, the United States and Japan are the world's two largest economies, accounting for around 40 percent of global gross domestic product. Their relations not only impact each other but also have a big effect on world economic conditions. The U.S. and Japanese economies are increasingly intertwined by merchandise trade, trade in services, and foreign investments.[36]

Although Japan remains economically important to the United States, its importance has slid as it has been edged out by other trade partners. Japan is the United States' third largest merchandise export market (behind Canada and Mexico) and the fourth largest source of U.S. merchandise imports (behind Canada, China, and Mexico). At one time, Japan was the largest source of foreign direct investment (FDI) in the United States but it slipped to second place, after the United Kingdom, in late 2004. At that time, Japan was the fifth largest target for U.S. FDI abroad. The United States was Japan's largest export market and the second largest source of imports in 2005.[37]

Japan's economy was anemic at best, and at times in decline, for most of the 1990s and into the first years of the twenty-first century. Economists and policy makers in Japan and the United States attributed Japan's difficulties to a number of factors. The United States and others pressured Japan to undertake deregulation in order to promote sustainable economic growth consistent with free market principles, and the Japanese economy, led by growing exports to China, the United States, and other markets, began to show growth by 2005.

Tensions in the U.S.-Japan bilateral economic relationship were much lower in recent years than was the case in the 1970s, 1980s, and early 1990s. A number of factors appear to have contributed to this trend: Japan's economic problems in the 1990s and first few years of this decade changed the general U.S. perception of Japan as an economic "threat" to one of a country with problems; the rise of China as an economic power caused U.S. policy makers to shift attention from Japan to China as a source of concern; the increased use by both Japan and the United States of the WTO as a forum for resolving trade disputes acted to depoliticize disputes and reduce friction; and the emphasis in the bilateral relationship shifted from economic to security matters.[38]

Foreign trade in general and trade with Japan in particular have long been of strong interest to Congress and the impetus for legislation. For many years, the relationship has been clouded by persistent and large U.S. trade deficits. The deficit in 1999 reached $74 billion, breaking the previous record of $65.7 billion set in 1994, and it was even larger, $81.3 billion, for 2000. It declined somewhat in subsequent years but started to rise again, reaching $82.7 billion in 2005 and $88.4 billion in 2006.[39]

Besides the growing imbalance in bilateral trade, the United States and Japan confront a range of economic issues. Disputes over the trade in steel products were contentious, especially at the end of the Clinton administration and in the first year of the George W. Bush administration, which featured antidumping measures against Japanese and other steel imports. The U.S. auto industry sometimes contrasted its large burden of health care and pension costs with the situation of its Japanese competitors that have fewer burdens in these areas because of Japanese government support. Japan's ability to keep the value of the yen from rising as the U.S. dollar declined against other currencies beginning in 2005 was a cause of concern in Congress, though China's alleged currency manipulation and much larger trade surplus with the United States received the largest share of congressional attention in this issue area.[40]

U.S. beef exporters and their often powerful representatives in the Congress took strong issue with Japan's restriction on U.S. beef imports stemming from what the Americans saw as unjustified Japanese suspicions that U.S. beef might be tainted with mad cow disease. After many years, Japan lifted the ban in late 2005, but then reimposed it in early 2006. After much controversy and discussion, Japan in June 2006 again lifted its ban on U.S. beef imports.[41]

Japan and the United States are major supporters of the Doha Development Agenda (DDA), the latest round of negotiations in the WTO. However, the two took divergent positions in some areas of the agenda. For example, the United States, Australia, and other major agricultural exporting countries pressed for reductions or removal of barriers to agricultural imports and subsidies of agricultural production, a position resisted by Japan and the European Union. At the same time, Japan and others argued on occasion that national antidumping laws and actions that member countries have taken should be examined during the DDA, with the possibility of changing them—a position the United States has opposed.[42]

Japan's Increased International Assertiveness

Under the leadership of Prime Minister Junichiro Koizumi and his successor Shinzo Abe, the Japanese government demonstrated a more assertive and active posture in international affairs than seen in previous years.

The new assertiveness was seen in at least four notable ways. First, under Koizumi, Japan intensified its cooperation with the United States, and Koizumi developed a strong personal relationship with President George W. Bush. Second, Tokyo hardened its policies toward Beijing, slashed its bilateral aid program, did not back down from territorial and historical disputes, and reoriented the U.S.-Japan alliance to give both countries more flexibility to respond to perceived and actual threats from China. Third, Japan attempted to exert more influence in Southeast Asia and elsewhere in the Asia-Pacific and on the global stage, as evidenced by its pursuit of a permanent seat on the UN Security Council and its negotiation of free trade agreements (FTAs) with a number of Southeast Asian countries. Fourth, Japanese leaders sought to make Japan a more "normal" country by legitimizing the military's ability to participate in collective security arrangements and take actions—such as firing at hostile foreign ships in Japanese waters—that most other countries take for granted.

The Bush administration generally encouraged Japan's growing assertiveness. The Japanese actions tended to mesh with U.S. interests in the Asia-Pacific, although U.S.-Japanese differences emerged from time to time over their respective tactics and approaches vis-à-vis North Korea, relations with rising power China, the importance of Asian multilateral groups, and their respective independent military modernization efforts. On the whole, however, Japan's greater activism occurred within the context of close U.S.-Japan collaboration and cooperation.[43]

The advent of the administration of Prime Minister Yasuo Fukuda in 2007 amid a decline in support for the ruling Liberal Democratic Party in Japan called into question a continuation of the recent Japanese assertiveness abroad. Fukuda seemed more in line with earlier Japanese practice of trying where possible to avoid disputes both with Asian neighbors and at home that would arise from pushing forward controversial foreign policy initiatives.[44]

PRIORITIES AND ISSUES IN U.S. RELATIONS WITH SOUTHEAST ASIA AND THE PACIFIC

U.S. policy concerns and issues of debate in Southeast Asia and the Pacific have been less important than the range of issues seen in U.S. relations with China, Korea, and Japan. In part this is because U.S. policy makers and opinion leaders generally saw less at stake for U.S. interests in Southeast Asia and the Pacific than in Northeast Asia. U.S. military presence, trade and economic relations, and Great Power politics inevitably gave pride of place to Northeast Asia in American calculations. Moreover, the opportunities for U.S. interests in Southeast Asia appeared limited at times. The region recovered somewhat from the Asian economic crisis of 1997–1998 but was subject to persistent political instability and economic uncertainty that curbed U.S. and other foreign investment. The instability and uncertainty also sapped the political power and importance of the Association of Southeast Asian Nations (ASEAN) and its leading members, even though ASEAN more recently has been at the center of growing Asian multilateral activism dealing with salient regional economic, political, and security issues.[45]

U.S. attention to the region rose in the first decade of the twenty-first century. The U.S.-led Global War on Terrorism broadened and intensified U.S. involvement and concerns throughout Asia. Southeast Asia for a time became a "second front" in the U.S. struggle against terrorism. The United States worked closely with allies Australia, the Philippines, and Thailand, as well as with Singapore, Malaysia, and Indonesia, among others, in various efforts to curb terrorist activities in the region.[46]

Following the Asian economic crisis, a variety of Asian regional multilateral groupings centered on ASEAN and its Asian partners were formed and advanced significantly. China's stature and influence in these groups and among ASEAN states grew rapidly amid burgeoning intra-Asian trade and investment networks involving China in a central role, and attentive and innovative Chinese diplomacy. China's increasing prominence was seen by many to steer the region in directions that reduced U.S. influence and worked against U.S. interests.[47] On the other hand, the massive and effective U.S.-led relief effort in the wake of the tsunami disaster in South and Southeast Asia in December 2004 showed unsurpassed American power and influence and underlined the continuing importance of the United States for regional stability and well-being.[48]

Evolving U.S. Policy Concerns

At the turn of the twenty-first century, U.S. policy concerns in Southeast Asia were scattered, focused on individual countries and their specific circumstances. They generally involved much smaller groups of U.S. policy makers and concerned U.S. observers than those involved in debates and discussions over U.S. policies toward China, Korea, and Japan.

Heading the list of regional trouble spots was Indonesia. The economic crisis of the late 1990s brought down the previous authoritarian rule of President Suharto, but a stable new order emerged slowly amid leadership maneuvering, mass demonstrations, persistent corruption, economic mismanagement, and an overall decline in governance. Jakarta's handling of the East Timor issue at this time drew strongly negative U.S. and other international responses.[49]

The government of President Joseph Estrada in the Philippines revived the cronyism of the Ferdinand Marcos era and seemed inattentive to fundamentals of good economic management. Estrada lost the support of most Philippine elites, who in 2001 rallied around his vice president, Gloria Macapagal Arroyo, in a successful and constitutionally extraordinary effort to push him from office. Arroyo took power and endeavored to promote reforms, but also faced repeated challenges to her rule from Philippine elites jockeying for power and influence.[50]

The January 2001 elections in Thailand brought to power a ruling coalition inclined to soft-pedal recent economic reforms and engage in corrupt practices of the past. Malaysia's weak economic recovery added to political challenges to Prime Minister Mahathir Mohamad's rule, notably within his ruling party. Mahathir usually responded to such challenges with a hard line, suggesting a degree of continuing political uncertainty about how the process of selecting his successor would add to economic difficulties in Malaysia.[51]

As its leading member states went through difficulties and turmoil, the ten-member ASEAN appeared to decline. The loss of Indonesia's Suharto was a major blow to the association's leadership. Intra-ASEAN bickering increased as members pursued contradictory agendas.[52] Foreign investors, including U.S. businesses, shifted away from the region. China in 1999 captured 61 percent of FDI in emerging Asian economics while ASEAN had 17 percent—a reversal of the shares ten years earlier. FDI in ASEAN declined 22 percent in 1999, after dropping 21 percent in 1998.[53]

Against this backdrop, U.S. policy concerns focused on particular issues in individual countries. The controversy over the Indonesian government's handling of East Timor dominated debate over U.S.-Indonesia relations. Democracy and human rights issues drove the U.S. discussion about policy toward Burma. Lower-level dialogue and debate marked issues in U.S. relations with other states in Southeast Asia and the Pacific.

Indonesia and East Timor

U.S. officials endeavored to influence the broad, important, and dramatic changes in Indonesia following the demise of President Suharto's long authoritarian rule in 1998. However, U.S. policy debates in this period tended to center more narrowly on this populous and strategically located country's treatment of East Timor, the Portuguese colony that Indonesia had occupied following Portugal's withdrawal in 1975 and annexed in 1976.

International pressure on the interim Indonesian government following Suharto's demise in 1998 led President B. J. Habibie to promise a referendum in East Timor. This took place on August 30, 1999, amid widespread intimidation efforts supported by opponents of East Timor independence within Indonesian security forces and elsewhere. East Timorese voters rejected an Indonesian plan for autonomy in the referendum, thus expressing a preference for independence. Anti-independence East Timorese paramilitary groups, backed by the Indonesian military, then instituted a wave of violence and terror. In response, an UN-approved international peacekeeping force entered East Timor in October 1999.[54]

The U.S. Congress often was ahead of the White House in pressing for greater resolve in defense of East Timor against Indonesian-backed violence and oppression. In response to Indonesian military units massacring peaceful demonstrators in Dili in November 1991, Congress terminated Indonesian military participation in the U.S. International Military Education Training (IMET) program in 1992 and placed special conditions on Indonesian participation when it worked out an agreement with the Clinton administration in 1995 to restore Indonesian participation. In 1994, Congress included in the fiscal year (FY) 1995 foreign operations appropriations bill (P.L. 103-306) a ban on the export to Indonesia of light arms and crowd control items until the secretary of state reported to Congress "significant progress" on human rights in East Timor. In 1996 and 1998, congressional criticism was influential in blocking the Clinton administration's planned sale of F-16 aircraft to Indonesia and in bringing about the cancellation of U.S. military exercises with Indonesian special forces units. Furthermore, significant numbers of members of Congress went on record as supporting self-determination for East Timor.[55]

In response to the 1999 violence in East Timor, the Clinton administration, backed by Congress, pressured the Indonesian government to accept international peacekeepers. It also suspended U.S. military-related programs with Indonesia, supported decisions by the International Monetary Fund (IMF) and the World Bank to suspend their assistance programs to Indonesia, dispatched three hundred U.S. military personnel to East Timor to provide transportation and communications support; and issued warnings to Indonesia that U.S. military-related programs would not be resumed and that Indonesia could face additional U.S. sanctions unless it cooperated with the international peacekeeping force.[56]

Foreign operations appropriations legislation for FY 2000 (P.L. 106-113) and 2001 (P.L. 106-429) prohibited Indonesian participation in the IMET program and U.S. foreign military sales of arms to Indonesia. The laws provided for resumption of these activities only after the president certifies that the Indonesian government and military have taken judicial action against East Timorese militia members and Indonesian military personnel responsible for the post-referendum atrocities and have allowed displaced East Timorese in Indonesian West Timor (then numbering more than 100,000) to return home.[57]

Burma (Myanmar)

At the beginning of the current decade, U.S. policy continued to focus on Burma's political situation since a military junta took power in September 1988 and repressed civilians. The regime suppressed political opposition and reportedly inflicted a wide array of human rights abuses against the populace. The U.S. policy debate focused on how much pressure the U.S. government should apply against the military regime. The Clinton administration strengthened existing sanctions in May 1997 by banning new U.S. private investment in Burma despite opposition from major U.S. corporations. Allied governments imposed varying restrictions in dealing with Burma, but Australia and Japan favored a strategy of engagement with Burma.[58]

The Burmese junta took power in 1988 following twenty-six years of military rule under Ne Win. The junta, known after December 1997 as the State Peace and Development Council (SPDC), suppressed pro-democracy demonstrators in September 1988, killing hundreds. It changed the country's official name from Burma to Myanmar (a change not officially accepted by the United States). The regime allowed elections for a National Assembly in 1990, but then nullified the results when the opposition National League for Democracy (NLD) won most of the seats. Subsequently, the government suppressed political liberties and reportedly jailed thousands. Aung San Suu Kyi, the leader of the NLD, was placed under house arrest and restricted in her movements.[59]

President Clinton issued an executive order on May 20, 1997, prohibiting U.S. private companies from making new investments in Burma, specifically barring U.S. oil companies from investing in new oil and natural gas projects there. Investments made prior to May 20, 1997, were not affected, however. The order added to existing sanctions that the Ronald Reagan and George H. W. Bush administrations had instituted after the Burmese military's repression of September 1988. These included a suspension of aid to Burma, including antinarcotics aid; suspension of Burma's trade benefits under the Generalized System of Preferences; termination of a U.S.-Burma textile agreement; suspension of Export-Import Bank loans to Burma; suspension of U.S. government insurance to U.S. businesses operating in Burma; opposition to new loans to Burma by the World Bank, the IMF, and the Asian Development Bank; and an informal arms embargo among G-7 countries and other allies.[60]

Secretary of State Madeleine Albright was a strong advocate of the Clinton administration's harder line. She criticized the SPDC at international conferences attended by officials from Burma, and she and other U.S. officials refused to meet bilaterally with Burmese counterparts. Albright also urged the secretary-general of the United Nations to pressure the SPDC to negotiate with Aung San Suu Kyi. The administration sponsored resolutions in the UN Human Rights Commission and the International Labor Organization condemning Burma and rejected SPDC offers to reduce opium production in return for the United States resuming antinarcotics aid (although the administration did contribute money to the UN Drug Control Program in Burma). The tough U.S. stance against Burma did not change substantially under George W. Bush.[61]

The European Union also continued limits on diplomatic contacts, refused to accept full Burmese participation in meetings between the EU and ASEAN, of which Burma is a member, and maintained trade sanctions.[62]

However, the Australian and Japanese governments diverged from the United States and pursued policies of engagement with Myanmar. Meanwhile, the United States opposed Burma's admission to ASEAN in 1997. The ASEAN countries, following Thailand's lead, adhered to a policy of engagement toward Burma. They argued that normal relations and expanded economic relations were the best means of influencing the SPDC to moderate its internal policies.[63]

Vietnam

Controversy and debate marked every step of the U.S. path toward normalizing relations with Vietnam. The effort began after the Vietnam War of the 1960s and 1970s and Vietnam's withdrawal from Cambodia in the face of U.S.-backed pressure in the late 1980s and early 1990s. The controversy and debate became less active during the 1990s, though concerns remained. The issues involved Vietnam's continued authoritarian political system, human rights violations, economic obfuscation, corruption and protectionism, and cooperation in resolving inquiries into the status of U.S. prisoners of war and service personnel listed as missing in action since the war.[64]

A U.S.-Vietnam bilateral trade agreement was signed on July 13, 2000. It provided for the restoration of "normal trade relations," other bilateral trade-regulating measures as required by U.S. law, and comprehensive additional commitments by Vietnam in the areas of market access, intellectual property rights, trade in services, and investment. It was submitted by the president to Congress for approval, where it elicited some debate over the issues in U.S.-Vietnam relations noted above, though the agreement was approved in 2001.[65]

Cambodia

U.S. concerns in Cambodia tended to include criticism of the often harsh and authoritarian methods of the ruling administration of Prime Minister Hun Sen and suspicions over its intention to follow through on promises to support a tribunal made up of Cambodian and foreign jurists investigating crimes committed by the former Khmer Rouge leaders of Cambodia. It appeared that the Hun Sen government was maneuvering to avoid significant actions by the tribunal in order to assuage ex-members of the Khmer Rouge important to its rule and to avoid offending China, the major foreign backer of the Khmer Rouge and a key supporter of the Phnom Penh government.[66]

Australia, New Zealand, and the Pacific Islands

There was little controversy in the United States over the close U.S. alliance with Australia and good relations with New Zealand and Pacific Island countries. There was concern with political instability and anti-democratic movements in such key Pacific Island countries as Fiji and the Solomon Islands, but U.S. policy attention to Oceania was minimal. U.S. policy makers tended to see the troubles in the region as more a responsibility of Australia and New Zealand, with the U.S. role as largely one of concerned monitoring and political support.[67]

The War on Terrorism in Southeast Asia

There was little opposition in the United States to the increased U.S. military and other counterterrorism cooperation with Southeast Asian governments after the September 11, 2001, terrorist attack on America. Nonetheless, several years of strong antiterrorism efforts combined with the U.S.-led war in Iraq prompted Southeast Asian leaders to complain that the United States was conducting the war on terrorism in the wrong way. American actions were seen as radicalizing Asia's Muslims and strengthening domestic opposition to Southeast Asian governments friendly to the United States. Meanwhile, Southeast Asian leaders also complained that U.S. preoccupation with the war in Iraq and the broader war on terrorism made U.S. leaders inattentive to Southeast Asia and the priorities leaders there put on nation building, economic development, and cooperation in an emerging array of regional multilateral organizations.[68]

The U.S. actions against terrorism in Southeast Asia were primarily bilateral. Some attention focused on regional organizations such as the ASEAN Regional Forum (ARF), Asia Pacific Economic Cooperation

(APEC), and ASEAN itself. With U.S. encouragement, APEC members in particular undertook obligations to secure ports and airports, combat money laundering, secure shipping containers, and tighten border controls. Meanwhile, the Australian government of Prime Minister John Howard was a staunch U.S. ally in most aspects of the U.S.-led war on terrorism, including the conflict in Iraq. New Zealand also supported various U.S. initiatives and contributed forces to antiterrorism actions in Afghanistan. Both Australia and New Zealand received strong U.S. support for their military and other interventions designed to calm recurrent instability in several Pacific Island states during this period.[69]

The U.S. military presence in Southeast Asia declined markedly with the closing of U.S. bases in the Philippines in 1992 after the end of the Cold War. The U.S. military endeavored to gain temporary access for transit and training. Extensive U.S. exercises continued with Thailand, and a small but important permanent U.S. presence was arranged with Singapore. No Southeast Asian state agreed to provide locations for prepositioned U.S. supplies until the Philippines negotiated a new visiting forces agreement late in the 1990s.[70]

The U.S. military took the lead after 9/11 in arranging for close cooperation with Philippine security forces to deal with terrorists in the country. U.S. military supplies to the Philippines increased markedly. Joint and prolonged exercises allowed hundreds of U.S. forces to help train their Philippine counterparts to apprehend members of the terrorist Abu Sayyaf Group, which was active in the southwestern islands of the Philippines. Other U.S. military training activities helped to strengthen Philippine forces to deal with other terrorist and rebellious groups. These included members of Jemaah Islamiyah, which was reportedly training terrorists in the Philippines. The United States awarded the Philippines the status as a "major non-NATO ally," provided increased U.S. military assistance, and welcomed the small contingent of Philippine troops in Iraq. The contingent was withdrawn in 2004 to save the life of a kidnapped Philippine hostage.[71]

The Bush administration also awarded increased military aid and major non-NATO ally status to Thailand, which sent nearly five hundred troops to Iraq. Thailand also reversed its refusals of the 1990s and offered sites for the forward positioning of U.S. military supplies. Cobra Gold, the annual U.S.-led military exercise in Thailand, attracted participation from other Asian countries. Meanwhile, Singapore developed a new security framework agreement with the United States, involving counterterrorism cooperation, efforts against proliferation of WMD, and joint military exercises.[72]

The United States also supported a Southeast Asian antiterrorism center in Malaysia. U.S. support for Indonesia focused at first on the Indonesian Police Counter-Terrorism Task Force and broader education and other assistance designed to strengthen democratic governance in Indonesia in the face of terrorist threats. Restrictions on U.S. assistance to the Indonesian military were slowly eased, despite continued reservations in Congress over the military's long history of abuses. Popular sentiment in Malaysia and Indonesia was strongly against a perceived bias in the Bush administration's focus against radical Islam as a target in the war on terrorism. This added to the unpopularity of American policies toward Iraq and the Palestinian-Israeli dispute. Nonetheless, the Bush administration worked hard to improve relations with Malaysia and particularly Indonesia, the world's largest Muslim state, whose government emphasized moderation and democratic values. U.S. aid, military contacts, and high-level exchanges grew as the Indonesian democratic administration made progress toward more effective governance.[73]

Asian Multilateralism and the Rise of China

By the middle of the first decade of the twenty-first century, U.S. policy makers and nongovernment specialists concerned with Asia actively debated approaches to the emerging challenges and opportunities for the United States posed by advances in Asian multilateralism and China's growing role in these organizations. U.S. allies and friends in Japan, Australia, Southeast Asia, and elsewhere urged Washington to adopt a more active stance toward Asian multilateralism. The focus of U.S. discussion and debate was on Southeast Asia and Asian multilateral groupings that gave prominence to ASEAN, and this focus was maintained even though key members of ASEAN—notably the three largest of the founding members, Indonesia, the Philippines, and Thailand—were preoccupied with serious internal problems and unable to lead the organization effectively.[74]

Regional groupings involving Central Asia, particularly the Shanghai Cooperation Organization led by China and Russia, did not include the United States. The United States participated as an observer in the main South Asian regional group, the South Asia Association for Regional Cooperation. Northeast Asian cooperation in the Six-Party Talks also had the potential to develop into a workable regional grouping in the future, but the talks remained focused on dealing with the protracted process of ending North Korea's nuclear weapons program.

Asian multilateralism based on ASEAN had two foundations. The first was economic cooperation, which was growing. It involved various free trade and regional monetary agreements. These arrangements reflected a quest for business profits, economic stability, and higher rates of growth, which were deemed very important to Asian entrepreneurs and to the Asian government leaders who depended on economic growth to shore up support for their continued political leadership. The Asian economies carried out a variety of free trade agreements. An ASEAN FTA in 1992 lowered, but did not eliminate, intraregional tariffs. Singapore negotiated ten FTAs with various countries, with more expected in the future. Indonesia, Thailand, Malaysia, the Philippines, and Vietnam sought various such agreements, as did Japan, South Korea, and Taiwan. China set the pace in 2002 by launching the process of establishing an FTA with ASEAN. Japan, India, South Korea and others followed with FTAs or similar trade schemes for their respective relations with ASEAN.[75]

China and South Korea favored a plan that would develop a free trade agreement among the ten members of ASEAN plus China, South Korea, and Japan. This was part of efforts, especially by China, to strengthen and develop the "ASEAN+3" grouping, begun in the late 1990s, into Asia's premier regional grouping. One proposal called for the creation of an East Asia Economic Community based on the ASEAN+3 members. Meanwhile, the ASEAN+3 members developed cooperative financial arrangements following the adverse effects of the 1997–1998 Asian economic crisis. Under the rubric of the Chiang Mai Initiative, they created a growing web of bilateral swap arrangements, by which short-term liquidity was available to support participating ASEAN+3 countries in need. In 2006, the network involved China, Japan, South Korea, and the five leading ASEAN economies.[76]

Though supportive of ASEAN+3, Japan was wary of China's growing role in Asian regional groupings and sought to involve other powers in these groups. In 2006, Japan proposed a sixteen-nation Asian free trade area to be coordinated by an organization similar to the Organization for Economic Cooperation and Development (OECD) in Europe. The sixteen members would include the members of ASEAN+3 along with India, Australia, and New Zealand. The membership was identical to that of the East Asia Summit (EAS) regional grouping, discussed below, that began in 2005. That grouping indicated a willingness to accept the United States and Russia as members in the future.

Japan said it planned to launch negotiations in 2008 for an Asia FTA among the sixteen Asia-Pacific nations. The concept was welcomed by India and ASEAN, but China and South Korea indicated that their first priority was the ASEAN+3 FTA. Japan actively encouraged the United States to join the EAS. Japan was not enthusiastic about U.S. support for APEC, seeing the latter group as large and unwieldy and excluding India, an important Asian power in recent Japanese calculations.[77]

For its part, the Bush administration gave priority to continued strong U.S. support for APEC. Founded in 1989 as an international organization focused on facilitating economic growth, cooperation, trade, and investment in the Asia-Pacific region, APEC for a time included twenty-one members: China, Japan, South Korea, seven members of ASEAN (Burma, Laos, and Cambodia were not members), Taiwan, Hong Kong, Australia, New Zealand, Papua New Guinea, Russia, Canada, Mexico, Peru, Chile, and the United States. APEC continued to grow. The United States favored a broad pan-Pacific membership that included the United States and that allowed Taiwan, a friend of the United States, to participate despite China's broad efforts to isolate Taiwan from formal international organizations and contacts. U.S. and other leaders valued the annual APEC summit, begun by President Clinton in 1993, which allowed for discussion of relevant international issues at the highest level. President Bush used the APEC summit in October 2001 to pursue an agenda fostering international efforts to combat terrorism. APEC efforts at trade and investment liberalization, business facilitation, and economic and technical cooperation tended to slow in recent years, though Bush used the summit in 2006 to propose an APEC-based pan-Pacific FTA.[78]

The second foundation of Asian multilateralism was political and security cooperation. This foundation was decidedly weaker than the robust economic cooperation. The most progress was made in groups with ASEAN playing the role of convener, notably the ASEAN Security Community, the ARF, the EAS, and ASEAN+3. The ASEAN Security Community involved the ten members of ASEAN. ASEAN also played a leading role in broader Asian groups. ASEAN often could take the lead in building multilateral institutions because it was viewed as more neutral and nonthreatening than China, Japan, the United States, or other major powers.[79]

The ASEAN Regional Forum was established in 1994 with the purpose of bringing non-ASEAN nations from the Asia-Pacific region together with ASEAN officials to discuss political and security matters and to build cooperative ties. The participants included all ten ASEAN members, China, Japan, the United States, the European Union, Russia, Australia, Canada, New Zealand, South Korea, North Korea, India, Pakistan, Mongolia, Papua New Guinea, East Timor, and Sri Lanka. The Asian region had little experience with broad security cooperation. ARF was created to complement U.S. security guarantees that appeared to be weakening in the early 1990s, as evidenced by the U.S. withdrawal from bases in the Philippines. And it endeavored to deal with uncertainties caused by changing power relationships in Asia, particularly the ascent of China. Since the member states tended to be independent minded and wary of one another, ARF was characterized by minimal institutionalization and the "ASEAN way" of gradualism and decisions by consensus. The ARF process began with transparency (through the publication of military spending and deployment information), dialogue, and confidence-building measures; then moved to preventive diplomacy (discussion and mutual pledges to resolve specific disputes solely through peaceful means); and, in the long term, hoped to develop a conflict resolution capacity.[80]

In the past decade, most of the ARF measures have focused on dialogue and confidence building. The annual ARF ministerial meeting provided an opportunity for foreign ministers to meet and discuss current issues. Significantly, defense ministers did not participate in the dialogue. This perceived gap was addressed in part by an informal group, the International Institute of Strategic Studies' Shangri-La Dialogue, meeting annually in Singapore. The dialogue attracted senior defense officials from most ARF members and elsewhere to discuss relevant security questions.[81]

The East Asian Summit met first in Malaysia in December 2005. Attending were leaders of the ten ASEAN states, China, Japan, South Korea, India, Australia, and New Zealand. Russian President Vladimir Putin came as a guest. The meeting was timed to follow the 2005 ASEAN summit as well as bilateral meetings between ASEAN and Russia, Japan, South Korea, and India. China at first played a strong role in promoting the EAS and was reportedly motivated in part by a desire to use the grouping to offset U.S. influence in the Asia-Pacific. Japan, Singapore, and Indonesia reportedly pushed to have Australia and India included in order to avoid feared dominance by China. As the latter efforts succeeded, China reduced support for the EAS and focused positive attention instead on ASEAN+3, where China had a stronger position.

The EAS said it was open, inclusive, transparent, and outward looking, with ASEAN as the leading force in the group. Several members encouraged the United States to meet the initial requirements for membership, namely, signing the ASEAN Treaty of Amity and Cooperation, becoming a formal dialogue partner of ASEAN, and having substantive cooperative relations with ASEAN. The United States met the conditions except for the signing of the treaty.[82]

Meanwhile, ASEAN+3 had security as well as economic importance. It came about in 1997 as a result of a Japanese proposal to create a regular summit process between ASEAN and Japan with an economic, political, and security agenda. Concerned with possible negative reactions from other Asian nations, ASEAN subsequently broadened the proposed summit to include China and South Korea. The ASEAN+3 members met regularly after each ASEAN summit to discuss finances, economics, and security. As noted earlier, China reportedly favored this organization over the East Asian Summit because it was not open to U.S. membership and did not include India, though Beijing continues to support the EAS, APEC, and other groups.[83]

U.S. Policy Choices and Recent Actions

Given the variety of regional groupings focused on ASEAN and Southeast Asia, U.S. policy choices in dealing with Asian multilateralism in this region are complex. Elsewhere in Asia, as noted earlier, the prevailing circumstances of Asian multilateral groupings involving Central Asia, South Asia, and Northeast Asia did not call for significant U.S. policy action on multilateral groupings in these parts of Asia.

In the case of the Southeast Asian–oriented groupings, the U.S. policy debate revolved around a basic choice: Should the U.S. government continue its recent level of activity in the region, or should it take steps to further advance the American profile in regional groupings? Spurred on by the growing Chinese influence in Asian multilateral groups and by the strong encouragement of Japan, Australia, Singapore, and others that the United States play a more prominent role in the Asian groups, the U.S. government increased its involvement in these organizations as it took a variety of steps to shore up U.S. relations with Southeast Asian governments.[84]

The Bush administration by 2006 developed U.S. initiatives to individual Southeast Asian nations and to the ASEAN regional organization and related regional multilateral groups. These initiatives were based on the U.S. position as the region's leading trading partner, foreign investor, aid donor, and military partner. U.S. initiatives to ASEAN represented in part Bush administration efforts to catch up with ASEAN's free trade agreements and other formal arrangements with China, Japan, and other powers. Strong U.S. opposition to the military regime in Myanmar continued to complicate U.S. relations with the ASEAN group. That regime's crackdown on large demonstrations led by Buddhist monks in 2007 saw the Bush administration take the lead in pressing the United Nations and individual states to initiate actions against the repressive government.[85]

In contrast to other powers seeking closer ties with ASEAN, the United States did not agree to the ASEAN Treaty on Amity and Cooperation (TAC) and remained ambivalent on participation in the annual ASEAN-led East Asian Summit, which required agreement to the TAC as a condition for participation. U.S. officials also said they were not opposed to Asian regional organizations that excluded other involved powers such as the United States, but U.S. favor focused on regional groupings open to it and other concerned powers.

For one, the United States supported the ASEAN Regional Forum, the primary regional forum for security dialogue. Secretary of State Colin Powell duly attended ARF annual meetings. Though his successor Condoleezza Rice missed the annual ARF meeting in 2005, she went to extraordinary efforts to participate actively in 2006 despite an urgent crisis posed by warfare between Israeli and Hezbollah forces in Lebanon. Because of crises involving Iraq and the Middle East, Rice again missed the 2007 ARF meeting.

The Bush administration strongly supports Asia Pacific Economic Cooperation. President Bush at the APEC summit meeting in November 2006 urged APEC members to consider forming an Asia-Pacific Free Trade Area. The U.S. initiative was seen to underline its interest in fostering trans-Pacific trade groupings in the face of Asian multilateral trade arrangements that excluded the United States.[86] At the APEC summit in 2007, President Bush proposed the formation of a democratic partnership among eight democratically elected members of APEC and India.[87]

Regarding Southeast Asia, President Bush in November 2005 began to use the annual APEC leaders' summit to engage in annual multilateral meetings with attending ASEAN leaders. At this meeting, he and seven ASEAN heads of state launched the ASEAN-U.S. Enhanced Partnership, involving a broad range of economic, political, and security cooperation. In July 2006, Secretary Rice and her ten ASEAN counterparts signed a five-year plan of action to implement the partnership.

In the important area of trade and investment, the ministers endorsed the Enterprise for ASEAN Initiative (EAI) launched by the U.S. government in 2002 that provided a road map to move from bilateral trade and investment framework agreements (TIFAs), which were consultative, to free trade agreements, which were more binding. Significantly, these FTAs were seen by U.S. officials as markedly more substantive, involving a variety of tangible commitments and compromises, than the FTAs proposed by China and other powers. From the U.S. officials' perspective, such U.S.-style FTAs were harder to reach, but had a much more significant effect on existing trade relations. The United States already had bilateral TIFAs with several ASEAN states, and in August 2006 the U.S. special trade representative and her ASEAN counterparts agreed to work toward concluding an ASEAN-U.S. regional TIFA. Meanwhile, the Bush administration followed its FTAs with Singapore and Australia with FTA negotiations with Thailand and Malaysia, but those negotiations stalled by 2007.[88]

The initiation in 2005 of the U.S. presidential mini-summits with ASEAN leaders attending the annual APEC leaders' meeting conveniently avoided the U.S.-ASEAN differences over Myanmar, which was not an APEC member. President Bush met with ASEAN leaders attending the annual APEC meeting in 2006 and 2007, but postponed a special meeting with ASEAN leaders slated to take place in Singapore in 2007.[89]

The Bush administration for a time accepted a working engagement with Myanmar as an ASEAN member at lower protocol levels. Myanmar was represented in the ASEAN-U.S. Dialogue, and Rice shook hands with all ASEAN foreign ministers at the signing ceremony of the ASEAN-U.S. Enhanced Partnership in July 2006. Meanwhile, the Bush administration announced in August 2006 that it was planning to appoint an ambassador to ASEAN and that the Treasury Department intended to establish a financial representative post for Southeast Asia.[90]

Indonesia received notable U.S. attention with Rice and Defense Secretary Donald Rumsfeld making separate trips during 2006 and President Bush making a visit in conjunction with the APEC summit in November. U.S. assistance to Indonesia in FY 2006 topped $500 million. Following the U.S. waiver in November 2005 of the remaining legislative restrictions on military assistance to Indonesia, the Bush administration in March 2006 permitted sales of lethal military equipment on a case-by-case basis and the U.S. Pacific Command in March endorsed a "rapid, concerted infusion" of military assistance to the country.

Vietnam, the host of the November 2006 APEC leaders' meeting, also received notable U.S. attention. The United States took the lead in negotiations on Vietnam's successful entry into the WTO. The United States was a close second to China as Vietnam's leading trading partner, and it was the largest foreign investor in the country. Rumsfeld visited Vietnam in 2005, and Vietnam modestly strengthened its defense ties with the United States.[91]

U.S. military activism in the region also included participation by Rumsfeld and his successor Robert Gates at the annual Shangri-La defense forum in Singapore and by secretaries Powell and Rice at the ARF; a strong program of bilateral and multilateral exercises and exchanges between U.S. forces in the Pacific Command and friendly and allied Southeast Asian forces; an active U.S. International Military Education and Training program with regional governments; and the U.S. role as the top supplier of defense equipment to the leading ASEAN countries. The U.S. military maintained what was seen as a "semicontinuous" presence in the Philippines to assist in dealing with terrorist threats, and it resumed in November 2005 a "strategic dialogue" with Thailand. These moves added to progress made in U.S. security ties with Singapore (the largest regional purchaser of U.S. military equipment) and the upswing in U.S. military ties with Indonesia.

The September 2006 coup in Thailand prompted a moderate U.S. reaction calling for restoration of democratic rule. The leadership instability leading up to and following the coup hampered U.S.-Thai negotiations on a bilateral free trade agreement and progress in other areas, although President Bush met cordially with his Thai counterpart at the APEC summit in November 2006.[92]

The pace and scope of U.S. military activism in the region reinforced the tendency of America's allies and associates to find reliance on the

United States and its regional defense structures preferable to reliance on other nascent but rising Asian regional security arrangements. Australia and Japan in particular worked hard to provide support for a continued strong and prominent U.S. defense role in the region. They developed and engaged in a new ministerial trilateral strategic dialogue with the United States during the Bush administration. With U.S. support, they concluded in 2007 a bilateral security arrangement, the first by Japan with a non-U.S. partner. The three powers also engaged more in individual and collective security cooperation with India. Representatives of these four governments met for security consultations on the sidelines of the ARF ministerial meeting in May 2007.[93]

Numerous bilateral and multilateral U.S. military exercises were valued by Asian partners. They included Talisman Sabre with Australia, Balikatan with the Philippines, Keen Sword/Keen Edge with Japan, Cobra Gold in Thailand, and the multination Rim of the Pacific (RIMPAC) exercise. RIMPAC 2006 alone included 40 ships, 160 aircraft, and some 19,000 military personnel drawn from Australia, Britain, Canada, Chile, Japan, Peru, South Korea, and the United States.

The United States promoted maritime security cooperation in the area of the strategically important Strait of Malacca by working with the states bordering the strait—Singapore, Malaysia, and Indonesia—to develop a command, control, and communications infrastructure that will facilitate cooperation in maritime surveillance of the waterway. Malabar, an annual U.S. exercise with India, was broadened in 2007 to include forces from Japan, Australia, and Singapore in a large naval exercise near the eastern entrance of the Malacca Strait. It involved more than thirty warships, including two U.S. and one Indian aircraft carrier battle groups.[94]

U.S. foreign assistance to Southeast Asian countries increased, along with substantial increases in the U.S. foreign assistance budgets prompted by the war on terrorism begun in 2001 and the Bush administration's Millennium Challenge Account (MCA) and Global HIV/AIDS Initiative (GHAI) begun in 2004. MCA rewards countries that demonstrate good governance, investment in health and education, and sound free market policies. GHAI is focused on dealing with the worldwide health emergency caused by HIV/AIDS. In addition to Indonesia, noted above, which received the bulk of $400 million pledged by the U.S. government for relief from the December 2004 tsunami disaster in addition to a substantial U.S. aid program, other large recipients of U.S. assistance included the Philippines, Vietnam, Cambodia, and East Timor.[95]

Although the events listed above show clear direction in U.S. policy and interests in Southeast Asia, serious complications and uncertainties persisted. The ability and will of U.S. leaders to devote attention to regional bilateral and multilateral relations in Southeast Asia and the

Pacific remained in question, especially given the overriding U.S. policy preoccupations with the Middle East. What difference the change in U.S. administrations in 2009 would make in U.S. policy and practice toward Southeast Asia was also unclear. U.S. allies Japan and Australia were compelled to adjust to domestic pressures and elections that appeared to complicate their continued avowed interest in working closely with the United States in active and collaborative military and security ventures in Asian and world affairs. The emerging U.S. security partnership with India was clouded by serious obstacles to the completion of the centerpiece of the new relationship, the U.S.-India nuclear cooperation agreement.

NOTES

1. Richard Armitage and Joseph Nye, *U.S.-Japan Alliance: Getting Asia Right through 2020* (Washington, D.C.: Center for Strategic and International Studies, 2007).

2. Robert Sutter, "The United States and Asia in 2006: Crisis Management, Holding Patterns, and Secondary Initiatives," *Asian Survey* 47, no. 1 (January/February 2007): 12.

3. Michael Green, "U.S.-Japanese Relations after Koizumi: Convergence or Cooling?" *Washington Quarterly* 29, no. 4 (Autumn 2006): 101–10.

4. Emma Chanlett-Avery, *Japan-U.S. Relations: Issues for Congress*, CRS Issue Brief 97004 (Washington, D.C.: Congressional Research Service, Library of Congress, March 31, 2006); Francis Rosenbluth, Jun Saito, and Annalisa Zinn, "America's Policy toward East Asia: How It Looks from Japan," *Asian Survey* 47, no. 4 (July/August 2007): 584–600.

5. Chanlett-Avery, *Japan-U.S. Relations*, 9; Richard Cronin, *Japan-U.S. Relations: Issues for Congress*, CRS Issue Brief 97004 (Washington, D.C.: Congressional Research Service, Library of Congress, July 31, 2001).

6. Michael J. Green and Nicholas Szechenyi, "U.S.-Japan Relations: Distracted Governments Make Some Positive Progress," *Comparative Connections* 9, no. 4 (4th Qtr 2007): 17–20, http://www.csis.org/media/csis/pubs/0704q.pdf.

7. Institute for National Security Studies, *The United States and Japan: Advancing toward a Mature Partnership*, special report (Washington, D.C.: National Defense University Press, 2000); Armitage and Nye, *U.S.-Japan Alliance*.

8. Richard Samuels, "Japan's Goldilocks Strategy," *Washington Quarterly* 29, no. 4 (Autumn 2006): 111–27; Green, "U.S.-Japanese Relations after Koizumi."

9. James J. Przystup, "The Zhu Visit and After . . . Efforts to Steady the Course," *Comparative Connections* 2, no. 4 (4th Qtr 2000): 78–87, http://www.csis.org/media/csis/pubs/0004q.pdf.

10. Minxin Pei and Michael Swaine, *Simmering Fire in Asia: Averting Sino-Japanese Strategic Conflict* (Washington, D.C.: Carnegie Endowment for International Peace, 2005); James Przystup, "Politics in Command, Part 2," *Comparative Connections* 9, no. 4 (4th Qtr 2007): 109–18, http://www.csis.org/media/csis/pubs/0704q.pdf.

11. David Kang and Ji-Young Lee, "Lost in the Six-Party Talks," *Comparative Connections* 9, no. 4 (4th Qtr 2007): 123–29, http://www.csis.org/media/csis/pubs/0704q.pdf.

12. Richard Samuels, *Securing Japan* (Ithaca, N.Y: Cornell University Press, 2007), 86–108.

13. Green and Szechenyi, "U.S.-Japan Relations."

14. Chanlett-Avery, *Japan-U.S. Relations*, 2.

15. Green and Szechenyi, "U.S.-Japan Relations."

16. Chanlett-Avery, *Japan-U.S. Relations*, 2.

17. Armitage and Nye, *U.S.-Japan Alliance*, 18–20.

18. Chanlett-Avery, *Japan-U.S. Relations*, 3.

19. Alex Hetherington, "Asia-Pacific Climate Talks: Just Smoke and Mirrors?" *Business Day*, January 19, 2006, 1.

20. U.S. Department of State, U.S.-Japan Joint Statement on North Korea, February 19, 2005, available at http://www.state.gov/r/pa/prs/ps/2005/42491.htm; Green and Szechenyi, "Japan-U.S. Relations."

21. Green, "U.S.-Japanese Relations after Koizumi," 105; Matt Spentalick, "Bush, Fukuda Try to Smooth over U.S.-Japan Ties," Reuters, November 16, 2007.

22. Kent E. Calder, "China and Japan's Simmering Rivalry," *Foreign Affairs* 85, no. 2 (March/April 2006): 129–39; Pei and Swaine, *Simmering Fire*.

23. Feng Zhaokui, "PM Amends Diplomatic Policies," *China Daily*, October 26, 2007.

24. Chanlett-Avery, *Japan-U.S. Relations*, 5–6.

25. Samuels, *Securing Japan*, 63–85.

26. Brad Glosserman, "The Alliance Transformed?" *Comparative Connections* 7, no. 4 (4th Qtr 2005): 19–22, http://www.csis.org/media/csis/pubs/0504q.pdf.

27. Robert Sutter, "The United States and Asia in 2005: Managing Troubles, Sustaining Leadership," *Asia Survey* 46, no. 1 (January/February 2006): 18; Sutter, "United States and Asia in 2006," 16.

28. Richard Cronin, *Japan-U.S. Security Relations and the Revised Defense Cooperation Guidelines*, CRS Report 98-857 (Washington, D.C.: Congressional Research Service, Library of Congress, 1998).

29. Larry Niksch, "Security Issues," in Cronin, *Japan-U.S. Security Relations*.

30. Glosserman, "Alliance Transformed?"

31. Chanlett-Avery, *Japan-U.S. Relations*, 8.

32. Samuels, *Securing Japan*, 83–84.

33. Ibid., 46–48, 80–82.

34. Niksch, "Security Issues"; Chanlett-Avery, *Japan-U.S. Relations*, 8.

35. Cronin, *Japan-U.S. Security Relations*.

36. William Cooper, *U.S.-Japan Economic Ties: Status and Outlook*, Issue Brief IB97015 (Washington, D.C.: Congressional Research Service, Library of Congress, July 15, 2001).

37. William Cooper, *U.S.-Japan Economic Relations: Significance, Prospects, and Policy Options*, CRS Report RL32649 (Washington, D.C.: Congressional Research Service, Library of Congress, July 9, 2007), 3–9.

38. Ibid., 1.

39. Ibid., 3–5.

40. Chanlett-Avery, *Japan-U.S. Relations*, 9.

41. Cooper, *U.S.-Japan Economic Relations*, 12.

42. Chanlett-Avery, *Japan-U.S. Relations*, 11.

43. Kenneth Pyle, "Abe Shinzo and Japan's Change of Course," *NBR Analysis* 17, no. 4 (October 2006): 5–31.

44. Green and Szechenyi, "U.S.-Japan Relations."

45. Diane K. Mauzy and Brian L. Job, "U.S. Policy in Southeast Asia: Limited Re-engagement after Years of Benign Neglect," *Asian Survey* 47, no. 4 (July/ August 2007): 622–41; Donald Weatherbee, "Strategic Dimensions of Economic Interdependence in Southeast Asia," in *Strategic Asia, 2006–2007: Trade, Interdependence, and Security*, ed. Ashley J. Tellis and Michael Wills, 271–300 (Seattle: National Bureau of Asian Research, 2006).

46. Evelyn Goh, "Southeast Asian Reactions to America's New Strategic Imperatives," in *Asia Eyes America: Regional Perspectives on U.S. Asia-Pacific Strategy in the 21st Century*, ed. Jonathan Pollack, 201–26 (Newport, R.I.: U.S. Naval War College, 2007).

47. Bruce Vaughn and Wayne Morrison, *China-Southeast Asia Relations: Trends, Issues, and Implications for the United States*, CRS Report 32688 (Washington, D.C.: Congressional Research Service, Library of Congress, April 4, 2006); Dana R. Dillon and John J. Tkacik Jr., "China and ASEAN: Endangered American Primacy in Southeast Asia," Heritage Foundation Backgrounder 1886 (Washington, D.C.: Heritage Foundation, 2005).

48. Victor Cha, "Winning Asia: Washington's Untold Success Story," *Foreign Affairs* 86, no. 6 (November/December 2007): 98–113.

49. R. William Liddle, "Indonesia in 2000: A Shaky Start for Democracy," *Asian Survey* 41, no. 1 (January/February 2001): 208–20; R. William Liddle, "Indonesia in 1999: Democracy Restored," *Asian Survey* 40, no. 1 (January/February 2000): 32–42.

50. Sheila S. Coronel, "The Philippines in 2006: Democracy and Its Discontents," *Asian Survey* 47, no. 1 (January/February 2007): 175–82.

51. Michael J. Montesano, "Thailand in 2001: Learning to Live with Thaksin?" *Asian Survey* 42, no. 1 (January/February 2002): 90–99; Patricia Martinez, "Malaysia in 2001: An Interlude of Consolidation," *Asian Survey* 42, no. 1 (January/ February 2002): 133–40.

52. Sarah Eaton and Richard Stubbs, "Is ASEAN Powerful? Neo-realist versus Constructivist Approaches to Power in Southeast Asia," *Pacific Review* 19, no. 2 (June 2006): 135–56.

53. *Wrapup: ASEAN Ministerial Meetings, Regional Forum, and Post-Ministerial Conferences* (Washington, D.C.: U.S.-ASEAN Business Council, 2001).

54. Judith Bird, "Indonesia in 1998: The Pot Boils Over," *Asian Survey* 39, no. 1 (January/February 1999): 27–37; Liddle, "Indonesia in 1999."

55. Larry Niksch, *East Timor Crisis: U.S. Policy and Options*, CRS Report RS20332 (Washington, D.C.: Congressional Research Service, Library of Congress, November 5, 1999), 4.

56. Niksch, *East Timor Crisis*, 4–5.

57. Ralph L. Boyce, "The Bush Administration Will Be Taking Indonesia Seriously," Pacnet no. 30A (Honolulu: CSIS Pacific Forum, July 27, 2001).

58. Catharin E. Dalpino, "Human Rights in Southeast Asia: Issues for the Twenty-First Century," SAIS Policy Forum Series, report 10 (Washington, D.C.: Johns Hopkins University, School for Advanced International Studies, 2000).

59. David Steinberg, "Burma/Myanmar and the Dilemmas of U.S. Foreign Policy," *Contemporary Southeast Asia* 21, no. 2 (August 2, 1999): 283–311.

60. Larry Niksch, *Burma-U.S. Relations*, CRS Report RS20749 (Washington, D.C.: Congressional Research Service, Library of Congress, December 8, 2000), 2–3.

61. Nick Cumming-Bruce, "Powell Will Explain Bush's Asia Policy at Forum in Hanoi," *Wall Street Journal*, July 23, 2001.

62. Tin Maung Maung Than, "Myanmar (Burma) in 2000: More of the Same?" *Asian Survey* 41, no. 1 (January/February 2001): 152–55.

63. Niksch, *Burma-U.S. Relations*, 5.

64. Mark Manyin, *The Vietnam-U.S. Normalization Process*, CRS Issue Brief IB98033 (Washington, D.C.: Congressional Research Service, Library of Congress, August 29, 2001).

65. Vladimir Pregel, *Vietnam Trade Agreement: Approval and Implementing Procedure*, CRS Report RS20717 (Washington, D.C.: Congressional Research Service, Library of Congress, October 30, 2000).

66. International Crisis Group, "Cambodia: The Elusive Peace Dividend," Asia Report No. 8 (Brussels: International Crisis Group, 2000).

67. John Baker and Douglas Paal, "The U.S.-Australian Alliance," in *America's Asian Alliances*, ed. Robert Blackwill and Paul Dibb, 87–110 (Cambridge, Mass.: MIT Press, 2000); Roger Thompson, *The Pacific Basin since 1945: A History of the Foreign Relations of Asian, Australasian and American Rim States and the Pacific Islands* (London: Longman, 1994).

68. Morton Abramowitz and Stephen Bosworth, *Chasing the Sun: Rethinking East Asian Policy* (New York: Century Foundation, 2006), 6; Stanley Foundation, "Economic Dimensions of New Power Dynamics in Southeast Asia," policy memo, July 12, 2007.

69. Mark Manyin, *Terrorism in Southeast Asia*, CRS Report RL31672 (Washington, D.C.: Congressional Research Service, Library of Congress, August 13, 2004).

70. Bruce Vaughn, *U.S. Strategic and Defense Relationships in the Asia-Pacific Region*, CRS Report RL33821 (Washington, D.C.: Congressional Research Service, Library of Congress, January 22, 2007), 22–23.

71. Temario C. Rivera, "The Philippines in 2004: New Mandate, Daunting Problems," *Asian Survey* 45, no. 1 (January/February 2005): 128–29.

72. Vaughn, *U.S. Strategic and Defense Relationships*, 23–25.

73. Weatherbee, "Strategic Dimensions"; Vaughn, *U.S. Strategic and Defense Relationships*, 26.

74. Joshua Kurlantzick, *Charm Offensive: How China's Soft Power Is Transforming the World* (New Haven, Conn.: Yale University Press, 2007); Bronson Percival, *The Dragon Looks South: China and Southeast Asia in the New Century* (Westport, Conn.: Praeger Security International, 2007). See also Hadi Soesastro, "East Asia: Many Clubs, Little Progress," *Far Eastern Economic Review* 169, no. 1 (January/February 2006).

75. Dick Nanto, *East Asian Regional Architecture: New Economic and Security Arrangements and U.S. Policy*, CRS Report RL33653 (Washington, D.C.: Congressional Research Service, Library of Congress, September 18, 2006).

76. Richard Stubbs, "ASEAN Plus Three: Emerging East Asian Regionalism?" *Asian Survey* 42, no. 3 (May/June 2002): 440–55.

77. Nanto, *East Asian Regional Architecture*, 22.

78. White House, "The President's Trip to Southeast Asia," November 2006, http://www.whitehouse.gov/asia/2006/.

79. Nanto, *East Asian Regional Architecture*, 18–26.

80. See the chairman's statements for the annual meetings of the ASEAN Regional Forum at the ASEAN website, http://www.aseansec.org/; the statement for the 14th ARF meeting on August 2, 2007, is at http://www.aseansec.org/20807.htm.

81. The website for the Singapore dialogue is http://www.iiss.org/conferences/the-shangri-la-dialogue.

82. Frank Frost and Ann Rann, *The East Asian Summit, Cebu 2007: Issues and Prospects*, Parliamentary Library of Australia E-Brief, December 20, 2006.

83. See chairman's statements on the annual ASEAN+3 ministerial and heads of government meetings on the ASEAN website, especially http://www.aseansec.org/18579.htm.

84. Sutter, "United States and Asia in 2005," 21; Sutter, "United States and Asia in 2006," 20–21.

85. Weatherbee, "Strategic Dimensions," 282–98; Peter Baker, "Bush Announces Sanctions against Burma," *Washington Post*, September 25, 2007.

86. White House, "President's Trip to Southeast Asia."

87. Cha, "Winning Asia."

88. The U.S. initiatives listed below and their status are discussed in Weatherbee, "Strategic Dimensions," 292–300, and Vaughn, *U.S. Strategic and Defense Relationships*, 14–26.

89. Sheldon W. Simon, "Burma Heats Up and the U.S. Blows Hot and Cold," *Comparative Connections* 9, no. 3 (3rd Qtr 2007): 61–70, http://www.csis.org/media/csis/pubs/0703q.pdf.

90. Sutter, "United States and Asia in 2006," 21.

91. Weatherbee, "Strategic Dimensions," 282–98.

92. Sutter, "United States and Asia in 2006," 21.

93. Simon, "Burma Heats Up."

94. Vaughn, *U.S. Strategic and Defense Relationships*, 14–26; Ralph A. Cossa and Brad Glosserman, "Multilateral Progress Pending on Multiple Fronts," *Comparative Connections* 9, no. 3 (3rd Qtr 2007): 1–18, www.csis.org/media/csis/pubs/0703q.pdf.

95. Thomas Lum, *U.S. Foreign Aid to East and South Asia: Selected Recipients*, CRS Report RL31362 (Washington, D.C.: Congressional Research Service, Library of Congress, January 3, 2007), 11–25.

4

✛

U.S. Priorities and Concerns Regarding South Asia, Central Asia, and Asian Russia

U.S. interest and issues in relations with South and Central Asia have reflected changing priorities in the post–Cold War period. The Soviet withdrawal from Afghanistan reduced U.S. attention to Pakistan, an on-again, off-again U.S. partner in Cold War competition with the USSR. India's close alignment with Moscow shifted with the collapse of the Soviet Union, and concurrent Indian economic reforms reinforced greater outreach to developed countries, notably the United States. The Indian and Pakistani nuclear weapons tests of 1998 saw the United States take the lead to deal with the danger of nuclear war. Initial sanctions against both governments were followed by an increase in U.S. interest in improving relations with India, as shown during President Bill Clinton's visit to India in 2000.

The collapse of the USSR left some newly formed Central Asian countries with nuclear weapons of great concern to the United States and with significant energy resources important to U.S. and other international companies. Russia's proximity, military presence, and control of energy pipelines, railways, and other means of communication from the Central Asian countries abroad made it the dominant power in Central Asia. Russia exerted generally secondary influence in other parts of the Asia-Pacific. It appeared preoccupied with other pressing concerns and unable to conduct major diplomatic, economic, or military initiatives. U.S. issues with Russia focused on concerns apart from the Asia-Pacific region.

The 2001 terrorist attack on America and the U.S.-led war against the Taliban regime in Afghanistan had a profound effect on U.S. interests and issues in South and Central Asia. Almost overnight, the United

States became deeply involved with Pakistan, a key base in the war against the Taliban. Together with a rapid increase in an ongoing improvement in U.S. relations with India, the United States emerged for the first time as the leading outside power in South Asia, a power in the unique position of having good relations with both of the long-standing South Asian rivals.

Russia initially was supportive of a rapid increase in U.S. military and other interchange with Central Asian states that focused on the war against the Taliban and stabilizing the region from the terrorist threat. Over time, however, Moscow became much more ambivalent about the U.S. military presence, at times joining with China and some Central Asian states to limit and diminish the U.S. role in the region. Whatever replay of the nineteenth-century "great game" of international competition in Central Asia that emerged at this time also included Russian and Chinese competition for energy resources and influence, even as the two powers occasionally teamed up to criticize U.S. policy and U.S. military presence there.

ISSUES IN U.S.-INDIAN RELATIONS

The end of the Cold War freed India-U.S. relations from the constraints of global bipolarity, but cooperation developed slowly for a decade on account of historical suspicions, the India-Pakistan rivalry, and nuclear weapons proliferation in both India and Pakistan. The U.S.-led war on terrorism and the conflict in Afghanistan saw a rapid improvement in U.S.-India relations. President George W. Bush came to call India a natural partner of the United States, and U.S. policy sought to assist India's rise as a major world power. In July 2005, President Bush and Indian prime minister Manmohan Singh issued a joint statement resolving to establish a "global partnership" between the two countries through increased cooperation on numerous economic, security, and global issues. Bush at the time called India "a responsible state with advanced nuclear technology" and pledged to achieve "full civilian nuclear energy cooperation" with India.[1]

American issues and interests in relations with India covered a wide array of subjects, ranging from the military dispute with Pakistan and weapons proliferation to concerns about regional security, human rights, health, and trade and investment opportunities. With the possible exception of the controversial Bush administration effort to carry out a nuclear energy agreement with India that required a reversal of three decades of U.S. nuclear nonproliferation policy, the issues with India generally were of secondary importance and posed no serious obstacles to the U.S. government's efforts to strengthen ties with this Asian partner.[2] The nuclear energy deal became more controversial in 2007 when it appeared that political opposition in India would block enactment of this centerpiece of the new U.S.-Indian partnership.[3]

In the 1990s, the demise of the Soviet Union had a big impact on India-U.S. relations. The USSR had been India's main trading partner and most reliable source of economic and military assistance for most of the Cold War. New Delhi responded to the new world order pragmatically, recognizing an immediate need to diversify international relationships, including the historically wary Indian relationship with the United States. At the same time, the Indian government in the early 1990s began what would turn out to be a significant series of economic reforms, moving incrementally toward free market practices that increasingly welcomed interchange with U.S. and other foreign entrepreneurs. India also faced deepening bitterness with Pakistan over the Kashmir dispute that added to the serious implications of Pakistan's and India's development of nuclear weapons and delivery systems for those weapons. Closely supporting Pakistan, China grew in power and importance in Asian affairs, and Indian strategists showed serious concern about long-term strategic rivalry with its powerful northern neighbor.[4]

Against this background, Indian and U.S. leaders explored possibilities for a more normal relationship between what they routinely cited as the world's two largest democracies. However, progress in relations was slow for over a decade. The Indian rivalry with Pakistan and the two powers' nuclear weapons programs headed the list of American concerns. The Indian administration faced numerous domestic separatist movements and strong sectarian tensions, leading to government crackdowns that prompted U.S. and other international complaints about abuses of human rights. In addition, the Indian economic reforms remained slow and halting, frustrating American business interests in the country.[5]

India initiated nuclear weapons tests in May 1998, which were followed promptly by similar tests by Pakistan. This was widely viewed as an important failure for U.S. policy. The United States took the lead in international efforts to condemn the tests and to apply sanctions to the two countries. At the same time, Deputy Secretary of State Strobe Talbott launched a series of meetings with Indian external affairs minister Jaswant Singh in an effort to bring the Indian government more in line with U.S. arms control and nonproliferation goals. India and the United States remained divided on India's nuclear weapons and ballistic missile programs, but Talbott and Singh developed a broader agenda on the wide scope of India-U.S. relations and met fourteen times over a two-year period. The improved mutual understanding between the Indian and U.S. administrations seemed to smooth India's acceptance of the United

States playing the key international role in defusing the 1999 Kargil crisis involving a serious Indian-Pakistan military confrontation in the disputed Kashmir territory. This laid the groundwork for President Clinton's visit to India in 2000.[6]

Clinton's March 2000 visit to South Asia focused on India, although he also made a brief stop, despite terrorist threats, in Pakistan. Among the results of the New Delhi visit, a U.S.-India Joint Working Group began in 2000, setting a foundation for closer antiterrorism cooperation between the two governments that would be significant after 9/11. Following Clinton's visit, Indian prime minister Atal Vajpayee visited the United States in 2000. He addressed a joint session of Congress and issued a joint statement with President Clinton in which India and the United States agreed to cooperate on arms control, terrorism, and HIV/AIDS.[7]

The George W. Bush administration built on the foundation of improved U.S.-Indian relations established in the last years of the Clinton government. It showed an interest in developing ties with the growing South Asian power for a number of reasons, including as a counterweight to possible negative implications for the United States coming from China's rising power.[8] Senior defense and foreign policy officials met repeatedly with their Indian counterparts. They smoothed past differences over the U.S. government's determination to build defenses against ballistic missiles and promoted closer cooperation between the U.S. and Indian militaries. In the wake of the September 11, 2001, terrorist attacks, India took the unprecedented step of offering the United States full cooperation and the use of India's military bases for counterterrorism operations.[9]

In November 2001, President Bush met with Prime Minister Vajpayee. The two leaders greatly expanded U.S.-Indian cooperation on a wide range of areas, including regional security, space and scientific collaboration, civil nuclear safety, and broadening economic ties. Notable progress came in security cooperation, marked by increasing collaboration on counterterrorism, joint military exercises, and arms sales. In late 2001, the U.S.-India Defense Policy Group met in New Delhi for the first time since India's 1998 nuclear tests. The group outlined a defense partnership based on regular and high-level policy dialogue. Bush's 2002 *National Security Strategy of the United States* declared that U.S. interests require a strong relationship with India.[10]

Follow-on events included Prime Minister Singh's visit to Washington in July 2005, which saw the joint U.S.-India statement establishing a global partnership and announcing determination to conclude an agreement on nuclear energy. President Bush visited India for three days in March 2006, pledging to follow through on the nuclear and other commitments and to advance further bilateral relations. By this time, U.S. leaders were routinely underlining U.S. interest in working to help India become a major world power in the twenty-first century. They conducted relations with India under the rubric of three major dialogue areas: strategic (including global issues and defense), economic (including trade, finance, commerce, and environment), and energy. The U.S. Congress saw India's importance increase. As supporters of improved U.S.-Indian relations, the Indian-American caucus represented the largest of all country-specific caucuses in Congress.[11]

Reflecting the scope and depth of U.S.-Indian relations at this time, Bush's March 2006 visit was followed by significant developments. The Indian foreign secretary visited Washington in late March, and counter-terrorism coordinator Henry Crumpton led a U.S. delegation in a two-day meeting of the U.S.-India Joint Working Group on Counterterrorism in April. Also in April, India's power minister visited with top U.S. officials in Washington. The fourth meeting of the U.S.-India Trade Policy Forum was held in May in New Delhi, at which officials discussed trade barriers, agricultural trade, investment issues, and intellectual property rights. In June, the U.S. chairman of the Joint Chiefs of Staff met with top Indian officials to discuss expanding U.S.-India strategic ties, and the U.S. special trade representative met with her Indian counterpart in Washington to agree on initiatives to strengthen U.S.-India trade relations. The president's initiative to establish nuclear energy cooperation with India despite India's development of nuclear weapons was approved in repeated congressional votes during the year. The high-profile nuclear deal ran up against serious obstacles on the Indian side in 2007, though, clouding prospects for quick approval.[12]

Specific Issues

High-Technology Trade

The Indian government had long pressed the United States to ease restrictions on the export to India of dual-use high-technology goods, as well as to increase civil nuclear and space cooperation. In January 2004, President Bush pledged progress in these areas, along with expanded dialogue on ballistic missile defense. In July 2005, the U.S. government allowed for greater bilateral cooperation on commercial satellites and removal and revision of some U.S. export license requirements regarding dual-use and civil nuclear items.[13]

Civil Nuclear Cooperation

Most of the above advances elicited little objection in the United States. The main exception was civil nuclear cooperation.

India's status as a nonsignatory to the 1968 Nuclear Non-Proliferation Treaty had kept it from accessing most nuclear-related materials and fuels on the international markets for more than thirty years. India's 1974 nuclear explosion spurred the U.S.-led creation of the Nuclear Suppliers Group (NSG)—an international export control regime for nuclear-related trade—and the U.S. government further tightened its own export laws with the Nuclear Nonproliferation Act of 1978.

The 1998 Indian and Pakistani nuclear weapons tests raised the specter of nuclear war in South Asia, reinforcing U.S. nonproliferation and broader security concerns. Nevertheless, the United States and the rest of the international community fairly quickly eased sanctions and improved relations. Reflecting this momentum, the Bush administration went against existing U.S. law and policy in urging a civil nuclear agreement with India. Some in Congress and the media expressed concern that U.S. civil nuclear cooperation with India might allow that country to advance its military nuclear projects and could be harmful to broader U.S. nonproliferation efforts. Despite these concerns, the Bush administration moved forward with adjustments in U.S. laws and policies in order to accommodate civil nuclear cooperation with India. Congressional votes in 2006 approved the administration's position. Civil nuclear cooperation with India still required that the two countries finalize a peaceful nuclear cooperation agreement, the NSG allow for such cooperation, and India conclude a safeguards agreement with the International Atomic Energy Agency. The main obstacle in this process in late 2007 was political opposition to the nuclear deal on the part of Communist parties in the coalition of Prime Minister Singh. Whether that opposition could be overcome remained unclear.[14]

U.S.-India Security Cooperation

The rapid advances in U.S.-India security cooperation in recent years included sophisticated military exercises and arms sales. Since 2002, the United States and India have held a series of unprecedented and increasingly substantive combined exercises involving all military services. These have included Indian air forces using advanced Russian Su-30MKI aircraft, Special Forces training in mountains near the China-India border, and annual naval exercises along the Indian coast. The scope of arms sales also has grown, with the Bush administration in 2005 welcoming Indian requests for advanced fighter aircraft and command-and-control, early warning, and missile defense equipment. The U.S. government also supported Israel's sale of the U.S.-Israeli Phalcon airborne early warning system to India.[15]

The U.S.-Indian rapprochement raises questions among some observers about the implications for U.S. relations with Pakistan, how India will use the new equipment and techniques learned through exercises with the United States, and what the strong U.S. tilt in favor of India means for American interest in relations with China. Some U.S. and Indian analysts praise increased U.S.-India security ties as providing a counterbalance to growing Chinese influence in Asia, but others are more ambivalent about the wisdom of relying on U.S.-India strategic cooperation as a viable and durable hedge against possible adverse consequences coming from China's rise to regional and global prominence.[16]

India-Iran and India-Myanmar Relations

As the United States firmly opposed Iran's efforts to develop nuclear weapons, the United States looked to India and other states with long-standing constructive relations with Iran to take a stand against Iran's nuclear ambitions. India wanted to sustain important energy and other beneficial relations with Iran, but in the end, it sided with the majority at United Nations sessions registering increasing concern about Iran's nuclear program. The U.S. and Indian governments were at an impasse in 2006 over India's determination to pursue large-scale projects to deliver Iranian gas to Indian consumers.[17]

Meanwhile, the brutal crackdown by the military government in Myanmar on mass demonstrations led by thousands of Buddhist monks in 2007 saw renewed U.S. pressure on India to use its growing influence in that country to urge more democratic reform and an end to repression. However, India felt its interests were better served by a policy of increasing engagement with the Myanmar regime.[18]

India's Economy and U.S. Concerns

India's economic reforms and greater conformity to trends in economic globalization have reinforced growth. Advancing at a rate of 7–8 percent in recent years, the Indian economy attracted strong U.S. and other foreign interest. Still, many problems remained, including inadequate infrastructure, hundreds of millions of poor residents, and weak public services in health care, education, power, and water supply. The Indian government also vacillates in its commitment to moving the economy in a free market direction, and excessive government control and bureaucracy are often cited in American complaints about doing business in India. As India's largest trade and investment partner, the United States strongly supported India's continuing economic reform policies. India was not a

heavily trade dependent economy, so levels of U.S. trade, while growing, have remained relatively low. Total trade, heavily in India's favor,
amounted to $27 billion in 2005.[19]

Dissidence and Human Rights

The Kashmir problem heads a long list of areas under Indian control that
saw recurring challenges to government authority and strong Indian
measures to maintain law and order. Maoist rebels continued to operate
in numerous states, and the Indian prime minister said in 2006 that these
insurgents represented "the single biggest internal security challenge"
ever faced by India. Repeated communal clashes between Muslims and
Hindus have prompted government crackdowns to restore order. International human rights groups focused on such persisting problems as
abuses by security forces and failure to contain violent religious extremism. The annual State Department human rights report has catalogued
a wide array of human rights shortcomings in India, some the direct
responsibility of the government and others a manifestation of bad practices in the broader society.[20]

U.S. Assistance

Though the U.S. government gave many billions of dollars of assistance
to India in the past, U.S. aid programs have been more modest in recent
years. U.S. Agency for International Development (USAID) programs for
India in 2006 were valued at $68 million. The United States also provided
very modest military training aid for India, while military sales agreements, pursued on a commercial basis and not involving U.S. Foreign
Military Financing, amounted to $288 million from fiscal year (FY) 2002
to FY 2005.[21]

Outlook

The growing "strategic partnership" between the United States and India
has a firm foundation based on shared values of democracy, multicultur-
alism, and the rule of law, along with increasing cooperation in counterterrorism, joint military exercises, high-technology trade, and numerous
economic, security, and global initiatives. The most controversial aspect of
the recent bilateral relationship was the agreement on full civilian nuclear
cooperation launched by President Bush in 2005. Yet, the accord received
endorsement late in the 109th Congress in votes that reflected bipartisan
support. Specialists nonetheless warned of possible "backsliding" by
India on implementing the understandings surrounding the U.S.-India
nuclear accord that likely would prompt congressional criticism. Also, if

key lawmakers did not find India sufficiently helpful on issues pertaining to the Iranian nuclear weapons program, their dissatisfaction with New Delhi could make legislative approval of the bilateral nuclear cooperation agreement with India more difficult. Meanwhile, the issue of anticipated major U.S. arms sales to India and what they mean for U.S. relations with nearby powers—Pakistan and China, in particular—appeared likely to concern the Congress. Congress, particularly its leading Democrats, also continued to be concerned with violations of human rights, including women's' rights and religious freedom in India, and with outsourcing of U.S. jobs to the country.[22]

ISSUES IN U.S.-PAKISTAN RELATIONS

U.S. relations with Pakistan have waxed and waned, depending heavily on the fluctuating degree of perceived congruence of the strategic interests of the two governments amid changing international circumstances. Their roots were in the Cold War and South Asian regional politics of the 1950s. U.S. concerns about Soviet expansionism and Pakistan's desire for security assistance against the perceived threat from India prompted the two countries to negotiate a mutual defense assistance agreement in 1954. In 1955, Pakistan aligned more closely with the West by joining the Southeast Asia Treaty Organization and the Central Treaty Organization. The country received nearly $2 billion in U.S. aid up to 1961.

Relations cooled markedly as a result of the Indo-Pakistani wars of 1965 and 1971, and the United States suspended security assistance to both sides. The United States again suspended U.S. assistance to Pakistan in 1979 as a result of Pakistan's efforts to build a nuclear weapon in response to the Indian nuclear test of 1974. However, after the Soviet invasion of Afghanistan in late 1979, Pakistan became a frontline U.S. ally in the effort to block Soviet expansionism. In 1981, the United States offered Pakistan a five-year $3.2 billion aid package. Pakistan was a key transit country for arms supplies to the Afghan resistance and home to three million Afghan refugees.

Congress nevertheless pressed for a restriction in U.S. aid on account of Pakistan's continued nuclear weapons development. In 1985 an amendment was added to the Foreign Assistance Act requiring the president to certify to Congress that Pakistan does not possess a nuclear explosive device during the fiscal year for which aid is being provided. With the Soviet withdrawal from Afghanistan, Pakistan's nuclear programs came under intense scrutiny, and in 1990, President George H. W. Bush suspended aid to Pakistan. Most bilateral economic aid and all military aid ended, and U.S. deliveries of military equipment stopped. During the 1990s, U.S.

attention shifted from the region. Pakistan consolidated its nuclear weapons capability, promoted a growing separatist insurgency in Indian-controlled Kashmir, and supported the Taliban movement in Afghanistan, where the radical Islamist group took control of Kabul in 1996.

Another dramatic shift in affairs came after al-Qaeda's attack on America in 2001. The United States refocused attention to the region after years of relative neglect. Faced with enormous U.S. pressure, Pakistan joined with the United States as a key ally in U.S.-led counterterrorism operations in Afghanistan and elsewhere.[23]

The checkered history and the important but relatively narrow foundation of U.S.-Pakistan relations result in a good deal of uncertainty and debate in the United States over the problems and prospects of U.S. ties with this South Asia power. In recent years, Pakistan has been the locus of three central U.S. foreign policy concerns: terrorism, weapons of mass destruction (WMD) proliferation, and democratization. There were also substantial issues over trade and economic reform and efforts to counter narcotics trafficking.

The congressional role in dealing with Pakistan is large, particularly as Congress reviews and approves foreign assistance to Pakistan. Pakistan was among the world's largest recipients of U.S. aid. It obtained more than $3.5 billion in direct assistance for FY 2002–2006, including $1.5 billion in security-related aid. Pakistan also received billions of dollars in reimbursement for its support of U.S.-led counterterrorism operations. In general, Congress joined with the administration in the often difficult balancing of an acute interest in Pakistan's continued counterterrorism cooperation—especially in regard to Afghanistan stabilization and the capture of al-Qaeda leadership—with concurrent concerns about weapons proliferation and perceived need to encourage development of a more democratic and moderate Pakistani state administration.[24]

The trade-offs and dilemmas of U.S. policy toward Pakistan reached crisis proportions in 2007 amid large-scale demonstrations against the authoritarian rule of President Pervez Musharraf and his resort to emergency measures and other forceful repression. The assassination of political opposition leader Benazir Bhutto in December 2007 compounded the crisis. What effect the crisis would have on U.S. support and large U.S. aid programs for Pakistan remained unclear.

Security Issues

Antiterrorism Cooperation

After the 9/11 terrorist attacks, Pakistan pledged and provided major support for the U.S.-led antiterrorist campaign. U.S. officials repeatedly praised Pakistan's unprecedented cooperation in allowing the U.S. military to use bases within the country, helping to identify and detain extremists, and tightening its border with Afghanistan. The Pakistani government also cracked down on militant groups involved in terrorist acts in Kashmir and India.[25]

Some of the results were mixed, prompting frustration and concern by U.S. officials regarding the Pakistani government's commitment to the antiterrorism effort. Al-Qaeda and Taliban leaders and forces were widely seen to be using Pakistani areas near Afghanistan to regroup and launch attacks against Coalition forces in Afghanistan. While many observers acknowledged a decrease in Pakistan's support for militants targeting Indian-controlled Kashmir, India continued to complain that the Pakistani government was not doing enough to curb these terrorist groups. Meanwhile, the Pakistani administration faced a daunting challenge of dealing with a wide range of domestic militants who used bombings, assassinations, and other terrorist attacks in opposition to the government and its policies, especially its close alignment with the United States.[26]

Pakistan-U.S. Security Cooperation

After the breakthrough in U.S.-Pakistan cooperation against terrorism in 2001, the United States quickly waived sanctions that had been imposed on Pakistan as a result of Pakistan's 1998 nuclear tests and the military coup in Pakistan in 1999 that brought the administration of then general and later president Pervez Musharraf to power. In October 2001, large tranches of U.S. aid began flowing into Pakistan. Direct assistance programs included training and equipment for Pakistan's security forces. In 2002, the United States began allowing commercial sales, which enabled Pakistan to refurbish at least some of its American-made F-16 fighter aircraft. In June 2004, President Bush designated Pakistan as a major non-NATO ally of the United States. In March 2005, the United States announced that it would resume sales of F-16 fighters to Pakistan after a sixteen-year hiatus.

In recent years, major government-to-government arms sales and grants have included C-130 military transport aircraft, aerostats and six TPS-77 surveillance radars, air traffic control systems, military radio systems, Harpoon antiship missiles, TOW (Target-on-Wire) antiarmor missiles, and surplus P-3C Orion maritime surveillance aircraft. Foreign military sales agreements with Pakistan were worth $344 million in FY 2003–2004 and $492 million in FY 2005. In June 2006, the Bush administration notified Congress of a possible sale to Pakistan of F-16 fighters worth $5.1 billion. This move prompted some congressional opposition and warnings that Pakistan would use the planes against India and might transfer the advanced technology of the planes to China.[27]

Nuclear Weapons and Missile Proliferation

American policy makers remain concerned with the arms race between India and Pakistan and the danger of nuclear war in South Asia. The May 1998 Indian and Pakistani nuclear tests were followed by continued development of weapons and delivery systems. Pakistan is believed to have enough fissile material, mainly enriched uranium, for fifty to ninety nuclear weapons; India's program focuses on plutonium and may be able to build a similar number of weapons. Both countries have aircraft capable of delivering nuclear bombs (U.S.-supplied F-16s in Pakistan's air force reportedly have been refitted to carry nuclear bombs). Pakistan has acquired short- and medium-range ballistic missiles from China and North Korea, while India has developed its own short- and intermediate-range missiles. All are assumed to be capable of delivering nuclear weapons.[28]

U.S. nonproliferation efforts in South Asia have been an issue of some controversy among U.S. policy makers in the administration and the Congress, though the recent trend has been to give them lower priority than in the period following the 1998 nuclear tests. At that time, President Clinton imposed full restrictions on all nonhumanitarian aid to both Pakistan and India as mandated under Section 102 of the Arms Export Control Act. However, Congress and the president acted almost immediately to lift certain aid restrictions and, after October 2001, all remaining nuclear-related sanctions on Pakistan and India were removed.

The United States continues to urge Pakistan and India to join the Nuclear Non-Proliferation Treaty as nonnuclear weapon states, and it provides no official recognition of their nuclear weapons capabilities. The Clinton administration set forth nonproliferation "benchmarks" for Pakistan and India. These included halting further nuclear testing, signing and ratifying the Comprehensive Test Ban Treaty (CTBT), halting fissile material production and pursuing negotiations to adhere to the Fissile Material Control Treaty, refraining from deploying nuclear weapons and testing ballistic missiles, and restricting all export of nuclear materials and technologies. The results were mixed, and the Bush administration set aside the benchmark framework. U.S. policy makers are concerned about Pakistan in particular, fearing onward proliferation from and internal instability in this nuclear weapons state.[29]

Media reports in 2002 suggested that Pakistan was assisting North Korea's covert nuclear weapons program by providing uranium enrichment materials and technology beginning in the mid-1990s. Such assistance was seen to call for ending all U.S. nonhumanitarian assistance to Pakistan, but the Bush administration said in 2003 that the relevant facts did not warrant imposition of sanctions under relevant U.S. laws. Libya's disclosure of its nuclear weapons program then showed Pakistani nuclear assistance, and in 2004 a Pakistani government investigation of Abdul Qadeer Khan, the founder of Pakistan's nuclear weapons program, said that Khan had confessed to involvement in an illicit international nuclear smuggling network involving sales of nuclear weapons technology and uranium enrichment materials to North Korea, Iran, and Libya. The Pakistan government's assurance to the United States and other concerned powers that it had no knowledge of the illicit activities met with a skeptical international response, but the Bush administration did not alter support for the Pakistan government, a key ally in the war on terrorism.[30]

Pakistan-India Tensions over Kashmir

U.S. policy makers showed special concern with the likely flashpoint of Pakistan-Indian war and possible nuclear conflict involving the intense dispute between the two countries over Kashmir. A separatist rebellion has been under way in the region since 1989. Tensions were very high in the wake of the so-called Kargil conflict of 1999, when an incursion of Pakistani soldiers led to a bloody six-week-long battle. In 2001, the bombing of the Jammu and Kashmir state assembly building in October was followed by a December assault on the Indian Parliament building in New Delhi. Both incidents were blamed on Pakistan-based terrorist groups. The Indian government mobilized 700,000 troops along the frontier with Pakistan and threatened war unless Pakistan ended all cross-border infiltration of Islamic militants. Under strong pressure from the United States and others, President Musharraf vowed to end the presence of terrorist entities in Pakistan and outlawed five militant groups. There were further flare-ups amid continued infiltrations and terrorist attacks, but the Indian and Pakistani governments, under strong pressure from the U.S. and other concerned governments, have endeavored with mixed results since 2003 to ease tensions, engage in dialogue, and promote confidence-building measures.[31]

Political Issues

Radical Islam and Anti-American Sentiment

The upsurge in anti-Americanism, xenophobia, and religious extremism fostered by politically active Islamic groups opposed to the administration of President Musharraf are viewed with concern by American policy makers. Those Islamic groups at times have controlled the assemblies of territories bordering Afghanistan, where they passed laws and took other actions in support of Islamic law that were at odds with the Musharraf administration. They particularly criticized the Musharraf government's shift in policy in favor of the United States after September 2001. They deemed that the alliance with the United States represented a fundamental threat to their values and to the sovereignty of Pakistan. Meanwhile, broader gauges of public opinion showed a decided anti-American trend. Worldwide polls measuring opinion of the United States showed Pakistan among those countries with the most negative view of the United States and its policies.[32]

Democratization and Human Rights

Administration and congressional policy makers in the United States continue to register concerns over the lack of progress toward greater democracy and human rights practices in Pakistan. In 2006, the often-cited nongovernmental organization Freedom House rated Pakistan as "not free" in the areas of political rights and civil liberties for the seventh year in a row. U.S. congressional committees periodically registered concerns about the slow pace of democratic development in Pakistan. The U.S. State Department's annual reports on human rights practices in countries abroad repeatedly registered a negative view of Pakistan's record, while the department's annual reports on religious freedom and trafficking in persons were similarly critical of Pakistan's performance.[33]

U.S. policy maneuvered awkwardly amid the crisis in 2007 posed by large-scale demonstrations against the authoritarian rule of Musharraf and the president's resort to emergency measures and other forceful repression. The Bush administration continued support for the beleaguered Pakistani leader and encouraged him to move toward political compromise with opponents and new elections. U.S. media and some U.S. political leaders more strongly opposed the Pakistan administration.

Economic Issues and U.S. Aid

Pakistan is a poor country that depends heavily on foreign aid. Since 2001, the United States has been the largest provider of aid to Pakistan. It is also the country's leading export market, taking in $3.25 billion worth of mainly cotton apparel and textiles in 2005. Output from Pakistan's industrial and service sectors has grown substantially since 2002, but the agricultural sector has lagged. Agricultural labor accounts for nearly half of the country's workforce. Pakistan's real gross domestic product (GDP) for the fiscal year ending June 2006 grew by 6.6 percent.[34]

U.S. assistance provides an important indicator of U.S. policy concerns regarding Pakistan. On the whole, administration and congressional actions show strong support for the Musharraf administration despite the nuclear and missile proliferation, political, human rights, and other concerns noted above. Efforts by some in Congress to reinstate some sanctions related to Pakistan's nuclear weapons proliferation occur from time to time, but have not been passed. Congress routinely extends the annual presidential waiver authority that allows aid to flow despite provisions that restrict U.S. aid to regimes abroad that have gained power through a coup, as did Musharraf in 1999.

It was unclear in late 2007 what effect the ongoing political crisis in Pakistan would have on possible congressional opposition to continued strong U.S. aid to Pakistan. A total of more than $15 billion in U.S. economic and military assistance went to Pakistan from 1947 through 2005. In June 2003, President Bush promised President Musharraf that he would work with Congress on establishing a five-year, $3 billion aid package for Pakistan. Annual installments of $600 million, split evenly between military and economic aid, began in FY 2005. The Foreign Operations FY 2005 Appropriations Act (P.L. 108-447) established a new program of $300 million for military assistance for Pakistan. When additional funds for development assistance, law enforcement, and other programs are included, the aid allocation for FY 2005 was about $688 million. Significant increases in economic support, plus U.S. funding for relief in response to an earthquake disaster in Pakistan, pushed the FY 2006 total to around $900 million. The administration's FY 2007 request called for $739 million in U.S. aid to Pakistan.[35]

With the support of the White House, Congress also appropriated billions of dollars to reimburse Pakistan for its support of U.S.-led counterterrorism operations in the country. U.S. Defense Department documents showed that Pakistan received about $3.6 billion in such payments from 2002 to 2005, an amount equal to one-quarter of Pakistan's total military expenditures during that period.[36]

A trade issue of great concern to the U.S. government is Pakistan's position as a major transit country for opiates that are grown and processed in Afghanistan and then distributed worldwide by Pakistan-based traffickers. The State Department indicates that the Pakistani government's cooperation with the United States on drug control is strong, and the U.S. government provides more than $50 million a year to support programs to enhance border security in order to curb the drug flow into Pakistan from Afghanistan, which is said to provide the majority of heroin to the world market.[37]

ISSUES IN U.S.–CENTRAL ASIAN RELATIONS

Since the 9/11 terrorist attack on America and the U.S.-led war against the terrorist-harboring Taliban regime in Afghanistan, U.S. officials, backed by Congress, have supported policies in Central Asia focused on three interrelated activities: the promotion of security, domestic reforms, and energy development. Contrary to a previous, less engaged U.S. policy approach toward Central Asia, after 2001 the U.S. government said it was critical to the national interests of the United States to greatly enhance American relations with the five Central Asian countries (Kazakhstan, Kyrgyzstan, Tajikistan, Turkmenistan, and Uzbekistan) to prevent them from becoming harbors of terrorism.

There remains considerable debate among U.S. specialists and knowledgeable policy makers regarding how deeply the United States should be involved with the countries in the region. There also are discussions and debates as U.S. policy makers endeavor to balance U.S. commitments to democracy and human rights with pragmatic needs to cooperate with authoritarian Central Asian states that are important for U.S. security and energy interests. U.S. security, energy, and political interests and involvement have run up against occasional opposition from some regional governments, including Russia and China, leading some observers to speculate about a revival of the nineteenth-century "great game" of international competition for influence in Central Asia. However, the signs of rivalry between and among the concerned powers remained limited, at least for the time being.[38]

Security Issues

U.S. security interests and involvement in Central Asia predated 2001. All the Central Asian states, except Tajikistan, had joined NATO's Partnership for Peace (PFP) program by 1994 (Tajikistan later joined in 2002). Central Asian troops thereafter participated in periodic PFP or PFP-related exercises in the United States, and U.S. troops participated in exercises in Central Asia beginning in 1997.[39]

A major U.S. concern after the breakup of the Soviet Union was to eliminate the nuclear weapons remaining in Kazakhstan and to control nuclear proliferation in the region. In December 1993, the United States and Kazakhstan signed the Cooperative Threat Reduction (CTR) umbrella agreement to allow for the "safe and secure" dismantling of 104 multiple-nuclear-warhead intercontinental ballistic missiles, the destruction of their silos, and related activities. In 1994, all bombers and their air-launched nuclear cruise missiles were removed, and in 1995 the last of more than a thousand nuclear warheads were transferred to Russia.

Kazakhstan announced it was a nuclear-free state in 1995, but work in this area with the United States continued. In 1999, the United States announced that 147 missile silos were destroyed. The two governments set up a U.S.-Kazakh Nuclear Risk Reduction Center in Kazakhstan in order to facilitate verification and compliance with arms control agreements and to prevent the proliferation of WMD.[40]

Besides Kazakhstan's nuclear weapons, U.S. attention focused on research reactors, uranium mines, milling facilities, and nuclear waste dumps in Kazakhstan, Kyrgyzstan, Tajikistan, and Uzbekistan, endeavoring to guard against theft. Kazakhstan and Uzbekistan had also hosted major chemical and biological warfare facilities during the Soviet era. U.S. CTR aid was used to transport weapons-grade uranium and enriched nuclear fuel to safekeeping in the United States, Russia, and elsewhere; to dismantle and secure anthrax and other biological warfare facilities; and to keep WMD weapons scientists employed in peaceful research.[41]

The U.S.-led war against the Taliban in Afghanistan saw U.S. military relationships with Central Asian countries grow rapidly. Kyrgyzstan provided basing for U.S. and Coalition forces at a facility at Manas, where in 2005 there were reportedly fifteen hundred U.S. troops. Until the expulsion of U.S. forces ordered by the Uzbek government in 2005, there were around nine hundred American personnel at a base at Karshi-Khanabad. Uzbekistan also hosted several hundred German troops in Termez and provided a land corridor for humanitarian aid to Afghanistan. Tajikistan permitted use of its international airport in Dushanbe for refueling and hosted a small contingent of French forces until 2005. Kazakhstan and Turkmenistan provided overflight permission and other support.[42]

The Uzbek government cracked down violently against demonstrators in the town of Andijon in May 2005. Dozens and perhaps hundreds of civilians were killed. The United States criticized the action and supported the airlifting of 439 people, who had fled to nearby Kyrgyzstan, from Kyrgyzstan to Romania, fearing that if they were forced to return to Uzbekistan they would be tortured. Uzbekistan's government then demanded the withdrawal of U.S. forces from the country, which was accomplished in November 2005. Russia and China strongly supported Uzbekistan's decision.[43]

U.S. security assistance to Central Asian countries grew after 2001. Security and law enforcement aid for the region was $188 million in FY 2002, $101 million in FY 2003, $132 million in FY 2004, and $148 million in FY 2005. The aid involved equipment and training, as well as border security aid to counter trafficking in drugs, humans, and WMD. U.S. funding to support the basing in Manas in Kyrgyzstan and Karshi-Khanabad in Uzbekistan came from separate accounts. The U.S. Central Command, responsible for U.S. military engagement in Central Asia, also launched a program in 2003 to enhance security assistance on the oil-rich Caspian Sea involving Kazakhstan and Azerbaijan. Meanwhile, the Defense Department was considering setting up long-term military facilities in Central Asia and nearby Mongolia known as "cooperative security locations." These sites might contain prepositioned equipment and be managed by private contractors with few if any U.S. military personnel present.[44]

Democratization and Human Rights

The falling out between the U.S. and Uzbek governments over U.S. criticism of and actions against the latter's crackdown on demonstrators in 2005 graphically illustrated the conflicts that frequently arose as U.S. policy makers tried to achieve goals of advancing democracy and human rights on the one hand while advancing security cooperation with the authoritarian Central Asian governments in the broad war on terrorism on the other. Each of the Central Asian states was led by ex-Communist Party officials who generally had little stake in the kind of democracy and human rights practices sought by the United States. Throughout the post–Cold War period, U.S. officials solicited pledges from the region's leaders to support democracy, but in practice the leaders seemed more comfortable with the authoritarian practices they were more familiar with and which they judged posed less danger to their continued hold on power.[45]

Turkmenistan and Uzbekistan were generally viewed as having the most repressive governments. It remained unclear in late 2007 if the death of Turkmenistan's despotic leader in late 2006 would lead to greater freedom in the country. Given the large U.S. security stake in Uzbekistan after 2001, the government's authoritarian domestic practices repeatedly ran up against congressionally mandated restrictions on U.S. assistance. Kazakhstan, perhaps the most important Central Asian country for U.S. energy interests, also came under negative congressional scrutiny that required the U.S. administration to waive aid restrictions on national security grounds.[46]

Economic and Energy Issues

U.S. private investment committed to Central Asian states has exceeded that provided to Russia and most other Eurasian states. Much interest has focused on the Caspian Sea and its energy riches. U.S. government policy endeavors to support the sovereignty of the energy-rich Central Asian states and their ties with the West. It backs U.S. private investment, promotes Western energy security by obtaining supplies from the region, assists NATO ally Turkey as a terminal point for pipelines from the region, and opposes outlets to Iran.[47]

According to the U.S. Department of Energy, Kazakhstan possesses the Caspian region's largest proven oil reserves and significant gas deposits. U.S. policy encouraged Kazakhstan to export oil through a pipeline ending in Turkey. Russia currently controls most existing export pipelines, although Kazakhstan opened a new pipeline to China in 2006. In October 2005, Kazakhstan and Azerbaijan agreed in principle to ship some Kazakh oil through a pipeline between Azerbaijan and Turkey.[48]

U.S. Aid to Central Asia

The United States gave $3.8 billion to Central Asia states from 1992 to 2005. The amounts given after 2001 were larger than those before, reflecting the higher priority the U.S. government placed on developing relations with this region of critical importance in the war on terrorism. In FY 2002, U.S. aid for purposes other than defense and law enforcement was $584 million. It declined to $302 million in FY 2005 and $125 million in FY 2006. The United States also provided aid through international financial institutions and conferred substantial aid to help Central Asian countries fight narcotics trafficking and production. Congressional deliberations over aid legislation allowed for considerable discussion and some debate regarding the implications of sometimes competing U.S. security, political, and energy interests and issues in the region.[49]

MONGOLIA

Mongolia straddles Northeast Asia and Central Asia. U.S. relations with Mongolia in the post–Cold War period have been good and generally without major controversy in recent years. Top-level visits have occurred frequently. President Bush visited Mongolia in 2005.

The United States has assisted Mongolia's movement toward democracy and market-oriented reform and has expanded relations with Mongolia primarily in the cultural and economic fields. In 1989 and 1990, the two countries signed a cultural accord, Peace Corps accord, consular convention, and Overseas Private Investment Corporation (OPIC) agreement. A trade agreement was signed in January 1991 and a bilateral investment treaty in 1994. Mongolia was granted permanent normal trade relations (PNTR) status and generalized system of preferences (GSP) eligibility in June 1999. In July 2004, the United States signed a Trade and Investment Framework Agreement with Mongolia to promote economic reform and more foreign investment.

The Agency for International Development plays a lead role in providing bilateral American assistance to Mongolia. The program emphasizes two main themes: sustainable, private sector–led economic growth; and more effective and accountable governance. Total USAID assistance to Mongolia from 1991 through 2007 was about $170 million, all in grant form.

The United States has also supported defense reform and an increased capacity by Mongolia's armed forces to participate in international peacekeeping operations. Mongolia has contributed small numbers of troops to Coalition operations in Iraq and Afghanistan since 2003. With U.S. Department of Defense assistance and cooperation, Mongolia and the United States jointly hosted Khan Quest, the Asian region's premier peacekeeping exercise, in 2006 and 2007.[50]

U.S. ISSUES WITH RUSSIA

The Russian administration of President Vladimir Putin, in power since 2000, saw significant improvement in Russian-U.S. relations during the early period of the George W. Bush administration. Differences regarding the Putin administration's tighter control over Russian politics and Russian energy resources and enterprises, and differences over salient international issues such as Iran's suspected nuclear weapons program, NATO expansion, and U.S. ballistic missile defense programs, were among the issues that soured relations by the latter part of Bush's tenure.[51]

Putin's government endeavored to play a more important role in Asia-Pacific affairs than the previous administration of Boris Yeltsin. Russia was active in important multilateral groups like the Six-Party Talks and the various multilateral meetings associated with the Association of Southeast Asian Nations (ASEAN), including the ASEAN Regional Forum. It was a leader along with China in the Shanghai Cooperation Organization (SCO), dealing with Central Asia. In contrast with Russian and Chinese cooperation with the United States and other powers in various Asian multilateral groups, Russia and China supported the SCO's stance that seemed to preclude the United States from joining the regional body. This was widely seen as reflecting Russian and Chinese wariness of the U.S. presence in Central Asia and their respective interests in balancing the growth of U.S. power in Asia since the advent of the war on terror in 2001.

Russia exerts important diplomatic leverage by virtue of its position as a permanent member of the UN Security Council. As one of the world's leading oil and energy exporters, Russia influences the energy security considerations of the United States and leading Asia-Pacific powers. Militarily, it has remained for many years the largest supplier of advanced military equipment to Asia's two rising powers, China and India.[52]

Putin's strong political control in Russia was seen in his reelection victory in 2004 in which he faced no serious competition. Pro-Putin political forces had clear majority control over the Russian Duma parliament. He brought television and radio under tight state control and virtually eliminated effective political opposition. Putin used state power to gain control over the important energy sectors of the Russian economy.[53]

The Putin administration's key objectives of strengthening the state and reviving the economy had notable results:

- Federal forces suppressed large-scale military resistance in Chechnya and in 2006 succeeded in killing most of the remaining top Chechen rebel military and political leaders.
- The economic upturn that began in 1999 continued. GDP and domestic investment grew impressively after a long decline in the 1990s. They were fueled in large part by profits from oil and gas exports. Inflation was contained, the budget balanced, and the currency was stable. Major problems remained, though, including almost one-fifth of the population living below the poverty line, low foreign investment, and pervasive crime, corruption, capital flight, and unemployment.
- Russian defense spending began to increase after massive declines over many years.
- Russia projected greater international confidence as an "energy superpower." It had mixed results in efforts to reassert dominance in and integration of former Soviet states.[54]

The U.S.-Russian "strategic partnership" of the early 1990s was replaced by increasing tension and mutual recrimination later in the decade. Key issues included NATO expansion, the U.S.-led war against Serbia, U.S. ballistic missile defense programs, and disagreements over Iraq, Iran, and other issues in the Middle East. In the first year of the George W. Bush administration, relations improved markedly. After a Bush-Putin summit, and particularly following the September 11, 2001, terrorist attacks on America, the two nations reshaped their relationship on the basis of cooperation against terrorism and Putin's goal of integrating Russia economically with the West.[55]

Since 2003, however, tensions have reemerged on a number of issues that again strain relations. Cooperation continued in some areas and Bush and Putin strove to maintain the appearance of cordial personal relations, but there appeared to be more discord than harmony in U.S.-Russian relations.

Russia's construction of nuclear reactors in Iran and its role in missile technology transfers to that country were critical sources of tension with the United States. Despite repeated warnings from the Bush administration and Congress that Iran will use the civilian reactor program as a cover for a covert nuclear weapons program, Russia refused to cancel the project, which neared completion. Moscow's position was that it intended to continue its civil nuclear power projects in Iran, while urging Tehran to accept intrusive international safeguard inspections and other guarantees that it will not produce nuclear weapons. Facing strong U.S. and European Union pressure to move the Iran issue to the UN Security Council, Russia went along with Security Council efforts beginning in 2006 to impose modest sanctions on trade with Iran's nuclear infrastructure and other restrictions and pressures designed to curb Iran's suspected nuclear weapons program. Russia, along with China, generally opposed more stringent sanctions supported by the United States.[56]

The United States clashed repeatedly with Russia over Iraq. After 9/11, Russia moved away from full support of Iraq against the United States. Then, as the United States moved toward military action against the Saddam Hussein regime, the Putin administration tried to balance competing Russian interests: protecting Russian economic interests in Iraq; restraining U.S. unilateralism and global dominance; and maintaining friendly relations with the United States. In early 2003, Russia aligned with France and Germany in opposition to U.S. military action and threatened to veto a U.S.-backed UN resolution authorizing military force against Iraq. It has continued criticism of U.S. behavior in the war in Iraq since.[57]

Vigorous Russian criticism of U.S. ballistic defense efforts and expanding alliances with NATO and with Japan subsided in 2001 amid closer U.S.-Russian cooperation over terrorism and other issues. Putin revived the strong criticism in 2007, seriously complicating U.S.-Russian summit meetings. Meanwhile, U.S. leaders, including President Bush, were outspoken in criticizing the Putin administration's perceived restrictions and reversal of political rights and economic freedom in Russia.[58]

U.S. Issues Involving Russia in the Asia-Pacific

The wide range of important domestic and international actions of the Putin administration that were noted above and posed significant issues for U.S. policy contrasted with the relatively less significant U.S. issues specifically involving Russian policy in the Asia-Pacific. Highlights of U.S. issues and concerns with Russian actions in the Asia-Pacific included:

- Russian leaders were often outspoken in criticizing the hard-line U.S. approach toward North Korea in the Six-Party Talks, and they welcomed the moderation the United States showed in reaching the February 13, 2007, agreement. Russia worked with China in softening the U.S.-backed UN Security Council resolutions dealing with North Korea's missile and nuclear tests in 2006.

- Russia sided with Uzbekistan as it resisted U.S. pressure on human rights issues and democracy in 2005 and expelled American forces from the country. It worked with China in the SCO to call for a deadline for the withdrawal of U.S. and Western military forces from Central Asia.
- Russia periodically joined with China in declaring strong opposition to U.S. "hegemonism" in Asia-Pacific and world affairs.
- In 2005, Russia carried out a large military exercise with China under the auspices of the SCO that seemed targeted against U.S. security interests in the Asia-Pacific.
- Russian sales of sophisticated arms to China amounted to $2 billion annually in recent years and severely complicated U.S. defense planning in the event of a military conflict with China over Taiwan.[59]

NOTES

1. White House, "President, Prime Minister of India Discuss Freedom and Democracy," press release, July 18, 2005.

2. Robert Sutter, "The United States and Asia in 2006: Crisis Management, Holding Patterns, and Secondary Initiatives," *Asian Survey* 47, no. 1 (January/February 2007): 18.

3. Satu Limaye, "Consolidating Friendships and Nuclear Legitimacy," *Comparative Connections* 9, no. 4 (4th Qtr 2007): 153, http://www.csis.org/media/csis/pubs/0704q.pdf.

4. Stephen Philip Cohen, *India: Emerging Power* (Washington, D.C.: Brookings Institution Press, 2001), 229–67.

5. Strobe Talbott, *Engaging India: Diplomacy, Democracy, and the Bomb* (Washington, D.C.: Brookings Institution Press, 2004).

6. K. Alan Kronstadt, *India-U.S. Relations*, CRS Report RL33529 (Washington, D.C.: Congressional Research Service, Library of Congress, July 31, 2006), p. 3.

7. Barbara LePoer, *President Clinton's South Asia Trip*, CRS Report RS20508 (Washington, D.C.: Congressional Research Service, Library of Congress, March 31, 2000); Indian Embassy, "Visit of Prime Minister Vajpayee to the United States," press release, September 2000.

8. U.S. Department of State, *Remarks at Sophia University by Secretary Condoleezza Rice*, Tokyo, Japan, March 19, 2005, www.state.gov (accessed November 21, 2007).

9. Kronstadt, *India-U.S. Relations*, 3.

10. Ashley Tellis, *India as a Global Power: An Action Agenda for the United States* (Washington, D.C.: Carnegie Endowment for International Peace, 2005).

11. Robert Sutter, "The United States and Asia in 2005: Managing Troubles, Sustaining Leadership," *Asian Survey* 46, no. 1 (January/February 2006): 19–20; Sutter, "United States and Asia in 2006," 18–19.

12. Kronstadt, *India–U.S. Relations*, 4.

13. Tellis, *India as a Global Power*.

14. Sharon Squassoni, *U.S. Nuclear Cooperation with India: Issues for Congress*, CRS Report RL33016 (Washington, D.C.: Congressional Research Service, Library of Congress, March 28, 2006).

15. Limaye, "Consolidating Friendships," 145.

16. John H. Gill, "India and Pakistan: A Shift in the Military Calculus?" in *Strategic Asia, 2005–2006: Military Modernization in an Era of Uncertainty*, ed. Ashley J. Tellis and Michael Wills (Seattle: National Bureau of Asian Research, 2005), 238–53.

17. Peter R. Lavoy, "India in 2006: A New Emphasis on Engagement," *Asian Survey* 47, no. 1 (January/February 2007): 121.

18. Limaye, "Consolidating Friendships," 148–50.

19. Kronstadt, *India–U.S. Relations*, 15–16.

20. U.S. Department of State, *India: Country Report on Human Rights Practices, 2006* (Washington, D.C.: GPO, 2007).

21. Kronstadt, *India–U.S. Relations*, 21–22.

22. Limaye, "Consolidating Friendships," 153.

23. K. Alan Kronstadt, *Pakistan–U.S. Relations*, CRS Report RL33496 (Washington, D.C.: Congressional Research Service, Library of Congress, July 27, 2006), 2–4; Stephen Philip Cohen, *The Idea of Pakistan* (Washington, D.C.: Brookings Institution Press, 2004), 1–15, 301–28.

24. Ashley Tellis, "U.S. Strategy: Assisting Pakistan's Transformation," *The Washington Quarterly* 28:1 (Winter 2004–2005) p. 97–116. Craig Cohen and Derek Chollet, "When $10 Billion Is Not Enough: Rethinking U.S. Strategy toward Pakistan," *Washington Quarterly* 30:2 (spring 2007) p. 7–19

25. John Gill, "Pakistan: A State under Stress," in *Strategic Asia, 2003–2004: Fragility and Crisis*, ed. Richard J. Ellings and Aaron L. Friedberg, 209–28 (Seattle: National Bureau of Asian Research, 2003).

26. Walter Andersen, "South Asia: A Selective War on Terrorism?" in *Strategic Asia, 2004–2005: Confronting Terrorism in the Pursuit of Power*, ed. Ashley J. Tellis and Michael Wills, 227–60 (Seattle: National Bureau of Asian Research, 2004).

27. Kronstadt, *Pakistan–U.S. Relations*, 7, 11–12.

28. Gill, "India and Pakistan," 250, 256–57.

29. Kronstadt, *Pakistan–U.S. Relations*, 12–13.

30. Charles H. Kennedy, "Pakistan in 2004: Running Very Fast to Stay in the Same Place," *Asian Survey* 45, no. 1 (January/February 2005): 107–9.

31. John Lancaster, "India, Pakistan End Talks Stalemated over Kashmir," *Washington Post*, September 7, 2004.

32. Adeel Khan, "Pakistan in 2006: Safe Center, Dangerous Peripheries," *Asian Survey* 47, no. 1 (January/February 2007): 125–28; "View of US's Global Role Worse," BBC World Service poll, January 2007.

33. U.S. Department of State, *Pakistan: Country Report on Human Rights Practices, 2006* (Washington, D.C.: GPO, 2007).

34. U.S. Department of State, "Background Note: Pakistan," May 2007, http://www.state.gov/r/pa/ei/bgn/3453.htm.

35. Craig Cohen and Derek Chollet, "When $10 Billion Is Not Enough: Rethinking U.S. Strategy toward Pakistan," *Washington Quarterly* 30, no. 2 (Spring 2007): 7–19.

36. Kronstadt, *Pakistan-U.S. Relations*, 21–22.

37. U.S. Department of State, *Pakistan*.

38. Kathleen Collins and William Wohlforth, "Central Asia: Defying 'Great Game' Expectations," in Ellings and Friedberg, *Strategic Asia, 2003–2004*, 291–320; Michael Milhaka, "Not Much of a Game: Security Dynamics in Central Asia, *China and Eurasia Forum Quarterly* 5, no. 2 (2007): 21–39.

39. Jim Nichol, *Central Asia: Regional Developments and Implications for U.S. Interests*, CRS Report RL33458 (Washington, D.C.: Congressional Research Service, Library of Congress, June 5, 2006), 14.

40. Ibid., 15.

41. Kenley Butler, "Weapons of Mass Destruction in Central Asia," Nuclear Threat Initiative (NTI) Issue Brief, October 2002, http://www.nti.org/e_research/e3_19a.html.

42. Lionel Beehner, "U.S. Military Bases in Central Asia," Council on Foreign Relations (CFR) Backgrounder, July 26, 2005, http://www.cfr.org/publication/8440/.

43. Jim Nichol, *Uzbekistan's Closure of the Airbase at Karshi-Khanabad: Context and Implications*, CRS Report RS22295 (Washington, D.C.: Congressional Research Service, Library of Congress, October 7, 2005).

44. Nichol, *Central Asia*, 18.

45. Jim Nichol, *Unrest in Uzbekistan: Context and Implications*, CRS Report RS22161 (Washington, D.C.: Congressional Research Service, Library of Congress, June 8, 2005).

46. Steven Lee Myers and Ilan Greenberg, "For Kazakh Leader's Visit, U.S. Seeks a Balance," *New York Times*, September 28, 2006; C. J. Chivers, "U.S. Courting a Somewhat Skittish Friend in Central Asia," *New York Times*, June 21, 2007.

47. Bernard Gelb, *Caspian Oil and Gas: Production and Prospects*, CRS Report RS21190 (Washington, D.C.: Congressional Research Service, Library of Congress, March 4, 2006).

48. Roger McDermott, "Kazakhstan's Partnership with NATO: Strengths, Limits and Prognosis," *China and Eurasia Forum Quarterly* 5, no. 1 (2007): 7–20.

49. Nichol, *Central Asia*, 18–19.

50. U.S. Department of State, "Background Note: Mongolia," February 2008, http://www.state.gov/r/pa/ei/bgn/2779.htm.

51. Stuart Goldman, *Russian Political, Economic, and Security Issues and U.S. Interests*, CRS Report 33407 (Washington, D.C.: Congressional Research Service, Library of Congress, January 18, 2007); Stephen Hanson, "Russia: Strategic Partner or Evil Empire?" in Tellis and Wills, *Strategic Asia, 2004–2005*, 163–99.

52. Elizabeth Wishnick, "Russia and the CIS in 2006: Asserting Russian Interests on Korean Security, Energy and Central Asia," *Asian Survey* 47, no. 1 (January/February 2007): 58–67.

53. U.S. Department of State, *Russia: Country Report on Human Rights Practices, 2006* (Washington, D.C.: GPO, 2007).

54. Celeste Wallander, "Russia: The Domestic Sources of a Less-than-Grand Strategy," in *Strategic Asia, 2007–2008: Domestic Political Change and Grand Strategy*, ed. Ashley J. Tellis and Michael Wills (Seattle: National Bureau of Asian Research, 2007), 139–76.

55. William Wohlforth, "Russia," in *Strategic Asia, 2002–2003: Asian Aftershocks*, ed. Richard J. Ellings and Aaron L. Friedberg (Seattle: National Bureau of Asian Research, 2002), 183–222.

56. Goldman, *Russian Political, Economic, and Security Issues*, 16.

57. Hanson, "Russia," 175–76.

58. Joseph Ferguson, "Putin Picks a Successor," *Comparative Connections* 9, no. 4 (4th Qtr 2007): 48–50, http://www.csis.org/media/csis/pubs/0704q.pdf.

59. Wishnick, "Russia and the CIS in 2006"; Richard Armitage and Joseph Nye, *U.S.-Japan Alliance: Getting Asia Right through 2020* (Washington, D.C.: Center for Strategic and International Studies, 2007), 11.

5

Determinants of Regional
Dynamics Important
to the United States

U.S. policy priorities and concerns in the Asia-Pacific region, including those that result from the ongoing and sometimes contentious U.S. domestic discussions and debates noted in the previous three chapters, often are important in determining the direction of U.S. relations with the region. At times, they have significant influence on the course of developments in the region. However, they are but one of several factors or sets of factors that influence broad regional trends, which establish regional conditions that determine whether U.S. policy faces greater challenges or opportunities in pursuing American interests in the Asia-Pacific.

The collapse of the Soviet Union and the end of the Cold War not only helped to empower U.S. domestic forces to exert greater influence in U.S. policy toward the Asia-Pacific and other world regions but also coincided with a marked upswing in Asian economic power and political assertiveness. Though dampened by setbacks during the Asian economic crisis later in the 1990s, regional initiatives and leadership have continued, mainly through national governments and the emerging regional groupings they foster. In China, India, Japan, and the economically advancing nations that make up the leading countries of the region, Asia-Pacific government leaders generally have endeavored to meet growing popular demand for greater economic development and nationalistic respect through balanced nation-building strategies that have placed a premium on encouraging economic growth beneficial to broad segments of their societies. Most tend to eschew radical ideologies and to emphasize conventional nationalism. Military power develops in tandem with economic power, but few administrations have emphasized the former at the expense of the latter in the face of international opposition and domestic pressures for more effective development of overall national wealth and power.

Regional government leaders remain well aware that failure to meet domestic expectations could result in being voted out of office in democratic states or widespread demonstrations and violence leading to regime collapse in authoritarian ones. People of the region generally recognize that national governments are important in advancing and protecting their interests and need to be effective to advance goals beneficial to citizens of the state. The people of the region tend to look to their governments to foster conditions beneficial to their livelihood and values, and they hold them accountable for perceived failures in these areas.

There are notable exceptions to these trends, but they generally remain secondary in determining overall regional conditions. The rulers of North Korea and Myanmar seem less concerned with balanced nation-building strategies and more focused on sustaining and developing military power as the prime means to maintain their hold on power. Many of the small Pacific Island states and some poor states on the Asian mainland (e.g., Laos) seem heavily dependent on foreign aid and in a weak position to set effective nation-building strategies. Even a large government like Pakistan's is heavily aid dependent and at times seems unable to cope effectively with internal and external challenges.

The greater power and assertiveness of Asia-Pacific nations come in the world's most diverse region, with a wide variety of cultural, historical, and other differences. Unlike Europe, Latin America, and Africa, mechanisms for substantial intraregional economic, political, and security cooperation are still in an early stage of development and are only beginning to rise in prominence and importance. The national governments generally see their interests well served with a wide range of experimenting with such mechanisms. Thus far, the governments generally have eschewed binding commitments in regional groupings that would compel cooperation and weaken the sovereignty or independence of action of individual national governments. The positive and cooperative atmosphere of a growing array of regional meetings fails to hide often intense competition and suspicion as larger powers maneuver for leadership positions and other advantages, and smaller powers maneuver to preserve their interests and independence.[1]

THE ASIA-PACIFIC AND GLOBAL TRENDS

Specialists have identified salient global trends that have affected and will continue to affect developments in the Asia-Pacific, along with other parts of the world. In general, the majority of Asia-Pacific regional governments are dealing with these trends pragmatically and effectively, although there are significant exceptions.[2]

Population

The Asia-Pacific countries on balance have demonstrated good control of population growth. In East Asia, population control remains a problem in Vietnam, the Philippines, and Indonesia. The large populations of South Asia are a major drag on development, though massive numbers of poor have not halted India's continued economic advances. Small states in the Pacific islands seem to have too many people given their very limited resources.

The region is not facing serious immediate problems posed by an aging population, except for Japan. As a result of its one child per married couple policy begun in the late 1970s, China is forecast to face a serious problem with a ballooning aging population and a limited cohort of working-age people by the second decade of the twenty-first century.[3]

There is labor migration among states, but generally it is controlled by national governments determined to preserve their sovereignty. Communal tension and minority issues are serious problems affecting countries like India, Pakistan, Indonesia, the Philippines, China, Thailand, and Malaysia. These problems may grow as information exchange increases and stokes minority and other grievances.

Infectious diseases, notably AIDS but also including new entrants like SARS and avian flu, have been or will become serious problems in most of the less advanced Asia-Pacific states, though overall they represent a sometimes serious complication rather than an overriding challenge to the nation-building agendas of most Asian governments.[4]

Energy, Food, and Water

The rapid economic development and ascension of China, India, and other Asian economies have prompted a rise in world oil and energy prices and a scramble among Asia-Pacific states to secure adequate resources. It is unclear if the mercantilist efforts of China, Japan, India, and other Asian governments and enterprises to secure international oil and gas reserves will be any more successful than the previous and generally unsuccessful efforts in the recent past. The competition for energy resources exacerbates tensions among the powers with respect to conflicting territorial claims involving energy, competition for control of or access to world supplies, and military efforts to secure sea lanes used for energy imports.[5]

Food security is generally adequate in the region, although there are major bottlenecks and difficulties in some places (e.g., North Korea). China will not consume world grain reserves—it can meet most needs with increasing imports that are not likely to cause substantial upset in world markets.

Competition for limited water resources remains a serious problem among Central and South Asian countries that regularly face problems because of inadequate rainfall and limited access to rivers and ground-water. Northern China faces a growing and serious water shortage, but it could be eased by changing the pricing and water usage system to make the cost of water conform to the market—China is moving slowly in this direction—and by taking other steps to divert water to the area from more well-watered territory.[6]

The Environment

The broad effects of widespread air and water pollution in the rapidly growing and inefficient-energy-using economies of China and India head the list of growing environmental problems weakening the prospects for sustained rapid growth in the region in the future. The Asian economies are in the lead in adding to emissions that will advance global warming and climate change that over time will have a major impact on Asia-Pacific populations, especially the large portion that continues to rely on agriculture for their livelihood. It also is likely to increase competition for water resources. Meanwhile, deforestation and the building of hydro-electric dams along Asian rivers in order to meet resource, energy, and transportation needs worsen overall environmental conditions and could so disrupt existing population and development patterns as to cause significant instability and turmoil among local populations.[7]

Economic Growth

Despite the longer-term environmental, demographic, resource, and other difficulties noted above, the Asia-Pacific region is projected to advance economically in the years ahead. By and large, the regional economies are following the path seen globally toward greater integration and greater growth. The splits between haves and have-nots in some countries, in-cluding China and India, will be a serious problem. There will be more migrants in the cities and gaps between rich and poor that will challenge some polities.

Given its overall assets, the Asia-Pacific is likely to grow in impor-tance in the overall world economy. Asian governments will see their growing economies become increasingly interdependent with other world economies—a clear advantage in times of global growth, but a possible liability in times of recession abroad.[8]

Permeation of Science and Technology

Information empowers greater civil society and enables economic growth by promoting scientific and technological advances that are important for national development. Because of the latter, even authoritarian Asian governments are likely to go along with this trend, though North Korea, Burma, and some others probably will continue to lag behind.[9]

Nation-State Power

The ability of Asia-Pacific states to promote authoritarianism, especially corporate control of social, economic, and political life, is in decline. The examples of Taiwan, South Korea, the Philippines, and Indonesia manifest this trend. At the same time, nationalism in the region is not declining and actually seems to be growing in intensity in recent years, and the nation-state seems to remain an essential vehicle for nationalism to be brought to fulfillment. Thus, a vibrant future for nationalism and the nation-state in the region seems likely.

While the nation-state is challenged by global business, international and local nongovernmental organizations, official international organizations, and terrorist, drug smuggling, and other criminal networks, the Asia-Pacific states, with some exceptions, remain coherent and often strong. They are not giving much authority to international organizations, regional groupings, businesses, or criminal or other networks, and they are adjusting to changed international circumstances and conforming more to regional and international norms. But at the same time, they work hard to preserve their independence and, where possible, to keep the policy initiative in their own hands.[10]

Continued U.S. World Leadership?

The ability and willingness of the U.S. government to sustain a leadership role in world affairs has been subject to sometimes intense debate in the post–Cold War period. The debate has intensified in recent years as a result of the major challenges faced by the U.S. government in dealing with the protracted and costly effort to militarily stabilize Iraq, the heavy responsibilities in the Global War on Terrorism, and ongoing large U.S. trade and budget deficits. These challenges are seen to be exacerbated in the Asia-Pacific region by the rise of China and the emergence of regional groupings that exclude or otherwise seem to undercut U.S. regional leadership.[11]

As noted in chapter 1, there has been a tendency among U.S. and other observers of Asia-Pacific regional affairs to see the United States as being in decline in the region in the face of newly rising powers. This book will provide an overall assessment of the status and outlook of continued U.S. leadership in Asia after assessing the challenges and opportunities posed by key regional trends and how well recent directions in U.S. priorities and policies meet those challenges and use those opportunities.

KEY DETERMINANTS

This study identifies five main determinants or sets of determinants that affect the recent policy environment in the Asia-Pacific region in ways relevant to U.S. interests and policy:

1. Reactions to changes in major regional power relationships, including China's rising power; India's rising power; Japan's on-again, off-again international assertiveness following a prolonged period of economic stagnation and political weakness; and Indonesia's slow comeback from weakness and leadership drift
2. Regional concern about sustaining economic growth amid growing challenges of economic globalization and related freer flow of information
3. Growing regional interest in and convergence around subregional and regional multilateral groups and organizations that address important economic and security concerns of Asia-Pacific countries
4. Regional reactions to broad security changes brought about by the Global War on Terror begun in 2001 and by changes on the Korean Peninsula prompted mainly by North Korea's provocative pursuit of nuclear weapons, ballistic missiles, and other weapons
5. Regional concern over U.S. security, economic, and political policies and objectives, ranging from apprehension over perceived excessive U.S. activism, unilateralism, and pressures on the one hand to worries over possible U.S. pullbacks and withdrawal from Asia-Pacific affairs on the other[12]

With the exception of the Global War on Terror, these determinants are not new, though all have become stronger in recent years. They have led to more fluid security and power relationships in the Asia-Pacific region than at any time since the Cold War. They also have strengthened the priority regional governments generally have given to shoring up their political legitimacy by effectively managing national and regional economic and political challenges.

The relative importance of each determinant or set of determinants depends on the circumstances and the priorities of regional leaders. Security determinants are of particular importance on those occasions—like the start of the war on terror in 2001 or the North Korean ballistic missile and nuclear weapons testing of 2006—when regional leaders have focused on their respective nation's security and relative power and position in a changing regional security situation.[13] Globalization and related information flows are of key importance when regional leaders face economic crises or social-political instability brought on by these forces.[14]

Taken together, the determinants provide impetus for greater activism by Asia-Pacific governments to foster their interests using an often wide array of means amid an increasingly challenging and fluid environment.

Regional Power Relationships

Asia-Pacific governments are watching carefully and taking measures to deal with several major changes in regional power relationships. These include:

- China is rising as a regional and global economic power, exerting ever-greater political influence in Asian and world affairs, and developing the leading military force in the Asia-Pacific. This expansion is likely to remain among the most important regional changes for years to come. It raises angst particularly in Taiwan and Japan, but also in varying degrees in several Southeast Asian nations and South Korea as well as the United States, Australia, New Zealand, India, and Russia. The implications of Beijing's political power and influence, developing in tandem with its economic and military power, coincide with concerns over Chinese internal stability. The authoritarian administration presides over remarkable economic growth but faces numerous internal problems associated with economic inequities, corruption, environmental problems, and political and ethnic dissidence fed by freer flows of outside information.[15]
- Like China, India also is increasing strongly in economic development, but from a lower level. International specialists forecast strong growth, but problems of poor infrastructure, bureaucracy, and continued mass poverty head the list of difficulties remaining to be overcome. India is a nuclear power with South Asia's dominant military force, and Indian leaders have embarked with some confidence on an international path pursuing advantageous and constructive contacts with the United States, Russia, China, and other world powers concerned with Asia-Pacific affairs.[16]

- Though remaining Asia's largest economy and possessing a strong and up-to-date military, Japan saw its influence in Asia decline after the Cold War. Japan's stagnant economic growth and political weakness in the 1990s undermined its regional leadership aspirations and capabilities, especially in comparison to China. The combination of China's growth and Japan's stagnation led recent Japanese leaders to adopt more assertive and competitive approaches to secure Japanese interests in an Asian order increasingly influenced by China and other powers.[17]
- Indonesia remains the largest power in the Association of Southeast Asian Nations (ASEAN) and for many years provided important leadership for the organization and for Southeast Asia. The democratic administration begun in the late 1990s drifted in weakness and uncertainty for several years following the toppling of the authoritarian regime that had ruled the country for decades. The gap in regional leadership was hard to fill, as other major ASEAN states such as Thailand and the Philippines faced significant internal problems and preoccupations. The result is an ironic situation of ASEAN recently gaining ever-greater regional prominence through the rapid growth of regional multilateral groupings in which ASEAN plays a leadership role at a time when many of ASEAN's leading states are undergoing major internal difficulties and crises. The situation adds to competition by China, Japan, India, the United States, and other powers as they work harder to secure an advantageous position in the fluid and uncertain regional situation.[18]

Other developments affecting regional power relationships include Russia's efforts, especially under President Vladimir Putin, to revive Russian influence in the Asia-Pacific, notably as an exporter of oil, gas, timber, and other commodities, as well as of advanced arms, which are needed by the regions' growing economies and militaries; the enhanced effort of the countries and leaders of the European Union since the 1990s to develop greater regional influence, largely to foster advantageous economic interchange; and the growing prominence of Middle Eastern and Central Asian countries in long-term Asia-Pacific economic and security calculations, related particularly to energy security.[19]

Economic Concerns and the Free Flow of Information

The record of improved performance of most regional economies following the 1997–1998 Asian economic crisis was a source of optimism to government leaders, but it failed to mask continued anxiety about future performance. The previous model of government-directed, export-oriented growth faced growing challenges from economic globalization and dependence on international markets, foreign investment, and limited energy and other resources. A variety of reporting showed that Japanese officials were particularly concerned about how to reform in order to generate growth after a decade of stagnation. China's strong economic growth was seen by Beijing as necessary to sustain social stability; this judgment seemed to place a continuing heavy imperative on continued growth. India's economic foundations were less developed than China's as it too sought rapid and sustained growth needed to meet forecasts and government ambitions of status as a major international economic power. Impressive recent growth in some other regional economies came without significant structural reform, possibly setting the stage for another downturn like 1997–1998, according to some economists.[20]

The Asian economic crisis not only hit regional economies hard but also seriously undermined social stability, challenged the standing of political regimes whose legitimacy rests heavily on providing economic growth, and weakened national security. It was a leading factor in the collapse of the Suharto government in Indonesia. It also prompted widespread popular and elite resentment over economic globalization and International Monetary Fund (IMF) rescue efforts. Years later, media reports and polling data show that Thai leaders and public opinion still harbor some resentment over the perceived belated and poorly conceived IMF effort to assist Thailand when it experienced the economic crisis in 1997. Malaysia's leadership also continued for many years to be critical of economic liberalization proposals of the IMF and others, favoring stronger government control.[21]

Nevertheless, governments in the region are often staffed by technocrats educated in the West, who tend toward pragmatism in economic policy. Most governments also accept the need to accommodate existing international norms on ownership, markets, trade, and investment. To seriously resist those norms could jeopardize economic development and thereby undermine domestic political support for Asian leaders whose political legitimacy rests heavily on their effectiveness in promoting economic growth and overall national power. Thus, although Chinese officials publicly supported Malaysia and other regional governments that attempted to diverge from Western development patterns at the time of the Asian economic crisis, they recognized that those patterns have an increasing influence over regional leaders and that China and others would need to conform to them in order to develop successfully in an increasingly globalized and interdependent world economy.[22]

The imperative of economic growth in an interdependent world economy has meant that regional states in general are accommodating the freer flow of information needed to modernize their economies, open markets, and promote common efforts to improve the environment and fight international crime and disease. To do otherwise risks economic downturn and stagnant development; these in turn could undermine the legitimacy and popular support of Asian governments that depend on improving economic conditions and living standards to support their continuation in power.[23]

The freer flow of information stemming from the global communications revolution nevertheless is likely to promote development of greater political pluralism, democracy, and respect for human rights that challenge Asian authoritarian regimes. Several of these governments are seeking to control the Internet and other forms of information exchange. They probably will continue to attempt to monitor, manipulate, and curb information to secure their political control—a preoccupation that saps state capacity for other goals.

Chinese authorities continue broad efforts to curb the use of the Internet by political dissidents and outlawed movements like the Falungong, which are seen to challenge the rule of the Communist Party. A wide range of dissidents, separatists, and political extremists in countries ranging from Pakistan to Indonesia continue to use available channels of communication to promote their respective messages to the detriment of existing state governance, cohesion, and stability.[24]

Regional authoritarian governments seek to preserve their prerogatives of power and resist trends toward democracy promoted through freer flows of information and other means. They attempt to find support from other regional advocates of conservative values and to develop common ground with other authoritarian regimes throughout the world that are under similar pressures by emphasizing their right to defend state sovereignty against outside interference. Noninterference in internal affairs remains a commonly emphasized principle in the international politics of Asia-Pacific governments. Even nonauthoritarian regional governments resist outside pressure to open to information flows deemed detrimental to national cohesion and sovereignty.[25]

Meanwhile, enhanced public access to a much broader range of information that accompanies economic development and interdependence associated with globalization also complicates the decision-making processes in democratic countries like Japan that previously had been dominated by political elites. Public officials increasingly have to take account of a broader array of opinion that can be brought to bear with expanding speed and effect on any given issue. For example, Japanese politicians who engage in sexual harassment or discrimination probably will be held more accountable by their constituents, who are influenced by international media critical of such practices. Most Asia-Pacific governments, authoritarian or not, remain concerned that the Internet and other means of communications can be used by ethnic, regional, religious, or other groups that challenge national identity and control and weaken the ability of the state to establish cohesive policies and programs.[26]

Asia-Pacific Multilateralism

The post–Cold War period has featured a remarkable growth in international, regional, and subregional organizations and groups of nations dealing with important economic, political, and security matters. As noted in the discussion in chapter 3 dealing with regional groups centered on ASEAN, regional bodies that deal with economic issues have tended to accomplish more than groups dealing with security. Broader groups including the United States and some nations from the eastern side of the Pacific emerged in the 1990s and continue to be active in dealing with economic and security issues. They include the Asia Pacific Economic Cooperation (APEC) forum, which hosts an important annual meeting of regional leaders, and the ASEAN Regional Forum, a regional group with broad membership that addresses security concerns.[27]

Some longer-standing subregional groups such as ASEAN (comprising ten Southeast Asian states), the South Pacific Forum (including Australia, New Zealand, and most Pacific Island countries), and the South Asia Association for Regional Cooperation (including South Asian states) have established observer status or dialogue mechanisms allowing participation of other regional and international powers. Other regional groupings are more exclusive. They include the Shanghai Cooperation Organization led by China and Russia and including four Central Asian states, with some geographically adjoining countries participating as observers; ASEAN+3, made up of ASEAN, China, Japan, and South Korea; and the Six-Party Talks, which represent the six countries (North and South Korea, the United States, China, Japan, and Russia) involved in negotiations concerning the crisis brought about by North Korea's nuclear weapons development. The East Asian Summit emerged in 2005 amid debate over the scope of its membership, with some favoring a more exclusive East Asian scope and others open to broader Asia-Pacific membership. A compromise allowed for broader membership by those Asia-Pacific countries willing to meet several requirements related to ASEAN and its Treaty of Amity and Cooperation.[28]

The significance of these and other regional groups and the overall trend of regional governments employing such multilateral means are widely debated. On one side are skeptics who acknowledge that these burgeoning groupings are useful meetings for the exchange of information and building relationships and perhaps a greater degree of trust among participating leaders but tend to see the groups as commonly unable to accomplish much of substance, in large measure because they are made up of generally independent-minded nationalistic governments that often are suspicious of their fellow members and are determined to preserve their independence and sovereignty in the regional groups. Moreover, regional powers (notably China and Japan, but also India and others) have shown a tendency to compete for regional leadership and to use the regional groupings as an arena for such competition. This tendency complicates efforts at regional cooperation.[29]

The importance of the emerging regional groups is highlighted by many Asia-Pacific government leaders as well as by specialists and commentators pointing to trends toward greater international cooperation among Asian governments. They see the governments as driven by common economic concerns and interests, especially growing trade and investment flows among them, and by common security problems that seem to require going beyond bilateral relations or other existing multilateral means to seek solutions. Some see the emergence of a new regional order in the Asia-Pacific that will rely on ever-closer cooperation among regional governments in their various groupings and will be less influenced than in the past by the power and policies of what are seen as nonregional powers, particularly the United States. They see an increasing convergence among regional leaders backed by emerging sizeable middle classes and elites in Asian cities that increasingly resemble each other, having similar lifestyles and common entertainment and communication networks.[30]

War on Terror and North Korean Provocations

Changes brought about by the Global War on Terror that began in 2001 and by North Korea's provocative pursuit of nuclear weapons, ballistic missile systems, and other systems represent the most significant security issues influencing the recent policy environment in the Asia-Pacific region in ways relevant to U.S. interests and policy.[31]

There remain other regional security hot spots. Off-again, on-again tensions over Taiwan pose the risk of a conflict or confrontation between China and the United States, possibly also involving Japan.[32] The conflict between India and Pakistan over contested claims to Kashmir has been the focal point of concern about possible nuclear war in South Asia.[33] There were significant upticks in tensions over these two disputes earlier in the decade, but they appeared by 2007 to have subsided under constraints imposed by concerned powers and by the countervailing interests of the governments concerned.

Concerns over the war on terrorism also seemed to subside as the decade moved on,[34] but its effect on the region was enormous. This was especially true in South and Central Asia, where the toppling of the Taliban regime in Afghanistan and continued armed struggle against Taliban and allied forces in the country saw a massive upswing in U.S. and NATO involvement that continues up to the present. The effect of the war on terrorism on the region saw the United States become Pakistan's most important foreign supporter, large deployments of U.S. and NATO forces in Afghanistan and much smaller deployments in some nearby states, and much closer U.S. security cooperation with India.[35]

For a while after the September 11, 2001, terrorist attacks on America, the United States pushed hard to make Southeast Asia a "second front" in the war on terrorism. It pressed for regional forums like APEC to move beyond their past focus on economic issues and to stress antiterrorism initiatives supported by the United States. It drove and assisted Southeast Asian states to do more to deal with terrorist groups in their countries. Prompted by terrorist attacks in Indonesia and the Philippines, these governments engaged in greater antiterrorist cooperation among themselves and with the United States and other concerned powers. This included enhanced efforts to prevent terrorists from disrupting the Malacca Strait and other important communication routes through Southeast Asia.[36]

Thus, the prominence of the United States in the region as a result of the war on terror significantly changed the Asia-Pacific environment. The war saw the United States become almost overnight the most important foreign power in South Asia, in the unprecedented position of having good relations with both India and Pakistan at the same time. And it increased U.S. involvement and importance, along with NATO, in Central Asia, and U.S. involvement in Southeast Asia. At the same time, however, the sometimes heavy-handed U.S. pressure for antiterrorist cooperation also affected the regional environment by alienating regional governments and broader elite and popular opinion. More importantly, as noted earlier in this book, the U.S. war in Iraq was very unpopular among Asia-Pacific leaders, elites, and public opinion. This changed the regional dynamics by strengthening the tendencies of regional leaders to keep the U.S. government at a distance and at times to seek solutions to regional problems in ways that would minimize the influence of or even exclude the United States.

Regarding North Korea, U.S. policies and practices and those of other concerned powers in dealing with the regime in Pyongyang in the post–Cold War period have followed an erratic pattern. The policies and practices have been driven in part by major shifts in North Korea's policies and practices during this period. The United States and concerned foreign powers have had difficulty coming up with ways to stop North Korea's advancing development of nuclear weapons, ballistic missiles, and related technologies and the serious consequence they pose for Asia-Pacific security. In late 2007, there was optimism that the United States and concerned powers had found a way to stop the advancement of the North Korean programs, but it remained to be seen whether their efforts would actually eliminate North Korean nuclear weapons. Overall, the North Korean programs remain a source of great importance and uncertainty in the prevailing regional environment.[37]

To recap the findings on U.S. policy toward North Korea discussed in chapter 2, the swings in U.S. and international approaches toward the North Korean administration and its nuclear weapons program during the post–Cold War period include the following highlights. U.S.-led confrontation over North Korea's nuclear weapons program led to negotiations and the Agreed Framework accord of 1994. The Agreed Framework was controversial in the United States, and suspected North Korean cheating, along with North Korea's provocative ballistic missile testing, prompted renewed negotiations led by former U.S. defense secretary William Perry in 1999.

North Korea's abrupt shift toward reconciliation with South Korea, resulting in a Pyongyang summit between North and South Korean leaders in 2000, had an important if temporary impact on the approach by the United States and other concerned powers to the North Korean administration. For a time, senior officials of these countries sought improved relations through widely publicized high-level dialogues.

This strategy changed with the new U.S. administration of George W. Bush. This administration's harder line stalled progress in U.S. relations with North Korea and divided the United States from South Korea, China, and Russia, which favored a more flexible stance toward North Korea. A crisis arose in late 2002 when North Korea responded to U.S. accusations that it was developing a clandestine highly enriched uranium nuclear weapons program and the United States cut off oil deliveries to North Korea provided for under the terms of the Agreed Framework. In response, North Korea publicly broke its promises in the Agreed Framework, withdrew from the Nuclear Non-Proliferation Treaty, and proceeded to openly produce nuclear weapons.

In a subsequent mix of U.S. pressure and negotiations, Bush administration officials worked with China—and later with Japan, South Korea, and Russia in the Six-Party Talks—seeking to curb or end North Korea's nuclear weapons program. Those talks went through twists and turns, mainly due to North Korean moves in reaction to U.S. steps that sometimes stressed a hard line toward North Korea and sometimes a more flexible approach.

An agreement on principles governing a settlement of the North Korean nuclear issues was reached in the Six-Party Talks in Beijing in September 2005. This was followed by stalemate and then a major crisis when North

Korea conducted seven ballistic missile firings in July 2006 and then on October 9, 2006, a nuclear weapons test. North Korea subsequently agreed to return to the Six-Party Talks, and an agreement reached in those talks on February 13, 2007, outlined steps to meet U.S. and North Korean concerns regarding the North Korean nuclear program and related issues. At this time, the United States showed itself to be more willing than in the past to meet North Korea's long-standing demand for direct bilateral negotiations with the United States.

The February 2007 agreement was widely seen as a first step in an uncertain process that held out a promise to manage the consequences of North Korea's nuclear weapons development and over time to curtail and ultimately end North Korea's nuclear weapons. In the interim, regional concern over North Korea's nuclear program and the ability of Pyongyang to take new provocative actions having a serious effect on the regional security environment remained high. At the same time, most concerned powers, including the United States, took steps and made pledges designed to ease tensions and promote accommodation with North Korea.[38]

U.S. Policy

After the Cold War, many countries in the region at first foresaw U.S. decline and withdrawal. This made some Asia-Pacific countries anxious, fearing instability and other adverse consequences accompanying a U.S. departure. In response, Asia-Pacific governments from Australia to Singapore endeavored to keep the United States interested and involved in regional affairs.

For their part, Chinese strategists predicted in more positive terms the emergence of a multipolar world following the end of the Soviet Union in 1991. The U.S. position as the world's sole superpower and U.S. power and influence in the Asia-Pacific were expected to decline as Asian and other powers, including China, Russia, Japan, and India were anticipated to take more prominent positions in regional and international governance once America's superpower status weakened and declined. This was depicted as a favorable development for China and Chinese interests, especially since Chinese commentators tended to see a consistent and often malign U.S. strategy of global domination and assumed a predatory U.S. hegemony in the Asia-Pacific and in world affairs.

Over time, this prediction was superseded by regional anticipation and uncertainty over resurgent U.S. strength and what it would be used for in Asia-Pacific and world affairs. Growing U.S. economic and military power seemed to be widening the gaps between the United States and other powers, including those in Asia that suffered direct and indirect negative fallout from the Asian economic crisis. It had become clearer to Chinese strategists by the mid-1990s that the world was not moving as quickly toward multipolarity as they had earlier supposed. Chinese analysts then tended to characterize the world power align- ment as "one superpower, many great powers." Continuing an awk- ward Chinese adjustment to resurgent U.S. power, by 1996, one Chinese observer remarked, "The superpower is more super, and the many great powers are less great."[39]

Further evidence of Asia-Pacific adjustment to expanding U.S. power and influence was seen at the start of the Kosovo crisis in 1999. Asia- Pacific observers did not expect the United States to use political, eco- nomic, and especially military power and influence to achieve goals that many did not see as warranting such a strong U.S. effort. Polling data and a variety of other reporting showed that the U.S. intervention in Kosovo reinforced uncertainty in the Asia-Pacific over U.S. objectives and per- ceived U.S. unilateralism.[40]

The Clinton administration's decisions in early 2000 to seek amend- ment of the Anti-Ballistic Missile (ABM) treaty and move forward with a National Missile Defense (NMD) program in conjunction with stepped- up Theater Missile Defense (TMD) programs in Asia divided the region. The subsequent deliberations delaying final decisions on missile defense reduced to some degree the urgency of this issue in the Asia-Pacific, but divisions and debate were increased when the incoming Bush administra- tion pushed forward with missile defense plans and programs.

China and Russia for a time were united and strongly opposed the U.S. missile defense plans. By early 2001, Russia compromised with the United States on amending the ABM treaty—a step China opposed. Although Japan had reservations about the U.S. NMD program, Tokyo nevertheless continued to move ahead with Washington to jointly develop TMD for Japan. South Korea, particularly sensitive to China's opposition, avoided endorsing the U.S. missile defense efforts. ASEAN governments, also feel- ing Chinese pressure, mildly criticized the U.S. plans or refrained from comment. India, like Russia, saw its interests best served with greater flexibility and less opposition to the U.S. initiative.[41]

After 9/11, the Bush administration pushed hard to get all participants at the APEC summit meeting in Shanghai during October 2001 to en- dorse a broad declaration against international terrorism. An assertive U.S. approach to Pakistan compelled Islamabad to reverse its policy as the U.S.-led war against the Taliban regime in Afghanistan began. Most Asia-Pacific governments went along with the string of many unilateral U.S. initiatives in the war on terror, though the U.S.-led military attacks against the Taliban in Afghanistan received a mixed reception. Indonesia and Malaysia were reluctant to antagonize significant elements of their large Muslim populations, who judged the U.S. military actions excessive and unjustified. Pakistan's government was placed in a particularly difficult position when it decided ultimately to side with the United States.[42]

The Bush administration's unilateral shift to a hard line against North Korea upset South Korea and China and complicated U.S. relations with Japan. Furthermore, the war in Iraq was broadly unpopular with elite and public opinion in the Asia-Pacific region. Most regional governments saw their interests better served by avoiding confrontation with the United States, though Russia joined France and Germany in opposing the U.S.-led invasion through maneuvers in the United Nations, and China joined them but avoided prominence in opposition to the United States.[43]

The Asia-Pacific governments and broader elite and public opinion also tended to view U.S. efforts to foster market economies and political issues and values such as human rights and democracy as driven by often unpredictable U.S. domestic interests that came at the expense of the national sovereignty of regional states. Even the closest U.S. ally in the region, Australia, privately voiced frustration over how perceived domestic interests influence U.S. policies in these areas. Australia has differed to varying degrees with the U.S. posture on human rights and democracy in regard to Myanmar, Cambodia, and China.[44]

As the Bush administration entered its final years, it came to be seen as beleaguered and weakened by Asia-Pacific and other commentators. In 2007, the war in Iraq was failing and seemed unsustainable; U.S. government spending deficits were very large and U.S. trade deficits were massive and ballooning out of control, raising fears of an economic crash or downturn of major proportions in the United States; and divided government between an often inflexible president and a newly empowered Democratic majority in Congress forecast gridlock and ineffective, confrontational governance.

As noted in the introduction of this book, commentators in the Asia-Pacific and elsewhere under these circumstances often saw the United States in a period of decline in Asia. The U.S. government was said to be inattentive to new and important developments in the region, notably the rise of interregional trade that seemed to diminish the economic importance of the United States for the Asia-Pacific region and the rise of regional multilateral groupings to govern important regional issues. The United States was thought to be losing out particularly to a rising China, which some predicted was emerging as the new central leader in Asia as a preoccupied and weakened United States waned in power and influence.

In sum, there have been remarkable shifts in perceptions of U.S. power and influence in the Asia-Pacific during the course of a decade and a half. These shifts in U.S. power and influence in the Asia-Pacific—from perceived weakness to resurgent strength to assertive unilateralism to newly perceived weakness—seriously impact the calculations of regional governments and their views of the regional environment that provide the context for their policies and behaviors.

Overall, these five broad categories of determinants of regional dynamics in Asia and the Pacific have their roots in and are reflected by the salient priorities of government leaders in the region. The following chapters examine those priorities in depth. They are followed by an assessment in chapter 9 that shows how regional dynamics, rooted in and reflected by individual governments' priorities, lead to several significant trends in Asia and the Pacific that pose major challenges and opportunities for the United States. On that basis, the chapter forecasts the outlook for U.S. relations with the region.

NOTES

1. In addition to the studies cited in the bibliography, see the following from the National Intelligence Council (NIC): *Mapping the Global Future: Report of the National Intelligence Council's 2020 Project*, NIC 2004-13 (Washington, D.C.: GPO, 2004), 27–40, 47–63; *Global Trends 2015: A Dialogue about the Future with Nongovernment Experts*, NIC 2000-02 (Washington, D.C.: GPO, 2000), 60–64; *East Asia and the United States: Current Status and Five-Year Outlook*, Conference Report CR 2000-02 (Washington, D.C.: GPO, 2000).

2. These global trends and the responses to them by Asia-Pacific countries are discussed in NIC, *Mapping the Global Future*, 8–36, 38–61, 74–78, 112–14; and NIC, *Global Trends 2015*.

3. NIC, *Mapping the Global Future*, 58–61.

4. NIC, *Global Trends 2015*, 19–26.

5. Erica Downs, *China*, Brookings Foreign Policy Studies Energy Security Series (Washington, D.C.: Brookings Institution, 2006); Peter Evans, *Japan*, Brookings Foreign Policy Studies Energy Security Series (Washington, D.C.: Brookings Institution, 2006); Tanvi Madan, *India*, Brookings Foreign Policy Studies Energy Security Series (Washington, D.C.: Brookings Institution, 2006).

6. NIC, *Global Trends 2015*, 26–32.

7. NIC, *Mapping the Global Future*, 52–58, 76–77.

8. NIC, *Mapping the Global Future*, 28–30; Naoko Munakata, *Transforming East Asia: The Evolution of Regional Economic Integration* (Washington, D.C.: Brookings Institution Press, 2006).

9. NIC, *Global Trends 2015*, 32–34.

10. Michael Leifer, *Asian Nationalism* (London: Routledge, 2000); NIC, *East Asia and the United States*, 3; NIC, *Global Trends 2015*, 38–49.

11. NIC, *East Asia and the United States*, 1–2; NIC, *Mapping the Global Future*, 64–72.

12. NIC, *East Asia and the United States*, 83–94; NIC, *Mapping the Global Future*, 25–72, 114–15.

13. Sheldon Simon, ed., *The Many Faces of Asian Security* (New York: Rowman & Littlefield, 2001); Tim Cook, *North Korea and Iran: Nuclear Futures and Regional Responses*, NBR Special Report no. 13 (Seattle: National Bureau of Asian Research, 2007).

14. Samuel Kim, *East Asia and Globalization* (Lanham, Md.: Rowman & Littlefield, 2000).

15. David Shambaugh, ed., *Power Shift: China and Asia's New Dynamics* (Berkeley: University of California Press, 2005); Bates Gill, *Rising Star: China's New Security Diplomacy* (Washington, D.C.: Brookings Institution Press, 2007); Susan Shirk, *China: Fragile Superpower* (New York: Oxford University Press, 2007).

16. C. Raja Mohan, "Poised for Power: The Domestic Roots of India's Slow Rise," in *Strategic Asia, 2007–2008: Domestic Political Change and Grand Strategy*, ed. Ashley J. Tellis and Michael Wills, 177–210 (Seattle: National Bureau of Asian Research, 2007).

17. Richard Samuels, "Japan's Goldilocks Strategy," *Washington Quarterly* 29, no. 4 (Autumn 2006): 111–27.

18. Bruce Vaughn and Wayne Morrison, *China-Southeast Asia Relations: Trends, Issues, and Implications for the United States*, CRS Report RL32688 (Washington, D.C.: Congressional Research Service, Library of Congress, April 6, 2006).

19. NIC, *Mapping the Global Future*, 55–58.

20. NIC, *Global Trends 2015*, 63; NIC, *Mapping the Global Future*, 27–63.

21. Michael J. Montesano, "Thailand in 2001: Learning to Live with Thaksin?" *Asian Survey* 42, no. 1 (January/February, 2002): 94–96, 98; Patricia Martinez, "Malaysia in 2001: An Interlude of Consolidation," *Asian Survey* 42, no. 1 (January/February, 2002): 136–38.

22. Marcus Noland, "Economic Interests, Values, and Policies," in *East Asia and the United States*, 73–82.

23. NIC, *Global Trends 2015*, 32–33, 61–63; NIC, *Mapping the Global Future*, 27–37.

24. William Watts, "Convergence/Divergence in Political Interests, Values, and Policies," in NIC, *East Asia and the United States*, 57–72; Martin Young, "Asia Battle against the Web," *Asia Times*, May 16, 2007.

25. Azar Gat, "The Return of Authoritarian Great Powers," *Foreign Affairs* 86, no. 4 (July/August 2007): 59–69.

26. NIC, *Global Trends 2015*, 32–33; NIC, *Mapping the Global Future*, 27–37.

27. Stanley Foundation, "New Power Dynamics in Southeast Asia: Issues for U.S. Policymakers," Policy Dialogue Brief, October 2006, http://www.stanleyfdn.org/publications/pdb/spcpdb06.pdf.

28. Dick Nanto, *East Asian Regional Architecture: New Economic and Security Arrangements and U.S. Policy*, CRS Report RL33653 (Washington, D.C.: Congressional Research Service, Library of Congress, September 18, 2006), 18–25.

29. Michael Yahuda, *The International Politics of the Asia-Pacific* (New York: RoutledgeCurzon, 2004), 223–39.

30. Joshua Kurlantzick, "Pax Asia-Pacifica? East Asian Integration and Its Implications for the United States," *Washington Quarterly* 30, no. 3 (Summer 2007): 67–77.

31. Ashley J. Tellis and Michael Wills, eds., *Strategic Asia, 2004–2005: Confronting Terrorism in the Pursuit of Power* (Seattle: National Bureau of Asian Research, 2004); Atlantic Council of the United States, *A Framework for Peace and Security in Korea and Northeast Asia* (Washington, D.C.: Atlantic Council of the United States, 2007).

32. Richard Bush and Michael O'Hanlon, *A War Like No Other* (Hoboken, N.J.: Wiley, 2007).

33. John H. Gill, "India and Pakistan: A Shift in the Military Calculus?" in *Strategic Asia, 2005–2006: Military Modernization in an Era of Uncertainty*, ed. Ashley J. Tellis and Michael Wills, 237–68 (Seattle: National Bureau of Asian Research, 2005).

34. Amitav Acharya and Arabinda Acharya, "The Myth of the Second Front: Localizing the 'War on Terror' in Southeast Asia," *Washington Quarterly* 30, no. 4 (2007): 75–90.

35. K. Alan Kronstadt, *Terrorism in South Asia*, CRS Report RL32259 (Washington, D.C.: Congressional Research Service, Library of Congress, August 9, 2004).

36. Mark Manyin, *Terrorism in Southeast Asia*, CRS Report RL31672 (Washington, D.C.: Congressional Research Service, Library of Congress, August 13, 2004).

37. Ralph A. Cossa and Brad Glosserman, "Multilateral Progress Pending on Multiple Fronts," *Comparative Connections* 9, no. 3 (3rd Qtr 2007): 1–4, http://www.csis.org/media/csis/pubs/0703q.pdf.

38. Donald G. Gross and Hannah Oh, "Agreement with North Korea, Progress with the South," *Comparative Connections* 9, no. 3 (3rd Qtr 2007): 41–47, http://www.csis.org/media/csis/pubs/0703q.pdf.

39. Rosalie Chen, "China Perceives America," *Journal of Contemporary China* 12, no. 35 (2003): 286.

40. Watts, "Convergence/Divergence"; Robert Manning, "The Perils of Being Number 1: East Asian Trends and U.S. Policies to 2025," in NIC, *East Asia and the United States*, 57–82, 83–94.

41. Atlantic Council of the United States, *Missile Defense in Asia* (Washington, D.C.: Atlantic Council of the United States, 2003).

42. Aaron L. Friedberg, "United States," in *Strategic Asia, 2002–2003: Asian Aftershocks*, ed. Richard J. Ellings and Aaron L. Friedberg, 18–30 (Seattle: National Bureau of Asian Research, 2002).

43. Robert Sutter, "United States: U.S. Leadership—Prevailing Strengths amid Challenges," in Ellings and Friedberg, *Strategic Asia, 2002–2003*, 33–52.

44. John Baker and Douglas Paal, "The U.S.-Australia Alliance," in *America's Asian Alliance*, ed. James Blackwill and Paul Dibb, 87–110 (Cambridge, Mass.: MIT Press, 2000). See also the discussion of Australian-U.S. differences in Jonathan Pollack, ed., *Asia Eyes America: Regional Perspectives on U.S. Asia-Pacific Strategy in the 21st Century* (Newport, R.I.: U.S. Naval War College, 2007).

6

✛

Chinese and Taiwanese Government Priorities

Those endeavoring to understand the priorities that determine the foreign policy of the People's Republic of China (PRC) after the Cold War have a wealth of books, articles, and other assessments and analyses by scholars and specialists in Chinese foreign policy. These works document ever-expanding Chinese interaction with the outside world through economic exchanges in an era of globalization, along with broadening Chinese involvement in international organizations dealing with security, economic, political, cultural, and other matters. They demonstrate a continuing trend toward greater transparency in Chinese foreign policy decision making and policy formation since the beginning of the era of Chinese reforms following the death of Mao Zedong in 1976. As a result, there is considerable agreement backed by convincing evidence in these writings about the course and goals of contemporary Chinese foreign policy and how they affect the United States.[1]

In the post-Mao period, Chinese Communist Party (CCP) leaders have focused on economic reform and development as the basis of their continued survival as the rulers of China. Support for economic liberalization and openness has waxed and waned, but the overall trend has emphasized greater market orientation and foreign economic interchange as being critical in promoting economic advancement and, by extension, supporting the continued CCP monopoly on political power. For a time, the leaders were less clear in their attitudes toward political liberalization and change, with some in the 1980s calling for substantial reform of the authoritarian Communist system. Since the crackdown at Tiananmen Square in 1989, there has been a general consensus among the party elite in favor of controlling dissent and other political challenges, allowing for only slow, gradual, and often halting political change that can be closely monitored by the authorities.[2]

In foreign affairs, post-Mao Chinese leaders retreated from the sometimes strident calls to change the international system and worked pragmatically to establish relationships with important countries, especially the United States and Japan but also China's neighbors in Southeast Asia and elsewhere, who would assist China's development and enhance Beijing's overall goal of developing national wealth and power. The collapse of Soviet communism at the end of the Cold War posed a major ideological challenge to Chinese leaders and reduced Western interest in China as a counterweight to the USSR. But the advance of China's economy soon attracted Western leaders once again, while the demise of the USSR gave China a freer hand to pursue its interests, less encumbered by the long-term Soviet strategic threat.[3]

Against this backdrop, Chinese leaders by 1997 were anxious to minimize problems with the United States and other countries in order to avoid complications in their efforts to appear successful in completing three major tasks for the year:

- The July 1, 1997, transition of Hong Kong to Chinese rule
- The reconfiguration of Chinese leadership and policy at the Fifteenth CCP Congress in September 1997, the first major party meeting since the death of senior leader Deng Xiaoping in February 1997
- The Sino-U.S. summit of October 1997, which China hoped would show people in China and abroad that its leaders were now fully accepted as respectable world leaders following a period of protracted isolation after the 1989 Tiananmen crackdown[4]

Generally pleased with the results of these three endeavors, Chinese leaders headed by president and party chief Jiang Zemin began implementing policy priorities for 1998. At the top of the list was an ambitious multiyear effort, begun in earnest after the National People's Congress (NPC) meeting in March 1998, to transform tens of thousands of China's money-losing state-owned enterprises (SOEs) into more efficient businesses by reforming them (e.g., selling them to private concerns, forming large conglomerates, or other actions).

Consequently, Beijing embarked on major programs to promote economic and administrative efficiency and protect China's potentially vulnerable financial systems from any negative fallout from the 1997–1998 Asian economic crisis and subsequent uncertainties. Thus, at the NPC meeting in March 1998, it was announced that government rolls would be drastically cut in an effort to reduce inefficient government interference in day-to-day business management. And China's new premier, Zhu Rongji, initiated sweeping changes in China's banking and other financial systems, designed to reduce or eliminate the vulnerabilities seen elsewhere in Asia.

As a result of the September 1997 CCP congress and the March 1998 NPC meeting, a new party-government team was in place, managing policy without the guidance and guidelines set by such powerful leaders of the past as Mao and Deng. There were problems reaching consensus on the power-holding arrangements made at the party and people's congresses, but on the whole, top-level leaders seemed to be working smoothly together in pursuing Chinese policy interests.

Making collective leadership work is an ongoing challenge for China's top leaders. Traditionally, a single senior decision maker has dominated the PRC. Periods of collective leadership, notably after Mao's death in 1976, were short and unstable. President Jiang gained in stature and influence, but his power still did not compare to that exerted by Mao and Deng. When it came time for Jiang and his senior colleagues to retire, there was a distinct possibility of a renewed struggle for power and influential positions by up-and-coming leaders. Thus, the leadership transition was handled cautiously, with Jiang slow to hand over the control of military power to the new generation of party leaders headed by Hu Jintao.

Once he had assumed the leadership of the Chinese party, government, and military by 2004, Hu moved carefully in consolidating his position. He seemed well aware that if a major economic, political, or foreign policy crisis were to emerge, leadership conflict over what to do, how to do it, and who to do it could be intense. Hu and his associates dealt with such major issues as the crisis caused by the outbreak of SARS in China in 2002–2003 and the North Korean nuclear crisis beginning in 2003 with generally effective policies that endeavored to support the leadership's interest in preserving Communist rule in China.

The results of the Seventeenth Congress of the CCP in October 2007 appeared to underline a continuing cautious approach to political change and international and domestic circumstances that was designed to reinforce Communist Party dominance.[5] There was little sign of disagreement among senior leaders over the broad recent policy emphasis on economic reform, though sectors affected by reform often resist strenuously. The ambitious plans for economic reform, especially of the SOEs, were needed if China's economy was to become efficient enough to sustain the growth rates that would justify continued Communist rule and develop China's wealth and power. Joining the World Trade Organization (WTO) in 2001 strengthened the need for greater economic efficiency and reform in China.

The reforms also exacerbated social and economic uncertainties, which reinforced the Chinese administration's determination to maintain a firm grip on political power and levers of social control. By late 1998, instability caused by economic change and growing political dissent prompted the PRC leadership to initiate significant suppression of political dissidents and opposition activities. The repression continued into the next decade and appeared likely to last for the duration of the economic reform efforts.

The Hu administration gave more emphasis than its predecessor to dealing with the many negative consequences of China's rapid economic growth and social change. The results of the Seventeenth CCP Congress in October 2007 strongly underscored this emphasis. These negative consequences included glaring inequities between urban and rural sectors and coastal and interior areas; pervasive corruption by self-seeking government and party officials; environmental degradation; misuse of scarce land, water, and energy resources; and the lack of adequate education, health care, and social welfare for hundreds of millions of Chinese citizens. Under Hu, the party leadership emphasized using scientific methods to promote sustainable development conducive to fostering a harmonious Chinese order under the leadership of the CCP. Documents and official commentary related to the party congress underlined these themes.[6]

Against this background, foreign affairs generally remained an area of less urgent policy priority. Broad international trends, notably improved relations with the United States, have supported the efforts by the Chinese authorities to pursue policies intended to minimize disruptions and assist their domestic reform endeavors. The administration remains wary of the real or potential challenges posed by a possible economic crisis, Taiwan, efforts by Japan and the United States to increase their international influence in ways seen as contrary to Beijing's interests, India's Great Power aspirations and nuclear capability, and other concerns. The PRC has voiced special concern over the implications for China's interests of U.S. plans to develop and deploy theater ballistic missile defense systems in East Asia and a national missile defense for the United States. Chinese officials also decried the downturn in U.S.-China relations at the outset of the George W. Bush administration, but appeared determined to cooperate with the U.S.-led antiterrorism campaign begun in September 2001.

In recent years, Chinese leaders are seen to be focused on promoting China's economic development while maintaining political and social stability in China. These efforts undergird a fundamental determination of the CCP to be an exception to the pattern of collapsing Communist regimes at the end of the Cold War and to reinvigorate and sustain its one-party rule in China. Foreign policy is made to serve these objectives by sustaining an international environment that supports economic growth and stability in China. This is done partly through active and generally moderate Chinese diplomacy designed to reassure neighboring countries and other concerned powers, especially the United States, the dominant world power in Chinese foreign policy calculations. Chinese officials try to demonstrate that their growing economic, military, and political power and influence should not be viewed as a threat, but rather as an opportunity for greater world development and harmony. In the process, Chinese diplomacy gives ever-greater emphasis to engagement with and conformity with the norms of regional and other multilateral organizations as a means to reassure those concerned with the possible negative implications of China's increased power and influence.[7]

Chinese foreign policy places great emphasis on seeking international economic exchange beneficial to Chinese development. A large influx of foreign direct investment, aid, technology, and expertise has been critically important in China's economic growth in the post-Mao period. In recent years, the country has become the center of a variety of intra-Asian and other international manufacturing and trading networks that have seen China emerge as the world's third largest trading nation and the largest consumer of a variety of key commodities and raw materials. In stark contrast to the "self-reliant" Chinese development policies of the Maoist period that strictly restricted foreign investment and limited Chinese economic dependence on the outside world, China today depends fundamentally on a healthy world economy in which Chinese entrepreneurs compete for advantage and promote economic development as an essential foundation for continued CCP governance. At the same time, the world economy depends increasingly on China. Now a member of the WTO and other major international economic organizations, China exerts ever-greater influence in international economic matters as a key manufacturing center for world markets and an increasingly prominent trading nation with a positive balance of trade and the largest foreign exchange reserves in the world.

Chinese nationalism and security priorities also are important determinants in the nation's contemporary foreign policy. The CCP has placed greater emphasis on promoting nationalism among the Chinese peoples as communism has weakened as a source of ideological unity and legitimacy following the collapse of the Soviet Union and other Communist regimes and the Chinese government's shift toward free market economic practices. Nationalism supports the CCP administration's high priority on preventing Taiwan independence and restoring this and other territory taken from China by foreign powers when China was weak and vulnerable during the nineteenth and twentieth centuries. Chinese leaders are forthright in building advanced military power and voicing determination to take coercive measures to achieve nationalistic goals, especially regarding

Taiwan, even in the face of opposition by the power of the United States and its allies and associates. More broadly, Chinese leaders seek to build what they call "comprehensive national power"—particularly economic, military, and political power—as China seeks an as-yet ill-defined leading role as a Great Power in Asian and world affairs.

Meanwhile, Chinese official and popular attention has focused with great national pride on Beijing's hosting of the August 2008 Olympic Games. The Chinese government has seemed determined to avoid actions at home or abroad that might complicate a successful Olympics. The administration is expected to use the occasion to showcase China's many positive accomplishments to wide audiences abroad and to reinforce the legitimacy and power of the Communist administration in the eyes of the Chinese people and international audiences.

DEBATE OVER CHINA'S PRIORITIES

Despite considerable agreement among specialists about the course and many of the goals in Chinese foreign policy after the Cold War, there also is extensive debate over the durability of China's recent approach. Some specialists judge that China's leaders are following a firm strategy that will last well into the twenty-first century, while others argue that China's approach is subject to change, particularly as major uncertainties and variables push Chinese foreign policy in directions different than the recent course.[8]

Chinese government officials and some Chinese and foreign scholars and specialists emphasize that the mix of Chinese government priorities and prevailing conditions in the post–Cold War period provide the basis of a Chinese strategy of peace and development that will last for decades. The Chinese leadership is seen as determined to avoid confrontation in foreign policy as it pursues economic development at home and abroad in the interest of enhancing the legitimacy and standing of the CCP. China's cooperative diplomacy and international activism will grow as China seeks the role of a responsible world power endeavoring to preserve and enhance China's international rights and privileges while it pulls its weight with greater international contributions, commitments, and obligations.

Chinese leadership priorities regarding economic development and domestic stability also favor a foreign policy that is inclined to accept the world situation as it is and avoid the often disruptive and assertive Chinese initiatives in world affairs of the Maoist period. Thus, China's strategy is said to accept the prevailing international and regional balance of power and influence that is often dominated by the United States. It pursues China's advantage by working with existing regional and other international economic organizations and by cooperating more closely with international groupings dealing with security, politics, culture, the environment, and other matters.[9]

The State Council of the PRC issued a white paper from its Information Office in December 2005 that provided an outline of this view of China's strategy in foreign affairs. Entitled "China's Peaceful Development Road," the document stressed that achieving peaceful development has been the "unremitting pursuit" of the Chinese people and administration for almost thirty years and that China's approach will remain along these lines and compatible with Chinese and international circumstances for decades to come. Key features of the Chinese approach were said to include striving to sustain a peaceful international environment helpful to Chinese development and the promotion of world development and peace; achieving development beneficial to China and its economic partners through growing economic interchange conforming to economic globalization; and doing China's part to build a harmonious world with sustained peace and common prosperity featuring more democratic international decision making than prevailed in the past. While acknowledging problems and conflicts in contemporary world affairs, the overall optimistic assessment said that "there are more opportunities than challenges" in the world today and that the rise of China was one of the most salient international opportunities, as "China's development will never pose a threat to anyone."[10]

Among the more detailed assessments of China's overall foreign policy strategy by prominent Chinese officials and specialists was an article published in 2006 by two prominent specialists of the Chinese Academy of Social Sciences.[11] This study said there were four core concepts underpinning China's strategy in world affairs:

1. A drive for Great Power status in world affairs
2. A need for a stable international environment supportive of China's economic development
3. Restraint on the part of Chinese leaders in world politics in order to avoid onerous obligations and commitments that would hamper China's growth and development (this restraint was strong during the leadership of Deng Xiaoping in the 1990s)
4. A recognition by post-Deng (d. 1997) leaders that China's success at home and abroad depends on ever-closer interaction with world affairs, which requires China to take up more international responsibilities than in the past

It went on to highlight four features of China's current strategy. These are related to the four concepts above. They are:

1. Great Power diplomacy involving strong Chinese efforts to maintain good relations with the United States and other international powers and to underline China's image as a Great Power at home and abroad
2. Active and positive diplomacy and other interaction with China's neighbors to create a buffer and hedge of protection in the event the ups and downs of U.S.-China relations cause the United States to resume negative pressure against the Beijing government
3. A growing but still incomplete Chinese interaction with regional and international organizations, many of which were viewed with suspicion by China in the past but have come to be seen recently as more beneficial for Chinese economic, security, and other objectives
4. A selective but growing Chinese willingness to undertake international responsibilities and commitments that in the recent past had been shunned as costly drains on Chinese development

In practice, according to the two Chinese specialists, the Chinese strategy involves several important initiatives:

- Seeking comprehensive cooperation and partnerships with all states around China's periphery and important governments elsewhere in the world
- Emphasizing and demonstrating Chinese self-restraint in order to add to a benign image of China as not a threat but an opportunity for the world
- Willingness to put aside past repeated and vocal complaints against U.S. dominance and "hegemony" in world politics so long as the United States does not challenge core Chinese interests regarding Taiwan, Communist Party rule in China, and related issues
- A Chinese approach to economic development that opens the Chinese economy ever more widely to international influence so that as China rises in economic importance, the benefits of its expansion are spread widely throughout the world and China's new position is less likely to be seen as a threat to the international economy or to the economies of countries that interact with China
- Ever-greater Chinese involvement with regional and other multilateral bodies, designed to enhance China's international profile on the one hand while channeling Chinese power into these institutions,

thereby reducing the suspicions of neighbors and significant world powers, notably the United States

Among foreign assessments, a cogent analysis by the prestigious Institute for International and Strategic Studies entitled *China's Grand Strategy: A Kinder, Gentler Turn* was published in late 2004 and focused on the growing concerns in the United States and among some of China's neighbors in Asia over the rise of Chinese economic, military, and political power and influence as a key driver in contemporary Chinese strategy in world politics.[12] The strengthening of negative perceptions of China's progress by the United States and other powers would inevitably lead to the establishment of new balancing coalitions against China, the report averred, upsetting China's still incomplete efforts to develop and accumulate comprehensive national power sufficient to secure Chinese internal and international interests. Thus, a core objective in China's strategy in world affairs is to assure the continued smooth growth of Chinese wealth and power, while simultaneously preventing the emergence of counterbalancing alliances that might arise in response to such growth.

To accomplish its goals, China has settled on an approach affirming Beijing's permanently peaceful intentions; emphasizing good neighbor relations designed to wean states, especially neighboring ones, away from potentially balancing behavior or coalitions; using China's economic strength as leverage to increase dependence on China by potential rivals; and accommodating and appeasing the reigning hegemon, the United States—at least until the point where Beijing can cope with American power independently—while exploiting Asian and international dissatisfaction with the United States in order to enhance China's own efforts to create buffers and guard against U.S. pressure and dominance. China's broader international goals include giving notice of its arrival as a Great Power, forging friendly relations with more distant governments for the purposes of developing new allies and access to needed commodities, and preempting these countries from aiding the United States in any future effort to pressure China.

In contrast to the above assessments of a coherent strategy in Chinese foreign relations based on clear priorities of Chinese leaders are the findings of foreign specialists, including this writer, who emphasize complications and uncertainties in Chinese foreign policy that make it far from certain that the prevailing moderate Chinese approach will continue without interruption. In the area of Chinese national security, Thomas Christensen argued at the start of this decade that, while the priorities of the Chinese leadership seemed clear, "many of the means to reach the regime's domestic and international security goals are so fraught with complexity, and sometimes contradiction, that a single, integrated grand plan is almost certainly lacking, even in the innermost circles of the Chinese leadership compound."[13] Christensen summed up China's strategic goals along lines widely accepted by other specialists and commentators:

1. Regime security
2. Preserving territorial integrity
3. Gaining prestige, power, and respect on the international stage[14]

But he pointed out that this simple list contains "a rich menu of sometimes contradictory goals in a complex world that does not allow for a unified master plan."[15]

A graphic example of such contradictions and complexity involves Taiwan. China's commitment to territorial integrity and related Chinese nationalism drive the Chinese administration to give top priority to preventing Taiwan's moves toward independence. In the event of such Taiwanese movement, Chinese leaders repeatedly state that the PRC will use its burgeoning military buildup opposite Taiwan and attack the island and its U.S. military supporters, despite the catastrophic effect this would have on China's peace and development, the otherwise central objective in China's contemporary foreign policy.[16]

U.S. government assessments have repeatedly underlined the uncertainty about China's strategy and longer-term objectives and what they mean for the United States. Throughout the often white-hot debates in the United States over policy toward China during the Clinton administration (1993–2001), U.S. leaders from the president down emphasized that the U.S. policy of engagement with China was premised on the belief that firm and constructive U.S. interaction with the Chinese leadership would steer Beijing away from possible assertive and disruptive policy leanings, which were major concerns for U.S. leaders, toward policies of accommodation and cooperation with the United States and the prevailing international order.

The George W. Bush administration adopted somewhat tougher policies than Clinton's in trying to deter possible Chinese aggression against Taiwan and on other issues, but on balance it carried out a policy emphasizing firm and positive engagement with China that was designed to steer the Chinese government along paths compatible with U.S. interests.

Speaking in Japan in March 2005 during her first trip to Asia as secretary of state in the second term of the Bush administration, Condoleezza Rice affirmed the basic judgment in U.S. government circles that, while China's growth in economic, military, and political power and influence was a reality, it was unclear whether the Chinese government had determined to use this power in ways that benefited or undermined U.S. goals of regional and international stability and cooperation. She described China's rising power as "a new factor" in world affairs that "has the potential for good or for bad," and she asserted it was the role of the United States and its partners to "try and push and prod and persuade China toward the more positive course."[17]

Rice cited China's integrating into the WTO and working closely with the United States and others in talks dealing with North Korea, antiterrorism, and the United Nations as examples of the positive convergence of Chinese and U.S. policies. But she cautioned: "China's internal evolution is still underdetermined. And as we look at issues of religious freedom, issues of human rights, as we look to the relationship between Taiwan and China, we see that there are matters of concern that still might take a bad turn." She added that the United States needed to use its power and influence, and work closely with Japan and other allies and partners, to create in Asia and the world "an environment in which China is more likely to play a positive role than a negative role."[18]

Bush administration discourse on China emphasized the positive during the president's second term. Deputy Secretary of State Robert Zoellick did so in September 2005 in a speech calling on China to behave as a "responsible stakeholder" in sustaining an international order beneficial to China and others.[19] Secretary of Defense Robert Gates said in 2007 that he did not view China as an adversary. At the same time, however, the United States took military preparations and other steps widely seen in China and abroad as contingency plans or hedges in the event of aggressive Chinese military or other actions.[20]

UNCERTAINTIES INFLUENCING
CHINA'S POLICY IN WORLD AFFAIRS

This writer and others who argue for caution in defining and assessing Chinese strategy in contemporary world affairs are supported by a variety of recent scholarship and evidence highlighting major uncertainties governing Chinese foreign policy and behavior.[21] For one thing, there is plenty of evidence that the course of Chinese policy leading to the current emphasis on peace and development has not been smooth. Even in the brief period since the end of the Cold War, there have been many twists and turns, along with various international crises and policy debates in China, on the best course to take in prevailing circumstances. Chinese leaders decided to pursue a much more assertive stance against outside powers than that espoused by the current peace and development line when they launched China's tough stance and provocative military actions in the Taiwan Strait in 1995–1996. They openly debated whether or not to adopt a tougher stance against U.S. "hegemonism" following the U.S. bombing of the Chinese Embassy in Belgrade in 1999. And the Chinese government for several days allowed illegal violence against Japanese diplomatic and business installations during an upsurge of anti-Japanese sentiment in China in April 2005.

For another, foreign specialists cannot come up with a clear view as to whether the prevailing Chinese approach to world affairs reflects confidence, strength, and determination to continue the current course or vulnerability and uncertainty in the face of circumstances at home and abroad that could prompt change in China's international approach. The result is a mixed and often confusing situation pointing to Chinese leaders' confidence in some areas and uncertainty in others, with the level of confidence or uncertainty in some key policy areas prone to vary over time with changing circumstances. For example, those who track Chinese officials' asserted confidence or uncertainty over the key issue of Taiwan have documented several cycles of optimism and pessimism in recent years brought on by different policies of the Taiwan administration.[22]

Examples of such mixed assessments are seen in 2005's *Power Shift*, a compendium by prominent international specialists on China's increasingly important role in Asia. One article by Bates Gill highlighted ever-growing Chinese confidence in dealing with Asian affairs, seen notably through the Chinese evaluations in periodic government white papers that deal with international affairs. Overall, Gill detected a recent Chinese policy approach of constructive interaction with neighbors and other powers in bilateral and multilateral arrangements that "are both cause and effect of China's more confident perception of its international and global situation."[23]

By contrast, Jonathan Pollack emphasized that "beneath the confident veneer about China's economic success and its enhanced international standing, a more contingent forecast predominates." He noted that Chinese wariness and uncertainties flow from many unsettled questions about the new regional order, with the "longer-term U.S. strategy toward China being uppermost among these uncertainties." According to Pollack, the three broad objectives of China's regional strategy are defensive in nature, reflecting worries that the regional environment could change in directions adverse to Chinese interests.[24] Thus, he said:

> First, China is attempting to limit its exposure in America's strategic headlights, thus deflecting a direct U.S. focus on China's political-military capabilities and strategies. Second, China hopes to prevent any countervailing strategy that could limit the country's future military options and strategic reach. Third, China seeks to forestall or discourage coordinated regional responses to its enhanced economic power, military capabilities, and political influence.[25]

Yong Deng and Fei-ling Wang endeavored in their edited volume on Chinese foreign policy published in 2005 to add domestic Chinese leadership considerations to what Wang characterized as China's "peculiar sense of insecurity in a secure world." Wang asserted that despite recent accomplishments, "an increasingly strong sense of China's 'vulnerability' and even 'insecurity' is clearly present in Beijing." This sense came from the Chinese Communist administration's strong sense of being under siege following the collapse of Soviet and international communism at the end of the Cold War and a strong sense of nationalism that challenged the administration's ability to manage Chinese foreign policy in ways constructive for its interests. Wang advised that there would be a continuing "mixture of insecurity and secrecy" in Chinese domestic politics and decision making, and Chinese foreign policy would remain "deeply politicized." Thus, "foreign events and actions were often judged by the CCP's political consideration rather than by China's national interests. Foreign criticism is often met with defensive and ultra sensitive counterattacks."[26]

U.S.-CHINA RELATIONS ADD TO
UNCERTAINTY IN CHINESE FOREIGN POLICY

Relations with the United States are widely acknowledged as the most important bilateral relationship and a key determinant in Chinese foreign policy. Whether China's approach to international affairs continues along the self-proclaimed strategic direction of peace and development or veers toward assertiveness and confrontation or in some other direction is widely seen in China and abroad to depend heavily on the state of play in China's relations with the United States.

Lack of clarity in predictions of the future course of U.S.-China relations underlines the ambivalence about the future direction of Chinese foreign policy. Professor Aaron Friedberg, a prominent international affairs specialist and former deputy director of the U.S. vice president's national security staff, wrote an assessment in late 2005 dealing with underlying uncertainties in U.S.-China relations.[27] He questioned whether U.S.-China relations over the next decades would be marked by convergence toward deepening cooperation and peace or by deterioration leading to growing competition and possibly war. Assessing the enormous consequences of either path for China, the United States, and the international order, Friedberg warned that despite these consequences and the many studies of U.S.-China ties, the bottom line is profound uncertainty, with few willing to predict the outlook without major caveats and conditions.

Friedberg provided a matrix of the views of those specialists, officials, and others, mainly on the U.S. side, who participated in the discussion of future U.S.-China relations. He found a wide range of viewpoints, which he arranged in categories under the headings of main international relations theories: realism, liberalism, and constructivism; he subdivided each of those three categories to list those in the group who tended to be optimistic about the future course of U.S.-China relations and those who tended to be pessimistic. Friedberg found the most common debate was between liberal optimists and realist pessimists, but that each of these schools of thought raised key determinants that Friedberg judged in the end might have an important impact on the course of U.S.-China ties. At this point, he was only able to offer informed speculation as to how the determinants seen as important by the respective schools of thought might combine in ways that would foster cooperative or contentious U.S.-China ties in the years to come. He offered no definitive conclusion.

In sum, the priorities of China's leaders have emerged gradually in the post–Cold War period. They appear to focus on preserving stability at home and abroad, while advancing economic exchanges and development that help to legitimate continued rule by the Communist Party. Also important are broader Chinese interests to exert greater influence in Asian and world affairs; to promote nationalistic goals, notably regarding Taiwan; and to develop China's military as well as economic and political power. These priorities sometimes come into conflict with one another. When this happens, Chinese policy tends to shift direction. Shifts also have occurred during important international crises in the past and presumably could occur as a result of future ones.

TAIWANESE GOVERNMENT PRIORITIES: IMPLICATIONS FOR CHINA AND THE UNITED STATES

Along with relations with the United States, Chinese leaders in the post–Cold War period consistently have given top priority to dealing with what they call the "Taiwan issue" in China's foreign relations. As in the case of Chinese relations with the United States, China's relations with Taiwan have followed a sometimes tortuous path since 1989. In a broad sense, China's approach has involved three main elements: positive incentives, mainly involving ever-growing economic exchanges; coercion, seen in the impressive Chinese military buildup focused on Taiwan; and unremitting Chinese efforts to isolate Taiwan internationally. At some times, Chinese leaders have appeared confident that the mix of positive and negative incentives will meet Chinese interests regarding Taiwan. But at other times, they have seemed deeply frustrated. Most notably, at several junctures, they have appeared uncertain about how to prevent Taiwanese moves toward permanent separation from China.[28]

Taiwanese maneuvers toward autonomy have waxed and waned in the post–Cold War period, but on balance the trend has been toward greater Taiwan independence from China. This seriously challenges a core concern of Chinese leaders, who are intent on preserving Chinese sovereignty and nationalistic ambitions while pursuing a path of peace and development in Asian and world affairs conducive to enhancing the legitimacy, power, and prestige of the CCP administration in China. In the view of Chinese policy makers, the former goal requires the large-scale buildup of Chinese military forces directed at Taiwan, the United States, and possibly others, like Japan, that might get involved in a military conflict over Taiwan. And it requires periodic assertions of China's determination to use forceful means to prevent Taiwanese independence. These actions naturally alarm Taiwanese, U.S., Japanese, and many other international leaders and undermine the credibility of China's avowed determination to follow a foreign policy of peaceful relations based on mutual accommodation. They demonstrate that the recent accommodating direction of China's declared strategy in international affairs could change quickly and sharply toward a more confrontational one, especially if leaders in Taiwan move toward permanent separation or independence from China. The volatility of the Taiwan hot spot and its unpredictable consequences for China's overall foreign policy are enhanced by the fact that China often has been unable to control the actions of the leaders in Taiwan, who have been undeterred in pursuing opportunities for independence.[29]

The election in 2000 and reelection in 2004 of Chen Shui-bian as president of Taiwan were serious setbacks for China's interests regarding the island. Chen advanced what were widely seen as the pro-independence initiatives of the previous president, Lee Teng-hui. His efforts caused a serious upsurge in tensions in cross-strait relations in 2003–2004. U.S. intervention, not Chinese policy, proved effective in curbing Chen's pro-independence initiatives in 2004. Subsequent actions by China, and by Chen's political opponents in Taiwan, seemed to add to U.S. policy in curbing Chen's pro-independence moves. The Taiwanese president also faced serious political problems and declining approval ratings caused by corruption charges directed at his administration and his family. Chen nonetheless launched a new round of pro-independence initiatives and challenges to China in 2006 and 2007 that focused on a referendum coinciding with the Taiwan presidential election in March 2008 on whether the country should seek entry into the United Nations as "Taiwan," rather than under its formal name, the Republic of China. Chinese officials reacted firmly against these maneuvers.[30] Chen's party lost badly in legislative elections in January 2008 and in the presidential election in March 2008, and Taiwanese leaders anxious to ease tensions with China took power. This suggested that the Taiwan hot spot would cool, although

Taiwan seemed to remain a volatile issue, with the ability to upset China's stated emphasis on a foreign policy approach emphasizing peace, accommodation, and economic development.[31]

CRISIS, INTERVENTION, AND STALEMATE, 2003–2007

Chinese officials observed with dismay as cross-strait relations turned for the worse in 2003–2004 as a result of the policy and behavior of President Chen Shui-bian. Even though the Chen government had agreed not to change the country's name, flag, or the few provisions in the constitution that identify Taiwan with China, in the months before the presidential election of March 2004, he and his supporters strongly veered toward greater political independence for Taiwan. They rejected the principle of "one China," condemned China's pressure tactics, and pushed hard for broad-ranging legal and institutional reforms in civil service practices, education, cultural support, public information, diplomacy, and other areas that ended past government practices identifying Taiwan with China and reinforced Taiwan's identity as a country permanently separate from China. In this context, they sought major constitutional changes.[32]

Chinese and American officials viewed the Taiwanese reforms as steps toward independence that made it increasingly unlikely that Taiwan ever would voluntarily agree to be part of the PRC.[33] Beijing focused on the possible change in provisions in the constitution that identified Taiwan with China, warning that removing those provisions and establishing a formal and legally binding status for Taiwan as a country permanently separate from China would result in China's use of force. Washington was anxious to avoid this outcome. Overall, the situation in the Taiwan Strait became more tense. China's leaders found that their mix of economic incentives, proposals for talks, military threats, and coercive diplomacy obviously had failed to stop Taiwan's moves toward greater autonomy from China.[34]

While the PRC's long-term objective was reunification, Chinese leaders for the time being, probably at least until the end of the Chen administration in 2008, seemed focused on preventing further steps by Taiwan toward permanent separation. Under proposals by Deng Xiaoping and Jiang Zemin, supported by current Chinese leaders, Beijing stated that Taipei could have a high degree of autonomy under future arrangements, but insisted Taiwan must recognize itself as part of one China. Although Beijing's vision of a unified China remained vague, it was more clear on what it would not tolerate, warning that Taiwanese actions toward greater separation, in particular a declaration of independence, would be met with force.

Among the reasons for the Chinese leaders' acute concern over Taiwanese independence was the fact that Taiwan's status remained a deeply emotional and nationalistic issue for Chinese leaders and citizens. The Communist Party leadership saw its own legitimacy entwined with its ability to show progress toward the goal of reunifying Taiwan with the mainland. It was reluctant to deviate from past positions widely accepted in China, sticking to the mix of hard and soft tactics that, unfortunately for China, on balance had the effect of driving Taiwan further away. Beijing also perceived Taiwan as a security problem; its alignment with the United States and possibly Japan posed a barrier to China's regional and global influence. Taiwan could serve as a base for subversion in case of domestic turmoil on the mainland.[35]

In Taiwan, political forces were divided on cross-strait issues. President Chen Shui-bian, his ruling Democratic Progressive Party (DPP), and their more radical allies in Lee Teng-hui's Taiwan Solidarity Union (TSU) party represented the so-called pan-green camp—one side of the political spectrum that continued to push for reforms that strengthened Taiwan's status as a country permanently separate from China. On the other side was the "pan-blue camp" made up of the formerly ruling Kuomintang (KMT) Nationalist Party and their allies the People First Party, who generally were more cautious in taking political steps that might antagonize China.

As President Chen pursued his anti-China and pro-independence initiatives in 2003 and 2004, Chinese officials initially reacted with alarm. They viewed Chen's proposed reforms involving changes in the Taiwan constitution as steps toward independence and a possible cause for war. Seeing the growth of instability and an increased danger of conflict in the Taiwan area, U.S. officials also were concerned with Chen's moves and took extraordinary steps to warn against them. Standing alongside Chinese premier Wen Jiabao, President Bush publicly rebuked the Taiwanese president in a meeting with reporters in Washington, D.C., on December 9, 2003. Afraid that Taiwanese popular opinion and pan-blue leaders were moving toward a tougher stance vis-à-vis the PRC, Chinese officials urged U.S. and international pressure to rein Chen in. They judged that among the few options acceptable to them, a strident public Chinese stance probably would be counterproductive for China's purposes as it would likely increase support for Chen in the prevailing atmosphere in Taiwan.

Chen's narrow reelection victory in March 2004 showed Chinese and other observers how far the Taiwanese electorate had moved from the 1990s when pro-independence was a clear liability among the broad populace. Chinese officials were pleased that U.S. pressure sought to curb Chen's more ambitious reform efforts that flirted with de jure Taiwan independence, but they pushed for more overt U.S. pressure, including restrictions on U.S. arms sales. American officials continued to press

Chen to avoid provocative actions, but remained firm in asserting military support for Taiwan to deter China from using force against Taiwan. The Americans were similar to their Chinese counterparts in focusing on what the Taiwan leader would actually do regarding proposed political reforms. They intervened repeatedly in the lead-up to the 2004 legislative elections to highlight differences between U.S. policy and the assertive positions of President Chen and his supporters.

Chinese officials appeared to judge that they were not in a strong position to influence the factors that would blunt the Chen administration's push toward greater independence, but at the same time they were not able to tolerate Chen's initiatives. Chen seemed to be driven by election politics, his own and his party's ambitions, and a basic sense in Taiwan that China's military threat was minimal, especially given strong U.S. military support for Taiwan.[36]

The Bush administration by 2003 and 2004 took repeated public and private steps to shake Taiwan's assurance of U.S. support and thereby restrain the provocative pro-independence posturing by Chen. Highlights of such U.S. displays include Bush's December 9, 2003, public rebuke of Chen's cross-strait policies, Secretary of State Colin Powell's admonition in October 2004 that the United States did not regard Taiwan as an independent state, and Deputy Secretary of State Richard Armitage's assertion that Taiwan represented a big problem, "a landmine," for U.S. policy.[37] Signs of decline in U.S. support and friction in Washington-Taipei relations upset public opinion in Taiwan, prompted pan-blue accusations against the Chen administration, and caused policy reviews within the Chen government.[38]

The Chen administration became more aware that the recent level of U.S. support for Taiwan could decline if it was seen by Washington to be provoking serious tensions with China. Continued U.S. preoccupation with the conflict in Iraq and U.S. reliance on China in dealing with North Korea were seen to restrict U.S. tolerance of Taiwanese reforms or other measures that upset China. Taiwanese officials also came to worry that the Bush administration might revert to past pressure on Taiwan to resume cross-strait dialogue on terms Taiwan was reluctant to accept or that the United States might seek arrangements to avoid war or other understandings with China that were adverse to Taiwan's interests.[39]

RENEWED STALEMATE AND OUTLOOK

U.S. officials and nongovernmental specialists and their counterparts in China and Taiwan gave some credit to repeated public U.S. interventions against Chen Shui-bian's pro-independence rhetoric during the legislative election campaign as helping to turn Taiwanese public opinion away from the president and his party. They also acknowledged that the elections were focused on local candidates and concerns rather than island-wide issues relating to cross-strait relations and Taiwan-U.S. relations.[40]

The poor showing of the DPP candidates in the legislative election of December 2004 was seen by President Chen as a public rebuke of his assertive stance; he and his party therefore reverted to the lower public profile on cross-strait issues that he had used prior to 2003. Even when Beijing's insistence on following through with a planned antisecession law at the annual meeting of the National People's Congress in March angered Taiwanese public opinion, Chen maintained a low profile on cross-strait questions.[41]

The dramatic visits of KMT chairman Lien Chan and pan-blue leader James Soong to China in the first half of 2005 saw Chinese president Hu Jintao and other Chinese officials mute China's past insistence on reunification under the "One Country, Two Systems" formula that also was used to govern Hong Kong's return to China and that had long been rejected by large majorities in Taiwan. Hu and other Chinese officials and commentators also avoided discussion of a possible timetable for reunification of Taiwan with the mainland. They instead focused on the need to avoid further steps toward Taiwan independence and promised various cross-strait economic, cultural, educational, and other benefits for the Taiwanese people.[42]

Amid favorable publicity for the Lien and Soong summits in China, President Chen for a time appeared to vacillate about renewing contacts with China, but he soon reverted to positions at odds with China's insistence on maintaining one China and halting moves toward independence. Indeed, the Taiwanese president seemed to have revived his confidence following the May 14, 2005, National Assembly elections in which DPP candidates did better than in the December 2004 elections despite waves of publicity for pan-blue leaders visiting China, renouncing Taiwan independence, and criticizing the Taiwan's government stance on cross-strait relations.[43]

Looking out to the end of the Chen Shui-bian administration in May 2008, it seemed that constraints on Chen's resuming pursuit of pro-independence initiatives that could risk conflict with China would remain strong. Among the drivers and brakes affecting the Taiwanese president's policy and overall cross-strait relations, the United States continued to loom large. Bush administration policy appeared set to follow the outlines of existing efforts to deter China from attacking Taiwan and to keep Taiwan from unilaterally disrupting the status quo with provocative moves toward independence.[44] This dual deterrence policy was balanced with U.S. reassurances to China of support for a one-China policy as defined by the United States and opposition to Taiwan independence, along with U.S. reassurances to Taiwan of continued support and protection.[45]

Although the Chinese military buildup opposite Taiwan continued, the Bush administration policy was seen as providing effective deterrence to a Chinese attack.[46] The more recent U.S. efforts to curb pro-independence moves by President Chen and his administration also were widely viewed as effective. In general, the U.S. policy was seen as an important reason why cross-strait tensions would remain within bounds until 2008. China would appear to have no good reason to confront U.S. forces militarily, barring a provocation from Taiwan.

Chen's revival in 2006 and 2007 of political initiatives that antagonized China and concerned the U.S. government suggested that the Taiwanese president saw his interests best served by resurrecting pro-independence initiatives amid divided politics in Taiwan. However, anticipated U.S. intervention as seen in the 2003–2004 election campaigns suggested that such a course would run up against strong opposition from Taiwanese voters who were concerned about alienating the United States at a time of tension in relations with China.[47]

U.S. officials at the highest levels were said to be comfortable with the prevailing balance in U.S. policy between the PRC and Taiwan. President Bush appeared to understand and fully embrace the policy,[48] which was followed with greater consistency and rigor from late 2003 than in the earlier years of the Bush administration.

The goals of U.S. policy were limited.[49] Unlike in the case of North Korea, the U.S. administration was not trying to change circumstances; rather, it was trying to preserve stability by maintaining a rough status quo in cross-strait relations. U.S. officials would have liked to see dialogue between the Taiwanese and Chinese governments as a means to reduce misunderstanding and ease tensions—and if that were to lead to agreements reducing tensions, the United States would welcome that, according to U.S. officials. However, the Bush administration saw no need to mediate between the two governments or to take other extraordinary efforts to "fix" the Taiwan problem. Washington seemed content to manage cross-strait tensions so that they did not escalate, but it saw risks in deeper U.S. involvement in cross-strait relations or shifting U.S. policy. Those risks included serious complications in the Bush administration's relations with China, Taiwan, and the U.S. Congress at a time when American foreign policy remained heavily focused on the difficulties in Iraq and the broader war on terrorism.[50]

Meanwhile, there appeared to be some common ground to allow progress based on China's recent positive initiatives toward Taiwan, including permitting more Chinese tourists to visit Taiwan, Taiwanese farmers to sell fruit in Chinese markets, and other increased exchanges and communications to take place across the strait. China's practical measures were well received in Taiwan, and the Taiwanese government may see its interests best served by welcoming at least some of them. At a minimum, the Chinese initiatives improved the atmosphere in cross-strait relations, even if obstacles continued to block formal dialogue between the two governments. Presidential candidates for the March 2008 election seemed open to such improvements in cross-strait relations.[51]

As the U.S. government was seeking flexibility from both the Taiwanese and Chinese governments to resume dialogue, President Chen Shui-bian also found himself facing considerable domestic pressure to revive cross-strait talks. The Taiwanese president was on the defensive politically on account of serious charges, investigations, and trials of his close aides and his wife in 2006 and 2007 on grounds of corruption. His approval ratings remained very low, and there were mass demonstrations calling for his resignation.

On the other hand, Chinese leaders faced little domestic pressure to resume talks with Chen. China's military buildup opposite Taiwan continued to grow rapidly.[52] The pace and scope of Chinese purchases of sophisticated arms from Russia had advanced markedly since the late 1990s. U.S. leaders and military planners were not persuaded by the arguments of those who judged that China's buildup was mainly designed to intimidate Taiwan and that Chinese leaders had no intention of using these forces. They prepared resolutely to fight China over Taiwan if necessary, built up U.S. forces in the region to deter and if needed engage Chinese forces, and worked closely with their Taiwanese counterparts to encourage Taiwan to build defenses sufficient to hold out in the event of a Chinese attack. Publicly, U.S. defense officials registered disappointment with Taiwan's defense preparations, especially the decline in Taiwanese defense spending.

Meanwhile, China and Taiwan's rivalry and conflict in international affairs continued without letup. Despite the bad publicity associated with China's refusal to allow Taiwan representation of any sort with the World Health Organization (WHO) at the time of the 2003 SARS epidemic that originated in China, Beijing continued to block Taipei from interacting with the WHO, even as a "health entity" rather than a state government.[53] In recent years, the PRC outmaneuvered Taiwan to gain diplomatic recognition from Caribbean and African states. Taiwan won over tiny Nauru, which had switched to Beijing's side only three years earlier, but Costa Rica switched to the PRC, and Panama, Haiti, and the Vatican were seen as wavering in their alignment to Taiwan.[54]

In China, the Hu Jintao leadership continued to consolidate its power but appeared wary of taking positions at odds with long-standing nationalistic positions of the Chinese government that were backed by powerful leadership and popular sensitivities. The passage of the antisecession law seemed counterproductive to China's policy toward Taiwan following Chen Shui-bian's setback in the December 2004 legislative elections, but Chinese officials repeatedly claimed that nationalistic sensitivity made it very difficult to halt the passage of the law.[55] In this atmosphere, it appeared less than likely that the Hu administration would make significant overtures to Chen, barring a significant compromise by the Taiwanese leader. Hu's remarks and other Communist Party pronouncements on the Taiwan issue at the time of the Seventeenth CCP Congress in October 2007 reaffirmed this position.[56]

In Taiwan, President Chen was aware of a continued sharp split in domestic politics between pan-green and pan-blue adherents over cross-strait and other issues. This might compel him to stay with his political base in opposition to China's one-China policy. If China made no significant overtures to the Taiwan government and continued the strong military and diplomatic pressure widely seen as obnoxious by Taiwanese public opinion, Chen might see the best political course as using Taiwanese sentiment against China and those pan-blue leaders that chose to collaborate with the mainland.

It was unclear in 2007 how the various corruption scandals in his administration would affect Chen's approach to cross-strait relations. They clearly undermined popular support for the president and his party, weakening their ability to launch effective initiatives that might challenge the status quo in relations with the PRC.[57] In 2006 and 2007, Chen appeared weak in the face of mass demonstrations and legislative moves calling for his resignation as prosecutors brought to trial some of his top aides and his wife.

In sum, prevailing circumstances in late 2007 provided some assurances that cross-strait tensions would stay within bounds and avoid military conflict for the next few years. PRC leaders remained very reluctant to confront the United States militarily, unless provoked by egregious moves by Taiwan toward independence. Instead, they appeared to be waiting for the end of the Chen administration, anticipating a new president in Taiwan who will be easier to deal with. In this regard, the pan-blue leader, former KMT chairman Ma Ying-jeou, was viewed with private approval by officials and specialists in China.[58] In the interim, President Chen and his entourage may choose to revive their pro-independence agenda and take major risks in the process, but U.S. intervention proved effective in turning back such initiatives in 2004, and U.S. officials remained vigilant and prepared to do so again. The prevailing political mood in Taiwan also looked as if it was working against a successful revival of a pro-independence agenda by Chen and the DPP. Chen supported the referendum proposed for March 2008 calling for voters to decide whether the administration should seek entry into the United Nations as "Taiwan," as opposed to the "Republic of China." This vote presumably represents a test of strength between pro-independence forces in Taiwan and their opponents.[59] In the event, the candidates of Chen's political party and his proposed referenda were defeated in the elections of January and March 2008.

There is uncertainty in assessing how far the Taiwanese and Chinese governments might go in easing tensions and resolving their differences. Prevailing circumstances include a sharply divided polity in Taiwan, with the Chen administration and its political backers still strongly committed to a pro-independence agenda despite setbacks since late 2004 and 2008. The election of March 2008 likely will result in more moderation in Taipei on cross-strait issues. The Chinese leadership, while flexible in some respects on some issues, remains constrained by nationalistic imperatives and leadership sensitivities from taking major steps toward reconciliation with the Chen government. China likely will try to seek some common ground with the new Taiwanese president. The U.S. government favors cross-strait dialogue in order to help ease tensions, ensure regional stability, and preserve the status quo in Taiwan-China relations. For the time being, the potential costs and risks for the leaders of all three governments seem too great to expect any of them to make major moves to change existing policies until after Taiwan's presidential elections and inauguration of the new president on May 20, 2008. After that, there are possibilities of progress on smaller steps, including enhanced cross-strait economic and personnel exchanges and perhaps a revival of formal dialogue through the existing mechanisms, moribund since 1999, or other means. Even if such talks accomplished little, they would provide a means of more accurate communication between the two governments and perhaps a way to ease misunderstanding and miscalculation in an uncertain and potentially quite dangerous situation. Moreover, a renewed positive dialogue between Taipei and Beijing could lead to more significant progress in cross-strait relations, as both seem more ready than in the past to calm the turmoil of recent years.

NOTES

1. For sources and examples, see Robert Sutter, *Chinese Foreign Relations: Power and Policy since the Cold War* (Lanham, Md.: Rowman & Littlefield, 2007), 2.

2. David Shambaugh, "China's 17th Party Congress: Maintaining Delicate Balances," Brookings Northeast Asia Commentary, November 2007, http://www.brookings.edu/opinions/2007/11_china_shambaugh.aspx.

3. Denny Roy, *China's Foreign Relations* (New York: Rowman & Littlefield, 1998).

4. Robert Sutter, *Chinese Policy Priorities and Their Implications for the United States* (Lanham, Md.: Rowman & Littlefield, 2000), 18. See also the review of this period in Barry Naughton, *The Chinese Economy* (Cambridge, Mass.: MIT Press, 2007), and Tony Saich, *Governance and Politics of China* (London: Palgrave, 2004).

5. Kerry Dumbaugh, "China's 17th Party Congress, October 15–21, 2007," Congressional Research Service memorandum, October 23, 2007.

6. Maureen Fan, "China's Party Leadership Declares New Priority: 'Harmonious Society,'" *Washington Post*, October 12, 2006.

7. These developments and determinants are reviewed in Sutter, *Chinese Foreign Relations*, 2–3.

8. See the divergent assessments in Bates Gill, *Rising Star: China's New Security Diplomacy* (Washington, D.C.: Brookings Institution Press, 2007), and Susan Shirk, *China: Fragile Superpower* (New York: Oxford University Press, 2007).

9. Reviewed in Sutter, *Chinese Foreign Relations*, 3–4.

10. People's Republic of China, State Council Information Office, "China's Peaceful Development Road," *People's Daily Online*, December 22, 2005.

11. Yunling Zhang and Shiping Tang, "China's Regional Strategy," in *Power Shift*, ed. David Shambaugh, 48–70 (Berkeley: University of California Press, 2005).

12. Institute for International and Strategic Studies (IISS), *China's Grand Strategy: A Kinder, Gentler Turn* (London: IISS, 2004).

13. Thomas Christensen, "China," in *Strategic Asia, 2001–2002: Power and Purpose*, ed. Richard J. Ellings and Aaron L. Friedberg (Seattle: National Bureau of Asian Research, 2001), 27.

14. Ibid., 30.

15. Ibid., 28.

16. Ibid., 27–70.

17. U.S. Department of State, *Remarks at Sophia University by Secretary Condoleezza Rice*, Tokyo, Japan, March 19, 2005, www.state.gov (accessed November 21, 2007).

18. Ibid.

19. Robert B. Zoellick, "Whither China: From Membership to Responsibility?" remarks to the National Committee on U.S.-China Relations, New York City, September 21, 2005.

20. "Gates: China Not a Strategic Adversary," *China Daily*, March 8, 2007.

21. Reviewed in Sutter, *Chinese Foreign Relations*, 8–12.

22. Richard C. Bush, *Untying the Knot: Making Peace in the Taiwan Strait* (Washington, D.C.: Brookings Institution Press, 2005).

23. Bates Gill, "China's Evolving Regional Security Strategy," in Shambaugh, *Power Shift*, 247–65.

24. Jonathan Pollack, "The Transformation of the Asian Security Order: Assessing China's Impact," in Shambaugh, *Power Shift*, 329–46; quotes on 337 and 336.

25. Ibid., 330.

26. Fei-ling Wang, "Beijing's Incentive Structure: The Pursuit of Preservation, Prosperity, and Power," in *China Rising: Power and Motivation in Chinese Foreign Policy*, ed. Yong Deng and Fei-ling Wang, 19–50 (Lanham, Md.: Rowman & Littlefield, 2005); quotes on 20, 19, and 22.

27. Aaron Friedberg, "The Future of U.S.-China Relations: Is Conflict Inevitable?" *International Security* 30, no. 2 (2005): 7–45.

28. See review and sources in Sutter, *Chinese Foreign Relations*, 189.

29. Shirk, *China*, 181–211.

30. Bonnie S. Glaser, "Product Safety Plagues the Relationship," *Comparative Connections* 9, no. 3 (3rd Qtr 2007): 30, http://www.csis.org/media/csis/pubs/0703q.pdf.

31. Richard Bush and Michael O'Hanlon, *A War Like No Other* (Hoboken, N.J.: Wiley, 2007). For an alternative view, see Robert Ross, "Taiwan's Fading Independence Movement," *Foreign Affairs* 86, no. 2 (March/April 2006): 141–48.

32. For overall assessments of this period and Taiwan's policies, see, among others, Robert Sutter, "The Taiwan Problem in the Second George W. Bush Administration: U.S. Officials' Views and Their Implications for U.S. Policy," *Journal of Contemporary China* 15, no. 48 (August 2006): 417–42; and Robert Ross, "Explaining Taiwan's Revisionist Diplomacy," *Journal of Contemporary China* 15, no. 48 (August 2006): 443–58.

33. For a more detailed assessment of the twists and turns in Taiwan-China-U.S. interaction during this period and a detailed description of the sources and many interviews with U.S., Taiwan, and Chinese officials used in this review, see Sutter, *Chinese Foreign Relations*, 200–215.

34. David G. Brown, "Campaign Fallout," *Comparative Connections* 6, no. 4 (4th Qtr 2004): 89–96, http://www.csis.org/media/csis/pubs/0404q.pdf.

35. Christensen, "China," 47–51.

36. International Crisis Group, "China-Taiwan: Uneasy Détente," Asia Briefing No. 42 (Brussels: International Crisis Group, 2005).

37. Brown, "Campaign Fallout."

38. Interviews with U.S. government specialists on Taiwan, March–May 2005, and with Taiwanese and U.S. government and nongovernment specialists, Taiwan, May–June 2005.

39. Ibid.

40. International Crisis Group, "China-Taiwan."

41. Sutter, "Taiwan Problem," 425, 433.

42. The Chinese proposals are reviewed in International Crisis Group, "China-Taiwan."

43. "Chen's DPP Wins Taiwan Vote for National Assembly," Agence France-Presse, May 15, 2005; Keith Bradsher, "Few in Taiwan Bother to Vote on Constitutional Assembly," *New York Times*, May 15, 2005.

44. Sutter, "Taiwan Problem."

45. Ibid., 434–38.

46. Bush and O'Hanlon, *War Like No Other*, 163–64; Michael Chase, "U.S.-Taiwan Security Cooperation: Enhancing an Unofficial Relationship," in *Dangerous Strait*, ed. Nancy Bernkopf Tucker (New York: Columbia University Press, 2005), 162–85.

47. Thomas Christensen, "A Strong and Moderate Taiwan," speech to U.S.-Taiwan Business Council, Defense Industry Conference, Annapolis, Md., September 11, 2007, available at http://www.state.gov/p/eap/rls/rm/2007/91979.htm.

48. Consultation with a U.S. official knowledgeable of the president's views on this issue, March 30, 2005, and May 9, 2005.

49. Consultation with a senior U.S. official responsible for U.S. policy in East Asia and the Pacific, May 9, 2005.

50. Sutter, "Taiwan Problem," 438.

51. Yun-han Chu and Andrew Nathan, "Seizing the Opportunity for Change in the Taiwan Strait," *Washington Quarterly* 31, no. 1 (Winter 2007/2008): 77–91.

52. Bush and O'Hanlon, *War Like No Other*.

53. Charles Snyder, "Lone Letter Supports WHO Bid," *Taipei Times*, May 15, 2005; "Taiwan Blames China for Failed WHO Bid," Reuters, May 18, 2005.

54. These diplomatic changes are tracked by David G. Brown in the quarterly e-journal *Comparative Connections*, http://www.csis.org/pacfor. See also Elisabeth Rosenthal, "Hints of Thaw between China and Vatican," *International Herald Tribune*, May 22, 2005.

55. Bonnie Glaser, "The Anti-Secession Law and China's Evolving Taiwan Policy," *Taiwan Perspective E-Letter*, Institute for National Policy Research, Issue no. 67, March 21, 2005, http://www.tp.org.tw/eletter/story.htm?id=20007206.

56. Shambaugh, "China's 17th Party Congress."

57. Interviews with pan-blue and pan-green leaders, Taipei, May 2006.

58. Interviews in Beijing, Shanghai, and Guangzhou, May–June 2006.

59. Shelley Rigger, *Taiwan's Rising Rationalism: Generations, Politics, and "Taiwanese Nationalism"* (Washington, D.C.: East-West Center Washington, 2006); Ross, "Taiwan's Fading Independence Movement."

7

✛

Japanese and Korean Government Priorities

JAPANESE GOVERNMENT PRIORITIES

Japanese government priorities and behavior in foreign affairs after the Cold War have reflected changes at home and abroad that pulled Japanese policies in often contradictory directions and led to a general reduction in Japan's influence in Asian and world affairs. Japan's economic growth, the foundation of Japanese international influence in previous years, stalled for more than a decade as Asia's other large economies, notably China and India, rose in prominence. Reviving the Japanese economy required closer integration with China, South Korea, and other Asian economies, but Japanese relations with China and Korea were seriously complicated by burgeoning Japanese nationalism, which featured patriotic demonstrations by Japanese leaders that were grossly offensive to the peoples and leaders of those countries. Japanese officials and public opinion saw growing security threats to Japan posed by North Korea and China. This pushed Japan into a closer military relationship with the United States, even though Japanese leaders continued to be concerned that future shifts in U.S. policies could see the United States give less priority to Japan as it sought U.S. interests in Asian and world affairs.[1]

That the Japanese leaders were not settled on a clear set of post–Cold War priorities was reflected in scholarly assessments by Western specialists.[2] Japan was seen at first as a reactive state, responding to the course of world events rather than shaping them.[3] In the late 1990s, some specialists emphasized that Japan was becoming what was labeled a "reluctant realist," pursuing the more assertive and nationalist foreign policies

195

advocated by Japanese conservatives.[4] At the same time, however, other specialists saw continued Japanese tendencies to eschew military power in favor of diplomacy and international cooperation. Japan continued to secure access to outside markets through nonmilitary means such as diplomacy, trade, and foreign aid and tried to maintain diplomatic and trade relations with all nations as much as possible.[5]

For many years, Japanese and foreign specialists debated whether significant change was actually occurring in Japan. More recently, the debate focused on how significant the change is, how fast will it develop, how far will it go, what its principal drivers are, and what might it mean for the United States. The political system is undergoing major transformation, marked by the obsolescence of the one-party system, diminished bureaucratic power, increased influence of politicians, strained corporate-political ties, unprecedented volatility of the voting public, and unpredictability of politician behavior. In this environment, the United States has fewer direct levers of influence, but may have more indirect, nontraditional, or nongovernmental levers.[6]

Economic Trends

Japan's economic development appears to be the key to determining Japanese government priorities. The world's second greatest economic power, Japan remains very important to regional and global economic trends, but less so than in the past. Stalled growth from the early 1990s reduced Japan's international stature and undermined the confidence of Japanese business and government leaders. Globalization also forced Japanese economic elites to conduct more unconventional and pluralistic decision making in pursuit of policies that will work effectively in the new environment. They have been compelled to conform more to Western norms of behavior that depart from the past methods of "Japan Incorporated," but the record of reform remains mixed. Corporations and politicians are increasingly learning the lessons needed to restructure and are looking to outside experts for assistance. Still, the established rules and practices in Japan slow the economy's restructuring and serve to keep Japan from full engagement in the global trend to let the market dictate winners and losers.[7]

Economic experts continue to forecast a slow economic recovery in Japan. They doubt that the incremental and partial reforms seen thus far will be sufficient to significantly improve Japan's position as a leader in the global market. Factors that impede effective Japanese growth included heavy government and private indebtedness, a persisting dual economy consisting of a competitive export-oriented business sector and less competitive domestic enterprises, an aging society, and the perceived absence of an entrepreneurial spirit. At the start of the twenty-first century, some economic experts saw a more gloomy future of protracted stagnation caused by the possible failure of banking or other key sectors.[8]

The major problems of the Japanese economy were clear at the start of the twenty-first century. During the previous decade, Japan—after more than three decades of sustained high levels of economic growth—was mired in an economic slump that the government was ineffective in correcting. Poor economic performance put pressure on Japan's political system and depressed growth prospects in Asia. The Japanese government remained hard-pressed to implement a sweeping reform strategy because aggressive efforts to restructure Japan's economy initially would cause economic instability in the form of bankruptcies, unemployment, and probably recession.

Weak demand was producing a deflationary environment and eroding household and corporate balance sheets that were already burdened by large debt. This debt had a real value that was increasing by $160 billion—or 4 percent of gross domestic product (GDP)—each year. Deflation reinforced the Japanese cultural emphasis on saving, making government efforts to boost consumer spending increasingly difficult. The slowdown in the world economy in general, and the U.S. economy in particular, limited the boost that Japan was likely to receive from foreign purchases of its goods and services. Continued government efforts at fiscal stimulation may have been an effective tool for avoiding a steep downturn, but they were not able to restore growth. Increasing budget deficits—which annually equaled 6 percent of GDP—added to the gross public debt, which approached 135 percent of GDP in 2001.[9]

Japan's banking system was nearly insolvent, but the government leadership was hesitant to show the political resolve necessary to carry through with much-needed bank restructuring. Efforts to place the banking system on a solid financial foundation would, in the short run, almost certainly lead to bank closures and unemployment. Likewise, corporate restructuring would be difficult because of the traditional reluctance of managers to cut jobs. Gradual restructuring, however, appeared likely to occur, slowing new hiring and leading to unemployment, which would reinforce deflationary pressures.[10]

These structural and political barriers to economic recovery complicated Japan's efforts to achieve even modest levels of economic growth. Nevertheless, over the short term at least, Japan was not likely to suffer a sharp, destabilizing economic contraction. The government had the option to sustain the economy through monetary and fiscal policies. Tokyo still had the financial resources to prevent a systemic banking crisis, and the Bank of Japan had lent freely to failing banks in order to keep them afloat. The government could nationalize large insolvent banks if necessary. Japan had very little external debt; consequently, a precipitous fall in the value of the yen would not have created a foreign payments crisis such as several Southeast Asian nations faced during the 1997–1998 economic crisis.

Real GDP growth began to pick up in 2002. Until 2004, this recovery was heavily dependent on a boom in Japan's exports to China. Breaking the drag of the deflationary cycle that had held back Japanese growth over the previous decade seemed to require an increase in Japanese domestic demand. Strong signs of domestic-led growth began to show in 2004. After years of retrenchment, Japanese corporations saw profits rise, and they began to hire workers on a full-time basis and pay higher wages. Real wages in Japan in 2005 grew for the first time since 1997. Meanwhile, Japanese businesses by 2005 reported that excess capacity—a drag on investment and growth for more than a decade—had largely disappeared. Capital spending grew by 7 percent. Nonperforming loans in Japanese bank portfolios dropped from 40 percent in 2001 to under 20 percent in 2004.[11]

In sum, Japan seemed by 2005 to have finally turned a corner after more than ten years of stagnation to experience more sustained economic growth. The process had been gradual and incremental. Japanese businesses and banks adopted more flexible employment practices and gradually dealt with massive amounts of bad debt. Corporate takeovers became more common. Foreign investors were allowed a greater stake in the Japanese economy. The Japanese government undertook some high-profile reforms, adding to the efficiency in use of capital in the Japanese economy.

On the whole, however, the Japanese economy was still regulated and insulated when compared to the United States and some other Western-oriented economies. What was continuing was an incremental trend to reduce the role of the state, allowing market forces to operate in the interests of greater efficiency.

Looking forward, there are still obstacles and few signs of big increases in overall economic growth. Monetary and fiscal policies need to be managed in ways that promote sustainable growth. Japanese fiscal authorities face large deficits, but tightening the monetary or fiscal policies prematurely or too severely could halt the recent progress. Higher energy and natural resources prices negatively affect the energy- and resource-intensive sectors of the economy. A major long-term brake on Japanese growth is the aging Japanese population and overall decline in the Japanese workforce. The Japanese government anticipates that the workforce will decline 0.7 percent per year and that the total population could decline from 128 million to 100 million by 2050. These trends will almost certainly hold back the expansion of the Japanese economy, though their negative effects can be offset to some degree by increases in worker productivity, and Japan may see more employment for women and immigrants.[12]

The implications of these trends for U.S. and international interests seem generally clear. In a scenario of incremental reform and a possibly mixed record on sustaining economic growth and banking bailout, the most likely implication for broad Japanese participation in international political and security affairs would be a continuation of the narrow focus of the past. The earlier postwar era of rather extreme Japanese passivity in global affairs is certainly over, but the nature of Japan's future participation remains uncertain. A scenario of partial reform also could leave the Japanese government favoring an international agenda that runs counter to the U.S.-backed global trend toward reinforcement of market principles.

A similar story could be told regarding international trade, with the Japanese government pursuing a frustrating go-slow agenda in the World Trade Organization and the Asia Pacific Economic Cooperation forum on trade and investment rules. The bilateral trade deficit persists as an issue with the United States. As more U.S. and other foreign companies invest in and participate in Japan's economy as a result of recent reforms, the United States has become more invested in the process and has a greater stake in the overall stability of the U.S.-Japan economic relationship.[13]

Incremental reform and slow growth hold potential negative consequences for strategic policy, as well. A Ministry of Finance worried about the large fiscal deficit despite weak economic performance will be seeking areas in which to cut spending. In this environment, expensive new military equipment development or procurement is problematical. This situation could cause difficulties if, for example, the U.S. government wants Japan to participate more actively in theater missile defense development or other expensive projects related to upgraded roles and missions in the bilateral relationship.

On the whole, however, economic trends probably will have only marginal implications for Japanese-U.S. security relations. The bilateral strategic relationship is not prone to sudden reversals, in part because there exist numerous brakes on abrupt changes in security policy, including strong domestic support for the U.S. alliance, cautious and status quo–oriented leaders, the requirement for consensus building, and strong pacifist sentiment.[14]

Changes in Japan's Security Posture

Continuing serious economic concerns combine with a number of recent security and other challenges to raise grave questions in Japan about the viability of its long-standing post–World War II national development-security strategy. The goal of Japan's postwar national strategy as laid out by Prime Minister Shigeru Yoshida was to gradually reestablish Japan's national power and preeminence. The strategy emphasized economic recovery and expansion to rebuild Japanese national wealth and, with that wealth, power and influence. The primacy of economics fit well with widespread Japanese postwar aversion to militarism and the use of force. But with the bipolar Cold War heating up, Japan could pursue economic growth only if its security were guaranteed. It thus relied on the United States for external security in exchange for hosting a large, permanent U.S. military presence.[15]

Japan's strategy was successful. Legally, politically, and socially constrained from rebuilding a credible military capability, Japan grew and became an economic superpower and leader by the 1980s. Not only did this strategy benefit Japan, but the bilateral security arrangement also supported the U.S. Cold War security strategy in the Pacific and was quietly endorsed by the rest of Asia as a check against future Japanese militarism.

Since the 1990s, this national development-security strategy has come under challenge and undergone change because of several key factors, described below.[16]

Post–Cold War Threats and Uncertainties

The end of the Cold War and collapse of the Soviet Union altered Japan's threat environment. It dismantled the Cold War strategic framework for the East Asian security equation, removed Japan's number-one security threat against which Japan's force structure had been configured, and took away the initial rationale for Japan's post–World War II geostrategic bargain with the United States.

Japanese leaders view the strategic situation in East Asia as being more unsettled than during the Cold War, with a number of near-term flashpoints and longer-term uncertainties shaping Japan's security calculus now and probably in the coming years:

- North Korea is the most pressing security issue. Pyongyang's Taepo Dong missile overflight of Japan in August 1998 galvanized a national sense of vulnerability. Japan previously had viewed North Korea as posing an indirect threat in terms of regional instability and refugee flows, as well as a potential problem for the alliance should rifts emerge with the United States over expected Japanese involvement in a Korean contingency. The missile launch, however, elevated North Korea to a direct, physical threat to Japan. Polling data and media reporting indicated that the psychological impact was profound, leaving Japan with a greater sense of immediate danger and highlighting the limitations of the U.S. alliance in deterring threats to Japan. In addition, the level of U.S. government concern over the launch was perceived by Japan as inadequate, raising questions over the degree of convergence of U.S. and Japanese security interests. Japanese attitudes toward North Korea have hardened as a result of the protracted crisis over North Korea's nuclear weapons program beginning in 2003 as well as the issue of accounting for Japanese citizens abducted by North Korean agents and detained in North Korea.

- The prospect of a unified Korea bears on Japan's efforts to prepare for future uncertainty. History makes Korea an important security concern for Japan. Despite efforts to improve bilateral ties with South Korea, Japan continues to be suspicious of Korea. The external orientation of a future unified Korea—how it relates to Beijing, the type of military capability it possesses, and the posture it assumes toward Japan—is seen in Japan as a major factor in the future security equation in Northeast Asia.[17]

- Taiwan is also a serious concern. Japanese leaders are aware that an outbreak of hostilities in the Taiwan Strait involving U.S. forces easily could draw Japan into it under the U.S.-Japan Defense Guidelines. The extent and role of Japanese involvement in a China-Taiwan-U.S. military conflict would require difficult decisions of Japan, weighing the need to support its ally against the costs such actions would entail for its future relationship with China. Japan faces the probability that it would emerge from a Taiwan crisis with either its U.S. or China relationship—or perhaps both—seriously damaged. In recent years, Tokyo has seemed to tilt against China as it has consulted closely with the United States in seeking to deter Chinese military action against Taiwan.

- China is a growing factor in Japan's security calculations. Japan's policy makers and public opinion are frequently critical of China's military buildup and intrusions by Chinese military forces into Japanese-claimed airspace and seas. Japanese leaders have not defined China as an inevitable threat, however. Public opinion polls, as well as Japanese officials and academic experts, are prone to place China more as an uncertainty for which Japan must actively position itself to deal on many fronts rather than as a threat to be actively countered. Some in Japan express concern primarily over the potential for China to become more aggressive and coercive—for example, in the disputed Senkaku/Diaoyu Islands. Others see China seeking to secure regional preeminence at the expense of Japan's leadership position. At the same time, there remains a long-standing Japanese concern over the potential for instability in China and worry about the physical and economic implications for Japan's security of a weak, fragmented, and unpredictable China.[18]

- Regional instability in Southeast Asia is a threat to Japanese political, economic, and security interests. It could jeopardize sea lines of communication, threaten Japanese nationals, and disrupt regional security dynamics. Japan's security interests are largely compatible with those of Southeast Asia—preventing regional hegemony, maintaining a regional U.S. presence as a stabilizing force, and endeavoring to carefully manage China's regional role as it grows in power. A stable and cooperative Southeast Asia can advance those interests better than a weak and divided region can. Recognizing the potential for broader instability, Tokyo has closely monitored the often unsteady political and economic conditions in Indonesia and has sought to play a positive political and economic role in stabilizing the situation.[19]

- Russia recently is low on the list of Japan's security worries, but this view could change quickly if Russian nationalism were to grow and to look eastward. One Japanese concern is Russian weapons proliferation and the problems this could pose in Asia, particularly Russia-China arms deals. Although the Northern Territories dispute remains a traditional security issue, Japan continues to deal with the problem in the diplomatic arena, subordinating it to the broader goal of good relations with Russia. Japan also competes with China over access to Russian oil.[20]

- In addition to country-specific worries, Japan also is sensitive to other emerging dangers. The Aum Shinrikyo gas attack in the Tokyo subway several years ago shocked the national consciousness not just as an act of domestic terrorism but also as a demonstration of chemical weaponry. The Taepo Dong missile launch highlighted the emergence of new, less geographically confined threats that not only are undeterred by the U.S. military presence but also could make Japan a target partly *because of* the U.S. military presence. Long-term energy and economic concerns drive much of Japan's diplomatic and economic activity in the Middle East. Japan saw its interests well served by strong support for the U.S.-led antiterrorism operations in Central Asia beginning in 2001. Japan also strongly supported the U.S.-led attack on Saddam Hussein's regime in Iraq in 2003.

Perceptions of U.S. Security Policy

U.S. security policy is a key question for Japan in the recent uncertain environment. Until the 1990s, Japanese policy makers appeared confident that the United States needed Japan—that the alliance was just as critical for Washington's security strategy as it was for Tokyo's. This confidence has been questioned, with Japan now unsure of its value to the United States. This uncertainty stems from several factors:

- Japanese academic writings and media commentary indicate that Japan is unsure how Washington defines its strategic role in the post–Cold War era. Less strategic clarity, compounded by such developments as U.S. action in Kosovo and the perceived divergence in Japanese and U.S. reactions to the 1998 North Korean missile launch, suggest to Japanese observers an inconsistency or unpredictability of U.S. security calculations that could prove problematic to Japan in the future. The updated U.S.-Japan Defense Guidelines and the strong pro-Japan leanings of the George W. Bush administration reassured Japanese leaders and helped to strongly solidify the U.S.-Japan alliance relationship. Nonetheless, the Japanese often remain insecure about the U.S. commitment to Japan. They can envision a crisis in the alliance erupting not only from Japan's failure to provide expected assistance to the United States in a contingency but also from a U.S. decision not to engage in a security issue important to Japan. Prime Minister Junichiro Koizumi endeavored to avoid any suggestion of Japan failing to provide assistance by adopting a high profile in support of the U.S. antiterrorism campaign in 2001–2002 and later for the U.S.-led military attack on Iraq. Japanese leaders seemed concerned with the U.S. decision in 2007 to abruptly put aside the past U.S. hard line and to show greater flexibility and moderation toward North Korea in the Six-Party Talks than Japan judged was warranted on the basis of North Korean behavior.[21]
- Japanese leaders assess that Japan's economic stagnation and slow growth have made the country less important to the United States. Because Japan has calculated its own national power largely in terms of economic strength since World War II, it follows that Tokyo would view the loss of power and influence resulting from economic difficulties as decreasing its importance abroad, particularly without the Cold War backdrop.[22]
- The Japanese are particularly sensitive about the U.S.-China relationship, as evidenced by the government's surprise and concern over President Bill Clinton's visit to China in 1998 without stopping in Japan. Japan is uncertain of U.S. policy on China. The George W. Bush administration worked hard to reassure Japan of its primacy in U.S. calculations in Asia, but as time has passed, the U.S. government has seemed much more involved with China than with Japan—a trend that some in Japan see as likely to continue after the U.S. election in 2008. A Japanese fear centers on a zero-sum dynamic

in which the United States could conclude that its long-term national interest depends most importantly on a strategic understanding with economically dynamic and increasingly influential China and could therefore pull back from Japan if it were an obstacle to this agenda. At the same time, however, many in Japan show concern that poor U.S. management of its China relationship could lead Washington to use Japan crudely and explicitly to counter growing Chinese power. The Japanese government in recent years has shown greater willingness to work with the United States and others in the Asia-Pacific to influence China toward channeling its energies in constructive ways and avoiding assertive and disruptive behavior. However, Japan presumably would oppose taking an overt role in any U.S. design to contain or hold back China's rise.[23]

Economic Conditions

Japan's economic stagnation in the 1990s severely shook the long-standing Japanese belief in economic power as the key lever of international importance and influence. As it recovered from World War II, Japan's approach to international relations was to exercise power and influence by establishing economic interdependence so that other countries would be inclined to cooperate with rather than to confront Japan when such a choice had to be made. Successive Japanese governments viewed this approach as successful, thus reinforcing the validity of the postwar strategy to concentrate on economics as the chief source of national power. The economic downturn and slow growth of the past fifteen years consequently has had a profound psychological effect on Japanese leaders. The moribund domestic market and fluctuations in outflows of Japanese direct investment and bank lending weakened Japan's economic influence with Asia and its other key trading partners. The government's efforts to compensate with greater official development assistance were increasingly hampered by budgetary constraints.[24]

Although Tokyo managed to marshal considerable resources for the region to address the Asian financial crisis, media reports indicate it began to realize that it had overrated the impact of economic leverage. The economic-based "comprehensive security policy" that Japan had touted began to look rather shallow, particularly in view of the new, more immediate threat from North Korea and the deeper uncertainties over regional security.

The impact of Japan's economic troubles on its security outlook is difficult to quantify, especially since the downturn occurred roughly at the end of the Cold War, which generated similar anxieties. Japan still has the world's second largest economy and thus remains powerful in relative terms. Tokyo probably has concluded that economic strength alone will not be sufficient to bring Japan the status, influence, and security it seeks in the post–Cold War period, but it will remain an essential ingredient.[25]

Domestic Political Environment

The Japanese political system within which government policies and priorities have been framed and decided for much of the past fifty years is undergoing major changes. The transformation of the political system is marked by:

- *Weakening of the party system.* Not only has the Liberal Democratic Party's monopoly on power been broken, but the structure of Japanese party politics has eroded, as well. Coalition politics will be a feature of the political landscape for the foreseeable future, in an environment in which party affiliations are fragile and alliances transitory.
- *Voter unpredictability.* The volatility of the Japanese electorate is unprecedented. Voter identification with political parties is weak, and traditional machine politics is dying. Social, economic, and technological changes have altered local political dynamics, leaving local elites unable to deliver the vote as in the past.
- *Decline of the bureaucrats.* The opening of the political system has increased the power of politicians at the expense of the bureaucrats—career subject experts who traditionally shaped public policy and were a strong force for continuity. Moreover, politician behavior increasingly reflects the volatile voting public.
- *Generational change.* A new generation of political leaders, reflecting generational change in Japanese society, is bringing new attitudes and policy concerns. Issues once considered taboo, such as constitutional revision, are now seriously debated and open to change.

The breakdown of the traditional political system has left a decision-making vacuum that is currently being filled by a variety of forces—public opinion, new interest groups, unusual tactical political alliances, and local political interests. In short, the political system is in flux, creating a decision-making environment that is more pluralistic and politically permissive and less predictable. The range of options has expanded, and policy outcomes cannot be taken for granted. Unexpected outcomes are increasingly possible.[26]

Popular Attitudes: Normalcy and Nationalism

Generational change is producing new dynamics in how the Japanese think about their country. The population is more confident in and proud of Japan's democracy and wants to demonstrate that pride, as illustrated by the official adoption of the national flag and anthem. Young Japanese are frustrated that Japan still seems to carry a pariah stigma; they believe it has earned the right to be a "normal" nation.

Growing nationalism in Japan is more of an expression of pride in Japan's postwar accomplishments and a desire to be viewed as a modern, responsible state than a desire for Japanese assertiveness or dominance, particularly in the security context. One component of this quest for normalcy is a greater popular acceptance of the Japan Self-Defense Forces (SDF) and more of a popular willingness to consider foreign missions for the SDF—within certain limits, as seen notably in Japan's support for the U.S.-led antiterrorism campaign from 2001 and deployment of Japanese forces to Iraq. Prime Minister Koizumi's visits to the controversial Yasu-kuni war memorial also were in line with this trend, though they caused so much controversy in Japan's relations with China and Korea that they have not been followed by his successors. Although a darker strain of nationalism does exist, it appears unlikely to grow significantly or gain popular acceptance unless there are dramatic changes in the regional situation and a major reordering of the political system.[27]

A balanced assessment of the likelihood of change in Japanese government priorities in policy areas important to the United States requires a careful review of the continuing constraints limiting the impact of the forces for change noted above. A variety of constraints exist that will dampen the prospects for substantial reprioritization of Japanese policies, especially regarding relations with the United States.

- A wide body of media and other reporting indicates a strong consensus that the U.S. alliance remains central to Japan's security, and public opinion polls show that popular support for the alliance remains high. Any deliberate actions that would directly undermine the alliance would be hugely controversial and unlikely to succeed.
- Consensus building in a democracy in which power is increasingly diffuse will be much more difficult to achieve than in a one-party-dominated, bureaucrat-controlled government, especially when virtually all subjects are debatable.
- Japanese leaders remain cautious and status quo oriented. In many ways, they are riding a wave of change, not driving it.
- Expected low economic growth will reinforce a status quo orientation and limit the resources available to substantially increase funding for Japan's current force modernization plans or other government spending initiatives.
- Although the political system is fluid, the political spectrum on key issues is generally bounded. On security issues, for example, the extreme left, as represented by the Socialists, has been marginalized

since the Soviet Union's collapse, leaving the political "center" somewhat more conservative. An abrupt upswing in leftist sentiment opposing the alliance is consequently less likely than other types of security shifts.

- Polling data indicates that antimilitarism and pacifist sentiment remain strong, especially among the elderly. This sentiment will dictate a cautious, incremental approach to any changes in how Japan uses its military, as demonstrated by the difficulties of achieving even modest changes in Japan's peacekeeping legislation.
- Japanese leaders also will be wary of drawing a negative reaction from Asian neighbors by moving to increase defense capabilities or taking steps that appear to pull away from the U.S. alliance. They expended considerable effort, for example, to explain the revised Defense Guidelines to regional neighbors to reassure them Japan was not adopting a more assertive security posture.

The strength of these limitations on changes to Japanese priorities is increasingly difficult to assess, given the magnitude and pace of transformation occurring in Japanese society, politics, economics, and the regional security situation. Absent dramatic changes in the external environment that would greatly heighten Japan's sense of vulnerability, these factors will continue to limit the country's freedom of action on key issues. Should the external environment markedly worsen, however, most of these constraints probably would weaken and some probably would be overwhelmed.

Recent Signs of Change

The volatile mix of forces, some pushing for change in Japanese policy priorities and others constraining change, has led to some significant signs of modifications in Japanese priorities in recent years that are relevant to U.S. interests.[28]

Anxiety over the U.S. Alliance

Japanese observers are raising serious questions over the nature, relevance, and flexibility of the alliance. The alliance remains central to Japan's security—Japan needs and wants the alliance to continue, and deeply fears the consequences if it does not. Nonetheless, Japanese leaders have continuing concerns, especially:

- *The depth of the U.S. commitment.* The perceived lack of a clear rationale for the alliance after the Cold War, combined with other anxieties regarding the U.S. and regional environment, has created ambivalence among Japanese leaders over the direction of the partnership. Absent a clear common threat, defining and articulating what the alliance stands for has become more difficult. Using it as an explicit counter against a threat from China remains difficult for both the United States and Japan. Tokyo does not question the continued need for the alliance given the near-term dangers, long-term uncertainties, and Japan's limited unilateral capabilities. It appears confident that the United States would react to major North Korean or Chinese aggression, although the 1998 Taepo Dong launch raised questions in Tokyo about the U.S. response in specific North Korean scenarios short of war on the peninsula. Nonetheless, some in Japan harbor a general unease that the United States will question the value of the alliance and ultimately pull back.

- *Asymmetry.* Despite its fears of fading U.S. interest, Tokyo periodically bristles at the unequal nature of the alliance. Japan seeks a more reciprocal arrangement in which Washington engages in prior consultations on security matters of importance and in which the United States does not seek to dictate Japanese government policies or actions related to the alliance, giving Japan greater autonomy. It is likely that Bush administration efforts to establish such a reciprocal arrangement lessened this Japanese concern, but the outlook for a future U.S. government is unpredictable.

Greater Assertiveness/Activism

Japan is demonstrating increased initiative in security and economic matters. The decision in 1999 to build indigenous reconnaissance satellites, an unusually aggressive response to the North Korean spy ship encroachment in early 1999, and the stepped-up pursuit of foreign military contacts and regional diplomacy exemplify this more forward-leaning posture. Japan for a time took the lead in the ASEAN+3 and other regional forums to devise mechanisms that excluded the United States and that helped to ensure regional economic well-being in the event of a recurrence of the 1997–1998 crisis. Activism also has been apparent within the alliance framework. Tokyo expended considerable effort to pass the Defense Guidelines legislation and sought new ways to cooperate with the United States in the antiterrorism campaign, though it was slow to engage in bilateral planning under the Defense Guidelines or to tackle a variety of other long-standing base-related issues.

Wider, More Active Security Debate

Even a few years ago, the notion that Japan would be seriously considering constitutional change to ease strictures against military activity seemed implausible. Debate on that issue is now accepted. In 2000, 90 percent of Diet members under the age of 50—nearly one-fifth of the total Diet membership—supported constitutional revisions; a study group was commissioned to explore options. The Japanese government in early 2007 moved forward with changes in the constitution, although subsequently in 2007, the defeat of the ruling party in upper house Diet elections and the inauguration of a new government under Prime Minister Yasuo Fukuda presumably slowed the move toward constitutional revision.

The public discussion of roles and missions necessitated by the Defense Guidelines legislation, including previously unspoken subjects such as Japan's potential response in a Taiwan contingency, is now an expected feature of the executive and legislative decision processes. Limits clearly exist, at least in public, as demonstrated by the immediate firing of a Japan Defense Agency vice minister in late 1999 for broaching the possibility of a future nuclear Japan. But prominent politicians raised the issue around the time of North Korea's nuclear weapons test in 2006, suggesting that it is probably only a matter of time before that subject, too, is no longer taboo. In a vibrant democracy, in which individuals more detached from Japan's wartime history are now moving into leadership positions, and in an uncertain strategic environment, freer debate on a widening range of security issues is inevitable.

Meanwhile, although Japan's public and government remain generally averse to the use of military force as a means of advancing national objectives, postwar hypersensitivity to military issues is lessening. The constitutional debate and moves to modify peacekeeping legislation demonstrate a growing maturity and normalcy in thinking about the purpose of the military. Humanitarian interventions and peacekeeping operations increasingly are viewed in Japan as valid roles for the SDF. Moreover, the firing of warning shots at North Korean spy vessels in early 1999 moved in the direction of using military force as a deterrent, while sending naval destroyers to South Asia during the antiterrorism campaign appeared to be a notable change.

KOREAN GOVERNMENT PRIORITIES

There have been periods of intense crisis and periods of remarkable thaw on the Korean Peninsula in the post–Cold War years. These periods have been hard to predict. They have depended on and have come about as a result of the policies and actions of the United States, China, Japan, and Russia—the four powers most involved with Korean issues. At bottom, however, they have depended on the policies and actions of the North Korean and South Korean administrations.[29]

North Korean Priorities

Though the weakest of the six governments directly involved with Korean affairs, the North Korean administration of Kim Jong-il has more often than not been in the lead in the post–Cold War period in determining whether developments on the peninsula move toward greater friction and confrontation or greater moderation and accommodation. As is explained in more detail in chapter 2, North Korea in the early 1990s created a major nuclear weapons crisis that was eventually eased with the Agreed Framework accord of 1994. In 2000, it shifted sharply in favor of accommodation with the government of South Korean president Kim Dae Jung, hosting a summit with the South Korean leader in Pyongyang. This set off rounds of high-level North Korean dialogue and détente with South Korea, the United States, and other concerned powers. In the face of the more hardline posture of the incoming George W. Bush administration, North Korea created a major international crisis by breaking previous agreements and overtly pursuing nuclear weapons development. The resulting nuclear weapons test of 2006 saw revitalization of the Six-Party Talks on North Korea's nuclear weapons development. All sides, including North Korea, registered renewed interest in using negotiations to ease tensions on the peninsula and have taken steps to do so in 2007.

North Korea has not been the only power to change policies in ways that add to or reduce tensions on the Korean Peninsula. The Bush administration hardened U.S. policy significantly in 2001 and sustained a tough posture until the North Korean nuclear test in 2006, when it changed course toward a more flexible and moderate approach involving direct U.S. engagement with the North Korean administration. Upon taking office in 1998, President Kim Dae Jung ended South Korea's past wary approach toward North Korea in favor of a policy of asymmetrical normalization known as the "Sunshine Policy." The policy remained controversial among conservatives in South Korea and was viewed with suspicion by the governments of the United States and Japan, which remained wary of North Korea. However, over time it became broadly accepted among South Korean ruling circles as the appropriate way for dealing with the North.

In general, the governments concerned with Korean Peninsula affairs, apart from North Korea, have found their policy choices bounded by strong interests that would be affected by significant shifts in their policies. Because of its status as a strict and authoritarian dictatorship with less commitment to existing policies and often with much to gain by shifting course, the Kim Jong-il regime has been less constrained than the other powers in changing course on the Korean Peninsula.[30]

North Korea's has remained one of the most secretive administrations in world affairs. As a result, its motives and goals have continued to be matters of discussion and debate. Given the structure of power in North Korea, a great deal appears to depend on the calculus of one person, Kim Jong-il, whose thinking has not been well known or understood.

Available circumstantial evidence and assessments by specialists[31] have shown North Korean motives to be focused on regime survival. This has required enormous military preparations for a country of North Korea's size, along with the development of weapons of mass destruction (WMD) sufficient to deter the United States and other powers from attacking or forcing regime change in North Korea. North Korea also seemed determined to use its growing WMD capabilities to bargain for international prominence, leverage, and material profit. Meanwhile, it used the specter of regime decay and collapse in North Korea to prompt its neighbors South Korea and China to provide advantageous trade and foreign assistance. The alternative was viewed as mass refugee flows and disruption of these countries. Indeed, North Korea endured economic collapse beginning in the 1990s that saw famine kill more than a million people by some estimates. The international response was large amounts of food aid and related assistance. This suggested North Korea was a failing state and was highly dependent on international assistance. However, the North Korean administration proved to be resilient and outside aid givers had little apparent success in using the aid as a means to change North Korea's nuclear weapons program and other policies and actions deemed undesirable by donor governments.

Throughout the post–Cold War period, the North Korean government sought direct dialogue with the United States. This presumably was a means to constrain the United States from using pressure to foster regime change in North Korea, thereby assuring the security of the authoritarian regime. The United States was also critically important in approval of any international aid program to North Korea on the part of major international financial institutions, and the United States would presumably exert considerable influence on any Japanese decision to follow through with stalled efforts to normalize relations with North Korea by paying large amounts of foreign assistance. U.S. engagement with and recognition of the North Korean regime also seemed likely to add greatly to the legitimacy of the Pyongyang administration both at home and abroad.[32] Over the longer term, some specialists discerned a North Korean goal of using its WMD capabilities and international prominence in interaction with the United States in order to sustain an independent position vis-à-vis the much more powerful and prosperous South Korea, and possibly to advance North Korean influence at the expense of South Korea.[33]

Kim Jong-il's Consolidation of Control and Calculus

North Korean leader Kim Jong-il used purges and other means to solidify his personal rule following the death of Kim Il-sung in 1994. His regime endured the multiyear famine in the 1990s with the support of foreign food aid. In 2000, he used summits with Chinese, South Korean, and Russian leaders and high-level meetings with the United States to reflect his ability to use personal diplomacy to secure important benefits for North Korea. He did so while preserving key interests involving internal regime control, military preparedness, WMD capabilities, and long-term goals regarding Korean unification.

Kim has long been seen to be committed ultimately to regime preservation, economic recovery, and a unified Korea in which the North is preeminent. Many specialists on Korean affairs were surprised by his changed approach to South Korea in 2000. Kim presumably judged that through greater détente with the South, his administration could seek economic advantage. South Korea reportedly smoothed the way for the summit with payments of several hundreds of millions of dollars. Kim also may have sought greater North-South agreement that Korea's future should involve two separate states for the foreseeable future.

Kim Jong-il's success with and satisfaction over the initial openings to South Korea and the international community might have provided momentum for further advances. He may have been undertaking a major change in policy direction that would have led to an extensive and constructive outreach to South Korea and foreign powers. However, Kim remained preoccupied with maintaining the existing power structure at minimum risk, and his approach was subject to abrupt change. Indeed, in the face of the tougher U.S. posture of the George W. Bush administration, Kim shifted to a much harder stance toward South Korea while pushing ahead openly with nuclear weapons development.[34]

Progress on the North's Goals

To meet the economic requirements needed to sustain the regime, North Korean leaders have relaxed some domestic economic controls and promoted economic interactions with South Korea and other donors. Food, fertilizer, electric power, foreign investment, and hard currency continue to head the list of regime needs. Positive movement in North Korea's relations with the United States, Japan, international financial institutions, and other possible donors could reinforce positive North-South momentum. Such improvement with the outside world also could be used by the North as leverage to extract more material benefit from the South Korean government, which does not wish to lose its position as a primary conduit to the North.[35]

Kim Jong-il's determination to maintain tight control of major developments in North Korea—control that inevitably would be challenged if Pyongyang opened to outside economic and other exchanges—potentially poses a major brake on forward movement in this area. Rising ferment in the North as a result of foreign contacts, for example, could prompt the North's leader to halt progress in external relations. Moreover, South Korea and other international interlocutors may not meet Kim's expectations for compensation—a significant element in negotiations on WMD programs. Kim also may decide to use improved ties with the United States, China, Russia, Japan, and others against the South, reverting to past practice in striving to marginalize Seoul's role in determining Korean developments.

Bureaucratic and Military Pressures

Bureaucratic and other differences could emerge in North Korea over the implications of détente with South Korea, and these in turn could impede advances in North-South relations. Though there is little reliable information about such differences, it is likely that at least some North Korean elites, including many in the military, an institution that has exerted greater internal influence in recent years, are strongly wedded to the past. They probably would place extraordinary emphasis on North Korean military and security preparedness and independence from foreign powers, and they could feel threatened by an extensive thaw in North-South relations and North Korean relations with the West, particularly if the pace of development appeared to be dictated by outside forces.

Weaknesses in Kim Jong-il's Approach

Despite its leading role in setting the agenda in international consideration of Korean Peninsula issues in recent years, the North Korean administration has made mistakes as it maneuvers for tactical advantage and demonstrates a greater tolerance of tension and confrontation than South Korea and the other powers concerned with the Korean Peninsula. For example, Kim Jong-il waited too long following the visit of U.S. Secretary of State Madeleine Albright to Pyongyang in 2000 to come to agreement on a proposed visit to North Korea by President Bill Clinton. Other perceived mistakes under Kim's guidance include North Korean negotiators' admission to their U.S. counterparts in October 2002 that North Korea did indeed have a clandestine highly enriched uranium program for developing nuclear weapons. The admission was used by Bush administration officials to place North Korea on the defensive and to strengthen international pressure against North Korea's WMD efforts.[36] Similarly,

Kim's admission to Japanese prime minister Koizumi in September 2002 that North Korea had abducted Japanese citizens did not improve North Korean–Japanese relations but actually hardened Japanese attitudes against the North Korean regime.[37] North Korean efforts to develop a special economic zone along China's border without adequate consultation with China prompted Beijing in 2002 to arrest the Chinese citizen slated to lead the North Korean zone.[38]

North Korea's frequently confrontational and erratic maneuvers have served to isolate it from the other concerned powers that—with the possible exception of the United States—are basically focused on nation-building agendas requiring regional peace and stability. Nevertheless, the North Korean administration has more or less effectively used three main cards—its WMD programs, the massive military deployments along the Korean demilitarized zone (DMZ), and the specter of North Korean collapse—to garner international leverage, recognition, and material advantage in the post–Cold War years.

South Korean Priorities

South Korean government priorities have been pulled in sometimes different directions in the post–Cold War period. The greater role South Korea has endeavored to play in managing and resolving tensions on the Korean Peninsula has been accompanied by vacillation and uncertainty in South Korea's continuing commitment to the alliance with the United States, a mix of simmering frictions, closer economic interdependence and greater cultural ties with Japan, and on-again, off-again enthusiasm over the importance of China's ascendance for South Korea's economic growth, national security, and broader influence in Korean and Asian affairs. Domestic preoccupations with sustaining economic growth amid a very competitive international environment of economic globalization, along with usually intense political competition among more conservative and more progressive political parties that was fed by various interest groups and the aggressive South Korean media, frequently overrode international concerns for Korean voters and political leaders.[39]

To recap the discussion in chapter 2, South Korean president (1998–2003) Kim Dae Jung carried out a major change in South Korean policy toward the North that continues to have a major effect on the Korean Peninsula. His so-called Sunshine Policy involved asymmetrical South Korean gestures and assistance designed to engage and eventually change North Korea; it won the support of the next president (2003–2008), Roh Moo Hyun, and appears likely to be followed by Roh's successor, as well.[40] Apart from this shift, however, South Korea during the post–Cold

War period has more often than not been in a reactive position in the face of North Korean maneuvers and the policies of other powers.

South Korean decision making on peninsular issues remains divided. There has been a wide gap on a range of important subjects between the administrations of Kim and Roh on one side and their conservative opponents on the other. The conservatives seem unlikely to overturn the Sunshine Policy following their victory in the December 2007 presidential election, but they appear likely to make adjustments on a variety of related issues, including the alliance relationship with the United States. Other topics that often get higher priority among South Korean citizens and voters than South Korea's relations with North Korea or the United States include the progress of the South Korean economy and the efficiency and integrity of governance in the country.

During the past two South Korean administrations, Seoul has shown a tendency to move further away from its formerly close alignment with the United States. During much of the George W. Bush administration, the two governments were clearly at odds in their respective approaches to North Korea. Younger voters were in the lead in South Korean opinion polls in seeing North Korea less as a threat and more as a needy brother requiring assistance. This view was in stark contrast with the Bush administration's hard-line statements against the threat posed by Pyongyang. Broader South Korean opinion also recognized that South Korea was in no position to handle the consequences of a collapse and absorption of indigent North Korea; South Korea thus sought to avoid regime change and reunification until well into the future.

Meanwhile, U.S.–South Korea alliance frictions added to bad feeling and contrasted markedly with improved South Korean relations with China. This prompted some in South Korea to view relying on China as an alternative to the alliance with the United States, and some South Korean leaders advocated a role for South Korea as a mediator or balancer between the two powers.[41]

Working against a serious split in South Korea's alliance with the United States were economic realities that required a strong alliance against North Korea if the South were to appear stable enough to attract needed foreign investment. The so-called silent majority of middle-aged and older South Korean voters viewed the possibility of their country going alone or relying on China as too dangerous in view of South Korea's relative small size and perceived need for U.S. backing to deal with North Korea and other sometimes difficult neighbors.[42]

South Korean relations with China cooled after reaching a high point in 2004. China loomed more as an international competitor to South Korean manufacturers. There were recurring differences with China over interpretations of historical territorial claims that received wide publicity in South Korea and were of great importance to South Korean leaders. Some in South Korea also saw China's growing economic interchange with North Korea as being opposed to South Korea's long-term goal of reunification. The Chinese actions were interpreted as efforts to shore up a North Korean administration that would then lean to China and avoid reunification with South Korea.[43]

South Korean relations with Japan continued to deepen economic interdependence and cultural and personal exchanges despite often intense differences over historical and territorial issues. Frictions subsided under the leadership of President Kim Dae Jung, rose in response to Prime Minister Koizumi's insistence on visiting the controversial Yasukuni Shrine, and subsided again with the more moderate and accommodating stance on historical issues adopted by later Japanese leaders.[44]

South Korean relations with the United States improved with the thaw in U.S. policy toward North Korea and efforts by both Seoul and Washington to moderate tensions and improve economic and other ties. Both governments emphasized the importance of the U.S.–South Korea Free Trade Agreement reached in 2007.[45]

In the end, South Korea's priorities appeared to focus on sustaining economic development amid continued intense political competition in South Korean domestic politics. It sought to avoid conflict and to reduce tension on the Korean Peninsula while continuing to use the asymmetrical Sunshine Policy. South Korea continues to rely on the alliance relationship with the United States and to develop closer ties with both Japan and China with a clear awareness of the differences South Korea has with both Asian neighbors.

The Priorities of Concerned Powers

The United States and China are the outside powers that have exerted the most important influence on the Korean Peninsula in recent years. The United States has shown division on how to deal with North Korea. The hard-line Bush administration policy was a change from the more moderate Clinton policy. It alienated the United States from South Korea and China, among others, and failed to halt North Korea's nuclear weapon development. Following the North Korean nuclear weapons test in 2006, the Bush administration shifted to a more flexible and accommodating position toward North Korea. This shift won the support of China and South Korea and opened the way for dealing with the North Korean nuclear program through negotiations in the Six-Party Talks.

Considerations that featured in U.S. calculations included the prevailing view among U.S. officials that North Korea's massive conventional military deployments along the DMZ seemed to rule out the United States using military force to destroy North Korea's nuclear capabilities or to force regime change in North Korea. At the same time, the U.S. government showed a strong aversion to compromise with a North Korean regime that was seen as part of an international "axis of evil" by President Bush and was assumed to be using its nuclear weapons to "blackmail" the United States and others for recognition and assistance.[46]

U.S. policy appeared to give priority to the following objectives:

1. Avoid war
2. Manage the North Korean nuclear program through negotiations in the Six-Party Talks
3. Endeavor to create a broader front in the Six-Party Talks in order to constrain and ultimately eliminate the North Korean WMD efforts
4. Use other U.S. leverage to press North Korea to change its WMD programs and other disruptive policies
5. Engage the North Korean regime warily, keeping in mind an ultimate U.S. goal of fostering regime change in North Korea[47]

U.S. options in recent years have ranged from standing firm against North Korean action to testing North Korea through negotiations and agreements. For much of the Bush presidency, U.S. policy was seen to be reactive to North Korean initiatives; American officials were at pains to show the United States endeavoring to manage the adverse consequences of North Korea's WMD programs through negotiations in the Six-Party Talks, while holding out hope for regime change later. When this reactive approach seemed to fail with North Korea's nuclear test in 2006, the Bush administration switched gears and activated an approach to engage North Korea and seek progress through direct U.S. talks with Pyongyang.[48]

The recent Bush administration approach should reduce U.S. differences with South Korea over policy toward North Korea. The United States has also endeavored to reduce alliance frictions with South Korea, compromising on such issues as ending the United Nations command in ways that were in accord with South Korean interests. The United States did abruptly withdraw one of its two combat brigades from South Korea for deployment in Iraq, but subsequently the U.S. government has worked to consult more closely with Seoul on such matters. South Korea in turn has maintained a large troop presence in Iraq despite strong popular opposition to the Iraq war in South Korea. Both the U.S. and South Korean governments have worked hard to approve a 2007 U.S.–South Korean Free Trade Agreement.[49]

China's priorities have been to sustain stability and avoid conflict on the peninsula. The danger of a U.S.–North Korea conflict seemed high in 2003, prompting China to take a more active role as a mediator in the three-party and later six-party negotiations. China sees North Korea's nuclear weapons program as being against its interests in regional stability, but it also opposes pressure on North Korea for fear that Pyongyang will lash out with dangerous consequences. In addition, China fears that a North Korean collapse would have major negative effects on nearby areas of China and could lead to the absorption of North Korea by South Korea backed by the United States.[50]

Among the foreign powers concerned with Korean affairs, China has the most effective relationships with both North and South Korea. The obvious signs of friction between China and North Korea diminish but do not offset the fact that China maintains its position as the outside power with the best relationship with Pyongyang. The costs to China include substantial aid and investment in North Korea.[51]

Meanwhile, China's economic, political, and sociocultural ties with South Korea have grown by leaps and bounds over the past decade. The improvement in China's relationship with South Korea is one of the most significant advances in Chinese foreign relations in the post–Cold War period, though as noted earlier, South Korean wariness of China has also increased in recent years. Overall progress in Chinese–South Korean relations adds significantly to Chinese leverage on Korean Peninsula issues and reduces Chinese concerns that the United States might somehow use its alliance relationship with South Korea as a means to counter or undermine Chinese interests on the peninsula.[52]

By virtue of its location and wealth, Japan should be playing an influential role on the Korean Peninsula. In fact, Japan has generally been shunned by North Korea, while its relations with South Korea have been negatively affected by historical and territorial issues. In common with other concerned powers, Japan seeks stability and the avoidance of war. It views North Korea's WMD programs as a serious and growing national security threat. Tokyo's ability to negotiate with Pyongyang is seriously hampered by the unresolved issues of Japanese abducted by North Korea. In general, the Japanese government has aligned with the tough posture of the Bush administration, and it was somewhat upset by the recent Bush administration shift toward greater engagement and accommodation of North Korea without any concession by the North Korean side. Over the longer term, Japanese officials are worried by China's rising influence in Korean affairs and are trying, with little apparent success, to position Japan more advantageously in Korean affairs.[53]

Because of economic problems and domestic and other international preoccupations, Russia has not been in a good position of influence in Korean affairs. It seeks international prominence in the Six-Party Talks and sees some possible economic advantages for itself in transportation and other schemes involving Korea. Russia has favored the South Korean approach of asymmetrical engagement with North Korea and negotiations as the best way to deal with the dangers posed by North Korean WMD programs.[54]

NOTES

1. Kenneth Pyle, *Japan Rising: The Resurgence of Japanese Power and Purpose* (New York: Public Affairs, 2007); Michael J. Green, *Japan's Reluctant Realism* (New York: Palgrave, 2001); Richard Samuels, *Securing Japan: Tokyo's Grand Strategy and the Future of East Asia* (Ithaca, N.Y.: Cornell University Press, 2007); Thomas Berger, ed., *Japan in International Politics: The Foreign Policies of an Adaptive State* (Boulder, Colo.: Lynne Reinner, 2006); Ellis Krauss and T. J. Pempel, eds., *The U.S.-Japan Relationship in the new Asia-Pacific* (Stanford, Calif.: Stanford University Press, 2004); Steven K. Vogel, *U.S.-Japan Relations in a Changing World* (Washington, D.C.: Brookings Institution Press, 2002).

2. Samuel Kim, *The Two Koreas and the Great Powers* (New York: Cambridge University Press, 2006), 161.

3. Kent Calder, *Crisis and Compensation* (Princeton, N.J.: Princeton University Press, 1988).

4. Green, *Japan's Reluctant Realism.*

5. Thomas Berger, "Japan's International Relations: The Political and Security Dimensions," in *The International Relations of Northeast Asia,* ed. Samuel S. Kim, 135–69 (Lanham, Md.: Rowman & Littlefield, 2004).

6. Reviewed in Robert Sutter, *The United States and East Asia* (Lanham, Md.: Rowman & Littlefield, 2003), 123.

7. Takatoshi Ito, Hugh Patrick, and David Weinstein, eds., *Reviving Japan's Economy: Problems and Prescriptions* (Cambridge, Mass.: MIT Press, 2005).

8. David Asher, *The Bush Administration's Japan Problem* (Washington, D.C.: American Enterprise Institute, 2001).

9. Adam Posen, "Pragmatic Policy Progress: Recent Changes in and the Outlook for Japanese Economic Policy," in National Intelligence Council, *Change in Japan: Implications for U.S. Interests,* Conference Report CR 2000-01 (Washington, D.C.: GPO, 2000), 9–22.

10. Edward Lincoln, "Implications of Economic Reform in Japan for U.S. Economic Interests," in National Intelligence Council, *Change in Japan,* 49–58.

11. William Cooper, *U.S.-Japan Economic Relations: Significance, Prospects and Policy Options,* CRS Report RL32649 (Washington, D.C.: Congressional Research Service, Library of Congress, May 14, 2007).

12. "Japan's Changing Demography: Cloud or Silver Linings?" *Economist,* July 26, 2007.

13. Cooper, *U.S.-Japan Economic Relations.*

14. Richard Armitage and Joseph Nye, *U.S.-Japan Alliance: Getting Asia Right through 2020* (Washington, D.C.: Center for Strategic and International Studies, 2007).

15. Michael Yahuda, *The International Politics of the Asia-Pacific, 1945–1995* (London: Routledge, 1996), 229–30.

16. These factors and developments are reviewed at length in, among others, Green, *Japan's Reluctant Realism*, and Samuels, *Securing Japan*.

17. Kim, *Two Koreas*, 157–224.

18. Minxin Pei and Michael Swaine, *Simmering Fire in Asia: Averting Sino-Japanese Strategic Conflict* (Washington, D.C.: Carnegie Endowment for International Peace, 2005).

19. Armitage and Nye, *U.S.-Japan Alliance*, 24.

20. Ibid., 11.

21. Richard Samuels, "Japan's Goldilocks Strategy," *Washington Quarterly* 29, no. 4 (Autumn 2006); Michael Green and James Przystup, "The Abductee Issue Is a Test of America's Strategic Credibility," Pacnet no. 47 (Honolulu: CSIS Pacific Forum, November 15, 2007).

22. Sutter, *United States and East Asia*, 133.

23. *Sino-Japanese Rivalry: Implications for U.S. Policy*, Institute for National Security Studies special report (Washington, D.C.: National Defense University Press, 2007).

24. Michael Green, "Japan's Changing Security Debate: Implications for U.S. Policy," in National Intelligence Council, *Change in Japan: Implications for U.S. Interests*, Conference Report CR 2000-01 (Washington, D.C.: GPO, 2000), 59–72.

25. Michael Mastanduno, "Back to Normal? The Promise and Pitfalls of Japan's Economic Integration," in *Strategic Asia, 2006–2007: Trade, Interdependence, and Security*, ed. Ashley J. Tellis and Michael Wills, 105–38 (Seattle: National Bureau of Asian Research, 2006).

26. Among recent assessments, see William Grimes, "The Changing Japanese Political System," *Journal of Japanese Studies* 33, no. 2 (Summer 2007): 565–69.

27. Benjamin Self, *The Dragon's Shadow: The Rise of China and Japan's New Nationalism* (Washington, D.C.: Stimson Center, 2006).

28. Samuels, *Securing Japan*; Kenneth Pyle, "Abe Shinzo and Japan's Change of Course," *NBR Analysis* 17, no. 4 (October 2006): 5–31; Sutter, *United States and East Asia*, 136–37.

29. Kim, *Two Koreas*.

30. National Intelligence Council, *North Korean Engagement: Perspectives, Outlook, and Implications*, Conference Report CR 2001-01 (Washington, D.C.: GPO, 2001), 3–6.

31. Donald Oberdorfer, *The Two Koreas* (Reading, Mass.: Addison-Wesley, 1997); Victor Cha and David Kang, *Nuclear North Korea* (New York: Columbia University Press, 2003); Robert Carlin and Joel Wit, *North Korean Reform*, Adelphi Paper 382 (London: International Institute for Strategic Studies, 2006).

32. Mitchell Reiss, "Avoiding Déjà Vu All Over Again: Some Lessons from U.S.-DPRK Engagement," in National Intelligence Council, *North Korean Engagement*, 11–25.

33. Daryl Plunk, "The New U.S. Administration and North Korea Policy: A Time for Review and Adjustment," in National Intelligence Council, *North Korean Engagement*, 27–38.

34. On varying perspectives on Kim's motives and goals, see, among others, Cha and Kang, *Nuclear North Korea*.

35. International Crisis Group, "Korea Backgrounder: How South Korea Views Its Brother from Another Planet," Asia Briefing No. 89 (Brussels: International Crisis Group, 2004).

36. Charles Pritchard, *Failed Diplomacy: The Tragic Story of How North Korea Got the Bomb* (Washington, D.C.: Brookings Institution Press, 2007), 40–44.

37. Ibid., 39.

38. Ming Liu, "China and the North Korean Crisis," *Pacific Affairs* 76, no. 3 (Fall 2003): 370–72.

39. Samuel Kim, "The Two Koreas: Making Grand Strategy amid Changing Domestic Politics," in *Strategic Asia, 2007–2008: Domestic Political Change and Grand Strategy*, ed. Ashley J. Tellis and Michael Wills (Seattle: National Bureau of Asian Research, 2007), 113–38; David Kang, "South Korea's Embrace of Interdependence in Pursuit of Security," in Tellis and Wills, *Strategic Asia, 2006–2007*, 139–72.

40. Aidan Foster-Carter, "Sunshine Deepened Only to Dim?" *Comparative Connections* 9, no. 4 (4th Qtr 2007): 83–84, http://www.csis.org/media/csis/pubs/0704q.pdf.

41. Kang, "South Korea's Embrace."

42. Jae Ho Chung, *Between Ally and Partner: Korea-China Relations and the United States* (New York: Columbia University Press, 2006).

43. Scott Snyder, "Teenage Angst: Fifteenth Anniversary of Sino-ROK Diplomatic Relations," *Comparative Connections* 9, no. 3 (3rd Qtr 2007): 107–12, http://www.csis.org/media/csis/pubs/0703q.pdf.

44. David Kang and Ji-Young Lee, "With a New Japanese Leader, New Opportunities?" *Comparative Connections* 9, no. 3 (3rd Qtr 2007): 125–31, http://www.csis.org/media/csis/pubs/0703q.pdf.

45. Donald Gross and Hannah Oh, "Progress, North and South," *Comparative Connections* 9, no. 3 (3rd Qtr 2007): 47–49, http://www.csis.org/media/csis/pubs/0703q.pdf.

46. Kim, *Two Koreas*, 225–96.

47. Ibid., 292–95.

48. Ralph A. Cossa and Brad Glosserman, "Tests Postponed, Pending, Passed, and in Progress," *Comparative Connections* 9, no. 2 (2nd Qtr 2007): 1–3.

49. Robert Sutter, "The United States and Asia in 2006: Crisis Management, Holding Patterns, and Secondary Initiatives," *Asian Survey* 47, no. 1 (January/February 2007): 17–18.

50. Kim, *Two Koreas*, 42–101.

51. Liu, "China and the North Korean Crisis," 347–73.

52. Scott Snyder, "Strategic Maneuvers for the 'Sandwich Economy,'" *Comparative Connections* 9, no. 2 (2nd Qtr 2007): 121–30.

53. David Kang and Ji-Young Lee, "Treading Water, Little Progress," *Comparative Connections* 9, no. 2 (2nd Qtr 2007): 147–54.

54. Kim, *Two Koreas*, 102–56.

8

✛

Priorities in Southeast, South, and Central Asia and Russia

The priorities of the governments in other parts of Asia generally have had less importance for Washington's relations with Asia than have the priorities of governments in China, Japan, and Korea. The United States has continued to play a leadership role in Southeast Asia, and the war on terrorism saw a marked upswing in the importance of the United States for the governments in South and Central Asia. Central Asia represented the Asian area where Russia exerted greatest influence, though Russian priorities in other parts of Asia also have had some impact on U.S.-Asian relations.

PRIORITIES OF GOVERNMENTS IN SOUTHEAST ASIA AND THE PACIFIC

As elsewhere in the Asia-Pacific region, the government leaders in Southeast Asia and the Pacific generally have endeavored to meet growing popular demand for greater economic development and nationalistic respect through balanced nation-building strategies. They have placed a premium on encouraging economic growth beneficial to broad segments of their societies. Most governments have tended to eschew radical ideologies and to emphasize conventional nationalism. The latter has seen some regional leaders, such as Malaysia's former prime minister Mahathir Mohamad, seek greater international prominence in defending their national interests in the face of perceived outside pressures or threats. Military power has developed in line with economic power, but few administrations in Southeast Asia and the Pacific have emphasized military power at the expense of economic development.

The post–Cold War economic and security environment witnessed major changes that created fundamental challenges and uncertainties for most governments in the area. The Asian economic crisis of 1997–1998 undermined the prominence of the area's newly industrializing economies, especially Thailand and Indonesia. What followed was a long and slow process of economic recovery under often weak administrations.[1]

Regional security seemed less certain following the withdrawal of U.S. forces from bases in the Philippines as demanded by the Manila government in the early 1990s. U.S. security interests in the area revived strongly after the terrorist attacks on the World Trade Center and the Pentagon in 2001. Some regional governments had strong differences with the coercive U.S. focus against terrorism in Southeast Asia, which the United States for a time emphasized was a "second front" in the Global War on Terrorism. The U.S.-led war in Iraq and other U.S. policies in the Middle East were widely criticized. At the same time, however, the United States managed to build upgraded military relations with most leading Southeast Asian governments, which quietly welcomed closer security ties with the United States in the uncertain regional security environment.[2]

China's growing economic and military advances initially were viewed with alarm in Southeast Asia. Over time, however, Beijing's good neighbor policies and cooperative economic proposals went far toward reassuring area governments about Chinese policies and behavior. Japan remained an important economic and political partner of Southeast Asian governments, as well, but Japan's prominence in the region declined with the stagnation of the Japanese economy throughout much of the post–Cold War period. India's expanding economy and growing military power on the whole were welcomed by Southeast Asian governments. The governments encouraged various powers—the United States, China, Japan, India, and others such as the European Union, Russia, and Australia—to deepen their involvement in the region and thereby create a security environment where the danger of one outside power dominating the region would be reduced.[3]

The Asian economic crisis had its most serious impact in Indonesia, bringing down the authoritarian Suharto government, but it also provided a central challenge to other leading states of the Association of Southeast Asian Nations (ASEAN). The founding members of ASEAN in 1967 were Indonesia, the Philippines, Thailand, Malaysia, and Singapore. Five notably weaker Southeast Asia states—Brunei, Burma, Cambodia, Laos, and Vietnam—joined later. Only Singapore, with its modern and globally integrated economy and efficient civil service, was relatively well positioned to weather the economic crisis and pursue its interests forthrightly in regional and world affairs. However, even this technically successful city-state was increasingly unsettled by the massive difficulties in neighboring Indonesia and by a broader cycle of economic and political weakness throughout ASEAN. It sought assurance through closer ties with the United States, Australia, the European Union, Japan, and China. While continuing to give public emphasis to fostering ASEAN unity, it sought a diversified range of security and economic contacts and guarantees that would help to sustain and preserve Singapore's interests in the prevailing atmosphere of economic and political uncertainty.[4]

At the start of the new millennium, prevailing trends seemed to forecast Southeast Asia's outlook of mixed recovery from the many consequences of the Asian economic crisis, along with continued political and economic uncertainty. The outlook posed challenges for democratic growth and interests in good governance, development, and regional cooperation. It reinforced the prevailing preoccupation of most regional governments with internal economic and political difficulties.[5]

ASEAN became more prominent as the venue and convener of a variety of emerging regional multilateral organizations that achieved greater prominence in this period. But the organization was seriously weakened by the collapse of the Suharto administration, ASEAN's previous leader, and Indonesia's slow revival and by serious internal weaknesses and problems in the Philippines and Thailand. These kinds of problems seemed likely to limit the effectiveness of ASEAN, particularly the ability of its member states to follow through on regional initiatives.

There was plenty of criticism of the United States and its policies, though the potential for regionwide anti-Western and anti-American activity remained low. Contests for political power in Indonesia, the Philippines, Thailand, and elsewhere were likely to generate sporadic protests and occasional violent clashes that increased the threat environment for U.S., Australian, and other Western nationals. Radical Islamic groups and others opposed to the U.S. antiterrorism campaign also threatened U.S. personnel and interests in several Southeast Asian nations.[6]

Among the key trends in the region were:

- "Short-term" presidencies in the Philippines and Indonesia early in the decade underlined the continued fragility of these polities. They were followed by serious political instability in Thailand, highlighted by a military coup backed by the Thai king, which replaced the elected government in 2006.
- Economic recovery and reform after the 1997 Asian economic crisis was hampered by a negative cycle seen in such leading regional states as Indonesia, the Philippines, and Thailand, where weak economic conditions fueled demands for political change that then

distracted the region's leaders from effective economic policy, furthering public discontent. Regional economies grew at an average rate of over 6 percent in 2000, but this declined markedly in 2001, before reviving later in the decade.[7]

- Democratic institutions and established political practices remained weak. The 2006 coup in Thailand and the slow restoration of democratic governance there underscored this trend. Traditions of authoritarianism were strong and prevented the development of cooperative legislative-executive relations. Testing the limits of constitutional amendments, decentralization laws, and other newly created political mechanisms added to the atmosphere of unpredictability.[8]
- The region's legacy of military-led politics remained in play: civilian leaders often were wary of military intentions but sought to cultivate military support.

Evidence of these trends and their negative consequences was prevalent among several of the leading governments in Southeast Asia in the middle of the decade.

Indonesia

Political and economic conditions appear to be stabilizing in Indonesia after several years of upheaval. Reforms continue to be implemented. The presidency of Susilo Bambang Yudhoyono is the most stable and effective government administration since Suharto's demise, though the president's popularity declined markedly when his government cut fuel subsidies in light of large oil imports at high prices. Corruption remains a major problem. A positive development was major progress in 2005–2006 in implementing a settlement of the protracted conflict with separatist forces in Aceh.[9]

The Indonesian economy witnessed growth of just over 5 percent in 2006. Unfortunately, this meant that the economy continued to fail to keep pace with population growth, which exceeded 6 percent. As a result, an ever-increasing number of Indonesians were in poverty. It was estimated that 80 million Indonesians are below a poverty level of a dollar a day. Nor is the outlook for more vigorous economic growth promising. Continued instability means that foreign investment remains low, as do Indonesian earnings from exports of natural gas and oil. Oil was being imported rather than exported because of poor infrastructure and lack of foreign investment. Tourism has been in a slump because of security concerns in the country.[10]

Indonesia's regional leadership remains weak. The country's neighbors were alienated by unregulated dry-season forest fires that sent clouds of choking smoke across the region. Relations with Australia are negatively affected by Australian immigration restrictions but have witnessed greater cooperation in military and antiterrorism activities. The United States has also moved to improve relations with Indonesia, notably by increasing military contacts and exchanges, and China is endeavoring to improve relations as part of its politically reassuring and economically growing presence in Southeast Asia. Indonesia reportedly sided with Japan and Singapore in opposing a Chinese-supported effort to limit the 2005 East Asian Summit to ASEAN+3 countries, which allowed India, Australia, and New Zealand to participate and left the door open for U.S. participation.[11]

The Philippines

Philippine president Joseph Estrada's ouster in January 2001 came in part after active duty and retired military officers shifted their support to then vice president Gloria Macapagal-Arroyo. Advised by former president and retired general Fidel Ramos, Arroyo was committed to tackling the country's economic problems. But she also needed to keep her disparate backers together as she faced continued opposition, including efforts by Estrada and his remaining supporters and other political rivals in the Philippine elites to undermine her.

By 2006, political instability had worsened, as a wide range of groups endeavored to force Arroyo from power. They failed when Arroyo resorted to proclamations, restrictions, and bans on political activities and demonstrations and sought the support of the military. The president appeared to be alienated from the political elites in Manila and relied on military leaders and alliances with provincial political leaders. In this uncertain political situation, there was widespread dissatisfaction with the Philippines' dysfunctional democracy but there was no consensus on how it should be reformed.[12]

The Arroyo administration added to the internal instability by launching an intensified conflict with the Communist Party of the Philippines and its armed wing, the New People's Army. The administration also carried out repression of leftist activists in various political and other organizations. This resulted in scores of "politically targeted extrajudicial executions," according to Amnesty International. At the same time, the government made progress in peace talks, brokered by Malaysia, to reach a settlement in the long-running conflict between the government and the Moro Liberation Front. That breakthrough came as the Philippine military, backed by U.S. troops deployed to the southern Philippines in recent years, continued efforts to wipe out the small extremist Abu Sayyaf Group, which has been linked to abductions and terrorist attacks and to connections with broader Southeast Asian terrorist groups.[13]

Arroyo's economic policies coincided with annual growth of 6 percent in 2006. Foreign direct investment increased substantially from past years, and there was a rise in remittances by an estimated eight million Filipinos overseas to a level worth $12 billion in 2006. This good news was offset by continued gross inequities that saw massive poverty and unemployment, widespread child malnutrition, and poor access to education.[14]

President Arroyo has improved relations with China while sustaining close security and other ties with the United States. She used her position as the rotating chair of ASEAN in 2006–2007 to enhance her international profile as a means to build greater legitimacy abroad and at home.[15]

Thailand

The January 2001 elections in Thailand—overwhelmingly won by the Thai Rak Thai party of Thaksin Shinawatra—were clouded by a corruption investigation. The courts eventually ruled in Thaksin's favor. Despite Thaksin's great popularity in rural areas, opposition politicians, academics, journalists, and middle-class residents of Bangkok showed growing concern that the prime minister's government was eroding the mechanisms and principles of democracy. Worries centered on developments such as the undermining of independent monitoring agencies that were supposed to be neutral, creating new emergency laws that overrode constitutional guarantees, and weakening the independence of the media. There also were widespread charges of extensive corruption involving the prime minister and his family and associates.[16]

The opposition boycotted the parliamentary election in April 2006 and triggered a constitutional crisis. Thaksin remained a caretaker prime minister. At the instigation of the king, the judiciary investigated the 2006 elections and found irregularities, and the Constitutional Court annulled the election. Fear of violence, along with perceptions of corruption and of undermining of democracy and royal authority, added to problems associated with the insurgency in the south and divisions within the military. These developments prompted military leaders to stage a coup in September and oust Thaksin before the expected elections on October 15. Although the coup leaders promised new elections and a quick return to parliamentary rule, they continued to focus on restoring stability by suspending the constitution, resorting to censorship, and curbing political rights.[17]

The prolonged tenure of the post-coup administration causes apprehension abroad and at home. After the coup, Thailand's new military leaders found themselves facing international condemnation from most Western nations for their overthrow of an elected government. The insurgency in the south continued. While the opposition and others hoped that the new administration would restore stability and deliver a more democratic constitution, the process has been slow and the results uncertain. The military leaders appear concerned that elections would bring Thaksin's supporters back to power.[18]

Amid political twists and turns, the Thai economy continues moderate growth following the 1997–1998 economic crisis. The Thai economy is export dependent, with exports of goods and services accounting for 68.6 percent of gross domestic product (GDP) in 2006. Thailand's recovery from the 1997–1998 Asian financial crisis relied largely on external demand from the United States and other foreign markets.

The Thaksin government took office in 2001 with the intention of stimulating domestic demand and reducing Thailand's reliance on foreign trade and investment. From 2001 to 2006, the Thaksin administration embraced a "dual-track" economic policy that combined domestic stimuli with Thailand's traditional promotion of open markets and foreign investment. Weak export demand held 2001 GDP growth to 2.2 percent. Beginning in 2002, however, domestic incentives and export revival fueled a better performance, with real GDP growth at 7.1 percent in 2003 and 6.3 percent in 2004. In 2005, the economy decelerated to a 4.5 percent annual growth rate due to the tsunami catastrophe, drought, and violence in the three southernmost provinces. For 2006, the rebound of production in agriculture and manufacturing, coupled with increasing numbers of tourists, boosted GDP by 5.0 percent (year-on-year).[19]

Malaysia

Political stability and economic development have been more positive in Malaysia and Singapore, the two smaller Southeast Asian nations that were among the five states founding ASEAN forty years ago.

Dr. Mahathir Mohamad was prime minister of Malaysia between 1981 and 2003, leading his parties to successive election victories. Mahathir emphasized economic development during his tenure, in particular the export sector, as well as large-scale infrastructure projects. He attributed the success of the Asian Tiger economies to the "Asian values" of its people, which he believed were superior to those of the West. The end of Mahathir's administration was marred by a falling out with his deputy and presumed successor, Anwar Ibrahim. Mahathir stepped down as prime minister in October 2003.

His successor, Abdullah Ahmad Badawi, called elections and won an overwhelming victory in March 2004, with his supporters taking 199 of 219 seats in the lower house of parliament. Since taking office, Abdullah, an Islamic scholar, has promoted the concept of "Islam Hadhari" or "civilizational Islam," emphasizing the importance of education, social harmony, and economic progress. His relationship with Mahathir eventually soured, and the former prime minister expressed regret at supporting Abdullah to be his successor.[20]

Since it became independent, Malaysia's economic record has been one of Asia's best. Performance peaked in the early 1980s through the mid-1990s, as the economy experienced sustained rapid growth averaging almost 8 percent annually. High levels of foreign and domestic investment played a significant role as the economy diversified and modernized. Once heavily dependent on primary products such as rubber and tin, Malaysia today is a middle-income country with a multisector economy based on services and manufacturing. It is one of the world's largest exporters of semiconductor devices, electrical goods, and information and communication technology products.[21]

The Malaysian economy went into sharp recession in 1997–1998 during the Asian financial crisis. It narrowly avoided a return to recession in 2001 when the economy was negatively impacted by the bursting of the dot-com bubble (which hurt the information technology sector) and slow growth or recession in many of its important export markets. The economy grew more than 7 percent in 2004 and more than 5 percent in 2005. Per-capita GDP exceeded $5,000.[22]

Regional cooperation is a cornerstone of Malaysia's foreign policy. A founding member of ASEAN, Malaysia served as the group's chair most recently in 2005–2006. It hosted the ASEAN summit and East Asia Summit in December 2005, as well as the ASEAN ministerial and the ASEAN Regional Forum in July 2006. Malaysia also is an active member of the Asia Pacific Economic Cooperation (APEC), the Organization of the Islamic Conference, the Non-Aligned Movement, and the United Nations. It is a frequent contributor to UN and other peacekeeping missions, including recent deployments to East Timor, Indonesia, Pakistan, Sierra Leone, Kosovo, and Lebanon.[23]

Singapore

Political stability in Singapore is underscored by the ruling People's Action Party, which has been in power since 1959. The vibrant economy has seen recent economic growth of more than 8 percent in 2004, over 6 percent in 2005, and almost 8 percent in 2006. Manufacturing and services are the twin engines of the Singapore economy and accounted for 26.9 percent and 63.2 percent, respectively, of Singapore's GDP in 2006. The electronics and chemicals industries lead Singapore's manufacturing sector, each accounting for about 32.5 percent of manufacturing output in 2006. To inject new life to the tourism sector, which faced a 20 percent fall in revenues between 1993 and 2000 and a declining share of East Asia-

Pacific tourism revenues from 8.2 percent to 5.8 percent, the government in April 2005 approved the development of two casinos that should result in investment of more than $5 billion.[24]

To maintain its competitive position despite rising wages, the government has sought to promote higher-value-added activities in the manufacturing and services sectors. It also has opened, or is in the process of opening, the financial services, telecommunications, and power generation and retailing sectors to foreign service providers and greater competition. In addition, the government has pursued cost-cutting measures, including tax cuts and wage and rent reductions, in order to lower the cost of doing business in Singapore. It has negotiated free trade agreements (FTAs) with sixteen key trading partners and has already concluded eleven FTAs, including one with the United States that came into force on January 1, 2004.[25]

Singapore is nonaligned. It is a member of the United Nations—occupying a rotational seat on the Security Council in 2001–2002—and several of its specialized and related agencies, as well as the Non-Aligned Movement and the Commonwealth of Nations. Singapore has participated in UN peacekeeping/observer missions in Kuwait, Angola, Namibia, Cambodia, and East Timor. It provided a training unit to assist in training Iraqi police and has deployed naval ships, air force transport planes, and refueling tankers to the Persian Gulf to support the multinational Coalition effort to bring stability and security to Iraq.[26]

The city-state supports the concept of Southeast Asian regionalism and plays an active role in ASEAN and the APEC forum. Singapore relies primarily on its own defense forces, which are continuously being modernized. The defense budget accounts for approximately 32 percent of government operating expenditures (or 5 percent of GDP). A career military force of 53,300 is supplemented by 300,000 personnel either on active national service, which is compulsory for able-bodied young men, or reserve status. The Singaporean armed forces engage in joint training with ASEAN countries and with the United States, Australia, New Zealand, and India. Singapore also conducts military training on Taiwan.[27]

Singapore is a member of the Five-Power Defense Arrangement together with the United Kingdom, Australia, New Zealand, and Malaysia. Intended to replace the former defense role of the British in the Singapore-Malaysia area, the arrangement obligates members to consult in the event of external threat and provides for stationing Commonwealth forces in Singapore.

The Singaporean government has consistently supported a strong U.S. military presence in the Asia-Pacific region. In 1990, the United States and Singapore signed a Memorandum of Understanding (MOU) that allows U.S. access to Singaporean facilities at Paya Lebar air base and the

Sembawang wharves. Under the MOU, a U.S. Navy logistics unit was established in Singapore in 1992, U.S. fighter aircraft deploy periodically to Singapore for exercises, and a number of U.S. warships visit Singapore. The MOU was amended in 1999 to permit U.S. naval vessels to berth at the Changi Naval Base, which was completed in early 2001. In July 2005, the United States and Singapore signed a Strategic Framework Agreement to expand cooperation in defense and security.[28]

Vietnam

Vietnam's Communist administration has pursued pragmatic economic policies that registered growth rates of better than 8 percent in 2005 and 2006. Vietnam joined the World Trade Organization (WTO) in 2006. In recent years, trade has grown at twice the rate of the economy. In 2005, exports amounted to 63 percent of Vietnam's GDP. The biggest export markets were the United States, Japan, and China. Foreign direct investment amounted to more than $8 billion in 2006. The Vietnamese administration has endeavored to restructure and streamline the large role played by state-owned enterprises in the economy and to improve education and human resources in order to make the economy more competitive.[29]

Vietnam's government has continued efforts in recent years to moderate border and other tensions with neighbors, notably China. It has integrated the country more closely into ASEAN and has played an active role in APEC and other regional groups. Relations with the United States have grown in importance. In 2006, the United States exported $1.1 billion of goods to Vietnam and imported $8.6 billion of goods in return. Similarly, U.S. companies continue to invest directly in the Vietnamese economy. During 2006, the U.S. private sector committed $444 million to Vietnam in foreign direct investment. This number was expected to rise dramatically following Vietnam's accession into the WTO.[30]

Myanmar

In power since 1988, the military-dominated Myanmar administration remains an exception to the pattern of Asian governments seeking legitimacy through pragmatic nation building, closer integration with the world economy, and convergence with international norms. Instead, 2006 saw a more entrenched and resilient military rule. The Myanmar authorities were defiant in the face of intense and growing pressure from the United States and the West, as well as from some neighbors in Southeast Asia. Instead of seeking reconciliation and accommodation with the political opposition, it has chosen a path of remaining in power indefinitely by coercive means.[31]

The military regime faced large-scale antigovernment demonstrations in major cities in Myanmar during September 2007. Thousands of Buddhist monks led the protests, attracting worldwide attention. The military rulers soon cracked down, killing some demonstrators and detaining thousands. The United States led the international outcry and sought sanctions in the UN Security Council. China and Russia opposed sanctions, however, and supported efforts by a UN mediator to ease tensions between the government and its opposition. Little tangible progress was evident by late 2007.[32]

The military-dominated regime is widely seen as exploiting the nation's economy and mismanaging economic development. Infrastructure continues to deteriorate and foreign investment is minimal. The majority of the people live on less than a dollar a day. Pervasive corruption means that much trade in timber and other resources is unrecorded, as is the large trade in illegal drugs. Western countries have imposed a range of economic sanctions against the junta. China remains the administration's main international backer, providing trade, aid, investment, military equipment, and political support. India and Japan also provide some aid and trade opportunities.[33]

Australia

Australia is now in its sixteenth year of uninterrupted economic expansion and enjoys a higher standard of living than any of the G-7 countries other than the United States. These economic conditions supported the long-serving government of Prime Minister John Howard, who provoked considerable controversy in Australia as a result of his strong support for the U.S.-led military invasion of Iraq and other strong U.S. actions in the Global War on Terrorism. Howard faced a stiff challenge in elections in late 2007 and announced he would retire soon, whatever the election outcome. He lost the election and opposition leader Kevin Rudd, a critic of Howard's support for controversial U.S. policies such as the war in Iraq, became Australia's new head of government. It remains to be seen how far Australian policy will change under Rudd on such controversial issues as close support for the United States in Iraq.

Three days after the terrorist attacks on the United States of September 11, 2001, Prime Minister Howard and President George W. Bush jointly invoked the ANZUS (Australia–New Zealand–United States) Treaty for the first time. Australia was one of the earliest participants in Operation Enduring Freedom in Afghanistan. The Australian Defense Forces also participated in Coalition military action against Iraq in Operation Iraqi Freedom. Australian military and civilian specialists continue to participate in the training of Iraqi security forces and the reconstruction of Iraq.

The United States in recent years has encouraged closer alliance cooperation with both Japan and Australia, and those two countries have in turn strengthened their mutual strategic ties.[34]

Australia has devoted particular attention to relations between developed and developing nations, with emphasis on the ten countries of ASEAN and the island states of the South Pacific. It is an active participant in the ASEAN Regional Forum, which promotes regional cooperation on security issues, and was invited to the East Asia Summit as an inaugural member in 2005. In September 1999, acting under a UN Security Council mandate, Australia led an international coalition to restore order in East Timor upon Indonesia's withdrawal from that territory and, in 2006, again participated in an international peacekeeping operation there. Australia led a regional mission to restore law and order in Solomon Islands in 2003 and again in 2006.

In 2006, the government committed to doubling Australia's official development assistance to US$4 billion a year by 2010. Australia budgeted US$2.48 billion as official development assistance in fiscal year (FY) 2006–2007 and has budgeted US$2.66 billion for 2007–2008. The Australian aid program is currently concentrated in Southeast Asia (Papua New Guinea is the largest-single recipient) and the Pacific islands.[35]

New Zealand

New Zealand has experienced good economic growth, averaging about 4 percent annually in recent years, and its unemployment rate has dropped below 4 percent. Its closest economic partners are Australia and the United States, and it trades actively with Japan and China. In the 1980s, New Zealand imposed conditions on U.S. warships visiting New Zealand ports that led to the U.S. suspension of alliance relations with the country. In recent years, the New Zealand administration has endeavored to improve relations with the United States, to enhance its military preparations in ways supported by the United States and Australia, and to take on other international commitments welcomed by the United States. Acknowledging the need to improve its defense capabilities, the government in 2005 allocated an additional US$3.19 billion over ten years to modernize the country's defense equipment and infrastructure and increase its military personnel. The funding represented a 51 percent increase in defense spending since the Labour Party took the reins of government in 1999.[36]

New Zealand is an active participant in multilateral peacekeeping. It has taken a leading role in trying to bring peace, reconciliation, and reconstruction to the Solomon Islands and the neighboring island of Bougainville. New Zealand also maintains a contingent in the Sinai Multinational Force and Observers and has contributed to UN peacekeeping operations in Angola, Cambodia, Somalia, and the former Yugoslavia. It participated in the Multilateral Interception Force in the Persian Gulf, as well. New Zealand's most recent peacekeeping experience has been in East Timor, where it initially dispatched almost 10 percent of its entire defense force. New Zealand participated in Operation Enduring Freedom and has fielded a Provincial Reconstruction Team in Afghanistan, as well as having deployed a frigate to the Gulf of Oman. In support of the effort to reconstruct Iraq, New Zealand deployed an engineering team to the country.

New Zealand participates in sharing training facilities, personnel exchanges, and joint exercises with the Philippines, Thailand, Indonesia, Papua New Guinea, Brunei, Tonga, and South Pacific states. It also exercises with its Five-Power Defense Arrangement partners—Australia, the United Kingdom, Malaysia, and Singapore.[37]

The Pacific Islands

Leading Pacific Island governments such as Fiji, Papua New Guinea, the Solomon Islands, and Vanuatu in recent years have faced major challenges from political instability, domestic violence and tensions, and poor economic performance. Outside powers led by Australia and New Zealand have repeatedly intervened in the affairs of these states, sometimes sending police and military forces, in order to calm violence and restore a semblance of order and stable governance. Unlike their much smaller and aid-dependent Pacific Island neighbors, these larger Pacific states have more resources that seem sufficient to promote viable economic development. But progress is slow and encumbered by corruption, political and ethnic divisions, and a variety of other problems. Meanwhile, intense competition between China and Taiwan for diplomatic recognition by small Pacific Island countries has seen transfers of assistance and other funds that are widely seen in Australia and New Zealand as fostering increased corruption, poor governance, and overall instability.[38]

SOUTH ASIAN GOVERNMENT PRIORITIES

Apart from Afghanistan, which is beyond the scope of this book, the priorities of the governments of India and Pakistan have had the most importance for U.S. relations with South Asia in the recent period.

India

The democratically elected Indian government has emerged as one of Asia's rising powers despite a variety of complications in India's domestic and foreign policies. Political stability is repeatedly challenged by terrorist attacks and threats, extremist political movements, separatism supported by armed insurgents, and sometimes weak political coalitions leading the government. India's widely publicized economic growth sometimes hides major problems of poor infrastructure, continued government interference, and excessive regulation. Massive poverty involving hundreds of millions of Indians calls for government spending on health, education, and welfare that is well beyond the limited capability of the government. Improvements in relations with the United States, China, and Pakistan have markedly enhanced India's international position. The Indian military is dominant in South Asia, though Pakistan's armed forces, backed by nuclear weapons, pose a major continuing challenge.[39]

The Indian government is a coalition of various parties led by the Congress Party. The leaders must therefore consult with a variety of members in its coalition, including some Marxists, before pursuing economic reforms or other controversial policies. This slows the economic reform process to some degree and complicates moves to establish closer relations with the United States, including Indian government approval of a landmark nuclear cooperation agreement with the United States. The next general election is slated for 2009.[40]

India has the world's twelfth largest economy—and the third largest in Asia behind Japan and China—with a total GDP of around $797 billion. Services, industry, and agriculture account for 51, 28, and 21 percent of GDP, respectively. Nearly two-thirds of the population depends on agriculture for its livelihood. About 28 percent of Indians live below the poverty line, but there is a large and growing middle class of 325–350 million with disposable income for consumer goods.[41]

India is continuing to move forward with market-oriented economic reforms that began in 1991. Recent reforms include liberalized foreign investment and exchange regimes, industrial decontrol, large reductions in tariffs and other trade barriers, reform and modernization of the financial sector, significant adjustments in government monetary and fiscal policies, and progress in safeguarding intellectual property rights.

Real GDP growth for FY 2005 (the fiscal year ending March 31, 2006) was 8.4 percent, up from 7.7 percent growth in the previous year. Growth for FY 2006 was about 8 percent. Foreign portfolio and direct investment inflows have risen significantly in recent years, contributing to the $166 billion in foreign exchange reserves India had accumulated by mid-September 2006.[42]

Economic growth in India is constrained by inadequate infrastructure, a cumbersome bureaucracy, corruption, labor market rigidities, regulatory and foreign investment controls, and high fiscal deficits. The outlook for further trade liberalization is mixed. India eliminated quotas on 1,420 consumer imports in 2002 and has announced its intention to continue to lower customs duties. The tax structure remains complex.[43]

The United States has been India's largest trading partner. Bilateral trade in 2006 was $32 billion. The rapidly growing software sector is boosting service exports and modernizing India's economy. In FY 2005, revenues from the information technology (IT) industry reached a turnover of $23.6 billion and software exports surpassed $22 billion. IT and business process outsourcing exports were projected to grow at nearly 27–30 percent during FY 2006. Personal computer penetration is 14 per 1,000 persons, the cellular/mobile market surged to 140 million subscribers by November 2006, and the country has 54 million cable television customers.[44]

The United States is India's largest investment partner, with a 13 percent share. India's total inflow of U.S. direct investment was estimated at more than $5 billion through FY 2005. India's external debt was $125 billion in FY 2005, up from $123 billion the previous year. Foreign assistance was approximately $3.8 billion in FY 2005, with the United States providing about $126 million in development assistance. The World Bank plans to double aid to India to almost $3 billion a year, with focus on infrastructure, education, health, and rural livelihoods.[45]

The Indian army numbers more than 1.1 million and fields thirty-four divisions. Its primary task is to safeguard the territorial integrity of the country against external threats. The army has been heavily committed in the recent past to counterterrorism operations in Jammu and Kashmir, as well as in the northeast. Its current modernization program focuses on obtaining equipment to be used in combating terror. The army often provides aid to civil authorities and assists the government in organizing relief operations.

The Indian navy is by far the most capable in the region. Its primary missions are the defense of India and of India's vital sea lines of communication. India relies on the sea for 90 percent of its oil and natural gas and more than 90 percent of its foreign trade. The navy currently operates one aircraft carrier, with two on order, fourteen submarines, and fifteen major surface combatants. It is capable of projecting power within the Indian Ocean basin and occasionally operates in the South China Sea, the Mediterranean Sea, and the Arabian Gulf. Fleet introduction of the Brahmos cruise missile and the possible lease of nuclear submarines from Russia will add significantly to the Indian navy's flexibility and striking power.

The Indian air force is becoming a twenty-first-century force through modernization, new tactics, and the acquisition of modern aircraft.[46]

Recent advances in Indian foreign relations focus on improved relations with Pakistan and China, sustained cooperative relations with Russia, and a marked improvement in relations with the United States. India-Pakistan affairs were advanced significantly in November 2003 when Prime Minister Atal Bihari Vajpayee and Pakistani president Pervez Musharraf agreed to a cease-fire—which still holds—along the line of control in Jammu and Kashmir. There have been numerous bilateral discussions and confidence-building measures that have improved relations since that time.[47]

Despite suspicions remaining from a 1962 border conflict between India and China and continuing territorial and boundary disputes, Sino-Indian relations have improved recently. Both countries have sought to reduce tensions along the frontier, expand trade and cultural ties, and normalize relations. Their bilateral trade reached $19 billion in 2005. China is India's second largest trading partner, behind the United States. The two powers have competed for economic advantage and political influence in Asia, notably with rival initiatives toward ASEAN. China has seemed lukewarm in rhetorically supporting India's bid for a permanent seat on the UN Security Council.[48]

A series of high-level visits between the two nations has helped to improve relations. In December 1996, Chinese president Jiang Zemin visited India on a tour of South Asia. While in New Delhi, he and the Indian prime minister signed a series of confidence-building measures along the disputed border, including troop reductions and weapons limitations. Chinese premier Wen Jiabao invited Prime Minister Vajpayee to visit China in June 2003. They recognized the common goals of both countries and made the commitment to build a long-term constructive and cooperative partnership to peacefully promote their mutual political and economic goals without encroaching upon their good relations with other countries. In Beijing, Vajpayee proposed the designation of special representatives to discuss the border dispute at the political level, a process that is still under way. In November 2006, President Hu Jintao made an official state visit to India, further cementing Sino-Indian relations. India and China are building on growing economic ties to improve other aspects of their relationship such as counterterrorism, energy, and trade.[49]

The collapse of the Soviet Union saw a big decline in India's trade with Russia as well as an end to Moscow's strategic backing for India. Nonetheless, Russia and India strongly support close mutual relations. Russia sells India more than $1 billion of advanced military equipment annually, and the two governments operate together on a variety of international issues.[50]

The most dramatic recent advance in India's foreign relations has come with the United States. Recognizing India as a key to strategic U.S. interests, the United States has sought to strengthen its relationship with India. The two countries repeatedly emphasize that they are the world's largest democracies, both committed to political freedom protected by representative government. India is also moving gradually toward greater economic freedom. The United States and India have a common interest in the free flow of commerce and resources, including through the vital sea lanes of the Indian Ocean. They also share an interest in fighting terrorism and creating a strategically stable Asia.

Differences remain, however, including U.S. antagonism toward India's nuclear weapons program and dissatisfaction with the pace of India's economic reforms. In the past, these concerns might have dominated U.S. thinking about India, but today the United States views India as a growing world power with which it shares many common strategic interests.[51]

In late September 2001, President Bush lifted sanctions that had been imposed under the terms of the 1994 Nuclear Proliferation Prevention Act following India's nuclear tests in May 1998. A nonproliferation dialogue initiated after the 1998 nuclear tests bridged many of the gaps in understanding between the countries. In a meeting between Bush and Vajpayee in November 2001, the two leaders expressed a strong interest in transforming the U.S.-India bilateral relationship. High-level meetings and concrete cooperation between the two countries increased during 2002 and 2003. In January 2004, the United States and India launched the Next Steps in Strategic Partnership (NSSP), which was both a milestone in the transformation of the bilateral relationship and a blueprint for its further progress.[52]

In July 2005, President Bush hosted Prime Minister Manmohan Singh in Washington. The two leaders announced the successful completion of the NSSP, as well as other agreements to further enhance cooperation in the areas of civil nuclear, civil space, and high-technology commerce. Other initiatives announced at this meeting included a U.S.-India economic dialogue, the Fight against HIV/AIDS, disaster relief, technology cooperation, a democracy initiative, an agriculture knowledge initiative, a trade policy forum, an energy dialogue, and a CEO forum. President Bush made a reciprocal visit to India in March 2006, during which the progress of these initiatives was reviewed and new initiatives were launched.

In December 2006, Congress passed the historic Henry J. Hyde United States–India Peaceful Atomic Cooperation Act, which allows direct civil nuclear commerce with India for the first time in thirty years. U.S. policy had opposed nuclear cooperation with India because the country had developed nuclear weapons in contravention of international conventions and never signed the Nuclear Non-Proliferation Treaty, but this legislation cleared the way for India to buy U.S. nuclear reactors and fuel for civil use. The agreement stalled in India in 2007 due to political opposition to the accord. Nonetheless, the U.S. and India elevated the strategic partnership further in 2007 to include cooperation in counterterrorism, defense, education, and joint democracy promotion.[53]

Pakistan

The Pakistani administration of President Pervez Musharraf has faced daunting challenges at home and abroad. Domestically, the administration has been forced to deal with numerous opponents, including armed extremists intent on killing the president. Violent opposition undermines central control in large areas of Pakistan, including along the border with Afghanistan. There, pro-Taliban sympathizers allow Taliban fighters to raid Afghanistan from Pakistan, causing major problems for the shaky Afghan administration and its supporters in the United States and the West. The poorly controlled border region reportedly also provides a haven for Osama bin Laden and his al-Qaeda followers. Efforts by the Musharraf administration to curb Kashmiri militants in order to keep relations with India on an even keel antagonize militants in Pakistan, who try to undermine the Musharraf regime.

In 2007, there was an upsurge of large peaceful demonstrations opposing the president's authoritarian rule and pressing for more political pluralism and democracy. The demonstrations reached a crisis level in late 2007, and Musharraf cracked down firmly but pledged to hold elections in 2008. His political opponents, led by former prime minister Benazir Bhutto, pledged continued resistance to his authoritarian rule. The crisis was gravely worsened with Bhutto's assassination in December 2007.

Following the October 12, 1999, ouster of the previous Pakistani government, a military-led government stated its intention to restructure the political and electoral systems. Two days later, General Musharraf declared a state of emergency and issued the Provisional Constitutional Order, which suspended the federal and provincial parliaments, held the constitution in abeyance, and designated Musharraf as chief executive. He appointed an eight-member National Security Council to function as Pakistan's supreme governing body, with a mixture of military and civilian appointees; a civilian cabinet; and a National Reconstruction Bureau to formulate structural reforms. On May 12, 2000, Pakistan's supreme court unanimously validated the October 1999 coup and granted Musharraf executive and legislative authority for three years from the coup date. On June 20, 2001, Musharraf named himself president and was sworn in. In a referendum held on April 30, 2002, Musharraf's presidency was extended by five more years. A handover from military to civilian rule came with parliamentary elections in November 2002, and the appointment of a civilian prime minister. Having previously promised to give up his army post and become a civilian president, General Musharraf announced in late 2004 that he would retain his military role.[54]

Musharraf's rule has seen economic conditions in Pakistan improve, notably as a result of large-scale international aid after 2001. U.S. assistance has played a key role in moving Pakistan's economy from the brink of collapse to setting record high levels of foreign reserves and exports, dramatically lowering its debt. In 2002, the United States led Paris Club efforts to reschedule Pakistan's debt on generous terms, and in April 2003 the United States reduced Pakistan's bilateral official debt by $1 billion. In 2004, approximately $500 million more in bilateral debt relief was granted.[55] The government has since reined in the fiscal mismanagement that produced massive foreign debt.

Weak world demand for its exports and domestic political uncertainty have contributed to Pakistan's high trade deficit. In 2004, growth of the economy rebounded to approximately 6 percent, with substantial improvement in public and external debt indicators, and it remained robust with 7.8 percent growth in 2005. Foreign reserves were at an all-time high of $11.5 billion. Pakistan's exports, which grew by 14.4 percent in 2005–2006, continued to be dominated by cotton textiles and apparel, despite government diversification efforts.[56]

On October 8, 2005, a magnitude-7.6 earthquake struck Pakistan, India, and Afghanistan. The epicenter of the earthquake was near Muzaffarabad, the capital of Pakistani-administered Kashmir, and approximately sixty miles north-northeast of Islamabad. An estimated 75,000 people were killed and 2.5 million were left homeless. The disaster of such a huge magnitude galvanized an international rescue and reconstruction effort in support of the affected region. The United States, among others, responded to Pakistan's call for assistance. At a reconstruction conference in Islamabad on November 19, 2005, the United States announced a $510 million commitment to Pakistan for earthquake relief and reconstruction, including humanitarian assistance, military support for relief operations, and anticipated U.S. private contributions.[57]

The earthquake cost Pakistan $1.1 billion to resettle those affected. Despite the earthquake, GDP growth remained strong at 6.6 percent in FY 2005. Consumer price inflation eased slightly to an average of 8 percent in FY 2005 from 9.3 percent in FY 2004.[58]

Low levels of spending on social services and high population growth have contributed to persistent poverty and unequal income distribution in Pakistan. The trends of resources being devoted to socioeconomic development and infrastructure projects have been improving since 2002, although expenditures remain below global averages. Pakistan's extreme poverty and underdevelopment are key concerns, especially in rural areas.

In foreign affairs, Pakistan's priorities changed dramatically in 2001. After the World Trade Center and Pentagon were attacked on September 11, Pakistan came under intense pressure from the United States. Musharraf pledged complete cooperation with the United States in the war on terror, which included locating and shutting down terrorist training camps within Pakistan's borders, cracking down on extremist groups, and withdrawing support for the Taliban regime in Afghanistan. The events of 9/11 and Pakistan's agreement to support the United States led to a waiver of the sanctions, and military assistance resumed, opening the way to providing spare parts and equipment to enhance Pakistan's capacity to police its border with Afghanistan and address its legitimate security concerns. In 2003, President Bush announced that the United States would provide Pakistan with $3 billion in economic and military aid over five years. This assistance package commenced during FY 2005.[59] Pakistani officials committed to using international assistance—including a major part of the $3 billion U.S. assistance package—to address Pakistan's long-term needs in the health and education sectors.[60]

Presidents Bush and Musharraf have affirmed the long-term, strategic partnership between their two countries. Since September 2001, Pakistan has provided extensive assistance in the war on terror by capturing more than six hundred al-Qaeda members and their allies. In 2004, the United States recognized closer bilateral ties with Pakistan by designating Pakistan as a major non-NATO ally. Bush visited Pakistan in March 2006, where he and Musharraf reaffirmed their shared commitment to a broad and lasting strategic partnership, agreeing to continue their cooperation on a number of issues, including the war on terror, security in the region, strengthening democratic institutions, trade and investment, education, and earthquake relief and reconstruction.[61]

The United States concluded the sale to Pakistan of F-16 aircraft in late 2006, further reflecting their deepening strategic partnership. When Musharraf visited Washington in September 2006, he held a bilateral meeting with President Bush and also participated in a trilateral meeting with Bush and President Hamid Karzai of Afghanistan.[62]

Bush and his senior aides publicly expressed support for Musharraf amid the political crisis in late 2007. U.S. media and congressional opinion was much more mixed, however, with many calling for a cutback in U.S. support and assistance until emergency rule was ended and movement toward democracy restored.

Relations between Pakistan and India have been characterized by rivalry, suspicion, and armed conflict. Although many issues divide the two countries, the most sensitive one since independence has been the status of Kashmir. Relations between India and Pakistan were particularly strained during the 1999 coup in Islamabad. Then, just weeks after 9/11, an attack on India's parliament on December 13, 2001, further strained this relationship.[63]

The prospects for better relations between India and Pakistan improved in early January 2004 when a summit meeting of the South Asian Association for Regional Cooperation (SAARC) permitted India's Prime Minister Vajpayee to meet with President Musharraf. Both leaders agreed to establish a "Composite Dialogue" to resolve their disputes. The Composite Dialogue focuses on several issues, notably confidence-building measures and Kashmir. Relations further improved when Musharraf met Indian prime minister Manmohan Singh in New York in October 2004. Additional steps aimed at improving relations were announced when Indian foreign minister Natwar Singh visited Islamabad in February 2005 and in April 2005 when Musharraf traveled to India. In a further display of improved relations, bus service commenced from Pakistani-controlled Kashmir to Srinagar in the Indian-controlled area in April 2005. After the destructive earthquake hit the Kashmir region in October 2005, the two countries cooperated with each other to deal with the humanitarian crisis.[64]

China has remained on friendly terms with Pakistan for decades. Indian officials have tended to see China using Pakistan as a means to hobble India's rising prominence in Asian affairs. Beijing provided Pakistan with important ingredients for its nuclear weapons and ballistic missile programs. China has muted in recent years its past support for Pakistan against India over the Kashmir issue and does not attempt to compete with the United States and other major donors to Pakistan.

Pakistan's relations with Afghanistan remain complicated by the Taliban fighters finding havens along the poorly controlled Pakistan-Afghanistan border. Pakistan's past support of the Taliban antagonized Iran, but relations have markedly improved recently. Pakistan historically has provided military personnel to strengthen Persian Gulf state defenses and to reinforce its own security interests in the area.[65]

CENTRAL ASIAN GOVERNMENT PRIORITIES

The Central Asian administrations of Kazakhstan, Kyrgyzstan, Tajikistan, Turkmenistan, and Uzbekistan have endeavored to stay in power and to achieve progress in economic development in the face of daunting security challenges at home and abroad caused to a large extent by crime, terrorism, and international competition for influence. The smaller, mountainous, and economically less well-endowed states of Kyrgyzstan (population about 5 million) and Tajikistan (7 million) have been seriously undermined by ethnic and regional tensions. Because of ample energy resources, the outlook for Kazakhstan (population 15 million) and Turkmenistan (5 million) in economic development is good, but both countries have had widespread corruption and political tensions.

Authoritarianism and poverty in Turkmenistan and Uzbekistan lay open the possibility of crises over political succession. The new government in

Turkmenistan, begun in late 2006, has sustained internal stability while opening more to the rest of the world. Kyrgyzstan has an emerging civil society seen to support the small nation in safeguarding its independence, and Turkmenistan is characterized by ethnic homogeneity that also seems to assist its integrity; both nations contain fractious regions and clans, however, that put national unity in question.

Uzbekistan appears to have the potential to become a regional power able to take the lead on policy issues common to Central Asian states and to resist undue influence from more powerful outside nations. It has a large territory and population (27 million), along with energy and other resources. However, tensions between Uzbekistan and other Central Asian states have thwarted regional cooperation.[66]

Among neighboring countries, the situation in Afghanistan has posed the most serious set of immediate problems for the Central Asian states. Particular concerns focus on the Islamic extremism and illicit drugs coming from Afghanistan. Central Asia's leaders do not want Islamic extremists to use bases in Afghanistan, as the militant opposition in Tajikistan did until recently. They objected to the refuge that the Taliban regime provided for the armed insurgents of the IMU (Islamic Movement of Uzbekistan) that threatened Uzbekistan and to its support for Osama bin Laden and his al-Qaeda operatives, who were thought to finance and train religious extremists determined to overthrow the existing governments throughout Central Asia. Meanwhile, historical trade routes have facilitated the smuggling of drugs and other contraband through the region to Russian, European, and other markets. The problem posed by the drug trade has increased because the post-Taliban Afghan government has been weak and unable to enforce antidrug production and trafficking measures.[67]

Central Asian governments have been concerned about Central Asian ethnic groups residing in northern Afghanistan, leading to a recent history of complicated interventions and alignments. During the rule of the Taliban, Uzbekistan's government was concerned with the 1.5 million ethnic Uzbeks in Afghanistan, and it supported an Uzbek paramilitary leader in Afghanistan. The leader was pushed out by Taliban forces in 1998 but returned to assist the Northern Alliance forces in defeating the Taliban in 2001.[68]

There are six million ethnic Tajiks in Afghanistan of concern to both Tajikistan and Iran. The comparatively weak administration in Tajikistan was strongly challenged by the Taliban's growing power, which added to concerns it had over neighboring Uzbekistan and Iran, who backed different sides in the long-running Tajik civil war. Tajikistan's instability and regional concerns caused the government there to rely more on Russia by granting it formal basing rights.[69]

Russia has remained the leading outside power in Central Asia. For Central Asian states, the challenge they face regarding Russia is to maintain useful ties with Moscow without allowing it undue influence. Kazakhstan, because of its shared 4,200-mile border with Russia and its relatively large ethnic Russian population (about one-fourth of a total population of 15 million), has remained vulnerable to Russian influence. Russia and Uzbekistan have improved relations following the Uzbek government's decision in 2005 to expel U.S. forces over a dispute caused by the authoritarian Uzbek regime's violent crackdown on political dissent earlier that year. However, Uzbekistan is interested in asserting its own power and limiting Russian influence in the region.[70]

The administration of President Vladimir Putin at first endeavored to strengthen Russian influence in the region while opposing the growth of U.S. and other influence. It later reversed policy and supported U.S. and NATO deployments in the region in the war against the Taliban regime in Afghanistan in 2001. This reflected a priority in stabilizing Afghanistan and Central Asia and enhancing Russian ties with the United States and the West over antiterrorism, economic cooperation, and other matters of importance to Moscow. The Russian government more recently has become much more cool to the U.S. presence in Central Asia.[71]

The Putin government also has used stronger control of energy resources and transportation routes linking energy sources in Russia and Central Asia with markets in the West and the Pacific Rim. The Central Asian region's continued economic ties with Russia are encouraged by the existence of myriad Moscow-bound and Russian-controlled transportation routes, the difficulty of trade through war-torn Afghanistan, and U.S. opposition to ties with Iran. Also, there are still many inter-enterprise and equipment supply links between Russia and these states. The Uzbek and Kazakh governments have sometimes criticized Russian tendencies to treat Central Asia as an unequal partner, but in general the Central Asian states have had only limited success in diversifying energy exports and developing alternative export routes apart from those involving Russia.[72]

China has emerged as Russia's leading partner in the Shanghai Cooperation Organization (SCO), a regional grouping formed in 2001 that includes Kazakhstan, Kyrgyzstan, Tajikistan, and Uzbekistan as full members. The SCO has focused on antiterrorist cooperation, mutual confidence building, and development issues. Beijing and Moscow periodically use SCO venues to voice opposition to U.S. policies. At the same time, they appear to compete in efforts to gain access to Central Asian energy resources. An oil pipeline from Kazakhstan to China opened in 2006, providing Kazakhstan with access to international oil markets via routes not controlled by Russia. China has signed agreements for natural gas imports from Turkmenistan that, if implemented, seem to represent a diversion from that Central Asian country's long-standing use of Russian supply lines. China's burgeoning foreign trade has made it an important trading partner with bordering Central Asian countries.[73]

Other foreign countries with an interest in Central Asia include Iran and Turkey. Iran was on the same side as Russia and most Central Asian states in backing the Northern Alliance against the Taliban regime in Afghanistan. Iran has good ties and rail and pipeline links with Turkmenistan. It also has improved relations with Kazakhstan, with whom it shares claims to the oil-rich Caspian Sea. Although the toppling of the Taliban benefited Iran, Tehran views the U.S. military presence and U.S. energy and pipeline activities in the region as contrary to its interests. The United States has supported pipelines between Central Asia and Turkey that would bypass both Russia and Iran. Turkey's ability to play a leading role among Central Asia's mainly Turkic peoples has been hampered by its domestic preoccupations with economic, ethnic, and insurgency problems.[74]

Adding to this complicated international mix, the Central Asian states have been compelled to deal with the expansion in U.S. influence in the region, especially following the upsurge in U.S. activism and involvement in the war against the Taliban regime in Afghanistan. The Central Asian states continue to rely on U.S.- and NATO-led efforts against the Taliban insurgents in Afghanistan. Major differences have arisen between the United States and Uzbekistan over U.S. condemnation of the authoritarian government's violent crackdown on political dissent in 2005, which resulted in the expulsion of U.S. forces based in the country. Russia and China publicly supported Uzbekistan's position. The SCO also went on record in 2005 in calling for a deadline for U.S. and NATO forces to leave the region once the Afghan situation stabilizes. Kyrgyzstan has demanded higher U.S. payments for the continued use of a base in that country.

Energy-rich Kazakhstan has welcomed unusual high-level Bush administration attention, including in recent years a very positive state visit by the Kazakh president to the United States and a visit by the U.S. vice president to Kazakhstan. However, the authoritarian government is seen to have strong reservations regarding the Bush administration's insistence that U.S. interests not only focus on security and energy development, which are compatible with Kazakh goals, but also stress fostering democratization and human rights that are at odds with the Central Asian administration's interests.[75]

MONGOLIA

Situated between Central and Northeast Asia, Mongolia is a large country with a small population (under three million). Following the demise of its main backer and controlling outside power, the USSR, the Mongolian government moved toward free market and democratic reforms. It has sought to maintain and develop good and mutually beneficial relations with its powerful neighbors Russia and China and with the newly independent republics of Central Asia. It has reached out to and gained support and assistance from the United States, Japan, South Korea, and other developed countries and international institutions. The Mongolian economy relies on agriculture and mining. Mongolia endeavors to participate actively in Asian regional organizations.[76]

RUSSIAN GOVERNMENT PRIORITIES IN ASIA

In addition to efforts to sustain Russia's leading influence in Central Asia, as noted above, the administration of President Vladimir Putin pursues arms sales, energy deals, and sometimes active diplomacy to benefit Russian economic interests and exert greater influence in Asia, an area of generally secondary concern in Russian foreign policy. Unlike the weaker and less organized Russian government during the tenure of President Boris Yeltsin, the Putin administration's stronger control of the Russian state apparatus and of the important energy assets in the country has combined with improved conditions in the Russian economy to provide a somewhat improved basis for Russia's efforts to influence Asian affairs in line with Russian interests.[77]

China and India receive top priority among Russia's Asian partners. Both receive more than $1 billion in advanced Russian arms annually, with India getting somewhat better access to them than China. Russia's trade with China has improved markedly from low levels of only a few years ago. It focuses on Russian oil sales to China. The oil is shipped by rail; proposed pipelines over the years have had very limited concrete results. Russia has vacillated on a proposed oil pipeline from Siberia to the east and now appears to have settled on a terminus on the Russian Pacific coast, favored by Japan, rather than in China, favored by Beijing.

Russia commonly takes international positions with China and India. It sometimes uses summit meetings with China to articulate criticisms of U.S. policies. At the same time, Moscow, Beijing, and New Delhi have shown in various actions that they give higher priority to their respective relations with the United States than they do with one another. Russia demonstrates little concern about possible strategic differences with India, but it remains wary of China as a rapidly rising power along Russia's sparsely settled east and in Central Asia, an area of top security and economic concern for Russia.

Putin's government gives lower priority to relations with Japan, though it was willing to accept Japanese blandishments in deciding to end the proposed oil pipeline on the Pacific coast, as Japan wished. At the same time, Putin remains uncompromising regarding the so-called Northern Territories, islands north of Hokkaido claimed by Japan but occupied by Russia. The Russian government joins with China and others in criticizing Japanese defense advances and closer alignment with the United States.

Russia is probably the least important participant in the Six-Party Talks. The Russian representatives tend to adopt positions in line with China and South Korea, urging greater flexibility by the United States in dealing with North Korea. Russia plays an active diplomatic role in nascent Asian multilateral organizations, though its ability and willingness to back up its diplomacy with substantive contributions remain low.

NOTES

1. Robert Sutter, *The United States in East Asia* (Lanham, Md.: Rowman & Littlefield, 2003), 169–96.

2. Sheldon Simon, "Southeast Asia's Defense Needs: Change or Continuity?" in *Strategic Asia, 2005–2006: Military Modernization in an Era of Uncertainty*, ed. Ashley J. Tellis and Michael Wills (Seattle: National Bureau of Asian Research, 2005), 269–304.

3. Evelyn Goh, *Meeting the China Challenge: The U.S. in Southeast Asian Regional Security Strategies* (Washington, D.C.: East-West Center Washington, 2005).

4. Jorgen Orstrom Moller, review of *Realism and Interdependence in Singapore's Foreign Policy*, by N. Ganesan. *Contemporary Southeast Asia* 28, no. 1 (April 1, 2006): 164–67.

5. Alan Collins, *Security and Southeast Asia* (Boulder, Colo.: Lynne Reinner, 2003).

6. Stanley Foundation, "New Power Dynamics in Southeast Asia: Issues for U.S. Policymakers," Policy Dialogue Brief, October 2006, http://www.stanleyfdn.org/publications/pdb/spcpdb06.pdf.

7. Donald Weatherbee, "Strategic Dimensions of Economic Interdependence in Southeast Asia," in *Strategic Asia, 2006–2007: Trade, Interdependence, and Security*, ed. Ashley J. Tellis and Michael Wills, 271–300 (Seattle: National Bureau of Asian Research, 2006).

8. *ISEAS Regional Outlook Forum, 2007: Summary Report* (Singapore: Institute of Southeast Asian Studies, 2007).

9. Damien Kingsbury, "Indonesia in 2006: Cautious Reform," *Asian Survey* 47, no. 1 (January/February 2007): 155–61.

10. U.S. Department of State, "Background Note: Indonesia," August 2007, http://www.state.gov/r/pa/ei/bgn/2748.htm.

11. Edward Cody, "East Asian Summit Marked by Discord," *Washington Post*, December 14, 2005.

12. Peter Wallace, "Philippines: Fragility and the Mixed Outlook," in *ISEAS Regional Outlook Forum*, 23–27.

13. Sheila S. Coronel, "The Philippines in 2006: Democracy and Its Discontents," *Asian Survey* 47, no. 1 (January/February 2007): 179–81.

14. U.S. Department of State, "Background Note: Philippines," May 2007, http://www.state.gov/r/pa/ei/bgn/2794.htm.

15. See President Gloria Macapagal-Arroyo's speech during the opening ceremony of the Fortieth ASEAN Ministerial Meeting, Manila, July 30, 2007, at http://www.aseansec.org/20758.htm.

16. "Opposition to Boycott Thai Vote on April 2," *International Herald Tribune Asia-Pacific*, February 27, 2006.

17. James Ockey, "Thailand in 2006: Retreat to Military Rule," *Asian Survey* 47, no. 1 (January/February 2007): 133–40.

18. Peter Brimble, "Thailand: Uncertainties and Turbulence," in *ISEAS Regional Outlook Forum*, 29–31.

19. U.S. Department of State, "Background Note: Thailand," June 2007, http://www.state.gov/r/pa/ei/bgn/2814.htm.

20. Claudia Derichs, "Malaysia in 2006: An Old Tiger Roars," *Asian Survey* 47, no. 1 (January/February 2007): 148–49.

21. U.S. Department of State, "Background Note: Malaysia," May 2007, http://www.state.gov/r/pa/ei/bgn/2777.htm.

22. Claudia Derichs, "Malaysia in 2005: Moving Forward Quietly," *Asian Survey* 46, no. 1 (January/February 2006): 171–72.

23. Derichs, "Malaysia in 2006," 153–54; U.S. Department of State, "Background Note: Malaysia."

24. U.S. Department of State, "Background Note: Singapore," April 2007, http://www.state.gov/r/pa/ei/bgn/2798.htm.

25. Song Seng Wun, "Singapore in 2007," in *ISEAS Regional Outlook Forum*, 32–33.

26. Amitav Acharya, *Singapore's Foreign Policy: The Search for Regional Order* (Singapore: World Scientific, 2007).

27. Singapore, Ministry of Defence, "Defense Policy," http://www.mindef .gov.sg/imindef/about_us/defence_policy.html.

28. U.S. Department of State, "Background Note: Singapore."

29. Hy V. Luong, "Vietnam in 2006: Stronger Global Integration and Resolve for Better Governance," *Asian Survey* 47, no. 1 (January/February 2007): 168–70.

30. Low Sin Leng, "Vietnam: Ready for a Take-off," in *ISEAS Regional Outlook Forum*, 25–29.

31. Ardeth Maung Thawnghmung and Muang Aung Myoe, "Myanmar in 2006: Another Year of Housekeeping?" *Asian Survey* 47, no. 1 (January/February 2007): 194–99.

32. Sheldon W. Simon, "Burma Heats Up and the U.S. Blows Hot and Cold," *Comparative Connections* 9, no. 3 (3rd Qtr 2007): 61, 64–65, http://www.csis.org/ pacformedia/csis/pubs/0703q.pdf.

33. Jurgen Haacke, *Myanmar's Foreign Policy*, Adelphi Paper 381 (London: Institute for International and Strategic Studies, 2006).

34. Ralph Cossa, "U.S.-Australia: Still Mates!" Pacnet no. 49A (Honolulu: CSIS Pacific Forum, December 19, 2007).

35. "Elements of Australian Foreign Policy," September 10, 2007, http:// australianpolitics.com/foreign/elements/.

36. Thomas Lum and Bruce Vaughn, *The Southwest Pacific: U.S. Interests and China's Growing Influence*, CRS Report RL34086 (Washington, D.C.: Congressional Research Service, Library of Congress, July 6, 2007), 21–23.

37. U.S. Department of State, "Background Note: New Zealand," May 2007, http://www.state.gov/r/pa/ei/bgn/35852.htm.

38. Lum and Vaughn, *Southwest Pacific*, 1–19.

39. Sharif Rangnekar and Manish Sharma, "India's Split Personality," *Far Eastern Economic Review* 169, no. 1 (2006): 18–21; Ashutosh Varshney, "India's Democratic Challenge," *Foreign Affairs* 86, no. 2 (March/April 2007): 93–106; Martin Walker, "India's Path to Greatness," *Wilson Quarterly* 30, no. 3 (Summer 2006): 22–30; C. Raja Mohan, "Poised for Power: The Domestic Roots of India's Slow Rise," in *Strategic Asia, 2007–2008: Domestic Political Change and Grand Strategy*, ed. Ashley J. Tellis and Michael Wills (Seattle: National Bureau of Asian Research, 2007), 177–210.

40. "Indian Politics: Ghandi's Girl," *Economist*, July 26, 2007.

41. U.S. Department of State, "Background Note: India," October 2007, http://www.state.gov/r/pa/ei/bgn/3454.htm.

42. Keith Bradsher, "India's Economy Is on the Verge of Overheating," *New York Times*, February 10, 2007.

43. Ranab Bardhan, "Globalization Hits Bumps in India," *YaleGlobal Online*, October 3, 2006, http://yaleglobal.yale.edu/display.article?id=8246.

44. K. Alan Kronstadt, *India-U.S. Relations*, CRS Report RL33529 (Washington, D.C.: Congressional Research Service, Library of Congress, July 31, 2006), 15–18.

45. Ibid., 21.

46. John Gill, "India and Pakistan: A Shift in the Military Calculus?" in Tellis and Wills, *Strategic Asia, 2005–2006*, 237–68.

47. Baldev Raj Nayar, "India in 2004: Regime Change in a Divided Democracy," *Asian Survey* 45, no. 1 (January/February 2005): 80–82.

48. Hugo Restall, "India's Coming Eclipse of China," *Far Eastern Economic Review* 169, no. 2 (March 2006): 12–17.

49. Satu Limaye, "Consolidating Friendships and Nuclear Legitimacy," *Comparative Connections* 9, no. 4 (4th Qtr 2007): 141–43.

50. Ibid.

51. S. Paul Kapur and Sumit Ganguly, "The Transformation of U.S.-India Relations: An Explanation for the Rapprochement and Prospects for the Future," *Asian Survey* 47, no. 4 (July/August 2007): 642–56.

52. Reviewed in Kronstadt, *India-U.S. Relations*.

53. Limaye, "Consolidating Friendships and Nuclear Legitimacy," 153.

54. K. Alan Kronstadt, *Pakistan-U.S. Relations*, CRS Report RL33498 (Washington, D.C.: Congressional Research Service, Library of Congress, July 27, 2006), 5–6.

55. Thomas Lum, *U.S. Foreign Aid to East and South Asia: Selected Recipients*, CRS Report RL31362 (Washington, D.C.: Congressional Research Service, Library of Congress, January 3, 2007), 26–29, 34–37.

56. Economist.com, "Country Briefings: Pakistan," August 20, 2007, http://www.economist.com/countries/Pakistan/.

57. U.S. Department of State, "Background Note: Pakistan," May 2007, http://www.state.gov/r/pa/ei/bgn/3453.htm.

58. Charles H. Kennedy, "Pakistan in 2005: Surviving Domestic and International Tremors," *Asian Survey* 46, no. 1 (January/February 2006): 125–26.

59. Lum, *U.S. Foreign Aid*, 34–37.

60. Kronstadt, *Pakistan-U.S. Relations*, 19–20.

61. Ibid., 4.

62. Sheryl Gay Stolberg, "Bush Plays Chaperon for Awkward Encounter," *New York Times*, September 28, 2006.

63. International Crisis Group, "India, Pakistan, and Kashmir: Stabilizing a Cold Peace," Asia Briefing No. 51 (Brussels: International Crisis Group, 2006).

64. Kronstadt, *Pakistan-U.S. Relations*, 6.

65. Ibid., 6–7.

66. Martha Brill Olcott, *Central Asia's Second Chance* (Washington, D.C.: Carnegie Endowment for International Peace, 2005); Daniel Burghart and Theresa Sabonis-Helf, eds., *In the Tracks of Tamerlane: Central Asia's Path to the 21st Century* (Washington, D.C.: National Defense University Press, 2004); Boris Rumer, *Central Asia at the End of the Transition* (Armonk, N.Y.: M. E. Sharpe, 2005). This assessment also draws from Jim Nichol, *Central Asia's Security: Issues and Implications for U.S. Interests*, CRS Report RL30294 (Washington, D.C.: Congressional Research Service, Library of Congress, January 7, 2005).

67. Olcott, *Central Asia's Second Chance*, 212–15.

68. International Crisis Group, *Uzbekistan: In for the Long Haul*, Asia Briefing No. 45 (Brussels: International Crisis Group, 2006).

69. International Crisis Group, *Tajikistan's Politics: Confrontation or Consolidation?* Asia Briefing No. 33 (Brussels: International Crisis Group, 2004).

70. Richard Weitz, "Averting a New Great Game in Central Asia," *Washington Quarterly* 29, no. 3 (2006): 155–67.

71. Elizabeth Wishnick, "Russia and the CIS in 2006: Asserting Russian Interests on Korean Security, Energy, and Central Asia," *Asian Survey* 47, no. 1 (January/February 2007): 66–67.

72. Peter Rutland, "Russia's Economic Role in Asia: Toward Deeper Integration," in Tellis and Wills, *Strategic Asia, 2006–2007*, 173–204.

73. Reviewed in Robert Sutter, *Chinese Foreign Relations* (Lanham, Md.: Rowman & Littlefield, 2007), 308–19.

74. Rollie Lal, *Central Asia and Its Neighbors: Security and Commerce at the Crossroads* (Santa Monica, Calif.: RAND, 2006).

75. Olga Oliker and David Shlapak, *U.S. Interests in Central Asia: Policy Priorities and Military Roles* (Santa Monica, Calif.: RAND, 2005; Robert Sutter, "The United States and Asia in 2006: Crisis Management, Holding Patterns, and Secondary Initiatives," *Asian Survey* 47, no. 1 (January/February 2007): 19–20.

76. U.S. Department of State, "Background Note: Mongolia," July 2007, http://www.state.gov/r/pa/ei/bgn/2779.htm.

77. This section is based on Celeste Wallander, "Russia: The Domestic Sources of a Less-than-Grand Strategy," in Tellis and Wills, *Strategic Asia, 2007–2008*, 139–76; Wishnick, "Russia and the CIS in 2006"; and Elizabeth Wishnick, "Russia and the CIS in 2005: Promoting East Asian Oil Diplomacy, Containing Change in Central Asia," *Asian Survey* 46, no. 1 (January/February 2006): 69–78.

9

Regional Trends
and Their Implications
for U.S. Leadership

Chapter 5 assessed the main determinants of regional dynamics in the Asia-Pacific of relevance to the United States and U.S. relations with the region. They can be summarized as follows:

- Reactions by regional governments to changes in major regional power relationships, including China's and India's rising power, Japan's greater international assertiveness, and Indonesia's slow emergence from weakness and drift
- The desire of regional governments to sustain economic growth amid growing challenges of globalization and the information revolution
- Increasing interest among regional governments in, and convergence over, subregional and regional multilateral groups and organizations that address important economic, political, and security concerns of Asia-Pacific countries
- Reactions of regional governments to broad security changes brought about by the Global War on Terror that began in 2001 and by changes on the Korean Peninsula prompted mainly by North Korea's provocative pursuit of nuclear weapons, ballistic missiles, and other destabilizing systems
- Regional concern over apparent swings in U.S. security, economic, and political policies and objectives, ranging from perceived excessive U.S. activism, unilateralism, and pressure to possible U.S. pullbacks and withdrawal from Asia-Pacific affairs

These drivers result from and work with the range of priorities of individual regional governments examined in chapters 6, 7, and 8. They lead to several trends of importance to U.S. relations with the Asia-Pacific that are likely to continue for at least the next five years and probably longer.[1]

GENERAL TRENDS

Proliferation of Regional Initiatives, Diffusion of Regional Prominence

The aforementioned determinants and the priorities of individual regional governments have resulted in a diffusion of regional initiatives and prominence, adding to the unpredictability of the types of tactical alliances or ad-hoc blocs that may emerge on specific issues. A variety of regional, subregional, and other multinational groups have emerged in the post–Cold War period as a result of initiatives from various large, and some smaller, Asian powers. This activism seems to reduce U.S. regional prominence; some of the groupings exclude U.S. participation, though none directly oppose the United States.[2]

No Coherent Regional Bloc

Regional security and economic trends push power relations in Asia in various and often complicated or seemingly contradictory directions. In this context, a static bloc of countries that dominates regional affairs is unlikely to emerge, though an increase in Asia-only and other regional and subregional forums as an outgrowth of intraregional interaction is evident.[3]

Defensive Motives of Regional Powers

The increase in policy initiatives coming from Asian governments has seemingly been based as much on insecurity and uncertainty over growing challenges and changing regional trends as on careful, long-term strategic plans. Even in the case of the region's main rising power, China, specialists discern strong defensive reasoning behind its recent initiatives in Asian affairs.[4] Meanwhile, regional activism by Japan, India, Russia, and other powers, including the United States, is driven of late partly by the perceived need to avoid falling behind China and one another in advancing their interests in regional affairs.[5]

National Governments—Key Agents of Change

The policy initiatives seen recently in Asia generally have reflected the policy priorities of individual governments. Many of these initiatives have been confined to specific areas (e.g., security, economic, or political). However, they often have had broader implications for regional trends affecting the United States and have prompted U.S. responses. Examples include:

- South Korean president Kim Dae Jung's opening to North Korea in 2000 not only eased tensions on the peninsula but also set off a spate of regional diplomatic maneuvering by the United States and other governments seeking advantage in the newly relaxed situation on the Korean Peninsula.[6]
- China's proposed free trade agreement (FTA) with the Association of Southeast Asian Nations (ASEAN) in 2002 prompted a flurry of activity as Japan, India, the United States, and others strove to develop their own trade arrangements with the Southeast Asian nations.[7]
- China worked with Malaysia and others to promote an Asian Leadership Summit in 2005 based on ASEAN+3 membership. This caused Japan to take the lead in working with Indonesia, Singapore, and others to propose a broader membership that would include India, Australia, New Zealand, and possibly the United States, Russia, and others. Seemingly in response, the United States emphasized an Asia-Pacific Free Trade Area based on the large pan-Pacific membership of the Asia Pacific Economic Cooperation (APEC) group.[8]

SPECIFIC TRENDS

Security Initiatives and "Hedging"

It is hard to avoid the term "hedging" when assessing recent discussions of security relations in Asia. The term is widely used to define patterns of interaction between and among regional states, and yet it remains poorly defined and often imprecise. Evelyn Goh, an academic specialist on Asia-Pacific security dynamics, advised that what is referred to as "hedging" is the norm in international relations. Most states adopt insurance policies, and while they establish military relationships with some states, they avoid committing themselves to potentially antagonistic stances toward other states most of the time, thereby preserving a maximum range of strategic options. During the Cold War, such behavior was severely limited by a need to line up with one side among contending blocs, but that era is now over.[9]

Another way to look at hedging is to see it as contingency planning. Asian governments face a complicated and uncertain security situation with many variables. Even though most of them seek to emphasize the positive in their recent security policy and initiatives with one another, historical experience reinforces prudence in supporting preparations for negative developments or contingencies at the same time.[10]

Hedging is defined in this study as a broad-ranging practice widely used by Asian governments seeking various domestic and international means at the same time in order to safeguard their security and well-being in the prevailing uncertain, but generally not immediately threatening, environment of post–Cold War Asia. The new Asian order has witnessed a tendency on the part of most governments in the region to emphasize nationalistic ambitions and independence. They eschew the tight and binding alignments of the past in favor of diverse arrangements with various powers that support security and other state interests in the newly fluid regional environment.[11] Three of the five determinants of recent regional dynamics cited above involve security issues that on the whole create an uncertain security situation in Asia. This environment is not so ambivalent that countries feel a need to seek close alignment with a major power or with one another to protect themselves, but it prompts a wide variety of hedging, with each government seeking more diverse and varied arrangements in order to shore up their security interests.

In this context, regional powers (i.e., China, Japan, India, Russia, and a wide array of smaller Asian governments) are continually hedging—using more diversified diplomacy, military preparations, and other means to ensure that their particular security interests will be safeguarded, in case the regional situation should change for the worse. All these governments want generally positive relations with the United States, the region's leading military and economic power, but some are wary of U.S. policy and seek diversified ties to enhance their security and other options. Meanwhile, they also remain cautious of one another and work with the United States and others to ensure their interests in the face of possible regional dangers posed by their neighbors. For example, China's rising prominence and power has prompted an array of recent hedging activities as China's neighbors endeavor to engage with Beijing constructively on the one hand, while preparing for possible contingencies involving China that would be adverse to their interests on the other.[12]

Economic Cooperation and Competition

Asian governments generally recognize the need to conform to the international economic norms that are broadly supported by the United States. To do otherwise would risk undermining the national economic development of their countries, which depends heavily on smoothly running international trade and investment. The political standing and legitimacy of the governments of Asia's export-oriented economies are based to a great degree on how well the governments manage economic affairs. Even entrenched authoritarian regimes, such as the Suharto administration in Indonesia in the 1990s, have been fatally undermined by failure to address competently pressing economic issues. However, Asian governments also seek to block or slow the perceived adverse consequences of economic globalization by means of greater cooperation with similarly affected governments inside and outside the region, through existing organizations such as ASEAN, APEC, and the World Trade Organization (WTO) and in emerging regional and broader groupings, notably ASEAN+3.[13]

Though the economic cooperation mechanisms and agreements seek mutual benefit, national rivalries remain vividly evident. As noted earlier, China was widely seen as stealing the lead from Japan and others in initiating in 2002 a free trade agreement with ASEAN. Japan, India, the United States, South Korea, Australia, and others have followed with FTA and other initiatives in order to keep pace with China's ascendance in Southeast Asia.

In this competitive environment, national governments seek their respective interests independently, even when they appear to be—and indeed are—cooperating, most noticeably in multilateral organizations in the Asia-Pacific. This can be seen in numerous instances:

- Based on its burgeoning economy, China has set the pace in recent years with economic cooperation initiatives in ASEAN, the Shanghai Cooperation Organization (SCO), and ASEAN+3, among others, that shore up its position as a regional leader.[14]
- The national governments that make up ASEAN encourage free trade and other economic arrangements between ASEAN and a variety of powers as a means to enhance constructive international interaction with Southeast Asia and to ensure that no single outside power will be in a position to dominate or dictate to the Southeast Asian states.[15]
- South Korea has endeavored to gain domestic economic and political benefits and to buttress its international economic position and overall importance through a negotiated FTA with the United States in 2007, followed by similar agreements proposed for China, the European Union, Japan, and others.[16]
- Major Asia-Pacific energy consumers, including China, Japan, and India, work assiduously and often in competition in seeking advantageous economic cooperation with Middle Eastern, Central Asian, and other major energy exporters.[17]
- Despite its closer alliance relationship with the United States, the Japanese government at times endeavors to foster greater economic cooperation in Asian organizations that exclude non-Asian powers.[18]

Political Trends

Opinion polling, focus groups, and other reports indicate that government transparency and accountability, the free flow of information, democracy, and an open society are supported by many in Asia. But reporting also shows that regional governments continue to strongly oppose outside pressure for political rights and democracy that come at the expense of national sovereignty and stability. Firm in their own convictions, regional powers—including U.S. allies—consult with one another at the United Nations General Assembly, the annual UN Human Rights Commission meetings in Geneva, and other forums in finding independent paths for dealing with regional human rights and other political issues. Some have appealed to nationalism—a powerful force in many of the newly emerged regional states—in efforts to mobilize their populations against the perceived outside pressure and domination by the United States or others.[19]

There was little regret in the region when the United States lost its seat on the UN Human Rights Commission in 2001. Furthermore, the George W. Bush administration's strong emphasis on democracy promotion in its second term received a very mixed reception in Asia. Some critics highlighted the seeming hypocrisy of the U.S. government promotion of human rights abroad while curbing such rights at home under the rubric of the war on terror. Others noted perceived U.S. expediency in doing little about human rights and democracy in authoritarian states such as Pakistan, China, and Kazakhstan, which were important for other U.S. interests, while focusing strong negative attention to smaller states like Myanmar.[20]

SPECIFIC CHALLENGES FOR U.S. LEADERSHIP

Opposition to U.S. Foreign Policies

Recent determinants and regional trends detailed above show that Asian governments, elites, and public opinion generally give priority to national development and greater prominence for their countries, and that they increasingly support regional collaboration and consultation in various multilateral groups. As explained in the introduction, Asians have tended to see Bush administration foreign policies as being at odds with these important regional interests and sensibilities.

Most Asians have opposed the U.S.-led war in Iraq. The U.S. emphasis on military means in the war on terror has been widely seen as excessive and myopic. The scandals and controversies surrounding American treatment of Iraqi prisoners and international terror suspects have severely damaged the U.S. image as a government committed to human rights and due process according to democratic principles. In addition, the strong U.S. support for Israel in its ongoing disputes with Palestinians has offended regional Muslim populations and their leaders. The hard-line Bush administration posture in negotiations over North Korea's nuclear weapons development that was prevalent until recently was also seen as misguided and received little regional support.

Perceived U.S. unilateralism in refusing to be bound by United Nations procedures regarding the war in Iraq and other matters, in refusing to sign the Kyoto Protocol on climate change, and in pushing U.S. initiatives to promote trade and democracy favored by the United States have offended many constituencies in Asia. The U.S. government has been widely seen in the region as being absorbed by the conflicts in Iraq, Afghanistan, and the broader war on terror, and therefore insensitive to Asian regional trends emphasizing cooperation, multilateral consultation, and development.

The contradictions between the priorities of regional governments and opinion and U.S. foreign policy and behavior have dominated recent public and private discourse about the United States in Asia. They have led to major declines in approval ratings of the U.S. government in opinion polls throughout the region. There have been occasional bright spots for the United States, such as broad approval in the region for the U.S. role in helping the victims of the 2004 tsunami disaster. But on the whole, specialists discern a clear undermining of the ability of the U.S. government to lead by example or to otherwise persuade the governments and peoples of the region to follow U.S. policies and initiatives on a variety of international issues. At a minimum, the specialists point to a serious decline in the U.S. government's image in Asia. Taken together, this mix of disputes, contradictions, and adverse trends appears to pose the most immediate and prominent challenge to contemporary U.S. relations with and leadership in Asia.[21]

Security Issues

The military power of the United States and the willingness of the U.S. government to bear the major security responsibilities that affect U.S. interests as well as those of Asian countries means that the United States is looked to by those countries to play a leading role in dealing with salient regional security issues and hot spots. Although Washington has received positive regional reactions to its handling of some issues, recent publicity has focused on sharp criticism and disapproval on salient security issues.

As noted above, the U.S. handling of the war in Iraq is roundly criticized, and there is sometimes strong disagreement by some regional governments with aspects of the broader U.S.-led war on terrorism.[22] The latter include opposition to U.S. initiatives regarding security in the Malacca Strait, military bases in Central Asia, and the Proliferation Security Initiative focused on North Korea and other potential proliferators of weapons of mass destruction. On the other hand, the Asian governments also continue to rely on U.S. leadership in dealing with the global terrorist threat. They seem to recognize that they are ill equipped to track and counter international terrorists and that they need to cooperate with the United States militarily and through intelligence, law enforcement, and other means.[23]

The U.S. handling of North Korea's nuclear weapons development has elicited more regional support and less criticism since the Bush administration moved from a hard-line stance to a more flexible negotiating posture.[24] Meanwhile, U.S. handling of the two other regional security hot spots, the Taiwan Strait and Kashmir, has been broadly accepted in the Asian region as conducive to sustaining regional peace and development.[25]

Alliance Management

The Bush administration has markedly advanced U.S. alliance relations with the governments of Japan and Australia. Japanese elite and popular opinion on the whole seems to welcome the closer ties with the United States, although there are still significant issues regarding U.S. bases in Japan, burden sharing, and the willingness of the Japanese government to depart from narrowly restrictive defense policies of the past in order to meet U.S. expectations.[26] For its part, the long-serving government of Australian prime minister John Howard faced considerable domestic resistance for his pro-U.S. security policies and actions. The outlook for U.S.-Australian relations was clouded by Howard's departure from political leadership.[27]

The United States has advanced its military relations with Singapore and India under the rubric of "strategic partnerships." It has also encouraged high-level security relationships between and among the United States, Japan, Australia, and India. Washington has striven diligently and with some success to build other webs of military connections with a wide variety of Asian states, devoting special attention to promoting ties with Indonesia and, to a degree, with Vietnam in Southeast Asia and Kazakhstan in Central Asia. Pakistan receives annually billions of dollars of U.S. support, advanced equipment, and other backing as a key ally against the insurgents in Afghanistan and the broader war on terrorism.[28]

The Bush administration has improved its alliance relationships with the Philippines and Thailand through training, provision of military assistance and equipment, security consultations, and high-level diplomacy focused on security issues of mutual concern. The advances have met with some setbacks, notably the Philippine decision to withdraw its modest troop contingent from Iraq because of a terrorist threat against a kidnapped Philippine citizen. Thai and Philippine support for the United States also is evidently tempered by their reluctance to be seen as siding with the United States at the expense of their other important international relationships, notably their close and growing relationships with China.[29]

The biggest regional alliance problem for the United States in recent years has been with South Korea. Over the past decade, major changes in South Korean politics, public opinion, and elite viewpoints have prompted a major shift in Seoul's approach to North Korea and attitude toward and interest in its alliance relationship with the United States. Under the Bush administration, U.S. policy toward North Korea appeared for many years to move in a direction opposite that of South Korea. South Korean–U.S. differences over policy toward North Korea, basing and burden-sharing issues, trade, and other issues have periodically reached crisis proportions. Leaders on both sides tend to see their interests being best served by continuing the alliance, but persisting friction and disputes mean that the formerly close U.S.–South Korean alignment on Korean Peninsula issues and other international affairs is a thing of the past.[30]

Asia-Pacific Multilateralism

There is a widely held perception in both Asia and the United States that the U.S. government has been insufficiently attentive to the remarkable growth in recent years of regional and subregional organizations and groups of nations dealing with important economic, political, and security matters. Though this perception is often disputed by U.S. officials and others, a common view is that the United States is losing out to China and other powers that have been more adept in positioning their governments to take advantage of trends toward the greater international cooperation among Asia-Pacific governments. This view sees Asian governments as driven by mutual economic concerns and interests—notably growing trade and investment flows among them—and by common security problems that seem to require going beyond bilateral relations or other existing multilateral means to seek solutions. Some see the emergence of a new regional order in Asia that will rely on ever-closer cooperation among regional governments in their various groupings and will be less influenced than in the past by the power and policies of what are seen as nonregional powers, including the United States. Asian and U.S. observers often see an increasing convergence among regional leaders backed by emerging sizeable middle classes and elites that increasingly resemble each other, having similar lifestyles and interests as well as extensive communication networks.[31]

To avoid being left behind in the wake of Chinese, Japanese, Indian, and other Asian regional initiatives designed to advance regional groups in ways advantageous to their respective national interests, the United States seemingly needs to work harder in order to "catch up." Too often, however, U.S. leaders are viewed as distracted with the war in Iraq, the broader war on terror, and other more immediate problems. They are thought to give insufficient attention to the need to conform more to the requirements and norms of the growing number of Asian organizations. Even such close American allies and friends as Japan, Australia, and Singapore strongly urge greater constructive U.S. involvement, but the results thus far are considered unsatisfactory, according to many regional observers and officials.[32]

Managing U.S. Domestic Pressures

In the post–Cold War period, the tendency of U.S. interest groups, constituents, and other domestic forces to work through Congress, the media, and other channels to push U.S. foreign policies in sometimes extreme directions has grown, and it is unlikely to subside soon. The trend did decline during the first years of the war on terrorism, but has revived in recent years. It has seriously challenged the Bush administration's policies on trade and China and has complicated U.S. initiatives toward India and interaction with countries such as North Korea, Indonesia, Pakistan, and Kazakhstan.

Gauging the importance of this challenge to U.S. policy toward Asia is difficult because it depends on U.S. reactions to unknowable future regional events and on the hard-to-predict outcome of U.S. elections. Prevailing circumstances seem to indicate that current and future U.S. administrations will continue to face major challenges from constituents concerned over the massive U.S. trade deficit and what this means for American economic interests and trade policies. It is less clear whether strong divisions in the United States over the war in Iraq will translate into greater pressure to restrict U.S. military deployments elsewhere, including in Asia. Thus far, they have not done so.[33]

THE RISE OF CHINA AND THE DURABILITY OF U.S. REGIONAL LEADERSHIP

In addition to the problems listed above, U.S. policy in the Asia-Pacific faces challenges posed by newly rising powers in the fluid regional policy environment. China is in the lead in this category. China's strengths in the Asia-Pacific include a burgeoning economy; it is the leading trader with most advancing regional economies, the largest recipient of foreign investment, and the largest holder of foreign exchange reserves. Attentive and adroit Chinese diplomacy fosters ever-closer ties with neighboring countries through bilateral and multilateral relations. Furthermore, China's rapidly improving military has become the region's leading force.[34]

In the United States, some specialists judge that the Chinese leadership is set on a goal of using its rising regional prominence to weaken and marginalize the United States while China seeks territorial and regional aims and prominence now blocked by U.S. power and influence. Others judge that China's administration seeks regional prominence for other reasons, but they also advise that the net effect of China's smooth diplomacy and collaborative policies with its Asia-Pacific neighbors shows the United States to be maladroit and ineffective by comparison. Still others judge that the United States need not feel defensive or threatened in the face of China's advancement, or that the United States can collaborate with a rising China as a means to secure U.S. interests in the Asia-Pacific region and elsewhere.[35]

Given the various challenges facing U.S. policy and the difficulties U.S. leaders have faced and will face in the fluid Asia-Pacific policy environment that are detailed above, it is natural that some specialists and observers have concluded that the United States is in decline in the Asia-Pacific region. This decline also seems underlined by China's success in advancing its prominence in regional affairs in recent years.

However, an important counterargument is made by some American and regional officials and specialists, who believe that U.S. power and influence in the Asia-Pacific region has not significantly declined.[36] They argue that assessments which conclude that there has been a U.S. decline due to China's rise and other reasons replicate erroneous predictions of U.S. decline in the region in the 1970s and 1980s.[37]

In order to determine which view is correct, the following discussion assesses in some detail how China, the most successful power to stand up in the post–Cold War Asia-Pacific region, has dealt with challenges in regional affairs that also affect the United States. It furthermore shows, through a comparison of China's strengths and weaknesses with those of the United States, how China's rise actually illustrates the resiliency of U.S. leadership in the Asia-Pacific.

Chinese' Advances and Accomplishments

In much of the post–Cold War period, the foreign trade of China's export-oriented economy has grown at about twice the rate of China's impressive overall economic growth. The result is that China became the leading trading partner, or at least one of the leading trading partners, of all its Asian neighbors. The advanced economies of South Korea, Taiwan, and Japan saw China emerge as their largest and increasingly important trading partner. China grew in importance in Southeast Asia and caught up with Japan and the United States to become the region's top import and export destination. Its trade also grew with India and the South Asian nations and with Central Asian countries, though geographic distance and the low level of development of many of those economies limited the scope and importance of these economic connections. China as well became increasingly significant to Russia and Australia, major exporters of energy and raw materials needed by China's manufacturers.[38]

The trading patterns that emerged among China and its neighbors have created webs of relationships and dependencies. Asia-Pacific producers of energy and raw materials found China to be a ready market for their goods. On the other hand, regional manufacturers of consumer products and industrial goods often found it difficult to compete in international and domestic markets with the low-cost and good-quality Chinese manufactured products. They therefore tended to integrate their enterprises with China by joining the wave of foreign investors that made China one of the largest recipients of foreign direct investment in the world. The developed economies of Asia have accounted for the majority of the $60–70 billion annual influx of foreign direct investment to China in recent years.[39]

What has resulted are networks of trading relationships characterized by so-called processing trade, which accounts for half of China's overall trade each year. Led by foreign-invested enterprises in China, consumer and industrial goods are produced in China with components imported from enterprises in other parts of Asia. It is often the case that the developing product crosses the Chinese border, sometimes several times, before it is completed. China is often the final point of assembly, but the value added in China would be relatively small in relation to the total value of the product. The final product frequently is exported to advanced Asian economies or even more frequently to China's largest export markets, the United States and the European Union.[40]

Through this process, China's importance as a recipient of Asian investment, a leading trading partner, and an overall engine of economic growth has risen dramatically in the Asia-Pacific. Its economic position is underscored by its rising trade surpluses with the world and unprecedented current-account surpluses (including foreign direct investment as well as large and growing trade surpluses) that show China to be the largest holder of foreign exchange reserves in the world. The advanced economies of the Asia-Pacific and other Asian export-oriented economies rely increasingly on trade and investment in China to sustain their economic growth.[41]

Adroit diplomacy that followed the lines of China's evolving "good neighbor" policy toward Asian countries has greatly improved Chinese relations with most of its neighbors.[42] High-level Chinese leaders are very active and attentive in frequent bilateral and multilateral meetings with Asia-Pacific counterparts. They are backed by an array of well-qualified and effective diplomats and other officials, who follow a "win-win" approach to Asia-Pacific countries: that China and Asia-Pacific partners should seek mutual benefit by focusing on developing areas of common ground while putting aside differences. China makes few demands on Asia-Pacific countries. With few exceptions, it does not expect them to do anything that they would not ordinarily do, and by the same token, China is not expected to do anything it would not do anyway. The exceptions involve China's strong opposition to foreign official interaction with Taiwan, the Dalai Lama, and the Falungong spiritual movement that is outlawed by the Chinese government.

China's approach has been greeted positively by Asia-Pacific countries, many of whom remember and seek to avoid a repetition of the assertive and disruptive Chinese policies of the past. Southeast Asian governments use Chinese involvement with the ASEAN regional organization and other means as part of a so-called Gulliver strategy, designed to tie China within a web of commitments and relationships that will ensure continuation of its recent moderate and accommodating approach.[43]

South Korea found that China's attentive diplomacy included an approach to the problems posed by North Korean development of nuclear weapons that seemed more respectful of and consistent with South Korean policy than that of its ally, the United States. Amid marked deterioration of U.S.–South Korean relations in the first years of the Bush administration, China followed an effective diplomatic approach that expressed understanding and support for South Korean policies that was warmly appreciated by South Korean public opinion.[44]

The Chinese ambassador to Australia enjoyed celebrity status in the Australian media as she rode a wave of positive publicity associated with an export boom of Australian energy and other raw materials to China.[45]

China's diplomacy has emphasized willingness to trade with and provide some aid, investment, and military support to countries with no strings attached. This means that, unlike Western governments, China imposes few conditions on its economic or other support. This approach has been well received by Asian governments in Myanmar, Cambodia, and elsewhere, which need foreign economic and other help but are loath to meet the conditions imposed by Western donors.[46]

Another feature of Chinese diplomacy has been the emphasis on Chinese language, culture, and personal exchanges. This includes Chinese support for Confucius Institutes throughout the region and the world that promote the teaching of Chinese language and culture. It also involves facilitating the travel of ever-larger numbers of Chinese tourist groups to neighboring countries and other foreign destinations.[47]

Regarding China's interactions with major powers in Asia, significant differences in Chinese relations with India have been managed in ways that allow the two governments to emphasize the positive aspects of their growing connection. Regarding relations with the United States, after the marked decline in official Chinese rhetoric critical of U.S. "hegemonism" in Asian and world affairs in mid-2001, the two countries managed to build a businesslike relationship that features continued emphasis on the positive aspects of U.S.-China relations. China's dealings with the Russian administration of Vladimir Putin developed in important military and energy areas, though they have not appeared as close as during the heyday of the China-Russia strategic partnership during the latter years of the Yeltsin administration.[48]

A salient feature of Chinese diplomacy has been more flexibility and activism in multilateral organizations and groups involving Asia-Pacific affairs.[49] In the past, Chinese leaders were seen to be wary of interaction with such bodies out of concern that they would hamper Chinese freedom of action and might be used by the United States and other powers to force change and commitments unwelcome by the Chinese administration. The prevailing assessment by international specialists shows that the new Chinese approach to such multilateral groups is designed to reassure China's neighbors that its growth is not a threat needing to be countered, to expand overall Chinese influence and prominence in the region, and to establish webs of regional relationships that will make it more difficult for the United States to win regional support for renewed pressure or so-called containment of China.[50]

Chinese leaders and officials have worked assiduously to build relations with ASEAN and with Asia-Pacific and other groupings based on ASEAN. China set the pace of international involvement with ASEAN by being the first to propose a free trade agreement with the association and the first to sign ASEAN's Treaty of Amity and Cooperation. Beijing reassured the ASEAN countries, many of which have claims to South China Sea islands that are also claimed by China, by reaching an accord on how to manage the disputes.[51]

China supports the ASEAN+3 regional grouping, which also involves Japan and South Korea, as its favored East Asian group. By definition, the group excludes the United States—an advantage for China, in the view of foreign observers. China had favored a more exclusive membership for the East Asian Summit when it emerged in 2005, but was compelled to acquiesce to efforts by Japan, Indonesia, Singapore, and others to broaden the scope of membership to include India, Australia, and New Zealand and to leave an opening for possible U.S. membership. China was the driving force and main backer behind the SCO, which includes Russia and Central Asian states, as well as Mongolia, India, Pakistan, Afghanistan, and Iran as observers, but excludes the United States. In addition, China works actively in important regional groupings that include and are favored by the United States, such as APEC and the ASEAN Regional Forum, and has also worked very closely with the United States in the Six-Party Talks to deal with the problem of North Korea's nuclear weapons development.[52]

Chinese efforts to reassure neighboring countries that its rise does not threaten them have led to public statements by Chinese officials and officials of most Asia-Pacific states playing down the significance of China's impressive military buildup. Chinese military officers have engaged in active diplomacy with their regional counterparts, endeavoring to build trust and reinforce China's moderate and accommodating posture despite the expansion of Chinese forces. The military modernization has placed an important emphasis on power projection, involving substantial increases in China's air and naval capabilities. Prevailing assessments judge that China has emerged as Asia's leading military power. This military advance presumably enhances China's power and influence in Asia, even though it was not frequently discussed in these terms by Chinese officials in interaction with Asia-Pacific counterparts.[53]

The overall record of Chinese diplomacy in recent years has witnessed major improvement in relations with much of Southeast Asia, South Korea, and Australia. Public opinion and leadership statements in these areas reflect positively on China. China's relations with Russia and Central Asian countries also continue to advance in various ways, as do Chinese-Indian ties. Its reputation in Asia-Pacific multilateral groups is one of an active participant that often sets the agenda for new initiatives.

Chinese Limitations and Weaknesses

Heading the list of limitations and shortcomings in China's rising influence in Asia is China's relations with both Japan and Taiwan.[54] The negative record in recent years shows that China has been unsuccessful in winning greater support in either country, despite many positive economic and other connections linking China with each. This has also had a negative effect on China's overall influence in the Asia-Pacific.

China's efforts to isolate Taiwan include strong pressure put on Asia-Pacific governments to avoid contacts with Taiwan that China opposes.

This is resented by some Asia-Pacific governments, although it causes few major controversies and has imposed few major obstacles in China's improving relations with the region.

China's efforts to isolate Japan from the rest of the Asia-Pacific over disputes involving history, territorial issues, competition for foreign energy supplies, Japan's growing military role in the enhanced U.S.-Japan alliance, and Japan's bid for a permanent seat in the UN Security Council have had significant detrimental effects for China's influence in the Asia-Pacific. These efforts continue despite some moves since September 2006 to improve China-Japan relations. Asia-Pacific governments have maintained, and sometimes strengthened, their connections with Japan and are reluctant to side with China against Japan. Chinese pressure on them to do so generally is not welcomed and appears to have undercut China's efforts to foster a benign and accommodating image for itself in the Asia-Pacific. The Chinese maneuvers have also energized Japanese efforts to work with the United States, Australia, India, and other powers and to use multilateral groupings and Japan's substantial economic, trade, and aid interactions to foster an Asia-Pacific order where China would not be in a position to dominate Japan.[55]

Strong Chinese nationalism and territorial claims complicate Chinese efforts to improve relations with Asian neighbors. South Korean opinion of China[56] declined sharply from a high point in 2004 because of nationalist disputes over whether a historic kingdom controlling much of the Korean Peninsula and northeast China was Chinese or Korean. South Korean officials dealing with China over the historical dispute privately voice sharp criticism of China's stance. Their distaste for China's hard stance on this issue influences their view of China's intentions toward North Korea. Some South Korean officials have come to view China's strategy toward North Korea as one intended to foster a continuation of an independent North Korean state under the economic, political, and security influence of China. Such an approach would be directly at odds with South Korea's prevailing Sunshine Policy, which envisions an eventual peaceful reunification of North Korea with a dominant South Korea. This South Korean concern with China's perceived approach to North Korea makes the Seoul government more wary of China.[57]

Chinese nationalism and territorial claims also underline a tough Chinese posture regarding differences with Japan. Chinese authorities failed to suppress anti-Japanese demonstrations in China in April 2005 that involved several days of violence against and destruction of Japanese diplomatic and private property in China. Disputed island and resource claims in the East China Sea, along with competing interests in Taiwan, have been accompanied by naval and other military maneuvers and statements by Japan and China that are seen as provocative, threatening, and indicative of a protracted rivalry between the two powers.[58]

Chinese diplomacy endeavors to play down Chinese territorial disputes in Southeast Asia and with India, but clear differences remain unresolved. On balance, the continued disputes serve as a drag on Chinese efforts to improve relations with these countries.[59]

China's remarkable military modernization and its sometimes secretive and authoritarian political system have raised suspicions and wariness on the part of a number of China's neighbors. They sought more transparency regarding Chinese military intentions, but were not reassured by China's refusal to join at a senior level with the United States and other Asian defense leaders at an annual conclave known as the Shangri-La Forum meeting in Singapore.

China's past record of aggression and provocative assertiveness toward many Asian countries is hard to live down. It has left few positive connections on which to build friendly ties with its neighbors. As a result, and also reflecting the state-led pattern of much of Chinese foreign relations, Chinese interchange with Asia-Pacific neighbors depends heavily on the direction and leadership of the Chinese government. Nongovernment channels of communication and influence are very limited.

An exception is the so-called overseas Chinese communities in Southeast Asian countries. These people tend to be comparatively well-to-do and entrepreneurial members of their respective countries. They provide important investment and technical assistance to China's development and represent political forces supportive of their home country's good relations with China. At the same time, however, it is clear to observers in Southeast Asia that the growing influence of this group, and evidence of close Chinese government association with them, runs the risk of a strong backlash. The dominant ethnic, cultural, and religious groups in Southeast Asia often have a long history of wariness of China and sometimes promoted violent actions and other discrimination against the economic and political power and influence of ethnic Chinese.[60]

The areas of greatest Chinese strength in Asia—economic relations and diplomacy—also show limitations and weaknesses.[61] Chinese trade figures are exaggerated because of the double counting associated with processing trade. Such double counting has been estimated to account for 30 percent of China's trade with Southeast Asia.[62] That half of Chinese trade is conducted by foreign-invested enterprises in China, that the resulting processing trade sees China often add only a small amount to the product, and that the finished product often depends on sales to the United States or the European Union also appears to undercut China's image in the Asia-Pacific as a powerful trading country.

The large amount of Asian and international investment that has gone to China was unavailable to other Asia-Pacific countries, hurting their economic development. China invests little in the Asia-Pacific apart from Hong Kong. While Chinese investment abroad grew fairly rapidly, it did so from a low base, amounting to just $16 billion for the entire world in 2006. Chinese aid to the Asia-Pacific was very small, especially in comparison to other donors, with the exception of North Korea and Myanmar. China's large foreign exchange reserves serve many purposes for the authoritarian Chinese administration that is trying to maintain stability amid massive internal needs, but they do not translate to big Chinese grants of assistance abroad. China's attraction to Asia-Pacific producers of raw materials is not shared by Asia-Pacific manufacturers. These entrepreneurs tend to relocate and invest in China and appear to do well, but their workers cannot relocate to China and appear to suffer.[63]

By definition, China's win-win diplomacy means that China will not do things that it ordinarily would not do. The sometimes dizzying array of meetings, agreements, and pronouncements in the active Chinese diplomacy in the Asia-Pacific does not hide the fact that China remains reluctant to undertake significant costs, risks, or commitments in dealing with difficult regional issues.

U.S. Weaknesses and Strengths

The weaknesses of the United States' position in the Asia-Pacific have been well publicized and are discussed thoroughly earlier in this book.[64] Prevailing discourse on the United States in the Asia-Pacific focuses on the widespread negative image of the United States among the public, elites, and many government officials in the region. The main cause of this poor image is the war in Iraq and other aspects of U.S. foreign policy.

In this negative atmosphere surrounding U.S. government actions and policies in the Asia-Pacific in recent years, it sometimes has been hard to discern evidence of U.S. strengths in the region. Several of these strengths have been publicly noted in the media and in specialist and scholarly assessments, and they are duly noted below. More important for this assessment were private interviews conducted with 175 Asia-Pacific affairs experts in the governments of nine Asia-Pacific states during four trips to the region in 2004–2007. An assumption behind the focus on interviewing Asia-Pacific officials knowledgeable about the regional order is one of the findings of this study—namely, that in this region, governments are seen as the key decision makers in foreign affairs. On the whole, the governments of the Asia-Pacific region are strong, the people look to the governments to make key foreign policy decisions, and government officials do so on the basis of careful consideration of their national interests. The findings of these interviews were reinforced in public speeches, briefings, and other interactions with audiences (amounting in total to three thousand) of informed Asia-Pacific elites in these nine countries during the course of two seven-week speaking trips in 2004 and 2006 and a two-week trip in 2007.[65]

These interviews—reinforced by the above-noted public speeches and briefings—underlined twin pillars of U.S. security and economic strength in the Asia-Pacific region. The United States continues to undertake major costs, commitments, and risks that are viewed by Asia-Pacific officials as essential to the stability and well-being of the region. No other power, including China, is even remotely able and willing to undertake these responsibilities, in the view of these officials.[66] America thus remains the indispensable leading power of the Asia-Pacific.

Asia-Pacific government officials interviewed during the 2004–2007 research trips were almost uniform in emphasizing the positive importance of the U.S. leading role as the Asia-Pacific region's security guarantor and vital economic partner. The few exceptions included a Communist Party of India (Marxist) official and, to a degree, some Chinese officials who criticized the U.S. security role in Asia.

Regarding security concerns, Asia-Pacific government officials hold the view that governments in the region generally do not trust each other. The kind of suspicion and wariness one sees today between China and Japan characterizes the relationships between most Asia-Pacific governments. And yet these governments need stability in order to meet their nation-building priorities. Economic development associated with effective nation building is seen as critically important to the legitimacy of most Asia-Pacific governments. In this context, the United States looms very large in their calculations. Unlike their Asia-Pacific neighbors, the United States does not want their territory and does not want to dominate them. It too wants stability and, in contrast with China's and other powers' inability or reluctance to undertake major risks and commitments, the United States is seen to continue the massive expenditure and major risk in a U.S. military presence in the Asia-Pacific region. This U.S. role is viewed as essential in stabilizing the often uncertain security relationships among Asia-Pacific governments.

Not only does the United States continue to occupy the top security position as the Asia-Pacific's "least distrusted power," but it also plays an essential economic role in the development priorities of Asia-Pacific governments. Most of these governments are focused on export-oriented growth. The United States continues to allow massive inflows of Asian imports essential to their economic development despite an overall U.S. trade deficit of more than $700 billion annually. Against this background, when asked if overall U.S. power and influence in the Asia-Pacific region were in decline, Asia-Pacific officials usually said no.

The interviews in the Asia-Pacific region were in stark contrast to the widely held perception of declining U.S. power and influence in world affairs evident since the string of setbacks and failures of the U.S. military occupation of Iraq. However, more detached assessments see the consequences of the Iraq failure for U.S. security commitments and power in the Asia-Pacific as limited.[67] They appear to support the judgment of the interviewed the Asia-Pacific officials that overall U.S. military power and the U.S. leading security role in the Asia-Pacific region have not diminished.

Meanwhile, evidence of U.S. economic difficulties and decline is widely seen in the United States, notably in the massive U.S. trade deficits and large government spending deficits. The argument here is that these problems will cause the United States to move in a decidedly protectionist direction that will significantly curb imports from Asia. Additional evidence was provided with the election of the Democratic-led 110th Congress in 2006. Democratic leaders Speaker Nancy Pelosi and Senate Majority Leader Harry Reid seemed to favor tougher and more restrictive trade measures against Asian exporters, especially China, the source of the largest U.S. trade imbalance. Nonetheless, more objective assessments showed Democratic Party divisions and weaknesses that made the adoption of significant protectionist measures unlikely, especially during a period of U.S. economic growth and prosperity. The effect of the U.S. economic downturn in 2008 on American trade policy remained to be seen. Overall, prevailing trends suggested that the leading U.S. role as Asia-Pacific's economic partner of choice would continue.[68]

Other strengths in the U.S. position, in comparison with that of China and other powers in the Asia-Pacific, were noted in the media and in specialist and scholarly assessments.[69] They included:

- Unlike China, the United States has not depended so heavily on government connections and government-led initiatives to exert influence in the Asia-Pacific. The United States has developed an extensive network of nongovernment business, educational, religious, and foundation connections established over many decades that undergird U.S. influence in the region. These have been supported by a wide-ranging web of personal connections that have grown following the U.S. decision in 1965 to end discrimination against Asians in U.S. immigration policy. This step resulted in the influx of many millions of Asians who settled in the United States and entered the mainstream of U.S. society while sustaining strong connections with their country of origin.[70]

- The U.S. military in recent years has been by far the most active U.S. government component in the Asia-Pacific. It followed quiet and methodical methods to develop ever-closer working relations with most Asia-Pacific governments, while endeavoring to reinforce the U.S. alliance structure in the region.[71] The ability of the U.S. military to quickly and effectively take the lead in the multilateral effort to bring relief to the millions of Asians afflicted by the tsunami disaster of December 2004 was based on the groundwork of connections and trust developed by the U.S. military leaders among Asian governments.
- As discussed earlier, the U.S. government continues to be seen in the Asia-Pacific as responsible for ensuring that the three major hot spots in the region—the crisis caused by North Korea's nuclear weapons program, the conflict between Taiwan and China, and the face-off between India and Pakistan over Kashmir—do not lead to war. The U.S. government's increased flexibility in dealing with North Korea since 2007 generally has been welcomed by regional governments and public opinion. The Bush administration's positions on Taiwan and Kashmir are broadly seen as sensible and as promoting the kind of stability sought by governments in the region.
- The U.S. government has developed a more active and positive stance toward multilateral groups in the Asia-Pacific, especially with ASEAN. The United States strongly supports the ASEAN Regional Forum, the primary regional forum for security dialogue, and APEC. President Bush in November 2005 began to use the annual APEC leaders' summit to engage in annual multilateral meetings with attending ASEAN leaders. At that meeting, the leaders launched the ASEAN-U.S. Enhanced Partnership, which involves a broad range of economic, political, and security cooperation. The Bush administration announced in 2006 its plans for a future Asia-Pacific FTA and that it would appoint an ambassador to ASEAN.[72]
- The Bush administration's success in improving U.S. relations with the major powers in Asia has added to the strength of U.S. leadership in the region and reinforced the U.S. government's ability to deal with crises on the Korean Peninsula and other regional difficulties, as well as negative implications coming from the rise of China in Asia. The United States having good relations with Japan and China at the same time is very rare. The United States being the dominant foreign power in South Asia and having good relations with both India and Pakistan is unprecedented, as is the current U.S. maintenance of good relations with both Beijing and Taipei.
- Effective U.S. policy toward China, emphasizing positive engagement while continuing to balance and hedge against the negative

implications of China's ascendancy, has helped to reinforce China's emphasis on peace and development and to constrain past Chinese objections and pressure against Asian governments interacting with the United States in sensitive areas. The prevailing circumstances in U.S.-Chinese relations have allowed the United States and Asian countries very sensitive to Chinese preferences and pressures (e.g., Vietnam and Mongolia) to develop closer relations involving such sensitive areas as military cooperation and related intelligence and information exchanges.[73]

Asian Hedging Reinforces U.S. Regional Leadership

There appears to be a contradiction between assessments of an emerging China-centered order in Asia and the prevailing post–Cold War regional pattern explained earlier that is characterized by many proud and nationalistic Asian governments seeking greater prominence and hedging warily against powers and trends, including a rising China, which might curb their independence and nationalistic goals. While it appears that the latter pattern has both positive and negative effects on China's growing influence in the Asia-Pacific, at bottom such hedging curbs any Chinese ability to dominate or lead the Asia-Pacific to the exclusion of other powers, particularly the United States.[74]

The post–Cold War Asia-Pacific order has witnessed a tendency on the part of most Asia-Pacific governments to emphasize nationalistic ambitions and independence. They eschew the tight and binding alignments of the past in favor of diverse arrangements with various powers that support security and other state interests in the newly fluid regional environment. On the one hand, China's generally constructive and accommodating approach to Asia-Pacific neighbors in bilateral and multilateral channels is welcomed by the regional governments seeking to diversify international options and integrate rising regional forces in ways that accord with their national interests. On the other hand, Asia-Pacific governments respond to China's powerful influence by taking steps to work with one another and other non-Asian powers, notably the United States, to ensure that their interests and independence will be preserved in the face of China's growing role in regional affairs. Both tendencies—to integrate and cooperate with China on the one hand, and to work with one another, the United States, and other powers to hedge against possible negative implications of China's rise on the other—have strengthened as China has become more prominent in regional affairs in recent years. One conclusion that comes from this is that few Asia-Pacific leaders or states appear ready to adhere to a Chinese-led order in Asia, and that China's rise adds to reasons for them to sustain and develop close relations with the United States and other powers useful in hedging against China's greater influence in regional affairs.[75]

Asia-Pacific government officials consulted in private interviews during 2004–2007 agreed that China's rise adds to the incentives for most Asia-Pacific governments to maneuver and hedge with other powers, including the United States, in order to preserve their independence and freedom of action. A Singapore official in May 2006 said that "hedging is the name of the game" in Southeast Asia, while an Indian official in June 2006 declared that Asian governments "are not going to put all their eggs in one basket." Asia-Pacific officials made clear that their governments hedge against the United States and other powers as well, but their recent focus has been on China's development. The governments tend to cooperate increasingly with China in areas of common concern, but they work increasingly in other ways, often including efforts to strengthen relations with the United States, to preserve freedom of action and other interests in the face China's rise.[76]

In an Asia-Pacific order featuring continued strong U.S. security and economic power and influence, such hedging by Asia-Pacific governments adds to factors that are seen to preclude Chinese leadership or dominance in the region and that reinforce U.S. leadership there. The majority of Asia-Pacific government officials that were interviewed privately assumed that China sought eventual "preeminence" in Asia; Chinese officials said no, though Chinese foreign policy specialists said that secret Chinese Communist Party documents over the years have continued to refer to a general goal of Asian leadership. When asked in May 2006 whether China sought leadership or domination in Asia, a senior Chinese official acknowledged the complications of U.S. power and influence and the role of many independent-minded Asian governments. He responded that "China can't dominate Asia; there are too many governments in Asia." He nonetheless went on to advise that China's influence in the region would continue to grow, as China's "weight" would become increasingly important to the governments in the region and China would have increasing success in reassuring Asian governments of benevolent Chinese intentions.[77]

In sum, the nationalistic ambitions of Asia-Pacific governments generally make them wary of coming under the dominant influence of their neighbors, most of whom they do not trust. This fact undermines the concrete advances for Chinese influence in the Asia-Pacific region. An inventory of Chinese influence compared with that of the United States detailed in recent assessments and scholarship shows that major regional powers such as Japan, India, and Russia continue to take measures to maintain their leadership ambitions and guard against coming under strong or dominant Chinese influence.[78] South Korea and a number of Southeast Asian states also have national and regional ambitions that require maneuvering and hedging to avoid coming under China's sway. As the most important power in the region, and one with no territorial or few other ambitions at odds with Asia-Pacific governments interested in nation building and preserving a stable regional status quo, the United States looms large in the hedging calculus of Asia-Pacific states dealing with a rising China.

NOTES

1. See the references listed in the bibliography and the sources in chapter 5, note 1.

2. Ralph Cossa, "East Asia Community Building: Time for the United States to Get on Board," Policy Analysis Brief, September 2007, http://www.stanleyfdn .org/publications/pab/CossaPAB07.pdf.

3. Of note is the recent competition between China and Japan over leadership in such regional groups as ASEAN+3 and the East Asia Leadership Summit. See Frank Frost and Ann Rann, *The East Asian Summit, Cebu 2007: Issues and Prospects* (Canberra: Parliamentary Library of Australia, 2006).

4. In particular, the Chinese administration seeks to reassure its neighbors of its benign motives in order to avoid a backlash in the region and a counterbalancing against it by its neighbors as China grows in power and influence. China also seeks to create a "buffer" of good relations around its periphery in order to block suspected U.S. efforts to pressure or constrain it. See Phillip C. Saunders, "China's Global Activism: Strategy, Drivers, and Tools," Institute for National Strategic Studies Occasional Paper 4 (Washington, D.C.: National Defense University Press, 2006).

5. Cossa, "East Asia Community Building"; Dick Nanto, *East Asian Regional Architecture: New Economic and Security Arrangements and U.S. Policy*, CRS Report RL33653 (Washington, D.C.: Congressional Research Service, Library of Congress, September 18, 2006).

6. National Intelligence Council, *North Korean Engagement: Perspectives, Outlook, and Implications*, Conference Report CR 2001-01 (Washington, D.C.: GPO, 2001), p. 3–6.

7. Lijun Sheng, *China-ASEAN Free Trade Area: Origins, Developments and Strategic Motivations* (Singapore: Institute for Southeast Asian Studies 2003).

8. Frost and Rann, *East Asian Summit.*

9. Evelyn Goh, "Understanding 'Hedging' in Asia-Pacific Security," Pacnet no. 43, (Honolulu: CSIS Pacific Forum, August 31, 2006).

10. Evan Medeiros, "Strategic Hedging and the Future of Asia-Pacific Stability," *Washington Quarterly* 29, no. 1 (Winter 2005/2006): 145–67.

11. Michael Yahuda, *The International Politics of the Asia-Pacific* (New York: RoutledgeCurzon, 2005), 237; Evelyn Goh, *Meeting the China Challenge: The U.S. in Southeast Asian Regional Security Strategies*, Policy Study 16 (Washington, D.C.: East-West Center Washington, 2005).

12. Robert Sutter, *China's Rise: Implications for U.S. Leadership in Asia* (Washington, D.C.: East-West Center Washington, 2006), 24–29.

13. Stanley Foundation, "New Power Dynamics in Southeast Asia: Issues for U.S. Policymakers," Policy Dialogue Brief, October 2006, http://www.stanleyfdn.org/publications/pdb/spcpdb06.pdf.

14. Yong Deng and Fei-ling Wang, eds., *China Rising: Power and Motivation in Chinese Foreign Policy* (Lanham, Md.: Rowman & Littlefield, 2005).

15. Goh, *Meeting the China Challenge.*

16. David Kang, "South Korea's Embrace of Interdependence in Pursuit of Security," in *Strategic Asia, 2006–2007: Trade, Interdependence, and Security*, ed. Ashley J. Tellis and Michael Wills, 139–72 (Seattle: National Bureau of Asian Research, 2006).

17. *Rising Energy Competition and Energy Security in Northeast Asia*, CRS Report RL32466 (Washington, D.C.: Congressional Research Service, Library of Congress, February 9, 2005).

18. Eric Heginbotham and Richard Samuels, "Japan," in *Strategic Asia, 2002–2003: Asian Aftershocks*, ed. Richard J. Ellings and Aaron L. Friedberg, 95–130 (Seattle: National Bureau of Asian Research, 2002).

19. Jonathan Pollack, ed., *Asia Eyes America: Regional Perspectives on U.S. Asia-Pacific Strategy in the 21st Century* (Newport, R.I.: U.S. Naval War College, 2007); Asia Foundation, *America's Role in Asia: Asian Views* (San Francisco: Asia Foundation, 2004); Suisheng Zhao, *A Nation-State by Construction: Dynamics of Modern Chinese Nationalism* (Stanford, Calif.: Stanford University Press, 2004).

20. Morton Abramowitz and Stephen Bosworth, *Chasing the Sun: Rethinking East Asian Policy* (New York: Century Foundation, 2006).

21. "View of U.S.'s Global Role Worse," BBC World Service poll, January 2007; "Come in Number One, Your Time Is Up," *Economist*, April 12, 2007, 12, http://www.the-economist.com/research/backgrounders/displaystory.cfm?story_id=9005261; Pew Research Center, "U.S. Image Up Slightly, but Still Negative: American Character Gets Mixed Reviews," June 24, 2005, http://pewglobal.org/reports/display.php?ReportID=247; Yaroslav Trofimov and Paul Beckett, "Singapore Prime Minister Urges U.S. to Bolster Its Ties in Asia," *Wall Street Journal*, April 18, 2007.

22. Amitav Acharya and Arabinda Acharya, "The Myth of the Second Front: Localizing the 'War on Terror' in Southeast Asia," *Washington Quarterly* 30, no. 4 (Autumn 2007): 75–90.

23. Goh, *Meeting the China Challenge.*

24. Ralph A. Cossa and Brad Glosserman, "Tests Postponed, Pending, Passed, and in Progress," *Comparative Connections* 9, no. 2 (2nd Qtr 2007): 1–4.

25. Abramowitz and Bosworth, *Chasing the Sun*, 49–59.

26. Richard Samuels, *Securing Japan* (Ithaca, N.Y.: Cornell University Press, 2007).

27. Ralph Cossa, "U.S.-Australia: Still Mates!" Pacnet no. 49A (Honolulu: CSIS Pacific Forum, December 19, 2007).

28. Daniel Twining, "America's Grand Design in Asia," *Washington Quarterly* 30, no. 3 (Summer 2007): 79–94.

29. Bruce Vaughn, *U.S. Strategic and Defense Relationships in the Asia-Pacific Region*, CRS Report RL33821 (Washington, D.C.: Congressional Research Service, Library of Congress, January 22, 2007), 22–25.

30. Victor Cha, "South Korea: Anchored or Adrift?" in *Strategic Asia, 2003–2004: Fragility and Crisis*, ed. Richard J. Ellings and Aaron L. Friedberg, 109–30 (Seattle: National Bureau of Asian Research, 2003).

31. Joshua Kurlantzick, "Pax Asia-Pacifica? East Asian Integration and Its Implications for the United States," *Washington Quarterly* 30, no. 3 (Summer 2007): 67–77.

32. Greg Sheridan, "China Wins as 'U.S. Neglects Region,'" *Australian*, September 3, 2007, 1.

33. Phillip Saunders, "The United States and East Asia after Iraq," *Survival* 49, no. 1 (Spring 2007): 141–52; Robert Sutter, "The Democratic-Led 110th Congress: Implications for Asia," *Asia Policy* 3 (January 2007): 125–150.

34. David Shambaugh, "China Engages Asia: Reshaping the Regional Order," *International Security* 29, no. 3 (Winter 2004/2005): 64–99; Bates Gill, *Rising Star: China's New Security Diplomacy* (Washington, D.C.: Brookings Institution Press, 2007); Abramowitz and Bosworth, *Chasing the Sun*; Joshua Kurlantzick, *Charm Offensive: How China's Soft Power Is Transforming The World* (New Haven, Conn.: Yale University Press, 2007).

35. Robert Sutter and Chin-Hao Huang, "China's Activism Faces Persistent Challenges," *Comparative Connections* 9, no. 2 (2nd Qtr 2007): 84.

36. For assessments detailing U.S. strengths in Asia in the face of China's rise and other perceived challenges, see Bronson Percival, *The Dragon Looks South: China and Southeast Asia in the New Century* (Westport, Conn.: Praeger Security International, 2007); Twining, "America's Grand Design"; Thomas Christensen, "Fostering Stability or Creating a Monster? The Rise of China and U.S. Policy toward East Asia," *International Security* 31, no. 1 (Summer 2006): 81–126; Yahuda, *International Politics*, 276–77; and Victor Cha, "Winning Asia: Washington's Untold Success Story," *Foreign Affairs* 86, no. 6 (November/December 2007): 98–113.

37. See the beginning of chapter 1 of this book.

38. These economic developments in Asia are discussed in sources cited earlier and listed in the bibliography. See also Dick Nanto and Thomas Lum, *The Rise of China and Its Effect on Taiwan, Japan and South Korea*, CRS Report RL31815 (Washington, D.C.: Congressional Research Service, Library of Congress, July 12, 2006); and Thomas Lum and Dick Nanto, *China's Trade with the United States and the World*, CRS Report RL31413 (Washington, D.C.: Congressional Research Service, Library of Congress, January 4, 2007).

39. Barry Naughton, *The Chinese Economy: Transitions and Growth* (Cambridge, Mass.: MIT Press, 2007), 401–23.

40. Ibid., 385–406.

41. David Shambaugh, "The Rise of China and Asia's New Dynamics," in *Power Shift: China and Asia's New Dynamics* (Berkeley: University of California Press, 2005), 1–21.

42. Kurlantzick, *Charm Offensive*.

43. Rosemary Foot, "China and the ASEAN Regional Forum: Organizational Processes and Domestic Modes of Thought," *Asian Survey* 38, no. 5 (May 1998): 425–40.

44. Jae Ho Chung, *Between Ally and Partner: Korea-China Relations and the United States* (New York: Columbia University Press, 2006).

45. Frank Frost, *Directions in China's Foreign Relations: Implications for East Asia and Australia*, Research Brief 9:2005-06 (Canberra: Parliamentary Library of Australia, 2005), 51–66.

46. Joshua Kurlantzick, "How China Is Changing Global Diplomacy," *New Republic*, June 27, 2005, 16–21.

47. Simon Montlake, "Chinese Tourists: Asia's New 'Ugly Americans'?" *Christian Science Monitor*, December 28, 2005.

48. Robert Sutter, *China's Rise in Asia: Promises and Perils* (Lanham, Md.: Rowman & Littlefield, 2005), 107–24, 231–48.

49. Jianwei Wang, "China's Multilateral Diplomacy in the New Millennium," in Deng and Wang, *China Rising*, 159–200.

50. Rosemary Foot, "Chinese Strategies in a U.S.-Hegemonic Global Order: Accommodating and Hedging," *International Affairs* 82, no. 1 (2006): 77–94.

51. Brantly Womack, "China and Southeast Asia: Asymmetry, Leadership and Normalcy," *Pacific Affairs* 76, no. 3 (Winter 2003/2004): 529–48.

52. Nanto, *East Asian Regional Architecture*, 22–23.

53. David Shambaugh, "China's Military Modernization: Making Steady and Surprising Progress," in *Strategic Asia, 2005–2006: Military Modernization in an Era of Uncertainty*, ed. Ashley J. Tellis and Michael Wills, 67–104 (Seattle: National Bureau of Asian Research, 2005).

54. Richard Bush, "Taiwan Faces China: Attraction and Repulsion," in Shambaugh, *Power Shift*, 170–86; Mike Mochizuki, "China-Japan Relations: Downward Spiral or a New Equilibrium?" in Shambaugh, *Power Shift*, 135–50.

55. Kent Calder, "China and Japan's Simmering Rivalry," *Foreign Affairs* 85, no. 2 (March/April 2006): 129–39.

56. Sutter, *China's Rise: Implications*, 49–51.

57. Scott Snyder, "Strategic Maneuvers for the 'Sandwich Economy,'" *Comparative Connections* 9, no. 2 (2nd Qtr 2007): 121–26.

58. Minxin Pei and Michael Swaine, *Simmering Fire in Asia: Averting Sino-Japanese Strategic Conflict* (Washington, D.C.: Carnegie Endowment for International Peace, 2005).

59. Barry Wain, "All at Sea over Resources in East Asia," *YaleGlobal.com*, August 14, 2007, http://yaleglobal.yale.edu/display.article?id=9546; Jo Johnson and Richard McGregor, "China Raises Tension in India Dispute," *FT.com*, June 10, 2007, http://us.ft.com/ftgateway/superpage.ft?news_id=fto061020071247219533.

60. Lijun Sheng, "China's Influence in Southeast Asia," Trends in Southeast Asia Series 4 (Singapore: Institute of Southeast Asian Studies, 2006).

61. Sutter, *China's Rise: Implications*, 17–24.

62. Robert Sutter and Chin-Hao Huang, "Chinese Diplomacy and Optimism about ASEAN," *Comparative Connections* 8, no. 3 (3rd Qtr 2006): 75–86.

63. Robert Sutter and Chin-Hao Huang, "Cebu Meetings, UN Veto on Myanmar," *Comparative Connections* 9, no. 1 (1st Qtr 2007): 73–82.

64. See especially the introduction.

65. These interviews are highlighted in Sutter, *China's Rise in Asia*, and Robert Sutter, *China's Rise and U.S. Influence in Asia: A Report from the Region* (Washington,

D.C.: Atlantic Council of the United States, 2006). The 2004 and 2006 trips involved visits to a total of twenty-two cities in Australia, China, India, Japan, New Zealand, Singapore, South Korea, and Taiwan. The 2007 trip included cities in China and Indonesia.

66. China's very modest contribution to the victims of the 2004 tsunami disaster underlined this point.

67. Saunders, "United States and East Asia after Iraq."

68. Sutter, "Democratic-Led 110th Congress."

69. Percival, *Dragon Looks South*; Twining, "America's Grand Design"; Christensen, "Fostering Stability"; Yahuda, *International Politics*, 276–77; G. John Ikenberry, "America in East Asia: Power, Markets, and Grand Strategy," in *Beyond Bilateralism: U.S.-Japan Relations in the New Asia-Pacific*, ed. Ellis Krauss and T. J. Pempel (Stanford, Calif.: Stanford University Press, 2004), 37–54.

70. Mark Borthwick, *Pacific Century: The Emergence of Modern Pacific Asia* (Boulder, Colo.: Westview Press, 2007).

71. Twining, "America's Grand Design."

72. Donald Weatherbee, "Strategic Dimensions of Economic Interdependence in Southeast Asia," in Tellis and Wills, *Strategic Asia, 2006–2007*, 282–300.

73. Christensen, "Fostering Stability."

74. Sutter, *China's Rise: Implications*, 24–29.

75. Goh, *Meeting the China Challenge*; Percival, *Dragon Looks South*; Foot, "China and the ASEAN Regional Forum"; Foot, "Chinese Strategies."

76. Sutter, *China's Rise and U.S. Influence*, 4.

77. Robert Sutter, *Chinese Foreign Relations: Power and Policy since the Cold War* (Lanham, Md.: Rowman & Littlefield, 2007), 404.

78. To keep track of recent developments in China's relations with the United States, Japan, Taiwan, Korea, Southeast Asia, and Russia, see the quarterly reviews of these subjects in *Comparative Connections*, available at http://www.csis.org/pacfor/.

10

✦

Outlook and
Recommendations

Academic specialists in the field of international relations have assessed recent dynamics and trends in the Asia-Pacific in an effort to discern the future order of the region. They find a very diverse region with many different cultures and types of regimes, varied and often contentious histories, shifting power balances, and rapid economic and social change. Against this background, they have found it hard to agree whether the course of development in the region will be peaceful or not, what kind of alignment of powers will predominate, and which of the leading schools of thought in the field of international relations—realism, liberalism, or constructivism—best explains and forecasts Asia-Pacific developments.[1] The mix of forecasts for the regional order include hegemonic order dominated by either China or the United States; a hierarchy of powers led by the United States or possibly China; two competing powers, usually seen as China and the United States; a U.S.-China condominium or a somewhat broader concert of powers involving the region's leading powers and the United States in cooperative efforts to manage regional issues; and broadly inclusive regionwide collective security and other multilateral groups to deal with regional affairs.[2]

This study does not forecast the regional order, nor discern whether the future of the region will be peaceful or not, nor determine which school of thought in international relations theory best explains regional dynamics. Its goals are more modest. This book assesses the background, status, and outlook of U.S. relations with the Asia-Pacific region. It provides an inventory of the major strengths and weaknesses in American dealings with the Asia-Pacific region and describes the significant points of agreement and disagreement between the United States and the governments and peoples of the region at the end of the George W. Bush administration. It focuses in particular on widely held views that see the United States in decline, with the U.S. leadership role in regional affairs undermined by a range of political, economic, and security problems.

This assessment carefully considers these views in the context of past U.S. difficulties and resilience in the region. It finds that recent U.S. difficulties have not fundamentally undermined the main foundations of the leadership, power, and influence that the United States has exerted in the region for many years. The study uses a comparison of Chinese strengths and weaknesses with U.S. strengths and weaknesses in the prevailing environment in the Asia-Pacific to determine the implications of China's rise for, and assess the resiliency of, U.S. leadership in the region. It shows:

- China is rising and probably will continue to rise in influence in the Asia-Pacific, the part of the world where China always has exerted greatest influence. But China also has major limitations and weaknesses and has a long way to go to compete for regional leadership.
- The power and interests of the United States and most Asia-Pacific governments work against China ever achieving dominance in the region.
- The U.S. image in the Asia-Pacific has declined in recent years, and U.S. foreign policy continues to be widely criticized. Nevertheless, U.S. ability and willingness to serve as the Asia-Pacific's security guarantor and its vital economic partner remain strong and provide a solid foundation for continued U.S. leadership in the region. According to Asia-Pacific officials interviewed in 2004–2007, overall American power and influence in the region have not declined. This judgment seems better grounded than those assessments by regional and U.S. commentators and specialists that emphasize U.S. weaknesses without giving appropriate attention to prevailing U.S. strengths in the Asia-Pacific region.
- Most Asia-Pacific governments maneuver and hedge against China's ascendance, and they find a strong U.S. presence in the region fundamentally important and reassuring.

Against this background, it appears that whatever new order is emerging in the Asia-Pacific region will have the United States as its leading power for many years to come. This forecast rules out some of the possible outcomes for the Asian regional order noted in the first paragraph of this chapter. Thus, China's dominance is precluded. Moreover, the U.S. role in any condominium, competition, or collective concert of powers in the Asia-Pacific would be that of its leading power.

Among the important variables to watch in U.S. and Asia-Pacific developments over the next few years are the policies and practices of new American and regional leaders. November 2007 to November 2008 will see important elections in Australia, South Korea, Pakistan, Taiwan, and the United States, as well as possibly Japan and others. What effect these elections will have on how well or poorly U.S. policies and practices mesh with those of the governments in the Asia-Pacific region remains to be seen.

U.S. presidential candidates thus far have given little attention to the region. They remain preoccupied with Iraq and the Middle East in their statements on foreign affairs. Their occasional remarks on China sometimes have been tough on trade issues and the perception of Chinese currency manipulation adding to the unacceptably large U.S.-China trade deficit. But there has been little talk of withdrawal of U.S. forces from Asia or sweeping trade protection that would seriously impact Asia-Pacific export-oriented economies.[3]

In the Asia-Pacific, meanwhile, there is little indication that incumbent or prospective leaders are prepared to undertake the major risks, costs, and responsibilities that the United States bears as the region's leading power. The leadership of China, the most likely candidate for this role, has just completed a major Communist Party congress amid clear indications that China is in no position to and has no interest in bearing these obligations as it seeks to manage a host of domestic issues and international complications in the years ahead.[4]

RECOMMENDATIONS FOR U.S. POLICY: SEEK CONFIDENT AND RESPONSIBLE STEWARDSHIP

The relatively sanguine judgments regarding the United States in contemporary Asian-Pacific affairs seen in this book do not support sweeping changes in U.S. policy in the region. Rather, they support the recommendation that the many problems and challenges for the United States in interaction with the region that are duly noted in this study should be dealt with by U.S. policy makers with a strong degree of confidence that U.S. leadership in the Asia-Pacific is not facing fundamental challenge.

- The contemporary problems in U.S. policy in the Asia-Pacific pale in comparison with those faced in earlier periods, notably at the start of the Cold War and after the U.S. war in Vietnam. Those past episodes saw U.S. leadership in the Asia-Pacific seriously challenged, but it was sustained and eventually strengthened.
- No Asian power or coalition of powers is able or willing to bear even a significant fraction of the large security and economic commitments,

costs, and risks that the United States provides, which are so important to the Asia-Pacific governments and represent a solid foundation
for U.S. leadership in the region. Despite widespread recent criticism
of U.S. foreign policy, most Asia-Pacific governments want the United
States to remain strong in the region and to continue to provide these
important security and economic benefits.

- Unlike rising China and other governments in the region, the U.S.
position in the region is not so dependent on government policy. It is
based to a large degree on many years of interaction by nongovernment American institutions and individuals in businesses, foundations, and educational and religious institutions. It also is based on
the unique strengths of multifaceted personal connections coming
from the many millions of Asians who have emigrated to the United
States and have integrated relatively smoothly into U.S. society in the
last forty years.[5]

The biggest challenges facing the security and economic foundations of
U.S. leadership in the Asia-Pacific lie within the United States. Thus far,
U.S. domestic pressure to erect protectionist trade and investment barriers that would significantly affect U.S.-Asian trade and investment has
been held in check. Domestic pressure to withdraw forces from Asia in
ways that would undermine the U.S. security role in the region appears
less significant. In the past, the U.S. policy process to deal with these
kinds of issues often has been contentious, notably in debates over U.S.
troop withdrawals from Asia after the lost war in Vietnam and over dealing with Japanese trade and investment practices in the 1970s and 1980s.[6]
Nevertheless, U.S. leadership in Asia was sustained and strengthened following those episodes. The challenges posed by domestic U.S. demands
today are less serious than those of the 1970s and 1980s.

- U.S. leaders will need to deal with the domestic challenges to the U.S.
economic and security positions in the Asia-Pacific in careful and
balanced ways that avoid catering to domestic political constituencies at the expense of broad U.S. international interests in securing a
favorable balance of power, smooth economic access, and promotion
of American values in the dynamic and increasingly important Asia-
Pacific region.

The U.S. government recently has established and carried out constructive initiatives and approaches to the Asia-Pacific region that should be
sustained and developed, including:

- The balance of engagement and hedging in the U.S. approach to
China is broadly seen in the United States and in the Asia-Pacific
region in positive terms and should be sustained.[7]

- Also to be continued are the U.S. advances in relations with Japan, India, Australia, Singapore, Indonesia, and Kazakhstan that strengthen U.S. interests without major negative consequences for U.S.-Asia-Pacific relations.[8]
- The recently more consultative and flexible U.S. posture toward North Korea has meant that U.S. management of the Asia-Pacific's three major hot spots—North Korea, Taiwan, and Kashmir—is positively assessed in the region and should be continued.[9]
- The growing web of U.S. military connections throughout the Asia-Pacific builds connections advantageous for the United States while avoiding significant adverse reactions from powers like China and Russia that are wary of U.S. security power and policies. The continued discreet expansion of these ties seems warranted.
- The detailed outlines of U.S. initiatives toward Southeast Asia in such proposals as the Enterprise for ASEAN Initiative and Joint Vision Statement for an ASEAN-U.S. Enhanced Partnership provide sound guidelines of future U.S. policy and should be pursued.

The many problems and challenges facing U.S. policy in the Asia-Pacific are best dealt with deliberately and methodically, without a sense of major crisis or undue alarm that the U.S. position in the region is at a tipping point and on the verge of major decline.

- An anxious U.S. superpower subject to abrupt change almost certainly would add to uncertainties and concerns among leaders in the Asia-Pacific about the future direction of the regional security and economic order and could easily add to, rather than reduce, the problems facing U.S. policies in the region.

Through strong policy debate and political pressure in Congress, the media, and U.S. elections, the American government has begun to reconsider and change many of the excesses and other aspects of its policy in the Middle East, the broader war on terrorism, and other areas of foreign policy that proved to be so offensive to leaders and public opinion throughout the Asia-Pacific. The results of these changes probably will not silence criticism of U.S. foreign policy in the Asia-Pacific region completely. Strong American support for Israel, U.S. military involvement in Iraq, and U.S. detention and interrogation of terrorist subjects head the list of topics that are likely to continue in U.S. policy and behavior and to exacerbate differences between the United States and the leaders and people of the Asia-Pacific.[10]

Nonetheless, with the successor to George W. Bush, the style as well as the substance of U.S. foreign policy appears likely to change in directions that will ease friction with the Asia-Pacific. The use of unilateral approaches backed by strong ideological tenets of a neoconservative school of thinking in U.S. foreign policy already has diminished markedly in the latter part of the Bush administration. This controversial trend in foreign policy has been replaced to a considerable degree by more pragmatic and consultative approaches that seek to work together with concerned governments and international stakeholders. This change is broadly welcomed in the Asia-Pacific region and reduces aggravation in U.S. relations with the governments and peoples of the region.

In the Asia-Pacific, the U.S. government recently has shifted to a much more flexible and consultative approach in dealing with the sensitive North Korean nuclear weapons issue, notably through bilateral talks with North Korea that are generally supported by the concerned powers in the Six-Party Talks.

- The United States needs to avoid excessive secrecy in bilateral negotiations with North Korea and remain open and aboveboard in dealing with the participants in the Six-Party Talks that have differing interests and approaches in regard to North Korea. In particular, helping key U.S. ally Japan to make progress on the abductee issue in its relations with North Korea and remaining sensitive to the threat Japan faces from North Korean weapons of mass destruction and delivery systems seem essential for U.S. interest in preserving a close alliance relationship with Japan.

The U.S. government has played down its past emphasis on Southeast Asia as a second front in the war on terrorism and increased attention to the development and security concerns of the regional governments. It also has shown more attentiveness to the Asian multilateral groupings favored by the governments and people of the region. In other areas, the United States has tried to meet regional and international objections to the U.S. stance against the Kyoto accord on global warming with initiatives involving other regional and concerned powers. It has worked with the United Nations in seeking a resolution to the human suffering in Darfur and has worked closely with the European Union and the United Nations in pressing Iran over its nuclear weapons program.

The Bush administration's strong rhetorical emphasis in its second term on democracy promotion has seen only limited policy action in the Asia-Pacific, primarily against the relatively small state Myanmar, while criticism of authoritarian governments important for other U.S. interests, notably China, Pakistan, and Kazakhstan, has been mild. This U.S. pragmatism regarding democracy promotion has avoided disruptions in important relations that would upset the regional order and would not be welcomed by many Asia-Pacific governments.[11]

- New U.S. leaders elected in 2008 should build on these changes, seeking wherever possible to consult with and accommodate the concerns of governments in the Asia-Pacific in pursuing pragmatic and broadly supported U.S. policies and initiatives affecting the interests of the Asia-Pacific nations and people.
- Promoting U.S. values and democracy remain a key goal of U.S. foreign policy. The incoming U.S. leaders will need to find ways and initiatives that balance U.S. actions supporting human freedom with broad U.S. security and economic concerns that require the cooperation of Asia-Pacific governments which disapprove of such U.S. initiatives.

The record of the recent past indicates that leaders of terrorist groups, as well as those of North Korea and possibly China, India, Pakistan and elsewhere, may take measures that will so endanger the regional order as to require abrupt and decisive U.S. action, including the use of military force. A strong record of U.S. consultation and accommodation with regional governments and leaders on foreign policy issues will reduce the possible negative backlash and help to reinforce the power and effectiveness of these unilateral U.S. policy actions.

- U.S. leaders should remain firm and prepared to deal expeditiously, and on their own if necessary, with serious challenges to the regional order, recognizing that a record of close consultation on regional matters with concerned governments will add to and not detract from the effectiveness of firm U.S. action.

The shift toward greater U.S. consultation and accommodation regarding regional concerns in the Asia-Pacific has not been accompanied by sufficient high-level U.S. attention or implementation in dealing with the Association of Southeast Asian Nations (ASEAN) and Asian multilateral groups. This lack of U.S. attention does not appear to reflect major differences between the interests of the United States and its existing alliance and bilateral relationships, on the one hand, and ASEAN and Asian multilateral groups, on the other.[12] Given the Bush administration's preoccupation with the problems of Iraq and related questions in the Middle East and the war on terror, it may be unlikely that the administration will be able to take sufficient steps to remedy this problem.

- U.S. leaders elected in 2008 should implement plans like the U.S.-ASEAN Enhanced Partnership and clearly determine and rigorously implement policies in support of U.S. interests in regional groups such as the ASEAN Regional Forum, Asia Pacific Economic Cooperation (APEC), and possibly the East Asian Summit.

Reduced support for the United States in the post–Cold War period on the part of U.S. treaty allies South Korea, Thailand, and the Philippines is consistent with the trend toward strategic hedging seen among various Asia-Pacific governments and seems unlikely to change substantially. Nonetheless, there remains a strong overlap of interests between the United States and each of these allies. For example, reflecting this overlap in interests, South Korea recently seems to have reversed recent efforts to distance itself from its U.S. ally and has implemented initiatives that will shore up the alliance with the United States. The rise of China provides each of these U.S. allies with reasons to distance themselves from close ties with the United States that might complicate their growing relationships with China. However, as is discussed above, China's rise also provides them with reasons to preserve and strengthen the U.S. ties as a means to maintain their independence in the face of China's power and other uncertainties.

- U.S. leaders should examine carefully the implications of strategic hedging by South Korea, Thailand, and the Philippines, determine the positive as well as negative implications for the United States, and deal with each treaty ally with an approach that endeavors to maximize American advantages based on overlapping interests while minimizing friction and costs.

In sum, the way ahead for the United States in the Asia-Pacific is far from smooth, and the room for improvement in U.S. policies and practices is large. However, the foundation of strategic and economic overlapping interests between the United States and the governments of the region remains strong. On this basis, carefully considered and executed U.S. policies that reflect sensitivity to the interests of the Asia-Pacific governments seem likely to go far in repairing some of the damage to the U.S. image in the region as a result of misguided policies of the outgoing U.S. administration and establishing momentum for greater U.S. cooperation with the region for some time to come.

NOTES

1. G. John Ikenberry and Michael Mastanduno, eds., *International Relations Theory and the Asia-Pacific* (New York: Columbia University Press, 2003); David Shambaugh, ed., *Power Shift: China and Asia's New Dynamics* (Berkeley: University of California Press, 2005); Aaron Friedberg, "The Future of U.S.-China Relations: Is Conflict Inevitable?" *International Security* 30, no. 2 (Fall 2005): 7–45.

2. David Shambaugh, "Asia in Transition: The Evolving Regional Order," *Current History* 105, no. 690 (April 2006): 153–59.

3. Council on Foreign Relations, *Campaign Blog: The Candidates and the World,* November 8, 2007, http://blogs.cfr.org/campaign2008.

4. David Shambaugh, "China's 17th Party Congress: Maintaining Delicate Balances," Brookings Northeast Asia Commentary, November 2007, http://www.brookings.edu/opinions/2007/11_china_shambaugh.aspx.

5. Mark Mather, "Education and Occupation Separates Two Kinds of Immigrants in the United States: Asian Immigrants Tend to Be More Educated and Highly Skilled," Population Reference Bureau, September 12, 2007, http://www.prb.org/articles/2007/EducationAndOccupationSeparatesUSImmigrants.aspx.

6. Robert Scalapino, *Asia and the Road Ahead: Issues for the Major Powers* (Berkeley: University of California Press, 1975); Bernard Gordon, *New Directions in American Foreign Policy in Asia* (London: Routledge, 1990); Edward Lincoln, *Japan's Unequal Trade* (Washington, D.C.: Brookings Institution Press, 1990); Robert Scalapino, ed., *Asia and the Major Powers: Domestic Politics and Foreign Policy* (Berkeley: University of California Press, 1988).

7. Council on Foreign Relations, *U.S.-China Relations: An Affirmative Agenda, A Responsible Course* (New York: Council on Foreign Relations, 2007).

8. Robert Sutter, "The United States and Asia in 2006: Crisis Management, Holding Patterns, and Secondary Initiatives," *Asian Survey* 47, no. 1 (January/February 2007): 10–21.

9. Ralph A. Cossa and Brad Glosserman, "Tests Postponed, Pending, Passed, and in Progress," *Comparative Connections* 9, no. 2 (2nd Qtr 2007): 1–3.

10. Sara Thannhauser, "A Dangerous Inheritance: Converging Challenges That Will Face the Next American President," America's Role in the World Working Group, Institute for the Study of Diplomacy, Georgetown University, February 26, 2007, http://isd.georgetown.edu/Inheritance_Feb_26_2007.pdf.

11. Robert Sutter, "The United States and Asia in 2005: Managing Troubles, Sustaining Leadership," *Asian Survey* 46, no. 1 (January/February 2006): 10–21; Sutter, "United States and Asia in 2006"; White House, "Environment: Protecting Our Nation's Environment," http://www.whitehouse.gov/infocus/environment/; White House, "President Bush Discusses Genocide in Darfur, Implements Sanctions," press release, May 29, 2007, http://www.whitehouse.gov/news/releases/2007/05/20070529.html; "Major Powers Send Iran Issue to UN Envoys for Talks," Agence France-Presse, March 4, 2007.

12. Stanley Foundation, "New Power Dynamics in Southeast Asia: Issues for U.S. Policymakers," Policy Dialogue Brief, October 2006, http://www.stanleyfdn.org/publications/pdb/spcpdb06.pdf; Ralph A. Cossa, "East Asia Community-Building: Time for the United States to Get on Board," Policy Analysis Brief, September 2007, http://www.stanleyfdn.org/publications/pab/CossaPAB07.pdf.

Selected Bibliography

As noted in citations throughout this study, readers with an interest in contemporary U.S.-Asia relations are urged to consult the annual volume *Strategic Asia*, published by the National Bureau of Asian Research; the quarterly review of regional developments in the e-journal *Comparative Connections*; the wide range of very valuable reports published by the Congressional Research Service; the annual survey of Asia in the January/February edition of the journal *Asian Survey*; and the very useful reports published by the International Crisis Group.

Abramowitz, Morton, and Stephen Bosworth. *Chasing the Sun: Rethinking East Asian Policy*. New York: Century Foundation, 2006.

Acharya, Amitav, and Arabinda Acharya. "The Myth of the Second Front: Localizing the 'War on Terror' in Southeast Asia." *Washington Quarterly* 30, no. 4 (Autumn 2007): 75–90.

Alagappa, Muthiah, ed. *Asian Security Order*. Stanford, Calif.: Stanford University Press, 2003.

Armitage, Richard, and Joseph Nye. *CSIS Commission on Smart Power: A Smarter More Secure America*. Washington, D.C.: Center for Strategic and International Studies, 2007.

———. *U.S.-Japan Alliance: Getting Asia Right through 2020*. Washington, D.C.: Center for Strategic and International Studies, 2007.

Bell, Coral. "The Twilight of the Unipolar World." *American Interest* 1, no. 2 (Winter 2005): 18–29.

Berger, Thomas, ed. *Japan in International Politics: The Foreign Policies of an Adaptive State*. Boulder, Colo.: Lynne Reinner, 2006.

Borthwick, Mark. *Pacific Century: The Emergence of Modern Pacific Asia*. Boulder, Colo.: Westview Press, 2007.

Bush, Richard. *Untying the Knot*. Washington, D.C.: Brookings Institution Press, 2005.

Bush, Richard, and Michael O'Hanlon. *A War Like No Other*. Hoboken, N.J.: Wiley, 2007.

Cha, Victor. "Winning Asia: Washington's Untold Success Story." *Foreign Affairs* 86, no. 6 (November/December 2007): 98–113.

Christensen, Thomas. "Fostering Stability or Creating a Monster? The Rise of China and U.S. Policy toward East Asia." *International Security* 31, no. 1 (Summer 2006): 81–126.

Chu, Yun-han, and Andrew Nathan. "Seizing the Opportunity for Change in the Taiwan Strait." *Washington Quarterly* 31, no. 1 (Winter 2007/2008): 77–91.

Cohen, Stephen Philip. *The Idea of Pakistan*. Washington, D.C.: Brookings Institution Press, 2004.

——. *India: Emerging Power*. Washington, D.C.: Brookings Institution Press, 2001.

Crosston, Matthew. *Fostering Fundamentalism: Terrorism, Democracy and American Engagement in Central Asia*. Burlington, Vt.: Ashgate, 2006.

Davis, Elizabeth Van Wie, and Rouben Azizian. *Islam, Oil, and Geopolitics: Central Asia after September 11*. Lanham, Md.: Rowman & Littlefield, 2006.

Dittmer, Lowell. "Assessing America's Asian Policy." *Asian Survey* 47, no. 4 (July/August 2007): 524–26.

Foot, Rosemary. "Chinese Strategies in a U.S.-Hegemonic Global Order: Accommodating and Hedging." *International Affairs* 82, no. 1 (2006): 77–94.

Friedberg, Aaron. "The Future of U.S.-China Relations: Is Conflict Inevitable?" *International Security* 30, no. 2 (2005): 7–45.

Gill, Bates. *Rising Star: China's New Security Diplomacy*. Washington, D.C.: Brookings Institution Press, 2007.

Green, Michael J. *Japan's Reluctant Realism*. London: Palgrave, 2001.

Ikenberry, G. John. "America in East Asia: Power, Markets, and Grand Strategy." In *Beyond Bilateralism: U.S.-Japan Relations in the New Asia-Pacific*, ed. Ellis Krauss and T. J. Pempel, 37–54. Stanford, Calif.: Stanford University Press, 2004.

Ikenberry, G. John, and Michael Mastanduno, eds. *International Relations Theory and the Asia-Pacific*. New York: Columbia University Press, 2003.

Institute for National Security Studies. *The United States and Japan: Advancing toward a Mature Partnership*. Special report, October 11. Washington, D.C.: National Defense University Press, 2000.

Jonson, Lena. *Vladimir Putin and Central Asia: The Shaping of Russian Foreign Policy*. London: Palgrave, 2004.

Kang, David. *China Rising: Peace, Power, and Order in East Asia*. New York: Columbia University Press, 2007.

Kapur, S. Paul, and Sumit Ganguly. "The Transformation of U.S.-India Relations: An Explanation for the Rapprochement and Prospects for the Future." *Asian Survey* 47, no. 4 (2007): 642–56.

Kim, Samuel. *The Two Koreas and the Great Powers*. New York: Cambridge University Press, 2006.

Krauss, Ellis, and T. J. Pempel, eds. *The U.S.-Japan Relationship in the New Asia-Pacific*. Stanford, Calif.: Stanford University Press, 2004.

Kurlantzick, Joshua. *Charm Offensive: How China's Soft Power Is Transforming the World.* New Haven, Conn.: Yale University Press, 2007.

———. "Pax Asia-Pacifica? East Asian Integration and Its Implications for the United States." *Washington Quarterly* 30, no. 3 (Summer 2007): 67–77.

Lal, Rollie. *Understanding China and India.* Westport, Conn.: Praeger, 2006.

Lim, Robyn. *The Geopolitics of East Asia: The Search for Equilibrium.* New York: RoutledgeCurzon, 2003.

Lincoln, Edward. *East Asian Economic Regionalism.* Washington, D.C.: Brookings Institution Press, 2004.

Medeiros, Evan. "Strategic Hedging and the Future of Asia-Pacific Stability." *Washington Quarterly* 29, no. 1 (Winter 2005/2006): 145–67.

Munakata, Naoko. *Transforming East Asia: The Evolution of Regional Economic Integration.* Washington, D.C.: Brookings Institution Press, 2006.

Nanto, Dick. *East Asian Regional Architecture: New Economic and Security Arrangements and U.S. Policy.* CRS Report RL33653, September 18. Washington, D.C.: Congressional Research Service, Library of Congress, 2006.

Olcott, Martha Brill. *Central Asia's Second Chance.* Washington, D.C.: Carnegie Endowment for International Peace, 2005.

Pei, Minxin, and Michael Swaine. *Simmering Fire in Asia: Averting Sino-Japanese Strategic Conflict.* Washington, D.C.: Carnegie Endowment for International Peace, 2005.

Percival, Bronson. *The Dragon Looks South: China and Southeast Asia in the New Century.* Westport, Conn.: Praeger Security International, 2007.

Pollack, Jonathan, ed. *Asia Eyes America: Regional Perspectives on U.S. Asia-Pacific Strategy in the 21st Century.* Newport, R.I.: U.S. Naval War College, 2007.

Pritchard, Charles. *Failed Diplomacy: The Tragic Story of How North Korea Got the Bomb.* Washington, D.C.: Brookings Institution Press, 2007.

Pyle, Kenneth. *Japan Rising: The Resurgence of Japanese Power and Purpose.* New York: Public Affairs, 2007.

Rozman, Gilbert. *Northeast Asia's Stunted Regionalism: Bilateral Distrust in the Shadow of Globalization.* New York: Cambridge University Press, 2004.

Rumer, Boris. *Central Asia at the End of the Transition.* Armonk, N.Y.: M. E. Sharpe, 2005.

Rumer, Eugene. *China, Russia, and the Balance of Power in Central Asia.* Washington, D.C.: National Defense University Press, 2006.

Samuels, Richard. *Securing Japan.* Ithaca, N.Y.: Cornell University Press, 2007.

Shambaugh, David. "China Engages Asia: Reshaping the Regional Order." *International Security* 29, no. 3 (Winter 2004/2005): 64–99.

———, ed. *Power Shift: China and Asia's New Dynamics.* Berkeley: University of California Press, 2005.

Shaplen, Jason, and James Laney. "Washington's Eastern Sunset: The Decline of U.S. Power in Northeast Asia." *Foreign Affairs* (November/December 2007): 82–97.

Shirk, Susan. *China: Fragile Superpower.* New York: Oxford University Press, 2007.

Stanley Foundation. "Economic Dimensions of New Power Dynamics in Southeast Asia." Policy memo, July 12. Muscatine, Iowa: Stanley Foundation, 2007.

——. "New Power Dynamics in Southeast Asia: Issues for U.S. Policymakers." Policy Dialogue Brief, October. Muscatine, Iowa: Stanley Foundation, 2007.

Sutter, Robert. *China's Rise: Implications for U.S. Leadership in Asia*. Washington, D.C.: East-West Center Washington, 2006.

Swaine, Michael. *Reverse Course: The Fragile Turnabout in U.S.-China Relations*. Policy Brief 22. Washington, D.C.: Carnegie Endowment for International Peace, 2003.

Talbott, Strobe. *Engaging India*. Washington, D.C.: Brookings Institution Press, 2004.

Tellis, Ashley. *India as a Global Power: An Action Agenda for the United States*. Washington, D.C.: Carnegie Endowment for International Peace, 2005.

Tow, William. "America's Asia-Pacific Strategy Is Out of Kilter." *Current History* 107, no. 701 (September 2007): 287–89.

Vaughn, Bruce, and Wayne Morrison. *China-Southeast Asia Relations: Trends, Issues, and Implications for the United States*. CRS Report RL32688, April 6. Washington, D.C.: Congressional Research Service, Library of Congress, 2006.

Vogel, Steven K. *U.S.-Japan Relations in a Changing World*. Washington, D.C.: Brookings Institution Press, 2002.

Yahuda, Michael. *The International Politics of the Asia-Pacific*. New York: Routledge-Curzon, 2005.

Index

Abdullah Ahmad Badawi, 229–30
Abe Shinzo, 89, 90, 92, 93, 100
Abu Sayyaf, 227
Aceh, 226
Afghanistan, ix, 16, 20, 34, 40, 44,
    161, 164; and Australia, 233–34;
    and Central Asia, 138–40, 244–45;
    Japan's role in, 87, 89, 91; and New
    Zealand, 235; and Pakistan, 131–37,
    240–43
Agreed Framework, 62, 63–65, 68, 73,
    89, 162, 210
Albright, Madeleine, 66, 67, 105–6, 213
al-Qaeda, 91, 244; and Pakistan, 132–
    33, 240–42
anti-ballistic missile (ABM) treaty, 164
anti-secession law, 55, 187, 190
Armitage, Richard, 19, 86, 87, 186
Arroyo, Gloria Macapagal, 103,
    227–28
article 9 of Japan's constitution, 96,
    97, 98
ASEAN+3 (APT), 110, 111, 112, 159,
    266
ASEAN Regional Forum (ARF),
    111–12, 113, 159
ASEAN Security Community, 111

ASEAN Treaty of Amity and
    Cooperation (TAC), 112, 113
ASEAN-U.S. Enhanced Partnership,
    114, 115, 273, 287
Asia-Pacific dynamics, 149–50;
    energy competition and security,
    151; environmental issues, 152;
    influence of global trends, 150–54;
    key determinants, 154–66, 253–54;
    outlook, 281–83; permeation of
    science and technology, 153;
    population trends, 151; recent
    trends—defensive motives of
    regional powers, 254; recent
    trends—economic cooperation
    and competition, 256–57; recent
    trends—no coherent regional
    bloc, 254; recent trends—political
    aspects, 258; recent trends—
    proliferation of regional initiatives,
    254; recent trends—role of national
    governments, 254–55; recent
    trends—security initiatives and
    "hedging," 255–56; U.S. power and
    influence, 153–54
Asia Pacific Economic Cooperation
    (APEC), 110–11, 159; and terrorism,

295

About the Author

Robert G. Sutter has been visiting professor of Asian studies at the School of Foreign Service, Georgetown University, since 2001. Prior to taking this full-time position, Sutter specialized in Asian and Pacific affairs and U.S. foreign policy in a U.S. government career of thirty-three years involving the Congressional Research Service of the Library of Congress, the Central Intelligence Agency, the Department of State, and the Senate Foreign Relations Committee. He was for many years the senior specialist and director of the Foreign Affairs and National Defense Division of the Congressional Research Service. He also was the national intelligence officer for East Asia and the Pacific at the U.S. Government's National Intelligence Council, and the China Division director at the Department of State's Bureau of Intelligence and Research.

A Ph.D. graduate in history and East Asian languages from Harvard University, Sutter taught part-time for more than thirty years at Georgetown, George Washington, and Johns Hopkins universities and the University of Virginia. He has published sixteen books, more than a hundred articles, and several hundred government reports dealing with contemporary East Asian and Pacific countries and their relations with the United States. His most recent previous book is *Chinese Foreign Relations: Power and Policy since the Cold War* (Rowman & Littlefield, 2007).